Words of the World

Most people think of the *Oxford English Dictionary* (*OED*) as a distinctly British product. Begun in England 150 years ago, it took more than 60 years to complete, and when it was finally finished in 1928, the British prime minister heralded it as a 'national treasure'. It maintained this image throughout the twentieth century, and in 2006 the English public voted it an 'Icon of England', alongside Marmite, Buckingham Palace, and the bowler hat. But this book shows that the dictionary is not as 'British' as we all thought. The linguist and lexicographer, Sarah Ogilvie, combines her insider knowledge and experience with impeccable research to show that the *OED* is in fact an international product in both its content and its making. She examines the policies and practices of the various editors, applies qualitative and quantitative analysis, and finds new *OED* archival materials in the form of letters, reports, and proofs. She demonstrates that the *OED*, in its use of readers from all over the world and its coverage of World English, is in fact a global text.

SARAH OGILVIE is Director of the Australian National Dictionary Centre, Reader in Linguistics at the Australian National University, and Chief Editor of Oxford Dictionaries, Australia. Prior to that she was Alice Tong Sze Research Fellow at Cambridge University. She holds a doctorate in Linguistics from the University of Oxford and worked for many years as an editor on the *Oxford English Dictionary* in England and the *Macquarie* and *Oxford* dictionaries in Australia.

Words of the World

A Global History of the *Oxford English Dictionary*

Sarah Ogilvie

CAMBRIDGE
UNIVERSITY PRESS

CAMBRIDGE UNIVERSITY PRESS
Cambridge, New York, Melbourne, Madrid, Cape Town,
Singapore, São Paulo, Delhi, Mexico City

Cambridge University Press
The Edinburgh Building, Cambridge CB2 8RU, UK

Published in the United States of America by
Cambridge University Press, New York

www.cambridge.org
Information on this title: www.cambridge.org/9781107605695

First published 2013

Printed and Bound in the United Kingdom by the MPG Books Group.

A catalogue record for this publication is available from the British Library.

Library of Congress Cataloging-in-Publication Data

Ogilvie, Sarah.
Words of the world : a global history of the Oxford
English dictionary / Sarah Ogilvie.
pages cm
ISBN 978-1-107-02183-9 (Hardback) – ISBN 978-1-107-60569-5 (Paperback)
1. Oxford English dictionary. 2. Encyclopedias and dictionaries–
History and criticism. 3. English language–Foreign countries. 4. English
language–Foreign words and phrases. 5. English language–Lexicography.
6. English language–Etymology.
I. Title.
PE1617.O94O44 2012
423.09–dc23

2012015672

ISBN 978-1-107-02183-9 Hardback
ISBN 978-1-107-60569-5 Paperback

For Jane Shaw

Contents

Illustrations

Appendix figures

Every word should be made to tell its own story – the story of its birth and life, and in many cases of its death, and even occasionally of its resuscitation.

Herbert Coleridge (1857), Editor from 1859 to 1861 of the dictionary that became known as the *Oxford English Dictionary*

Preface

Most people think of the *Oxford English Dictionary* (*OED*) as a distinctly British product. Begun in England one hundred and fifty years ago, it took more than sixty years to complete, and when it was finally finished the British Prime Minister heralded it as a 'national treasure'. It maintained this image throughout the twentieth century, and in 2006 the English public voted it an 'Icon of England', alongside marmite, Buckingham Palace, and the bowler hat.[1] Central to the rhetoric of OED-as-national-treasure is the collection of eccentric lexicographers who devoted their lives to the giant text. We have inherited the picture of a handful of devoted Englishmen huddled in a cold, damp Scriptorium on Banbury Road, Oxford, wrapping their legs in newspaper to keep warm. Scholars and the media never fail to focus on the nineteenth-century editor of the *OED*, James Murray (1837–1915), who laboured on the dictionary for nearly forty years and died on the letter T without knowing whether the whole dictionary would ever be finished. We are presented with a story of uncompromising persistence and dedication to produce a multi-volume dictionary of unrivalled scholarly rigour which future generations would hail as the definitive record of the English language.

All of this is true, except for the bit about the *OED* being a distinctly English product. The making of this dictionary was a transnational effort, and if you look closely at its pages you discover a distinctly international dimension. Not only were some members of the small band of Englishmen in the Scriptorium actually Scottish, not English, but they were supported by hundreds of men and women from around the world. The *OED* text was created by the work of hundreds of contributors worldwide. It is a distinctly global product, in a sense the original Wikipedia, coordinated by Royal Mail. What's more, Murray intended it to be so.

He reached out for words beyond the shores of Britain and was helped by hundreds of dedicated readers and editors around the globe. He actively sought the assistance of these men and women; he saw their words – loanwords (words borrowed into English from other languages) and World Englishes (varieties of English spoken around the world) – as legitimate members of the English language and wanted to include them in his new dictionary. Murray's actions and policies were criticized in his day, but he continued throughout his career to rebel against his critics.

In the second half of the nineteenth century, when the British Empire was reaching the zenith of its power, confidence, and size, Murray enlisted the help of people not only within the empire but also beyond it, creating a network that was truly global. He was fascinated by the differences that were emerging in the English language and wanted his dictionary to reflect and record the developments he witnessed. Contrary to what recent commentators have assumed, Murray was far from the Anglocentric Oxford don who merely wanted to preserve the 'Queen's English'. Instead, he was an outsider within Oxford who was excluded from university life and was never made a Fellow of an Oxford college. He saw himself as an innovator, a self-proclaimed 'pioneer' whose lexicographic efforts to describe global English were undeniably breaking new ground. In order to accomplish his aims, he corresponded with a global network of hundreds of collaborators who read local World English texts and sent words and quotations for inclusion in his dictionary. He formed transnational relationships by exchanging letters and books with contributors in regions as dispersed as Ceylon, Mexico, and New Zealand.

Over time, as small portions of the *OED* were gradually published, critics (both inside and outside his workplace) recognized the prevalence of non-British words in the dictionary and urged Murray to stop including them because, as one reviewer put it, 'there is no surer or more fatal sign of the decay of a language than in the interpolation of barbarous terms and foreign words; if a great dictionary is to be regarded as a treasury of the language it should give no currency to false and fraudulent issues'.[2] Murray answered his critics the way he knew best: by refusing to change his policy and by defiantly continuing to include words of the world. Although using the language of imperial exploration, Murray was nonetheless clear about his global lexicographic identity from the earliest days. He wrote in 1884 (while still editing the letter A), 'I feel that in many respects I and my assistants are simply pioneers, pushing our way experimentally through an untrodden forest, where no white man's axe has been before us.'

It was true that no one had written such a comprehensive dictionary of English before Murray and his team, and no one has since. However, the full extent of the dictionary's original scope – its generous inclusion of words from outside Britain – has never been fully appreciated. In fact, it has even been misunderstood and misrepresented – especially in the past forty years – by scholars and journalists who, on the basis of little evidence, have criticized Murray and the early editors of the *OED* for neglecting vocabulary from outside Britain. In contrast, these critics have praised a later *OED* editor,

Robert Burchfield (1923–2004), for his inclusion and treatment of loanwords and World Englishes.

This book challenges this narrative. Until now, no one has investigated the actual text of the dictionary to assess whether these generalizations are correct. By using a combination of statistical, textual, contextual, and qualitative analyses to compare versions of the *OED* from its inception until 1986, I discovered that the inverse is true.[3] There was no smooth story of progress within the *OED* text from imperialism to postcolonialism, in which coverage of words from outside Britain improved over time. Rather, I found that the early editors were less conservative in their policy and practice with regard to loanwords and World Englishes than usually assumed. And I found that the later editor, Burchfield, was less the champion of these words than he or others have claimed. The coverage of the dictionary has never been insular, and the story of Burchfield's pioneering efforts to open up the dictionary to the Englishes of the world in the third quarter of the twentieth century does an injustice to its editors from 1884 to 1933.

This book provides new insight into the coverage of words from outside Britain in the first edition and Supplement volumes of the *OED,* and the decision-making processes behind the lexicographic practice; it analyzes the relationship between editorial policy and lexicographic practice; and it demonstrates that it is in the slippage between policy and practice that a lexicographer's attitudes towards culture and language can often be found. In addition, a more nuanced picture of the *OED* editors emerges when the first edition of the *OED* is compared with a competitor dictionary, the *Stanford Dictionary of Anglicized Words and Phrases* (1892), and when Burchfield's *Supplement to the OED* (1972–1986) is compared with the dictionary upon which it was based, the *1933 Supplement*. More than a history of one of the greatest books ever written, this book takes as its starting point the actual dictionary text, surveying its treatment by the dictionary creators and using that as a window into the attitudes and lives of its makers – both those in Oxford and those continents away. This is the story of the global *OED*, its makers and its text.

ENDNOTES

1 http://www.icons.org.uk.
2 'The Literature and Language of the Age', *Edinburgh Review*, April 1889 p. 348.
3 See Coleman and Ogilvie (2009) for more on this method of dictionary analysis.

Acknowledgements

The process of writing this book opened many new worlds to me, for which I am very grateful. There were several unexplained discoveries that I made in the archives and in the dictionary itself, and my efforts to solve these mysteries took me to unexpected places: to a park in Brisbane, Australia, where I met one of the *OED*'s most prolific contributors; to a cemetery in Wolvercote, outside Oxford, where I identified the tombstone of James Murray beside that of his best friend James Legge; and to a large, rambling house in north Oxford where C. T. Onions had lived until his death in 1965. Onions ended up being a central character of the book, and I got to know his elderly daughter Elizabeth, who passed away while I was writing this book, and his son Giles, who had lived in the family house for more than eighty years. They both shared memories of growing up in literary Oxford, as well as Giles' experience of reading for Burchfield's *OED Supplement*, which all deserve a book of their own.

First and foremost I must thank my colleagues at the *Oxford English Dictionary* (*OED*). Although I still consult for the dictionary from amidst the fens in Cambridge, I do miss sitting with them in the large open-plan office and eating together each day in the OUP cafeteria. My years at the *OED* provided me with the best possible lexicographic training, and I must thank my colleagues, especially John Simpson and Edmund Weiner, for their guidance, inspiration, and advice over the years. This book has been improved by the advice and comments of many people, most notably Charlotte Brewer, Peter Gilliver, Terry Hoad, Sidney Landau, Rod McConchie, Sara Miles, Lynda Mugglestone, and Jane Shaw. I am indebted to others who commented on earlier drafts of chapters, especially Michael Adams, Dianne Bardsley, Paul Bogaards, Julie Coleman, David Cram, Victor Flynn, Bill Frawley, and Aditi Lahiri. These colleagues and friends devoted many hours to read and correct the text at several stages; they encouraged my scholarship and shared their ideas, but of course ultimately all opinions and errors in this book remain my own.

I would also like to thank others who have helped generously with their ideas and support: Cindy Allen, Martha Baer, Helen Barton, Gary Bolles,

Kingsley Bolton, Kate Brett, Keith Brown, Lesley Brown, Philip Bullock, Mike Clark, Jeanette Covacevich, Joanna Day, Mary Dalrymple, Kate Dobson, Valerie Crane Dorfman, Edith Esch, Stefano Evangelista, Paul Fromberg, Susan Froud, Mark Grace, Sarah Green, Rebecca Groves, Mark Gwynn, Rosa Lee Harden, Richard Harms, George Hecksher, Bernadette Hince, Sarah Hoem Iversen, Niels Hooper, Kasia Jaszczolt, Steve Jensen, Mari Jones, Elizabeth Knowles, James Lambert, Richard Mason, Marilyn McCord Adams, Jon McCormack, Rebecca McLennan, Robert Merrihew Adams, Kate Mitchell, Ben Morse, David Nash, Kateena O'Gorman, Georgina Paul, Stephen Pax Leonard, Pam Peters, Tamson Pietsch, Curtis Price, Joyce Reid, Alan Renwick, Judith Robertson, Julia Robinson, Antoinette Rossi, Rhian Samuel, Dave Shirt, Chris Stray, Barry Supple, Sandie Taylor, Caroline Thomas, Janet Todd, Mark Turin, Judith Unwin, Alison Vinnicombe, Trudy Watt, David Willis, and Beverley Yorke.

Because there is no electronic copy of the first edition of the *OED* and its separate supplement volumes, all the analysis for this book had to be done manually. This was a painstaking task which necessitated access to the original texts. Early on in this project, Miranda Curtis and Jane Shaw generously gave me a first edition of the *OED*, which helped immeasurably.

There is a great deal of archival material in this book, and I am grateful for the kind assistance of Bev Hunt and Martin Maw at the Oxford University Press (OUP) archives, and to the Delegates of OUP for permission to publish them. The images are reprinted by permission of the Secretary to the Delegates of Oxford University Press. Portions of this text are published in articles elsewhere and I am grateful for permission to use some of that material here. My research was funded by Lucy Cavendish College, Cambridge, the UK Arts and Humanities Research Council, and the Wingate Foundation. I also gratefully acknowledge the support of Trinity College and the Department of Linguistics, Philology, and Phonetics, Oxford; the Department of Applied and Theoretical Linguistics, Cambridge; as well as Visiting Fellowships at the Department of Linguistics, University of California–Berkeley, and the Research School of Humanities and the Australian National Dictionary Centre at the Australian National University, Canberra. I am grateful for access to the Murray Papers at the Bodleian Library, Oxford; the Onions Collection at the National Library of Australia, Canberra; the Craigie Papers at the National Library of Scotland, Edinburgh; C. T. Onions' Letters at Birmingham University Library; the Furnivall Papers at King's College London; and the Papers of the BBC Advisory Committee on Spoken English at the BBC Written Archives Centre, Reading. Thanks are also due to the archivists at Balliol College, Oxford, Exeter College, Oxford, Jesus College, Cambridge, and Magdalen College, Oxford.

1 Entering the *OED*

I thought, imagine if I could help get one word in the dictionary.

Mr Chris Collier, Reader for the Oxford English Dictionary
(and contributor of more than 100,000 quotations), Brisbane, Australia, 2006

In 2001, after ten years of writing dictionaries in Australia, I found myself walking through the cobbled streets of Oxford, England, to start a new job at the mother of all dictionaries: the *Oxford English Dictionary* (*OED*). I knew that there was no dictionary in the world that matched the *OED* for size and scholarly authority. I would share responsibility for words entering English from languages outside of Europe: it was the opportunity of a lifetime for any lexicographer, regardless of provenance.

I walked through the imposing stone arch of the majestic headquarters of Oxford University Press (OUP) into the front quad with its fountain and ancient oak tree. I had read *A Room of One's Own* so I knew not to walk on Oxbridge grass, but what I did not know was that you also should not smile at people who walked past you, and certainly not say 'g'day' if you had not met them before. There were many Australian mannerisms I would learn to control over the coming years while working on the *OED*, but this first day I was too excited to realise how 'colonial' I seemed to my new work colleagues. As soon as I met the Deputy Chief Editor – an elegant and handsome Englishman who had worked on the dictionary since coming down from Christ Church, Oxford, at the age of twenty-one, the same age I had started working for Oxford Dictionary in Canberra – he greeted me with the unforgettable 'Oh you're Australian.' I knew what he meant, and I was determined to show him that, once we entered the silent zone of the *OED* offices (there is no speaking in the office; if you want to speak you must go into a small glass booth) and started editing the actual text, there would be no difference in the quality of my work and that of any other editor on the floor.

The open-plan office was huge: seventy people in all, consisting of a team of forty editors who wrote the dictionary, an IT team of ten who supported the complex computer system, and twenty readers and typists who spent all day sorting and typing out quotations which were later reviewed by editors who used them to tease out a word's pronunciation, provenance, meaning, and use

Figure 1.1 The modern *OED* office, with its open plan. (Credit: S. Ogilvie)

over time. Although full of people, the office was completely quiet, and its glass and metal fixtures gave it a modern feel. The environment was nothing like the photographs I had seen of the *OED* in the nineteenth century in which James Murray (1837–1915) stood in his pokey Scriptorium surrounded by a thousand pigeon holes, each of which was crowded with 4 × 6-inch 'slips' of paper that recorded each entry of the dictionary (Figure 2.6), or indeed the other office in the regal, sandstone-columned Old Ashmolean building in Broad Street which housed Henry Bradley (1845–1923) and his team (Figure 1.6). In comparison, this modern office was large and sterile, despite the efforts that editors had made to brighten their desks with plants and fluffy toys (Figure 1.1).

At first, I found myself gravitating to others at the Press who had an accent, and it seemed everyone I met had a quirkiness that I found intriguing and irresistible, like the middle-aged gentleman on the reception desk, called a 'porter' in Oxford, with his handle-bar moustache and northern accent. He put me at ease immediately on my first day. Upon hearing my accent, he launched into a short history of falconry in Australia – he had gone to Australia to fly birds (who on earth goes to Australia to fly birds, I thought?). He was the first of many people I would meet at the Press who were world authorities on obscure topics. My favourite was Dave, who had written the science entries in the *OED* for twenty years. I was told he had camped on the shores of Loch Ness building a submarine. Dave not only specialized in English folk music but also real ales, and most Fridays over the coming years he and fellow lexicographer Mike would teach me everything they knew down at the Old Bookbinder's Arms.

Near the Press, surrounded by small terrace houses that were once the brothels of Jericho, this small, white pub was the traditional watering hole for the binders of the Press who for centuries drank there each day after work. Small and smelly, with a fireplace and sticky carpet, it had been featured in an episode of the TV detective series *Inspector Morse*, but other than that no one seemed to know about it. The Bookies became our escape each Friday afternoon, the place where we would unwind over a pint of Old Speckled Hen. Our conversation drifted from topics as disparate as the longest letters in the Chinese alphabet (Mike edited the famous *Oxford Chinese-English Dictionary* so was able to assert authoritatively that in the Pinyin Chinese writing system the largest letters are S, X, Y, and Z, as opposed to C, S, and P in English); to global inconsistencies in naming species of beetles and the difficulties this posed for disambiguation in dictionaries (entomology was one of Dave's many specialisms). The borrowing of foreign phrases in English was my own specialism. I would always have a new discovery to share with Mike and Dave, such as the expression *the mother of all* . . . which was a calque (direct translation) from Arabic *'umm al-ma'arik*, 'the mother of all battles', made famous by Saddam Hussein in the first Gulf War. At the *OED*, I had found soulmates and fellow editors who shared my own passion for the words we worked on and were just as enthusiastic to share their discoveries as to hear mine.

When I began to work there, we were revising the third edition of the *OED* (*OED3*). There had only been two editions previously – the first edition (*OED1*) published in 1928 and the second edition (*OED2*) in 1989 – and the second edition was not really a revision of the first edition but rather a combination of the first edition with various addition and supplement volumes.[1] The new third edition entailed the first thorough revision and re-editing of the original first edition of the dictionary, and therefore involved the re-working of some words or 'entries' that had remained untouched since the nineteenth century.

Generally the length of time since the word was last edited was directly proportional to the time needed to edit it because more citations had to be found, and given the mixed editing history of entries in *OED2* there was no telling how long each entry would take to edit for *OED3*. Although our bundles of slips were tied together according to each word or entry, an editor generally thought according to each sense, or individual meaning, of a word or entry. Some senses would take days to sort out, others mere minutes, and there was little way of guessing whether a sense might be 'quick'. Of course entries with multiple senses generally took longer as a whole, but the time spent on each sense of a word would vary: words with a single sense might take much longer to edit than one sense of a word with multiple senses. One colleague spent more than three months on the entry *put* while another laboured for two months on the word *party*. More recently, it took an editor nine months to work through the 645 senses of *run* which took over from the word *set* (579 senses, yet to be revised) as the largest entry in the dictionary.

I specialized in foreign words borrowed into English (known as 'loan-words') from languages outside of Europe and words from varieties of English around the world (known as 'World Englishes'). Many of my 'non-European' words had not been in English long enough to develop multiple senses, so I was often spared the difficult task of teasing out the finer nuances of meaning that separated multiple senses of a word. Although non-European words were generally single senses and therefore shorter than other entries, they were not necessarily quicker to edit because the task of tracing its etymology, finding written evidence in overseas sources, and checking the etymology and definition with a language specialist was all time-consuming. Some of the words had entered the language recently because of world affairs, and were new entries that needed drafting from scratch, such as *Talibanization* and *Talibanize* which were lexicalizations of *Taliban*, the fundamentalist Islamic movement that governed Afghanistan between 1996 and 2001. Other words with a much longer history in English entered so long ago, via explorers and missionaries who spoke Germanic or Romance languages, that most of us would never think of them as 'foreign' words. For example, the word *chocolate* came from Nahuatl, the language of the Aztecs, in 1604 via the Spanish Jesuit missionary Jose de Acosta. *Sugar* (1299) and *magazine* (1583) came from Arabic via Romance languages, and *coffee* (1598) came from Arabic via Germanic languages.

My work on words of the world called for knowing a little about a lot of languages, ranging from Sanskrit to Hebrew and Arabic, to the languages of the Amazon or Aboriginal Australia. Over six hundred languages are currently mentioned in the etymologies in the *OED*. Backed up by the support of language specialists around the world, I worked on all aspects of these words, describing how they entered the English language – their pronunciation, spelling variants, and meaning – as well as finding written quotations that illustrated their use in English contexts.

The biggest challenge and thrill for every *OED* editor is finding the first instance of a word in print. This involves scouring old texts for the first appearance of a word. The *OED* uses electronic corpora for this process, but also employs teams of people who sit each day in the Bodleian Library, British Library, Library of Congress, and major libraries in Toronto, New York, Boston, New Haven, and Riverside, California, reading old books and manuscripts for 'first quots'. It also relies on members of the public who send in quotations from books, magazines, and journals they have read. The reading programme has an eclectic collection of readers who specialize in words from particular genres and subject areas, and send in quotations on topics as varied as politics, surfing, pornography, or needlework.

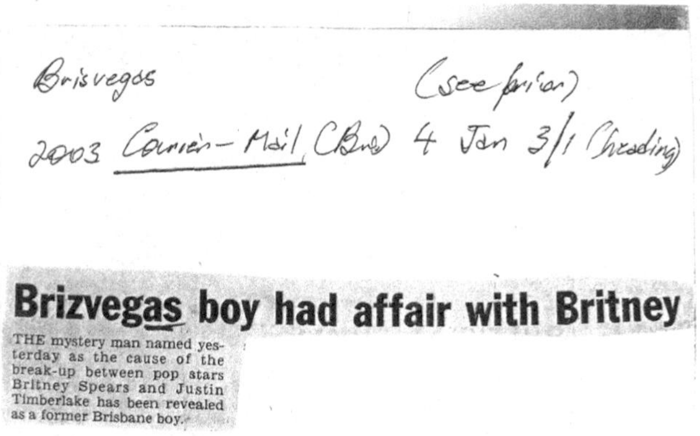

Figure 1.2 One of Mr Collier's slips showing the use of the word *Brizvegas* in Brisbane's *Courier Mail* newspaper with his annotations. (Credit: ANDC)

The *OED* and its 'satellite' national dictionary centres around the world have always depended on the contributions of the public.[2] We had a similar system in Australia, and one of the greatest contributions of the past few decades came from a man in my hometown of Brisbane. When I first worked on Australian Oxford dictionaries at the Australian National Dictionary Centre in Canberra, it was my job to open the bundle of quotations that Mr Chris Collier collected and sent each month. There was a veil of mystery surrounding Mr Collier, as no one had ever met him or heard his voice, so the only clues to his identity lay in the hundreds of 4 × 6-inch slips of paper he sent. Each bundle of slips was oddly wrapped in old cornflake packets, with bits of dog hair (or so we hoped) stuck to them. On each slip, he had cut out and glued a quotation, all of which had one thing in common: they were from the same source, Brisbane's main newspaper the *Courier Mail*. The year was 1990, and I vividly remember opening Mr Collier's packages, eager to see the words he had trawled that month: *comfort food, pooper scooper, environmentalism, fast-tracked, gurgler* ... there were hundreds of them (Figure 1.2). You can imagine my surprise, then, when on my first day at the job in Oxford, I was asked whether I knew Mr Collier. He had also been sending quotations to the *OED* all these years, and his reading of the *Courier Mail* had provided first quotations for the words *seajack* (1975), *petrolhead* (1980), *off-the-plan* (1986), *Neutralysis* (1989), *kit-off* (1992), and *Mad Max* (1996). We had no knowledge in Australia that Mr Collier had such an international reputation, and over the coming years I would learn that he was one of hundreds of devoted international readers who had contributed to the *OED*.

Figure 1.3 Mr Chris Collier, an Australian reader for the *OED* who contributed over 100, 000 quotations. (Credit: S. Ogilvie)

Most of these contributors remain faceless, if not nameless, but I made a point of meeting Mr Collier in 2006. I wanted to put a face to this faithful dictionary contributor and to find out more about him, but it was not easy to track him down as he only ever provided a postal box return address. On a trip to Australia to write a high school dictionary at the Australian National Dictionary Centre, I asked the staff about Mr Collier. I knew he was still sending quotations to Oxford, but was he still sending them to the Centre in Canberra? Oh yes, his collecting is as prolific as ever, I was told. As though he had heard my enquiry, the Centre soon after received a telephone call from Mr Collier! For the first time we were able to hear his voice, and I asked if I could come to Brisbane to meet him.

In September 2006, I met Mr Collier at a place of his choosing: a park behind the Paddo Tavern in the Brisbane suburb of Paddington, his 'office' as he put it (Figure 1.3). In his mid seventies when I had met him, Mr Collier had moved with his family to Paddington from Victoria when he was three years old. He was educated at the Milton State School, and spent most of his life working in the Queensland Patents Office. In 1975, he read an article in the *Courier Mail* about the then Chief Editor of the *OED*, the New Zealander Robert Burchfield (1923–2004), who was calling for public contributions to his Supplement volumes of the *OED* (Burchfield's *Supplement*). 'I thought, imagine if I could help get one word in the dictionary', Mr Collier told me. And so began the obsession that occupied him every day since. He supplied an average of 250 quotations every month, and sent more than 100,000 quotations in all. Not all of these have gone into the dictionary, of course, but it has meant that Brisbane's *Courier Mail* is the 584th most frequently quoted source in the *OED*, with more quotations than Virginia Woolf, T. S. Eliot, Winston Churchill, the *Book of Common Prayer*, *Daily Mirror*, or *National Geographic*.[3] Was there any chance of him coming to Oxford to see first-hand the work of the editors of the *OED*? 'No way', he replied, 'I couldn't face all the *Courier Mails* waiting for me on my return. I am going to be at Paddington for the rest of my days.'

And indeed Mr Collier did live alone in the same Paddington house his entire life. His collection of movie posters and words from the *Courier Mail* eventually took over his living quarters. 'He was the local naturist and a hoarder', explained his neighbour of forty-six years. 'Eventually there was only a single, narrow track through the house with piles of paper and newspaper lining each side.' Aged seventy-nine years old, Mr Collier went in to the Royal Brisbane Hospital on 20 June 2010 for a heart operation. He died on the operating table. His funeral was attended by his neighbours, none of whom knew the extent of his contribution to English scholarship.

Quotations like those submitted by Mr Collier are vital to any historical dictionary such as the *OED*. They tell lexicographers important things: who first used the word, where in the world it was first used, where its usage spread, and how it has been used since. The quotations for words of foreign provenance in particular show how and when a word starts being assimilated into English; in early quotations the word might be italicized, in inverted commas, or followed in the sentence by an explanation of its meaning, then – over time – the explanation is usually dropped, and finally it appears in roman type with no special treatment.

My etymological work on these words meant that most of the obscure dictionaries housed in our own little *OED* library were usually sitting on my desk. It also involved reading original diaries of explorers and early word lists compiled by missionaries. For example, I traced the word *Nootka* (the name of a Native tribe of North America on Vancouver Island) to Captain James Cook's *Journal*. The word seemed to have been misunderstood by him to be the local Native American people's name for the bay where they lived, whereas it may actually have been the Nootka word for 'to circle about', referring to a circle dance that was being performed to welcome Cook's party, or perhaps indicating that his ships should circle about to come into the harbour.

My work on the non-European words was backed up by a large group of about two hundred language specialists around the world to whom I could send my entries for checking. A hundred years ago, Murray was able to use Royal Mail to connect to the rest of the world: he would write by hand and wait for a reply from the consultant by Royal Mail. Thanks to email, our Khoekhoe specialist in Namibia often responded more quickly than our Tocharian specialist situated in Oxford. Every entry therefore passed through many hands over many months, years, or decades, before it was finally published. And it took quite a bit of evidence for a new word to get in the dictionary. We hesitated to state an official policy for new words, but usually a word only got admitted if it appeared in written texts more than five times over five years, and preferably in a variety of sources (i.e. not just newspapers but also magazines and books). It was important to discern if the word was a mere fad word that would die out after several months. Once a word entered the *OED*, it never left, so it was important for the word to show signs of longevity. If a word became obsolete, we would place a small dagger sign beside the headword in the dictionary but the actual entry would never be deleted from the text (this policy distinguishes the *OED* from most smaller dictionaries which are continually adding and deleting words in order to appeal to current markets).

Just as interesting as the words I edited were the people I worked with. Lexicographers have a reputation for being nerdy, conscientious, and borderline obsessive-compulsive, but that is a bit harsh. The diverse range of experiences and talents of this group of seventy people was particularly fascinating. Divided into four subgroups according to the kinds of words we edited, the most senior staff (Chief Editor and Deputy Chief Editor) sat at one end of the huge open-plan office followed by the bibliography group, the general words revision group, the science group, the etymology group, and a small band of IT specialists. Because I edited all parts of my non-European entries, my words did not go to the etymology group, and because my words spanned all types, including scientific and new words, I did not really belong to any one group. I spent the first couple of years sitting near the senior staff and later moved to sit with the new words group which was where the young and hip lexicographers tended to work. Young and hip for lexicographers may have its own definition, but each group certainly had its own character. The bibliographers tended to be older, more sensible, librarian types who knew their field better than anyone else in the world. Most of them had worked on the *OED* since the 'Burchfield days' of the 1970s and 1980s, and were more than happy to answer any question an editor had relating to an incomplete cited quotation or published edition. Most of them had started as library researchers or 'library checkers' who provided editors with information on the larger context of a quotation within a text or checked dictionary quotations for correct publication dates and page numbers. This is meticulous yet vital work that sometimes highlights errors in the editor's work such as a quotation that actually does not exist in the cited title or a previously misunderstood quotation that has led to a word being ill-defined.

The general words revision group and the science group were both mixes of all ages, and magnets for eccentric characters, including one who wore a different kilt for each Scottish feast day and would sometimes email me in Klingon, the language of *Star Trek* (we bonded early on about Klingon morphology because I was familiar with the grammar of Mutsun, a Native language of North America upon which Klingon was based). Many of the lexicographers sang in the Oxford Bach Choir and the OUP choir, some were Morris dancers in their spare time, and others followed their individual passions in the Bodleian Library after work each day. I would often bump into colleagues in the Bodleian Upper Reading Room who were researching for their own pleasure the history of Celtic ship names or the life of J. R. R. Tolkien before Bilbo. The editors in the etymology group were often from Scotland and Germany, places with universities that still taught philology. This eclectic mix of educational backgrounds and personal interests led to the *OED* submitting a very strong team for the 2004 series of *University Challenge: the Professionals*, an adaptation of the long-running BBC TV quiz, for members of professions and institutions rather than students. A bus load of lexicographers carrying mascot dictionaries and OUP teddy bears went to Manchester for the filming and to support our team, which made it to the final but narrowly lost to the British Library.

Positioned at the opposite end from the senior staff, the IT group was the generic prototype of pony-tailed, fast-talking techies surrounded by empty coke cans and crisp packets. The only difference was that these folks knew an adjective from an adverb, and created their own digital avatar alter egos out of historical *OED* lexicographers using 3D virtual worlds such as Second Life. I knew that the eating of junk food had a long tradition at the *OED* because I sometimes came across old slips in the archives that were written on the back of recycled chocolate wrappers. One of the early editors, Arthur Maling (b.1858), who had worked on the *OED* for thirty years after graduating in mathematics at Cambridge in 1886, had a habit of reusing waste paper of his own as slips, most of which were chocolate wrappers (his favourite brand seems to have been Harrod's Finest Mocha) (Figures 1.4 and 1.5).

Most of my colleagues at the *OED* had degrees in English literature or history, but there were also a couple of mathematicians and biologists. I was surprised to learn that I was the only linguist, and the Chief Editor jokingly explained that he liked it that way because linguists thought too much about things (the implication being that they would take too long to edit an entry).

We all got to know each other even though we sat each day in a silent zone. Silence is the golden rule at the *OED*, with several posters pinned on walls saying 'silence please'. And *everyone* obeys. If you want to speak, then you must go into one of several glass cases reserved for the purpose. Getting phone calls became tricky. Not only did the ringing sound distract others and prompt several dirty looks but I would then have to speak to the person, and over time my friends knew to stop ringing me since I could

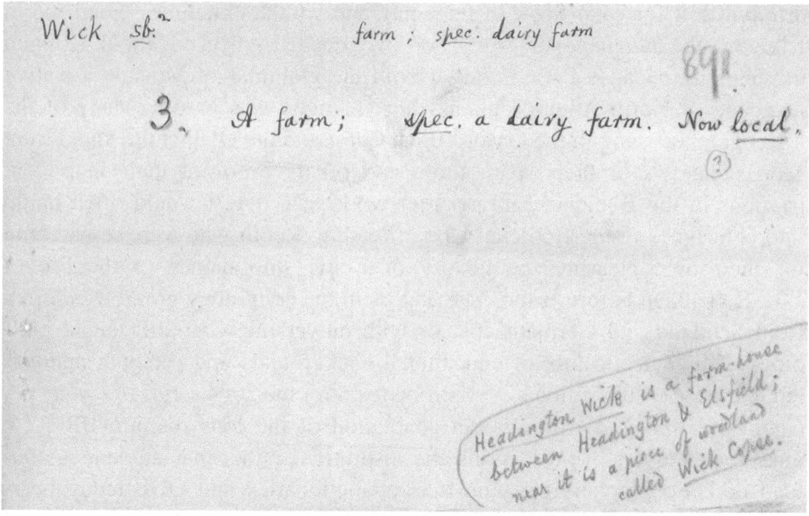

Figure 1.4 One of Arthur Maling's slips written on recycled chocolate wrappers. (Credit: OUP)

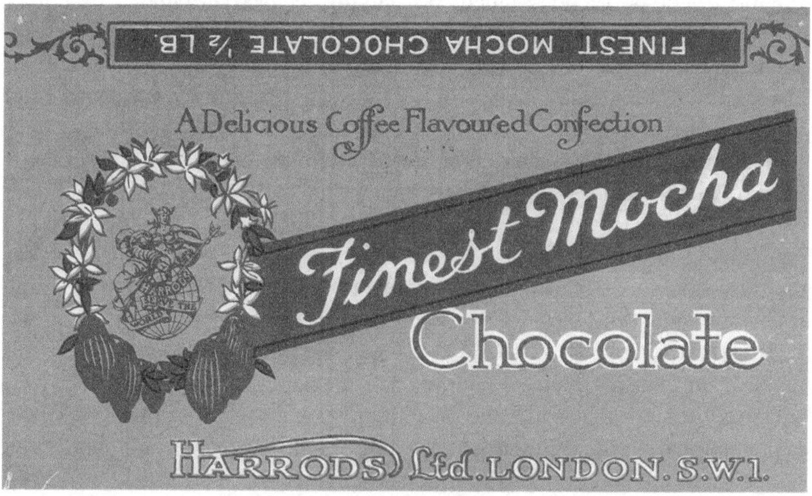

Figure 1.5 The reverse side of Arthur Maling's slip for *wick* showing one of many recycled chocolate wrappers. (Credit: OUP)

never say more than a whispered 'yes' or 'no'. My supervisor sat opposite me, our desks touching, but if I wanted to ask her a question I had to email her or save it for our weekly meeting in a glass case. This was a shock for me, as the office environments at the Macquarie Dictionary in Sydney and the Australian National Dictionary Centre in Canberra were more informal. If someone had a question about a pronunciation or definition, they would simply go and ask a colleague, or call out from room to room, or go to morning tea with a list of queries for everyone to share. The Australian offices were not air conditioned and in the sweltering summer temperatures, each lexicographer would peel off their shoes and clothing. I had been trained writing definitions in bare feet, and found myself in the formal setting of the *OED* offices unconsciously slipping off my shoes under my desk. I still can't define wearing shoes, but I did learn to put my shoes back on when I walked around the *OED*.

Editing the *OED* was a slow process, mainly because it was so thorough. It took nearly six years for forty of us to edit the letter M, and we partied at the home of the Chief Editor when it was finished. Even though it was in the middle of the alphabet, it was the first letter to be revised for the third edition. Why start at M? At the beginning of the new project, the editors decided not to superimpose their policy inconsistencies onto Murray's inconsistencies, and given that Murray started at the letter A, they decided to start at the middle of the alphabet by which time the editors of *OED1* would have been firmly in their lexicographic stride.

Raising a glass of wine with my fellow editors at the M party, I felt quietly chuffed that the last word to be edited in the letter M had been a non-European word. In fact, two Swahili words used in East African English brought the letter to a close: *Mzee*, an old person, and *mzungu*, a white person. I dared not mention it to the scientists, whose entry *myzostomid*, a type of parasitic worm, had been pushed to antepenultimate position. The significance of editing last words was something of a tradition for *OED* editors. Apparently one of the early editors, Charles Onions (1873–1965), often enjoyed boasting that he edited the last word in *OED1*: it was *Zyxt,* an archaic second-person singular indicative present form of the verb 'to see', but it has since been moved to the entry *see* so the ancient Egyptian beer called 'zythum' is the new last word. In theory, if work continues to be done alphabetically (and editors have already begun to edit some high-profile words outside the alphabetical range), the real last word for the editors of the third edition will be the last word in the letter L *lyxose*, a crystalline sugar, which might get the scientists excited but it does not have the same ring as *Zyxt,* which, given it was 'the last word', was later made the brand name of a soap which was advertised as 'the last word in cleanliness'. But, of course, for lexicographers there is never a last word in a good dictionary because, once you finish, you always start again.

Even now – over a decade since the launch of *OED Online* (third edition) – the editors will sensibly not name a finishing date. Somewhere in the vicinity of twenty years from now seems accurate. In the meanwhile, portions of the revised text are published quarterly online, and the dictionary is doubling in size. At this rate, it is often estimated that the final product will be over forty volumes in length – if indeed it is ever published in book form.

The thought of no end in sight can be debilitating to a lexicographer. Hence, when you work on such a large project it is important to set many short goals, and the slow pace of work at the *OED* was really hard to get used to at first. I was accustomed to working on smaller, synchronic dictionaries rather than a large, diachronic dictionary such as the *OED*. Diachronic dictionaries describe words 'across time', showing how a word is used historically by the use of quotation paragraphs after the definition. Synchronic dictionaries, on the other hand, give the reader a snapshot of a word at one point in time. These form the majority of dictionaries – smaller desktop dictionaries that give readers the pronunciation, etymology, and definition but no quotation paragraph. Synchronic dictionaries are faster to write because the lexicographer does not have to research a word's entire history and usage throughout time. They are also more stressful for lexicographers because the publishers set tighter schedules and are always pushing you to meet deadlines and to go faster.

There was less pressure at the *OED*, and at first it was difficult for me to adjust to the relaxed pace. Within a few months of instinctively setting my own deadlines and staying late or coming in to the office on weekends, as we were trained to do in Australia, I was politely taken into one of the glass cases by my supervisor and told to stop working long hours as it put too much pressure on other colleagues. I was told that *OED* editors must only work eight hours a day, five days a week. After several months, I realised that this was actually a smart working practice, because the nature of the work was so detailed and taxing on one's eyes and mind that it was sensible to control one's hours in order to last in the job over many years. When I began venturing into the *OED* archives and reading the old letters stored down there, I observed that the current *OED* regime of eight hours, five days a week, was not practised by the early editors.

As far as I could tell from the archives, the early editors worked phenomenally long hours. Murray started work in the early hours of the morning, before the sun rose, and worked until dinner time, often returning to his desk after dinner until late at night. He worked weekends, and I found several letters dated 25 December that showed he even worked on Christmas Day. Murray expected similar devotion from all his editors. Charles Onions was trained by Murray, and his son told me that his father worked all day at the office, only to return home and disappear into his study in the front room of the house. I began to learn that lexicography was an entire way of life, more than a job, for the early editors.

The history of the *OED* is scattered with stories of lexicographers whose mental health was compromised. One of Murray's sub-editors, John Dormer, was hospitalized in 1907 for mental illness after working on the largest letters of the alphabet (C and S). The famous contributor Dr. Minor (1834–1920), a convicted murderer, had mental health issues before contributing quotations from his cell in Broadmoor mental hospital. Less well-known is James McLeod Wyllie (1907–71) who worked at a manic pace on the first *Supplement to the OED* which was published in 1933 (hereafter referred to as '*1933 Supplement*'). He kept the *OED* files updated once the *1933 Supplement* was published, and worked on the *Oxford Latin Dictionary*, but the death of two of his children, combined with his irrepressible work ethic, led to several nervous breakdowns. He was finally hospitalized in the Warneford mental hospital in Oxford, and devoted the final decades of his life to self-published tracts that defamed OUP.[4]

I had come to work on the non-European words in the *OED* with the inherited notion that these words had been neglected by early dictionary editors.[5] Many of the entries I worked on had been untouched since Murray and the early editors wrote them, and yet their content did not reflect the popular image of the early editors as determinedly entrenched in nineteenth-century hierarchical views of language and culture. Not only were many loanwords and World Englishes already included in *OED1*, but when they were included they were dealt with surprisingly well. Considering some entries were over a hundred years old, the etymologies were thorough, the selection of quotations comprehensive, and the wording of most definitions surprisingly free of the racial and imperialistic presumptions of the period.

Dictionary-making, like all human activity, is inherently subjective, and the dictionary-maker inevitably leaves a trace of him- or herself in the text, but the traces that I found while editing the *OED* did not match the general consensus that the later editors were liberal in their inclusion of words of the world, and the early editors were conservative. But these were merely observations, and more detailed and careful analysis was needed in order to test these intuitions. For example, rather than exhibiting a neglect of loanwords, the first letter edited for *OED3*, the letter M, which was originally edited by Henry Bradley in 1906, contained over 800 foreign words, and we shall see in Chapter 3 that the letter P, which Murray originally edited, contained nearly 2000 foreign words. This equated to an average of 7% of the whole letter, which is approximately the same percentage as covered in *OED3* today – when the editors are making a concerted effort to cover this kind of vocabulary.[6] Murray's letter K had over 13% loanwords, which is much higher than the average coverage across the alphabet. Recent criticism that the earlier *OED* editions were UK-centric did not measure up against these kinds of figures. The more I edited the dictionary itself and the more

I researched, the more I realized that I may have to rethink my original view of the *OED* as a prototypically Anglocentric product of the Victorian period.

Discoveries in the archives

I first visited the *OED*'s archives because of the word *myall*. It was a word meaning 'stranger' which had entered English from an Australian Aboriginal language, and it had been included in *OED1* by Henry Bradley in 1908. I had expected very few Australian Aboriginal words in *OED1* but was surprised by how many there were. As I had spent a year living with an Australian Aboriginal community and had written a grammar and dictionary of a previously undocumented Aboriginal language, these were the words that I felt most confident editing. However, I had observed several fascinating differences between my editing of the word *myall* and Bradley's original efforts; for example, he had the etymology as 'from native name: Bigambel' which I changed to '< Dharuk (Sydney region) *maiyal* stranger, person from another tribe' along with a dated quotation taken directly from the original source (Collins 1798). The most significant change to the entry, however, lay in the structure of the rest of the entry and the use of definitional metalanguage to distinguish Australian Aboriginal from non-Aboriginal usage of the word in English contexts.

I wanted to see Bradley's original slips to see where he got his etymology and why he structured the entry the way he did. So I went down to the archives, located in the basement of the *OED*, to look at the original slips. Nothing is ever thrown out at the *OED*; even today, every slip that helps build an entry is stored in the archives for future checking. There were no windows in the archive, and the stuffy rooms were lined with hundreds of dusty boxes, each filled with slips and letters dating back to 1857 when the dictionary was first proposed.

There are few events in one's life that are so special that they seem to go in slow motion. As soon as I walked down the stairs into the dark basement, I knew I was in one of those moments. The archivist had kindly extracted the tattered bundle of *myall* slips, and they lay waiting for me under a lamp on a table. I could not believe I was touching the crumbling slips that the first editors had created, and reading their comments to each other. Each box around me contained new discoveries, like Murray's address book and list of correspondents and contributors – many of them from all corners of the globe – recording which books he sent them to read for the dictionary. It was a good thing that Murray's team of lexicographers in north Oxford worked separately from Bradley's team located downtown – it meant that members of Murray's team in the Scriptorium on Banbury Road were forced to write messages to Bradley's team in the Old Ashmolean Building on Broad Street.

Figure 1.6 The dictionary offices in the Old Ashmolean Building, Oxford, which housed Henry Bradley's team (at the front, second from the right). (Credit: OUP)

This provides an invaluable record of not only the work practices of the early editors but also the reasons and thought processes behind them.

Fans of any persuasion are liable to fetishize their subject. As soon as I held the bundle of slips for *myall* and untied the little piece of brown twine that kept each entry separate from the next, I romantically imagined that it had been tied by Bradley himself after he finished the entry in 1908. (Years later, I learnt more about the early work processes and realized that the early editors numbered each slip and sent them directly to the printer, so someone else in the press would have rebundled the slips and tied the string.) I read the top slip for the entry and presumed that the cursive handwriting was Bradley's, but later I got to learn the handwriting of the various editors, and recognized that this particular slip had been written by the editorial assistant John W. Birt (b.1890), not Bradley. It was probably pure fantasy that first hooked me into the archives, but, after that first visit for the word *myall* (which on this occasion actually gave me little extra information about the entry), I certainly wanted more.

I began to spend my lunch hours in the archives and frequently revisited after work. Issues would arise in my editing during the day and I would check and cross-check things in the archives or down the road at the Bodleian Library where the Murray Papers were stored. I began to discover that a dictionary was more than an alphabetical list of words; it was more like any other text that can be analyzed and probed for further meaning and context. The dictionary was not so much an immutable bible, but more like any other text in which an author, or in this case a lexicographer, imbues his or her work with his or her own perspective. I followed up these subjective fragments in the archival materials, and began to piece together the overlooked story of the *OED* as a truly global project that included the words of the world.

Re-evaluating the story of 'progress'

Whether editing the dictionary at my desk or digging through boxes in the archives, my days at the *OED* became one giant process of discovery. The story that unravelled was not only about the actual words but also about the *OED* lexicographers of the past whose voices came through the dictionary entries themselves and through the handwritten letters and slips stored in the archives. Ask any lexicographer who has revised a dictionary, and they will tell you how they get to know the person whose work they are revising. Murray seemed inclined to 'lump' definitions together (perhaps to save space on the page), rather than 'split' them into separate senses as was Bradley's habit. Onions seemed to be neither a lumper nor a splitter, and revelled in the detail of etymology. Craigie tended to write too much (thereby taking up too much space) and liked to distinguish transitivity, as many of the verbs he edited were described according to whether or not they took an object. The enjoyment of my own editing increased as I appreciated the privilege of being able to work on the same entries that these men (and most of them were men) had worked on. It was another way of getting to know them.

Before working on these words, I had believed the scholars and more popular media who had suggested that the early editors excluded these words because they were seen as peripheral to the central core of English.[7] In these critiques, the lexicographers were portrayed as: (1) having a view of the English language that was bound by the borders of Britain alone; (2) deliberately excluding non-British sources in preference for British texts in their collection of quotation evidence for the dictionary; and (3) ignoring international varieties of English to the extent that they were dismissed as peripheral and inferior, 'illegal immigrants' that deserved no place in an English dictionary.[8] As a consequence, the critics went on to praise Burchfield for being generous in his inclusion of words from outside Britain.[9] He was portrayed as: (1) having a global view of the English language; (2) deliberately seeking non-British sources as quotation evidence for the dictionary; and (3) including international varieties of English in the *OED* for the first time in its history. This view of the Anglocentric approach of early editors and the inclusive approach of later editors is still current.[10]

It is a view that fits a paradigm of 'progress': that Victorian lexicographers were conservative and imperialistic in their lexicographic policy, but that later editors were naturally more enlightened and 'liberal' in their coverage. And of course Burchfield's New Zealand identity seemed to lend further weight to the theory that he was the enlightened bringer of change who was more open to these words. Who was the original source of this story of 'progress'? And why had no one questioned it? Was it because the original source was regarded as reliable and authoritative?

All sources led back to 1972 and to one clear original source: Robert Burchfield himself. In the preface to the first volume of Burchfield's *Supplement*, he said that 'Readers will discover by constant use of the *Supplement* that the written English of regions like Australia, South Africa, and India have been accorded the kind of treatment that lexicographers of a former generation might have reserved for the English of Britain alone.'[11] No one before this date suggests this was the case, but *everyone* after this date follows Burchfield's line. It is a story we have all accepted for the past forty years.

Burchfield's presentation of himself as the champion of words of the world coincided, in the 1970s, with an increase in scholarly linguistic studies of varieties of English around the world. Scholars became more aware of the lexical, morphological, and syntactic similarities and differences between distinct varieties known as 'World Englishes'.[12] In the past twenty years, this linguistic work had been accompanied by a critique of the relations between these varieties and British English.[13] This analysis of the impact of the spread of English globally, combined with an increase in linguistic descriptions of World Englishes, had resulted in an interest in the lexicographic treatment of words from outside Britain in the *OED*. This interest had focussed mainly on the neglect of loanwords and World Englishes in the dictionary, especially in *OED1*, and on the ethnocentrism of definitions and choice of quotations within the dictionary.[14]

This book seeks to investigate the actual coverage given to non-European words by the early editors and Burchfield, the editorial methods of accessing and researching these words, and the editorial policies and practices relating to them. It looks at loanwords and words from varieties of English around the world, grouped together as 'words of the world', for two main reasons. First, they are words whose treatment in the dictionary has often been used by critics as a barometer of the editors' attitudes towards race, language, and goods away.

Nullafidian, variant of NULLIFIDIAN.

|| **Nullah** (nɒ·lă). *Anglo-Indian.* Also **nulla.** [Hindī *nālā* brook, rivulet, ravine.] A river or stream; a watercourse, river-bed, ravine.

1776 HALHED *Code Gentoo Laws* 52 When the water fails in all the *Nullahs.* **1793** HODGES *Trav. India* 20 This road is crossed by several nullahs, some of which have ferry boats stationed at them. **1834** MEDWIN *Angler in Wales* II. 16 A nullah, broader and swifter than usual, cut off my communication with the budgerow. **1859** R. F. BURTON *Centr. Afr.* in *Jrnl. Geogr. Soc.* XXIX. 206 Here and there are nullahs, with high stiff earthbanks for the passage of rain torrents. **1883** F. M. CRAWFORD *Mr. Isaacs* x, We had just crossed a nullah in the forest, full from the recent rains.

attrib. **1869** E. A. PARKES *Pract. Hygiene* (ed. 3) 71 Marsh or nullah water full of vegetable debris.

|| **Nu·lla-nu·lla.** Also **gnulla-, nullah-, nolla-.** [Native Australian.] A club of hard wood used as a weapon by the aborigines of Australia.

1838 T. L. MITCHELL *Exped. E. Austral.* I. 350 Striking him on the back of the head with a nulla-nulla. **1863** BEVERIDGE *Gatherings* 10 Wherein lay his Nullah-nullah. **1885** MRS. C. PRAED *Head Station* 176 The elder men beat their nulla-nullas, and waved their spears. **1890** LUMHOLTZ *Cannibals* 72 The nolla-nolla or club, the warlike weapon of the Australian native most commonly in use.

Nulle, will not: see NILL *v.*

Figure 1.7 Example of the use of tramlines in *OED1* on the Indian English word *nullah*, a river or stream, and the Australian English word *nulla-nulla*, a wooden club used traditionally by Australian Aborigines. (Credit: OUP)

culture. Second, they were grouped together by the editors themselves as 'words on or near the frontier line' whose inclusion and treatment in the dictionary often vexed them.

As with all words considered for the dictionary, the inclusion of loanwords and World Englishes depended on their use in written sources. Based on their degrees of naturalization in English written texts, the words were categorized according to four levels, which Murray described as 'naturals', 'denizens', 'aliens', and 'casuals'. His policy was to put two small parallel lines ||, known in-house as 'tramlines', beside the headword to indicate that the word was 'alien or not yet naturalized' on denizens, aliens, or casuals, but not on naturals (Figure 1.7). These categories were not immediately easy to understand, so Murray outlined them in the preface to the first volume of the dictionary. Naturals were 'native words' like *father* and 'naturalized words' like *street* and *parasol*. Denizens were words naturalized in use but not in form, pronunciation, or inflection, such as *aide-de-campe* and *locus*. Aliens were names of 'foreign objects or titles' with no English 'native equivalents', as with *cicerone*, an Italian guide, and *backsheesh*, the Persian and Arabic term for money or a tip. Murray described casuals as 'foreign words . . . not in habitual use, which for special and temporary purposes occur in books of foreign travel [and] letters of foreign correspondence'. He admitted that the boundaries between these groups were porous, and that words moved from one to another, usually moving 'upwards from the last to the first': from casual to alien to denizen to natural.[15] Murray's system for classifying a word according to its naturalization was followed not only by his fellow editors but also by Burchfield one hundred years later (tramlines only occur on two words in the *1933 Supplement,* as will be discussed in Chapter 5, and were dropped altogether in *OED3*).

By engaging in qualitative, contextual, and statistical analysis and comparison of dictionaries, this book shows that it is possible to access the relationship between lexicographic policy and practice, highlighting that it is in the disjunction between policy and practice that a lexicographer's attitudes can often be found. Ultimately, the *OED* text is shown to be the most reliable barometer of how those attitudes are worked out in practice. The results of my work provide an alternative perspective, and a corrective, to Burchfield's story of 'progress'.

This book is not a comprehensive survey of the nature of loanwords and World Englishes in the *OED1*, nor is it a critique of whether or not *OED1* was ethnocentric or imperialist in its definitions or metalinguistic coding.[16] My starting question for this study is twofold: (1) to discover whether the story Burchfield told of his predecessors was true, and (2) to discover whether the story Burchfield told of himself was true. This book, then, is an examination of the relationship between lexicographic policy and practice relating to loanwords and World Englishes. I was particularly interested in the disconnect between policy and practice, which can be gleaned by comparing the final text with archival, published, and historical evidence. In this sense, the book is clearly rooted in, and draws on, my own experience as a practising lexicographer.

The particular research questions that this study seeks to answer fall into three main groups. The first consists of questions specific to the *OED*, its compilation and content. I ask the questions: how did Murray and his fellow editors understand and categorize loanwords and World Englishes? How did their successor, Robert Burchfield, understand and categorize loanwords and World Englishes? How did the editors seek to document these words? What were their main sources and how did they find them? Did the editors exhibit biases towards words from certain languages, regions of the world, or semantic fields? How was the *OED*'s treatment of words of the world received by contemporaries? What variables influenced the editors and their treatment of loanwords? How did the *OED*'s coverage of these words compare with other dictionaries? What was the relationship between the *OED* and other dictionaries specializing in words from outside Britain?

The second group of research questions is more broadly concerned with the continuing development of dictionary research – especially methodological approaches to dictionary research – as a discipline.[17] In a way, this strand of the book is a by-product of the study as a whole: through my analysis of the *OED*, I was able to explore different methodological approaches to dictionary research. Areas explored include: dictionary case study sampling techniques; limits and problems of analyzing dictionaries with multiple editors and publication dates that span across decades; and pitfalls of relying too heavily on the lexicographers' own accounts of their lexicographic practices, or on one type of evidence in dictionary research at the expense of others (archival, textual, statistical, and contextual).

Third, the results of the case study in Chapter 6 allow a new exploration of questions relating to the history of the English language, particularly its loanwords and words from international varieties of English: are there trends in borrowing according to semantic field or donor language?

This book is laid out so as to proceed, where possible, chronologically. It begins by focusing on *OED1* (Chapters 2, 3, and 4) followed by the *1933 Supplement* (Chapter 5), and finally Burchfield's *Supplement* (Chapter 6). Chapter 2 provides a brief history of the early *OED* which shows that from its beginnings it was a transnational dictionary intent on 'flinging its doors wide', as one early editor put it.[18] Chapter 3 contextualizes *OED1* within the later nineteenth-century British Empire, revealing that Murray was influenced by Empire in nuanced and unexpected ways, thereby providing a counter-position to a black-and-white approach of seeing the *OED* as a distinct product of Empire in which the position of 'centre' defined and dominated the 'periphery'. It explores Murray's lexicographic vision and practice, and his view of what constituted the English language. In an attempt to test the recent criticism aimed at Murray and the early editors, this chapter probes the various internal and external pressures on the early editors to exclude foreign words; it discusses the differences in policy and practice between the early editors; and describes their context and place within Oxford and the academy. It shows that Murray was more inclusive of words of the world than recent scholars have suggested. There is not only evidence in the dictionary of his liberal inclusion of foreign words, but ample evidence in his own writings, letters, and lectures that his inclusive practice was rooted in a radical view of English as a global language that was worthy of representation and description in the dictionary.

Murray was not always consistent in his rhetoric and practice on foreign words, and there were limits to his inclusion policy. The best way to test these limits is to compare his work with that of his contemporaries, especially lexicographers working on other dictionaries that specialized in foreign words. Chapter 4 examines how Murray's treatment of loanwords compares with Charles Fennell's treatment of loanwords in the *Stanford Dictionary of Anglicised Words and Phrases* (1892). The results add texture and nuance to the picture of Murray presented in Chapter 3. He emerges as a complex and competitive man who was committed to including words from outside Britain in the *OED*, but whose inclusion policy could have gone further.

The lexicographic policies and practices devised by Murray in the early 1880s were more or less faithfully followed by all who succeeded him until 1986, except in the use of tramlines in the *1933 Supplement*. Chapter 5 investigates the use of tramlines in the *1933 Supplement*, and reveals unforeseen influences on the editors, William Craigie (1867–1957) and Charles Onions, from the Society of Pure English (SPE) which had an impact on their attitude towards foreign words, and, in turn, on their lexicographic practice.

A central aim of this book is to investigate whether scholars and the media were accurate in their criticism of early *OED* editors and their praise of later *OED* editors. In order to explore the accuracy and validity of this critique, Chapter 6 consists of a case study that compares the two *Supplements* (1933 and 1972–86). The case study examines in detail over nine thousand dictionary entries (10% of each dictionary) across nineteen parameters, and reveals that the lexicographic practice of Robert Burchfield did not always match his stated policies on loanwords and World Englishes.

By assessing the coverage of words from outside Britain in the *OED* from its inception until 1986, I hope this book allows readers to discover more about the various forces – in this case, global forces – that go into making a dictionary of the magnitude of the *OED*, as well as the decision-making processes behind lexicographic practice, and the places of slippage between a dictionary-maker's stated editorial policy and his or her actual practice.

ENDNOTES

1 The Supplement volumes were published in 1933, 1972 (A–G), 1976 (H–N), 1982 (O–Scz), and 1986 (Se–Z) respectively.

2 Until recently, there were satellite dictionary centres that produced national dictionaries of World Englishes in Australia, New Zealand, Canada, and South Africa.

3 Brisbane's *Courier Mail* is quoted 783 times in the *OED*. T. S. Eliot is quoted 676 times, Virginia Woolf is quoted 588 times, Winston Churchill is quoted 495 times, *Daily Mirror* is quoted 565 times, *National Geographic* is quoted 525 times, *Book of Common Prayer* is quoted 663 times. See http://www.oed.com/sources.

4 Wyllie (1965). See more on Wyllie in Chapter 5 and in Brewer (2007).

5 The early editors of *OED1* and the *1933 Supplement* are criticized in Burchfield (1972: xv; 1977: 61; 1986: ix, xi); Bailey and Görlach (1982: 4); Howard (1986: 12); Weiner (1987; 1990); Burchfield and Aarsleff (1988: 22); McArthur (1993: 332); 'Wimmin and Yuppies Earn Places in Oxford Dictionary Supplement', *The*

Globe and Mail (Canada), 9 May 1986 p. 9; 'A Supplement to the Oxford English Dictionary', *The New Leader,* vol. 68, 1 December 1986 p. 5; 'Interview with Burchfield on the Macneil/Lehrer', *News Hour*, New York, Tuesday, 27 May 1986; and Ackroyd (1987: 22). Praise for Burchfield can be found in all these sources, including Sledd (1973: 46); Sands (1976: 718); Görlach (1990: 312); McArthur (1993: 332); Brewer (1993: 326); Price (2003b); and Simpson (2008). These sources and Burchfield's own attitude towards his predecessors are discussed fully in Chapter 6.

6 This is a modest estimate, taking 'tramlines' (two small parallel lines beside the headword '||' used to signify that the word is 'alien or not yet naturalized') as a barometer, but there were hundreds more World English neologisms and adaptations not given tramlines, so the exact figures would be even higher. The inclusion of foreign words in *OED1* is discussed further in Chapter 3, and Murray's policy on tramlines is explained more fully later in this chapter and Chapter 3.

7 See e.g. Burchfield (1972: xv; 1977: 61; 1986: ix, xi); Bailey and Görlach (1982: 4); Howard (1986: 12); Ackroyd (1987: 22); Burchfield and Aarsleff (1988: 22); Weiner (1990: 500); and McArthur (1993: 332). See Chapter 6 for more detailed criticism aimed at the early editors.

8 Burchfield (1986: ix).

9 See e.g. Sledd (1973: 46); Sands (1976: 718); Bailey and Görlach (1982: 4); Görlach (1990: 312); Ackroyd (1987: 22); McArthur (1993: 332); Brewer (1993: 326); Weiner (1987, 1990); Price (2003b); and Simpson (2008). See Chapter 6 for more detailed praise of Burchfield.

10 Weiner (1987); Brewer (2007, 2009); Simpson (2008).

11 Burchfield (1972: xv). More of Burchfield's criticisms of the early editors are given in Chapter 6.

12 Key early studies that compared the similarities and differences between varieties of English were *Varieties of Present-Day English* (1973) by Bailey and Robinson (eds.); *International English: A Guide to Varieties of Standard English* (1982) by Trudgill and Hannah; *English as a World Language* (1982) by Bailey and Görlach (eds.); *The New Englishes* (1984) by Platt, Weber, and Ho; and *The Alchemy of English: The Spread, Functions, and Models of Non-native Englishes* (1986) by Kachru. More recent surveys include *Post-imperial English* (1996) by Fishman, Conrad, and Rubal-Lopez (eds.); *World English* (2002) by Brutt-Griffler; *The Oxford Guide to World English* (2002) by McArthur; *A Handbook of Varieties of English* (2004) by Kortmann and Schneider; *The Handbook of World Englishes* (2006) by Kachru, Kachru, and Nelson (eds.); *Postcolonial English* (2007) by Schneider; *World Englishes* (2007) by Kirkpatrick; and *World Englishes* (2008) by Mesthrie and Bhatt.

13 The landmark text in the critique of the spread of English and its global role is *Linguistic Imperialism* (1992) by Phillipson. Debate on the issue can be found in most of the recent publications listed in note 8, and in articles by Bisong (1995), Davies (1996), Pennycook (1994), and Brutt-Griffler (2005).

14 Criticism of ideological and cultural bias in the *OED* can be found in Weiner (1987, 1990), Moon (1989), Willinsky (1994), Algeo (1995), Benson (2001), Simpson (2008), and Brewer (2007, 2009).

15 Murray (1888: xix).

16 There already exist studies on cultural and ideological bias in the *OED* by Moon (1989), Willinsky (1994), and Benson (2001).

17 See Coleman and Ogilvie (2009) for more on dictionary research methodology, an article that, in part, grew out of the work I did on this book.

18 MP/9/11/1862. Furnivall Circular to the Philological Society, 9 November 1862, p. 3.

2 A global dictionary from the beginning

> Fling our doors wide! All, all, not one, but all, must enter.
>
> Frederick Furnivall (1862), Editor of the dictionary from 1861 to 1879

The first edition (*OED1*) was officially proposed in 1857, and completed seventy-one years later in 1928. A first *Supplement* volume was published in 1933, and a second *Supplement* was published in four volumes in 1972 (A–G), 1976 (H–N), 1982 (O–Scz), and 1986 (Se–Z). The second *Supplement* was combined with 5000 extra entries in 1989 to form *OED2*. In 1993 and 1997, three volumes of *Additions to the Second Edition* were published. Work began on *OED3* in 1993 – the first complete revision of the first edition and the *Supplement* volumes – and *OED Online* was launched in 2000, which allowed users to search either second edition entries or revised third edition entries, as they were published quarterly.

The original idea for the dictionary came in the middle of the nineteenth century from three members of the Philological Society – the oldest learned society in Britain devoted to the study of language. More than a century later I joined it myself, soon after starting at the *OED*. Once a month I travelled to London by train for its meetings at the School of Oriental and African Studies (SOAS) in Russell Square. The meetings were like something out of another century: they began with tea and sandwiches, and an announcement of the people who had expressed the wish to join since the previous meeting. The members who were present – most of whom were elderly men in tweed jackets – were urged to speak up if they objected. Tea was always excruciating for me because no matter what the topic of conversation I found that the elderly men never looked at me. I remember one conversation about early Maori dictionaries, a personal interest of mine, in which the old man addressed his entire conversation to my young male friend who was a specialist in Old Icelandic and knew absolutely nothing about the topic. Tea was always followed by a lecture on any topic pertaining to historical and comparative linguistics.

I suspect the format of meetings had changed little since the mid nineteenth century when the idea for the dictionary was first proposed by three men:

Figure 2.1 Richard Chenevix Trench (1807–86) who proposed the concept of a 'new dictionary' to the Philological Society. (Credit: OUP)

Herbert Coleridge (1830–61), Frederick Furnivall (1825–1910), and Richard Chenevix Trench (1807–86). Grandson of the poet Samuel Coleridge, Coleridge was a young barrister and specialist in Sanskrit and Icelandic who had been educated at Eton and the University of Oxford (Figure 2.2).[1] Furnivall was five years older than Coleridge; he was a lawyer and literary scholar who had graduated from the University of Cambridge and University College, London (Figure 2.3). He was a Christian Socialist who had founded the Working Men's College with F. D. Maurice and others.[2] Trench was a prominent clergyman and scholar of English who was twenty years older than the other two (Figure 2.1). He was Professor of Divinity at King's College, London, had been educated at Harrow and the University of Cambridge, and later became Dean of Westminster, and then Archbishop of Dublin.[3]

Figure 2.2 Herbert Coleridge (1830–61), first editor of the dictionary from 1859 to 1861. (Credit: OUP)

The three men were dissatisfied with existing English dictionaries, and formed an 'Unregistered Words Committtee' to search for words missing from current dictionaries. Their work culminated in the idea for a dictionary of their own that would completely re-examine the language from Anglo-Saxon times onward. Trench presented the idea of the new dictionary at a meeting of the Philological Society in 1857.[4] Two years before that, he had published five lectures on the English language, entitled *English: Past and Present* (1855). Originally delivered to his students at King's College, London, the lectures give an insight into Trench's view of language in general, and his view of foreign words in English in particular, and help to reveal the thinking behind his proposal for a new dictionary.

Figure 2.3 Frederick Furnivall (1825–1910), editor of the dictionary from 1860 to 1879, photographed rowing on the Thames. (Credit: Furnivall Sculling Club)

In the mid nineteenth century, it was firmly believed that Britain was the intellectual centre of the English-speaking world, and while many commentators saw the borrowing of foreign words as a menace with the potential to decay, Trench saw it as an opportunity for the reception of new words. His first lecture was devoted to English as a 'composite language' in which 'changes have resulted from the birth of new words or the reception of foreign words'. He was well aware of the proportion of foreign words in the English language, explaining:

Suppose the English language to be divided into a hundred parts; of these, to make a rough distribution, sixty would be Saxon, thirty would be Latin (including of course the Latin which has come to us through the French), five would be Greek; we should thus have assigned ninety-five parts, leaving the other five, perhaps too large a residue, to be divided among all other languages from which we have adopted isolated words.[5]

He then went on to describe these loanwords in detail, by explaining that Hebrew words were 'mostly, if not entirely, belonging to religious matters, as "amen", "cabala", "cherub", "ephod", "hallelujah", "jubilee", "manna", "Messiah", "sabbath", "seraph".' He described the large proportion of mathematical and astronomical loans from Arabic, such as *algebra*, *cipher*, *zero*, *zenith*, *nadir*, *talisman*, *almanach*. 'The Arabs were the chemists, no less than the astronomers and arithmeticians of the middle ages', he explained, listing other examples such as *alkali*, *alembic*, *elixir*, and *alcohol*. 'Add to these the names of animals or articles of merchandize first introduced by them to the notice of Western Europe', wrote Trench, listing thirty words which included *giraffe*, *gazelle*, *saffron*, *lemon*, *orange*, *syrup*, *jar*, *coffee*, *sugar*, *jasmin*, *assassin*, *divan*, *sofa*, and *magazine*. He discussed Persian words (*bazaar*, *lilac*, *pagoda*, *caravan*, *azure*, *scarlet*, *taffeta*, *saraband*); words from Turkish (*tulip*, *turban*, *chouse*, *dragoman*); and words from the 'new world' such as *tobacco*, *chocolate*, *potato*, *maize*, *condor*, *hamoc*, *cacique*, *wigwam*, and *hurricane*.[6]

In 1857, the year the three men proposed the new dictionary, Trench gave two famous lectures to the Philological Society, published as *On Some Deficiencies in our English Dictionaries*, in which he and his colleagues proposed a radically new framework for lexicography. His proposal was inspired by the emergence of major European dictionaries in the early to mid nineteenth century, and was a reaction against what was perceived as the prescriptivism and inconsistencies of Samuel Johnson's *Dictionary of the English Language* (1755) and the deficiencies of Charles Richardson's *A New Dictionary of the English Language* (1836–7).[7] Johnson's approach had been typical of the linguistic climate of the eighteenth century in which scholars tried to 'fix' the language; dictionaries often included personal judgements and opinions of the lexicographer, and were often more about prescription and proscription than description. A century later, however, Trench suggested an approach that was evidence-based and scientific. He believed that a dictionary should describe the language in a systematic way, founded on the new scientific and historical principles of the day. In addition to providing full etymologies, he wanted the usage of each word in the dictionary to be based on a variety of written sources, not merely on a predictable canon. Trench believed that a dictionary should not be a 'standard' for the language as the French *Dictionnaire de l'Académie française* had aimed to be, but rather it should describe the language.[8] 'It is no task of the maker [of a dictionary] to select the *good* words of the language', wrote Trench, '... if he fancies that it is so, and begins to pick and choose, to leave this and to take that, he will go astray.' Obsolete words should be recorded.[9] He recommended that, unlike Johnson's and Richardson's dictionaries, a dictionary should include or exclude a word for systematic, rather than ad hoc, reasons:

> The business which he [the lexicographer] has undertaken is to collect and arrange all the words, whether good or bad, whether they do or do not commend themselves to his judgment, which, with certain exceptions hereafter to be specified, those writing in the language have employed, he is an historian of it, not a critic.[10]

Coleridge had a similar vision, which he explained in a letter to Trench, published in the *Transactions of the Philological Society* in 1857: 'Every word should be made to tell its own story – the story of its birth and life, and in many cases of its death, and even occasionally of its resuscitation.'[11] This quotation (which I had pinned above my desk at the *OED*) suggests that lexicographers write biographies of words: that words have lives unto themselves and are dynamic entities, which we endeavour to track and describe as best we can.

These men were proposing a shift in thinking about dictionaries. Not only would these texts describe rather than prescribe, but they would be inclusive and cover all English. Trench said that he also wanted to create a *Lexicon totius Anglicitatis*, a dictionary of *all* English.[12] This expression was an allusion to a well-known four-volume Latin dictionary by Guido Forcellini called *Lexicon totius Latinitatis* (1771). The term was re-appropriated as *Dictionarium totius Anglicitatis* and *Lexicon totius Anglicitatis* in the mid nineteenth century to refer to the ideal of a comprehensive dictionary that recorded every word in the English language.[13]

Trench's *Lexicon totius Anglicitatis* would start from scratch and not be based on any pre-existing text. It was to be 'an entirely new Dictionary; no patch upon old garments, but a new garment throughout'.[14] He articulated the need for 'drawing as with a sweep-net over the whole extent of English literature' so that 'innumerable words ... which are lurking in every corner of our literature, will ever be brought within our net'.[15] According to him, 'the business which [the lexicographer] has undertaken is to collect and arrange all words ... whether they do or do not commend themselves to his judgement'.

The Philological Society agreed to gather citations and compile materials for this 'new' dictionary, which would later be called the *New English Dictionary on Historical Principles, founded mainly on the materials collected by the Philological Society*. It was published under this title until 1933, and generally referred to as the *New English Dictionary* or *N.E.D.*, despite having been known informally as the 'Oxford English Dictionary' since the 1890s. The entire dictionary was not officially called the *Oxford English Dictionary* until 1933, when it was re-issued with the *1933 Supplement*.[16]

A dictionary of this scale was new for Britain but not for Continental Europe, where three major national historical dictionaries were already in progress: in Germany, the Brothers Grimm had begun *Deutsches Wörterbuch* in 1838; in France, Emile Littré began work on *Dictionnaire de la langue française* in 1841, and in the Netherlands, Matthias de Vries had started *Woordenboek der Nederlandsche Taal* in 1851.[17]

In his lectures and his book, Trench showed an appreciation of the presence of loanwords and regionalisms in English, and, interestingly, his attitude towards the place of foreign words in an English dictionary changed between the publication of *On Some Deficiencies* in 1857 and the publication of *Canones Lexicographici, Or Rules to be Observed in Editing the New English Dictionary* in 1860. In *On Some Deficiencies*, in the context of criticizing the inclusion of 'purely technical terms' pertaining to 'some special art or science', Trench spoke against the inclusion of 'hideous exotics' and 'rubbish'. He stated that provincialisms and regionalisms 'had no right to a place in a Dictionary of the English tongue' unless they were 'citizens', i.e. unless they had spread nationally or had previously held national status.[18] He argued that words that were once citizens but now localized to one region should be included (not on the basis of their current status as regionalisms but because of their previous status as 'citizens'), such as *spong*, a Suffolk term for 'an irregular narrow and projecting part of a field'; *hazle*, an East Anglian term for 'the first process in drying washed linen';[19] and the North Country verb *flaite*, 'to scare, to terrify'.[20] However, there was a change of policy by the time of *Canones Lexicographici* (1860), three years later, which Trench wrote with Coleridge, Furnivall, and five others who comprised the Dictionary Committee.[21] In *Canones Lexicographici*, provincialisms and regionalisms were recommended for admittance to the main dictionary 'whether furnished or not with the otherwise indispensable passport of a quotation'.[22] In addition, Americanisms were to be admitted to the dictionary 'on the same terms as our own words', as were foreign words with an etymological appendix for the roots and 'primitive bases' ('all forms which represent the last origin that can be assigned to a word').[23] The change in policy represented by the second text may have been the result of Furnivall's involvement in its composition, because he was always keen to include as many words as possible in the dictionary.

Apart from the mention of Americanisms in *Canones Lexicographici*, neither text referred to any other global varieties of English which would have been emerging at this time. Would Trench have dismissed them in principle in the same way that he seems to have dismissed British regionalisms that were not 'citizens'? The answer hinges on whether Trench's sense of the priority of national language, as opposed to regional language, extended to all nations or just to England. If it extended to all nations, then Trench would have welcomed words from varieties of English outside Britain as long as they were 'once current over the whole land.'[24] If Trench's view was truly focused on England alone, then he would have lumped 'World Englishes' with 'provincial or local words', and proposed omitting them all from the dictionary unless the unlikely prospect arose that they were once written and spoken in all of England.

After Trench delivered his speeches, the Philological Society agreed to compile the *New English Dictionary* and the youngest of the three men, Herbert Coleridge, aged twenty-eight years old, was chosen to be the first editor. In 1859, the same year that Charles Darwin published *On the Origin of Species*, Coleridge began work on the dictionary. Under his leadership, two important systems were instituted which still exist at the *OED* today. First, he managed the reading programme that had been initiated by Trench and the Philological Society, and targeted specific texts to be read by the public and members of the Society. Second, he decided that these quotations should be written on slips of 4 × 6-inch paper (corresponding to the *fiche* of the French and the *zettel* of the Germans),[25] with the headword and part of speech written in the upper left-hand corner, and the citation in the centre. This exact practice, on the same sized paper, was still in use when I worked on the *OED* 142 years later, and it remains in use.

On words from outside Britain, Coleridge's editorial policy was sometimes more conservative and less inclusive than his colleagues envisaged for their dictionary, but a system was put in place where Coleridge gave feedback and sought the advice of Philological Society members. In one such paper, *On the Exclusion of Certain Words from a Dictionary* (1860), which requested feedback on his inclusion policy, Coleridge stated that his starting point for inclusion was that 'every word is prima facie to be looked upon as admissible, till its inadmissibility be satisfactorily established'. But he identified certain classes of words that ranked as 'probationers on trial' whose inclusion was not automatic; one such class was imperfectly naturalized foreign words and words introduced from Latin and Greek 'in cases where a word exactly expressing the sense required already exists in familiar use such as *psychologer* for *psychologist*.[26] Coleridge proposed relegating all such words to an alphabetical list at the end of the dictionary, but it is striking that the Philological Society members opposed his solution and insisted that '*all* words should be admitted into the proposed Dictionary'. As reported by Furnivall in an appendix to Coleridge's paper, 'though they [the members] allowed that a discretion was reserved to the Editor to exclude some words, they desired that it should be exercised sparingly'.[27]

These early editors were extraordinarily optimistic about how quickly they expected the dictionary to be finished, as their correspondence shows. Coleridge presumed that the first part of the dictionary would be published in two years, and in 1857, he reported to the Philological Society that 'in two years we shall be able to give our first number to the world. Indeed were it not for the dilatoriness of many contributors ... I should not hesitate to name an earlier period'.[28] However, within two years of his editorship, Coleridge died of consumption at the age of thirty, and the dictionary was left without an editor.

The first part of the dictionary, A–ANT, took another twenty-six years to be completed and published. The reason for the delay lay with Coleridge's successor, Frederick Furnivall. Furnivall is perhaps the most colourful yet underrated figure in the history of the *OED*. He has been portrayed as immature and irresponsible, as someone who came up with good ideas but did not follow them through. Perhaps history has treated Furnivall badly because, on the face of it, the *OED* made very slow progress in those twenty-six years. But these criticisms are unfair because he instituted policies and lexicographic practices that outlived him and are still employed at the *OED*. He also made things happen for other scholars and was one of those rare 'big' people who help and enable others rather than compete with them; he was, for example, responsible for getting James Murray his job as editor of the dictionary. Importantly for *OED1*, Furnivall believed in including as many words as possible.

As one of the three members of the Philological Society who had originally proposed the dictionary, not only did Furnivall know its vision, but he had helped shape it. When Coleridge had asked members of the Philological Society for advice on the treatment of 'probationers on trial', such as imperfectly naturalized foreign words, it was Furnivall who had pushed that '*all* words should be admitted into the proposed Dictionary'.[29]

Furnivall saw the dictionary's boundaries as without limits, 'Fling our doors wide! all, all, not one, but all, must enter', he had declared shortly after Coleridge's death.[30] For Furnivall, words in the dictionary were like guests at his parties, which were famous throughout London for welcoming all regardless of provenance or type. As explained by his friend Francis Bickley: 'There was no selection about his parties. University professors were expected to fraternize with girls from the tea-shop; and, under the spell of their host's personality, they did fraternize.'[31] His inclusive view of the dictionary was typical of his personal openness to all ideas and people. In John Gross' biography of Furnivall, *The Rise and Fall of the Man of Letters* (1969), he described him as 'an ardent old-fashioned socialist, who refused to be bound by snobbish convention' as characterized by the fact that one of the contributions in the memorial volume published after his death was from a waitress in the ABC tea shop in Oxford Street which he frequented.[32]

Furnivall remained the nominal editor of the *OED* until 1879, by which time his disparate interests in other activities such as founding the Early English Text Society (1864), the Chaucer Society and Ballad Society (1868), the New Shakspere Society (1874), and his training of the world's first women's rowing team (one of whom became his second wife), meant that he devoted time to amassing materials for the dictionary but not editing it (Figure 2.4).[33] Furnivall's industrious enthusiasm and leadership are deftly captured in Gross' description of him as 'one of the great rock-blasting entrepreneurs of Victorian scholarship, the kind of man who if his energies had taken another turn might have covered a continent with railways'.[34]

Figure 2.4 Furnivall photographed with the world's first women's rowing team whom he coached. (Credit: Furnivall Sculling Club)

Furnivall put this enormous energy into organizing a band of readers and sub-editors for the dictionary, and the activities that distracted him from editing the dictionary were, in the end, to benefit the dictionary in unfathomable ways.[35] For example, having observed the dearth of printed texts in the pre-1500 period, he founded the Early English Text Society, which in turn supplied the *OED* with quotations from pre-1500 texts, thereby immeasurably boosting its coverage of Old and Middle English.

Furnivall remained closely associated with *OED1* until his death in 1910. 'His interest in the dictionary', wrote Henry Bradley in tribute to Furnivall in 1911, 'amounted to a passion'.[36] He contributed more than 30,000 quotations, many of which were taken from his daily reading of newspapers. As remarked in the OUP in-house journal, *The Periodical*, 'if the Dictionary at one period quotes the *Daily News* and at another the *Daily Chronicle*, it is because Furnivall had changed his paper in the meantime'.[37] These quotations were not written on conventional, clean slips of 4 x 6-inch paper, but were characteristically written on anything at hand, similar to the postcards he sent friends, described by his friend, the English literary critic Caroline Spurgeon, thus:

I heard from him on picture post cards of a varied and sometimes startling kind, on the backs of other people's letters, on half-sheets carefully torn from his vast correspondence, on Museum slips, and on the edge of newspaper cuttings. ... I asked him once why he was so frugal about paper, and he said it was a habit he had started at a time when paper was very dear. This peculiarity, like many another of his, was very characteristic of the man. It illustrates his disregard of convention, as well as his pertinacity, and his readiness to work with any tools.[38]

Furnivall's reading for the dictionary shows a particular interest in travellers' tales and books on other cultures, which provided quotational evidence for many loanwords and words pertaining to life in remote parts of the world. He read *Travels in West Africa, Congo Français, Corisco and Cameroons* (1897) by the explorer Mary Kingsley, which contributed words such as *lhiamba*, West African hemp, *koko*, a West African taro plant, and *ju-ju*, a West African charm.[39] Many of the books that Furnivall read for the dictionary were topical and controversial, drawing attention to the injustices of British colonial rule. Some, such as *Froudacity* (1889) by John Jacob Thomas, became seminal liberation texts. Furnivall's immediate reading of this controversial polemic on the domination of the black population of the West Indies elicited Caribbean English words such as *colour-domination*, discrimination of black West Indians, and *colour-dread*, the feeling of dread at the thought of the success of a black West Indian, which Murray promptly published in the 1891 fascicle *clo-consigner* (the dictionary was gradually published in small alphabetical portions called 'fascicles').[40] Other words followed in later fascicles, such as *drogherman*, someone who steers a West-Indian boat, and *plantocracy*, the dominant class of plantation owners in the West Indies.[41] Furnivall had a particular eye for lexicalization of loanwords in English, such as *tarbooshed*, wearing a Muslim felt hat, used by Charles Godfrey Leland in *The Egyptian Sketch Book* (1873).[42] His penchant for the polemical or 'outlandish' shows that *OED* editors could not be accused of *not* reading a text because of its controversial nature or non-canonical provenance. Further proof of the impartiality of the reading programme is the fact that the controversial book to which *Froudacity* was a critical response, *The English in the West Indies* (1888) by J. A. Froude, was also read for *OED1* and provided quotations for general vocabulary such as *masthead* and *with an eye to*.

By 1879, the dictionary had already been worked on for twenty years, but not a word had been published. The original publishers, Macmillan Press, wanted a smaller dictionary than the Philological Society envisaged, and Furnivall recognized that the project needed a new publisher and a new editor. Turned down by Cambridge University Press (CUP) in 1877, the eventual publisher of the dictionary was Oxford University Press.[43] The new editor was James Murray, a school master at Mill Hill School in London (Figure 2.6).[44]

When James Murray took over from Furnivall in 1879, he immediately focused on the task of editing the dictionary. Unlike Furnivall, Murray was not educated at Oxbridge, and he had no formal philological qualification, studying only for an external BA from London University. Murray had worked as a bank clerk and headmaster of a school before publishing a dictionary of his Scottish dialect called *The Dialect of the Southern Counties of Scotland* (1873). For the first time, the dictionary was passing into the hands of a practised lexicographer, and someone who personally and intellectually understood the variation that existed in English. Murray worked on the dictionary part-time while still working at Mill Hill School until 1885, when he moved to Oxford and became full-time editor.

On the suggestion of his wife Ada, Murray built a shed in the back garden of his house in north Oxford and set it up as his Scriptorium, which would house the dictionary project for the next thirty-six years.[45] The Scriptorium was demolished long ago, but if you walk past 78 Banbury Road you will see a blue plaque erected in 2002 to mark the historical site.

Murray spoke often of Trench's vision and of his own responsibility to honour his legacy:

> This dictionary superadds to all the features that have been successively evolved by the long chain of workers, the historical information which Dr Trench desiderated. It seeks not merely to record every word that has been used in the language for the last 800 years, with its written form and signification, and the pronunciation of the current words, but to furnish a biography of each word.[46]

In his editing, Murray endeavoured to follow the principles set by Trench and Coleridge that 'every word should be made to tell its own story'. His comments on the proofs for the obsolete word *abaisance*, a bow, show how literally he took the task of 'furnishing a biography of each word'.[47] Murray had included two quotations from other dictionaries (Bailey 1721 and Johnson (1755), and a final quotation from Dickens, which was square-bracketed because it illustrated the word *obeisance* not *abaisance*. Beside these quotations, a hand resembling Arthur Maling's wrote, 'These are not examples of *Abaisance*.' But Murray responded, 'NO! But they illustrate the statement of the history made above. They show that *abaisance* had a beginning and end. Trench and Coleridge *greatly* valued this kind of quotation. The quotations are not merely *examples* – they are *illustrations*, *evidence* etc.'[48]

This entry for *abaisance* appeared in Murray's first fascicle A–ANT, published in 1884, but he developed a more finessed and complex policy, as can be seen in later fascicles (and is still followed today in *OED3*) in which quotations that illustrate the same meaning but a variant spelling of the headword, such as the one from Dickens in *abaisance*, would not be square-bracketed (Figure 2.5). The form would either be chosen as the headword spelling (if it represented the most recent and frequent usage, which in this case the form *obeisance* does not) or it would be listed as a variant form. And in the case of a development of usage that was based on confusion with a warde beside forth, & the kynge ne the lands never abailled.

† **Abaisance** (ăbēⁱ·săns). *Obs.* [a. OFr. *abaissance* abasement, humility, n. of action f. *abaissant* pr. pple. of *abaisser* to lower: see ABASE. From the earliest period confused in Eng. with *obeisance*, Fr. *obéissance*, obedience, n. of action f. *obéir* to obey. A few writers in 7–8 tried in vain to restore the etymological distinction.] The bending of the body as a mark of respect; a bow.

[**1393** GOWER *Conf.* III. VI. iii. 75 And ate last he gan to lout And obeisaunce unto her make.] **1671** SKINNER *Etymol. Ling. Ang.* To make a low abaissance. **1675** *Art of Contentment* IV. XV. 199 Haman can find no gust in all the sensualities of the Persian court, because a poor despicable Jew denies his abaisance. **1721** BAILEY An Abaisance, a low Conge or Bow, a stooping down. **1755** JOHNSON Obeysance is considered by Skinner as a corruption of abaisance, but is now universally used. [**1838** DICKENS *Nich. Nick.* (C.D. ed.) xxiv. 193 Miss Snevellicci made a graceful obeisance.]

Abaisch, abaish, abaisse, obs. forms ABASH.

Abaise, obs. form of ABASE.

Figure 2.5 Murray's entry for *abaisance*. (Credit: OUP)

word of slightly different meaning (e.g. *abaisance* from Old French 'humility' being confused with *obeisance* from Anglo-Norman 'authority, obedience') the variant forms list would consist of more than one section (e.g. α showing the variant forms based on *abaisance*, and β showing the variant forms based on *obeisance*). But in the early days, Murray was still working out his lexicographic principles, and clearly he looked to his predecessors for guidance and took their vision quite literally.

Murray sought readers, both nationally and internationally, to read their local texts and send him quotations.[49] As we will see in the next chapter, he cast his net globally for quotations because he always believed that the English language was broader than that of the language spoken by the average person living in England: 'None of us know everything,' he told the Philological Society in 1880, 'the names of the things we do not know are not part of *our* English, but we should be bold men to make the limit of our general knowledge, the limit of the English language'.[50]

In addition to corresponding with hundreds of readers around the world, Murray sought specialist advice on etymology and meaning; he gathered around him a small group of assistants; and he devised a system to categorize

Figure 2.6 James Murray (1837–1915), editor of the dictionary from 1879 until his death in 1915, pictured in his Scriptorium in north Oxford surrounded by his slips. (Credit: OUP)

loanwords. He devoted his life to creating a dictionary that he described as 'permeated through and through with the scientific method of the century'.[51] He sent his first batch of copy to the printer on 19 April 1882, and until his death on 26 July 1915, Murray managed to edit one-half of the dictionary himself: letters A–D, H–K, O, P, and T.[52] He viewed his lexicographical method as unsurpassable, and stated in his Romanes Lecture at Oxford in 1900 that in the making of *OED1*, 'Lexicography has for the present reached its supreme development.'[53] He was knighted in 1908. However, despite all his lexicographic successes, Murray was never fully embraced or appreciated by the University of Oxford. He did receive an honorary doctorate from

Figure 2.7 Henry Bradley (1845–1923), who followed Murray as editor of the dictionary from 1915 until his death in 1923. (Credit: OUP)

Oxford the year before he died, but by then, as we shall see in Chapter 3, he had compensated for his exclusion from university life by active involvement in civic life.

After the publication of the first volume of the dictionary in 1884, a particularly insightful review had appeared in the *Academy* journal written by Henry Bradley, a forty-year-old autodidact who had spent twenty years working as a clerk in a Sheffield cutlery company (Figure 2.7).[54] He had no formal academic training, not even an external BA like Murray, but had taught himself languages, and in 1884 had moved to London for economic reasons, supporting his family with miscellaneous literary work such as reviewing for *The Academy*. The review displayed Bradley's knowledge of etymology and philology, and impressed Murray so much that he invited Bradley to join him on the dictionary in 1886. Appointing Bradley on the basis of his knowledge of philology, rather than relying on the old boys' network (of which he was not really a part), proved to be a characteristic of Murray's leadership throughout his working life. Bradley worked for two years as Murray's assistant, became the second in charge in 1888, and remained at the dictionary until his death in 1923 (the last eight years, after

Murray's death, as Chief Editor). In those forty years, he edited the letters E–G, L–M, and parts of S and W. Bradley initially worked on the dictionary from London until 1896, when he moved to Oxford and worked for five years in the Clarendon Press, followed by a larger, permanent setup on the ground floor of the Old Ashmolean in Broad Street.[55]

It was Bradley's knowledge of Arabic and Spanish and his ability to connect historical events with language contact and transmission of loanwords that had, in part, first impressed Murray. In his review, Bradley had queried Murray's treatment of the word *alpaca*: Murray's etymology read (and still reads today, because it has not yet been amended): '[a. Sp. *alpaca* or *al-paco*, f. *al* Arab. article often prefixed to names + *paco*, prob. a native Peruvian name].' Bradley had questioned the ultimate Arabic etymology of *alpaca*: 'It is true that in Spanish the prefix *al-* seems to have been applied (probably out of pedantic affectation) to a few nouns of non-Arabic origin; but, considering the late introduction of the word "alpaca", this explanation appears here inapplicable.'[56]

Bradley was President of the Philological Society in 1890–93, 1900–03, and 1909–10. He was given an honorary DLitt by Oxford University at the same time as Murray in 1914, and was made a Fellow of Magdalen College in 1916. His writings show an appreciation for the cultural contact that resulted from the expansion of the British Empire: 'The progress of colonization, in which England has borne so great a part, has made known to our countrymen the languages, customs, and products of the most distant regions of the earth'. He acknowledged that this contact brought benefits for the language: 'hence it has come to pass that the modern English vocabulary includes words derived from every civilised language of Europe, and from innumerable languages of Asia, Africa, America, and Australia'.[57] In his book *The Making of English* (1904), Bradley wrote in defence of the inclusion of loanwords and World Englishes in the dictionary, regardless of whether or not Englishmen were familiar with the words: 'The many languages of our Indian Empire are abundantly represented in our English dictionaries. The number of Malay words in English is surprisingly large, and though most of them are probably known to few people, the list includes the familiar *gingham, gong, gutta-percha, lorry, orang-outan, amuck, ketchup.*'[58]

Bradley's view of English, however, was slightly different from Murray's. While we will see that Murray believed that unfamiliar loanwords classified as 'English', Bradley believed that they were not really English but still deserved a place in an English dictionary. For Bradley then, words were only 'English' once they were naturalized. He wrote, 'China has given us tea and the names of various kinds of tea; a good many other Chinese words figure in our larger dictionaries, though they cannot be said to have become really English.'[59] Bradley appreciated that many foreign objects and concepts would

Figure 2.8 C. T. Onions (1873–1965), who worked on the first edition of the *OED* and co-edited the 1933 *Supplement to the OED*. (Credit: G. Onions)

be adopted into English and would then take on new 'naturalized' meanings. 'For Japan', he wrote, 'besides the terms relating to the art and the institutions of that country, we have *rickshaw*, which seems likely to become naturalized in an application unknown in its native land.'[60] Hence, the naturalization process figured highly in Bradley's view of English and he took seriously the lexicographic device of applying tramlines to signify the stage of a word's naturalization: 'The languages of the New World have contributed some hundreds of words; and although many of these, such as *squaw* and *wigwam* are used only in speaking of the peoples to whose tongues they belong, there are not a few (e.g. *tobacco, potato, toboggan, moccasin, pemmican*) which we never think of regarding as foreign.'[61]

In 1895, Murray and Bradley were joined by an assistant editor, Charles Talbut Onions, who had recently graduated from Mason College in Birmingham (which became the University of Birmingham in 1900) (Figure 2.8). He initially worked under Murray, later switching to Bradley's team, a change which he described thus: 'it was to pass from the practical professional teacher to the philosophical exponent.' The switch may have happened because of a misdemeanour committed by Onions when he was twenty-six years old, which is alluded to in archive documents but never fully explained. Onions had cause to leave Oxford for some 'queer' reason in 1899. As Murray explained in a letter to the Secretary to the OUP Delegates (the prestigious decision-making committee that runs the Press and comprises distinguished Oxford academics from various disciplines): '[Onions] had an extensive visiting acquaintance here [in Oxford], and as it is generally known that "something queer" has happened.' Murray felt that it may have been difficult and embarrassing for Onions to return to the city and the Press because, as he put it, 'there would be considerable embarrassment, on behalf of friends and acquaintances, and probably a good deal of difficulty for himself'. However, Murray reassured Cannan that if Onions did return to Oxford, 'I would doubtless take him back, asking no questions, and fully believing that all that is said to have happened has been a grave error of judgement, into which no thought of evil entered'.[62] Onions did return to Oxford and resumed his work on *OED1*. It did, however, take him fifteen years to be promoted to the position of an independent editor (in contrast with Craigie, who was promoted within four years), at which point he edited parts of the letters S and W and all of X–Z. It may be that the event in 1899 had something to do with the delay of his promotion.

In 1911, Onions produced the *Oxford Shakespeare Glossary* (many times reprinted), and, in 1918, he took time out from editing the *OED* to work for British intelligence. In 1920, he was appointed Lecturer in English at Oxford, and in 1923 became a Fellow of Magdalen College (taking up Bradley's old Fellowship).[63] After the final publication of the dictionary in 1928, Onions co-edited the *1933 Supplement*, the *Shorter Oxford Dictionary* (1933), and his *Oxford Dictionary of English Etymology* (1966) was published a year after his death in 1965 (with assistance from G. S. Friedrichsen and R. W. Burchfield). From 1940 to 1955, Onions was Fellow Librarian of Magdalen, famously sitting each day by the dictionary bay of the library with a blanket wrapped around his shoulders to stave off the cold. It was here in the 1950s that he met and encouraged the young Rhodes Scholar, Robert W. Burchfield, to become the next Chief Editor of the *OED*.

In 1907, Onions had married Angela Blythman (1883–1941) and they had ten children (Figure 2.9). His youngest child, Giles, recalled his father frequently entertaining the famous writers C. S. Lewis (1898–1963) and J.R.R. Tolkien (1892–1973) or 'Jirt' as the family called him (after his initials J.R.R.T.). At the very start of his career, Tolkien had worked as an editor on *OED1* from 1919 to 1920. He had worked with Onions on the letter W, and the two men became firm friends (despite the fact that they both went for the same job to replace Craigie as Rawlinson and Bosworth Professor of

Figure 2.9 C. T. Onions and his wife Angela with nine of their ten children (Giles is in his mother's arms and Elizabeth is second from the right). (Credit: G. Onions)

Anglo-Saxon at Oxford, for which Tolkien was chosen over Onions). After Onions' death, Tolkien described him as 'my dear protector, backer, and friend' who 'was the last of the people who *were* "English" at Oxford and at large when I entered the profession'.[64]

Unlike C. S. Lewis and Tolkien, Onions was not a member of the Inklings, the Oxford literary discussion group that met regularly at the Eagle and Child pub, but Onions' son recalled many of the Inklings visiting their house. On one occasion, Tolkien was visibly shocked by the chaos of Onions' life with ten children: 'Jirt was over for lunch and my brother John was hitting golf balls in the back garden', recalled Giles Onions. 'One came up through the ventilator, bounced around the dishes on the table, and nobody took any notice. Jirt always remarked how funny it was, but for us it was normal.' Giles and his sister Elizabeth described a father who was largely absent from family life, forever worried about money, and thoroughly devoted to the dictionary.[65] Onions' work is discussed in Chapters 5 and 6, and he emerges as far and away the most inclusive of all the editors until the present day of loanwords and World Englishes.

In 1897, the project was joined by William Craigie, the most formally educated of the editorial team, who had graduated from Oxford and St Andrews, and was a specialist in classics, philosophy, Icelandic, Scandinavian, Celtic, and Germanic languages (Figure 2.10). Initially working under Bradley, the thirty-year-old Scot became the third independent editor after just four years

Figure 2.10 William Craigie (1867–1957), who joined the dictionary in 1897 and co-edited the 1933 *Supplement to the OED* with Charles Onions. (Credit: OUP)

of working on the project. In addition to editing letters N, Q, R, U, V, and parts of S and W in *OED1*, Craigie went on to co-edit the *1933 Supplement* with Charles Onions. Craigie held the appointments at Oxford of Taylorian Lecturer in Scandinavian Languages from 1905 to 1916, and of Rawlinson and Bosworth Professor of Anglo-Saxon from 1916 to 1925.[66] While still working on the *OED*, he moved to Chicago in 1925 to found and edit two other major dictionaries: the *Dictionary of the Older Scottish Tongue* (1931–2002) and the *Dictionary of American English* (1936–44).[67] He was knighted in 1928 on completion of *OED1*.

The completion of *OED1* in 1928 was a national event, and the Prime Minister's speech at the celebratory dinner was to be broadcast live on the radio.[68] As it turned out, the BBC filled the slot instead with a talk by Lady

Lawrence, 'Across the Sind Desert'.[69] Perhaps this was just as well, considering the word *radio* was not yet in the dictionary (the letter R had been published in 1904, just a few months after the famous radio exchange between King Edward VII and President Roosevelt, and two years before the word *radio* was used for a *wireless*). Neither were other words in current use, such as *aeroplane, African, appendicitis, cinema, jazz*, or *radium*. The latter provides an interesting case because, in 1902, Murray had advised Craigie to delete *radium* from the proof sheets in case its definition as 'a new metal' turned out to be false; he feared 'it may turn out to be a regrettable blunder'.[70]

In his speech, the Prime Minister Stanley Baldwin reminded everyone that the mammoth task was not exactly over: a supplement volume was pending. The *OED*'s long gestation meant that, by 1928, it was more than forty years after the first fascicle had been published, and all that time the editors had been collecting slips for hundreds of additions and revisions for all parts of the alphabet. 'If ever a dictionary were destined for eternity', said Stanley Baldwin, 'it is the *OED*, because no sooner have we . . . drawn our last cheque, had it cashed, and seen it honoured, and had the last volume delivered, than we are told that supplements are about to begin; and Oxford with that sure touch of the modern generation, is appealing to us to buy this new book because there is going to be a little article in it on appendicitis'.[71]

A *Supplement to the OED* was published in 1933, edited by Craigie and Onions, and, apart from J. M. Wyllie continuing to gather quotations and to manage dictionary files, the dictionary project more or less lay in abeyance until 1957 when Robert Burchfield, Lecturer in English Language at Christ Church, Oxford, was appointed editor of a second *Supplement* (Figure 2.11).[72] Originally from New Zealand, Burchfield had come to Oxford as a Rhodes Scholar in 1949. He remained Chief Editor until the publication of the fourth and final volume of the *Supplement* in 1986.[73] In 1986, two of Burchfield's editorial assistants, John Simpson (b.1953) and Edmund Weiner (b.1950) became co-editors of the *OED*, preparing *OED2* which comprised *OED1*, Burchfield's *Supplement*, and 5000 new entries.[74]

The editors who came after Murray all strove to follow his lexicographic policies and practices. The dictionary's remit was, as Murray articulated it, to give each word 'as nearly as possible the date of its birth or first known appearance, and in the case of an obsolete word or sense, of its last appearance, the source from which it was actually derived, the form and sense with which it entered the language or is first found in it, and the successive changes of form and developments of sense which it has since undergone.'[75] All these were derived from historical research, and Murray had set up a team of editorial assistants, sub-editors, re-sub-editors, consultants, and readers, each of whom had a specific role and many of whom were volunteers.

Figure 2.11 Robert W. Burchfield (1923–2004), chief editor of the *OED*, 1957–86. (Credit: OUP)

Murray instituted a complex editorial system that more or less still endures to the present day. When a reader sent slips to Murray, they were initially checked for any obvious errors in citational style or content, in which case the issue was addressed with the reader directly.[76] The slips were then sorted by 'sorters' into alphabetical and chronological order, and, depending on the skill of the sorter, also into senses and parts of speech.[77] Originally some of the sorters were Murray's eleven children, who earned pocket money from the task (starting rate of one penny an hour), but eventually the dictionary employed more paid assistants, and this process continues to the present day (Figure 2.12).[78]

The slips were then posted around the country to various sub-editors who further divided the slips according to senses, sometimes with provisional definitions per sense.[79] Sub-editors included Miss Janet Brown (d.1907) of Cirencester and Henry Hucks Gibbs (Lord Aldenham) (1819–1907) of

Figure 2.12 James and Ada Murray with their eleven children, who were paid one penny an hour to help sort slips. (Credit: OUP)

London. Miss Brown contributed over 8000 quotations and was described by Murray as 'one of the most devoted and enthusiastic of our volunteer helpers'.[80] They became good friends and she left Murray £1000 in her will. The dictionary engaged the intellect and skill of many such women for nearly sixty years, in a period when women were only just gaining access to Oxford University.

The first choice of quotations fell to the editorial assistants, even though their decisions may have ended up being overruled by their editor. The editorial assistants, such as Arthur Maling or John Birt, would also create a 'top slip' which was the first slip for each entry consisting of the headword, part of speech, etymology, list of spelling variants, and definition. The sub-editor also sometimes attempted to write definitions. A re-sub-editor read through the sub-editor's definitions with new slips to hand, and was instructed 'to modify the definitions or re-arrange the meanings'.[81]

Finally the editor checked the entire entry, fine-tuned the sense divisions, chose the final quotations, wrote the pronunciation, improved the definition, wrote the etymology, and sought expert advice from etymological consultants such as the linguist James Platt (1861–1910) and Sanskrit and Hindi scholar Dr. Fitzedward Hall (1825–1901), and subject consultants such as the anthropologist E. B. Tylor (1832–1917) or the Australiana expert Edward Petherick (1847–1917).[82] Unlike slips for Burchfield's *Supplement* and *OED3*, no editor of *OED1* or the *1933 Supplement* signed his name or initials on any slip, so researchers of these texts have to rely on identification of handwriting, based on matching examples shown on signed letters and memos with that on slips.

When an editor chose the final quotations, he put the rejected slips into a file called 'Superfluous'. There was more material rejected than accepted for *OED1*, so the size of the Superfluous file (rejected slips) is much larger than the Copy file (slips of published entries): in the OUP archives, there are 294 boxes of copy slips but 337 boxes of superfluous slips.[83] The Superfluous file is large because it contained not only slips for rejected quotations of accepted words but also slips for entire entries or senses of words which were deemed not fit for inclusion, usually on the policy of lack of frequency or distribution of use. This system is still in use today, as nothing is thrown out at the *OED*, and every superfluous slip is kept and stored (either on paper or electronically) for future reference. If words or corrections came to light after the relevant *OED1* alphabetical range had been published, then the evidence was written on slips and put in a file called 'Supplement'. These were set aside for the day when a proper supplement volume would be published.

Interestingly, the *1933 Supplement* was based primarily on all the slips in the Supplement file; the Superfluous file was not accessed. We do not know why the editors of the *1933 Supplement* did not use the Superfluous slips, but the decision had both positive and negative consequences. On the positive side, it meant that many of the slips in the Superfluous file remained more or less untouched since the *OED1* editors put them there. This allows researchers of *OED1* a rare glimpse into a record of which words and quotations the *OED1* editors deemed unfit for inclusion. It also provides researchers with rare access into the editors' inclusion policies. Of course, as with the copy slips, researchers must be sensitive to the reality that both copy slips and superfluous slips were moved around – even shipped to America and back – during and after the compilation of *OED1*. For example, 430,000 Middle English slips were sent in 1930 to the University of Michigan, via Cornell, for the Middle English Dictionary project. The slips were always sent back to Oxford, but it is impossible to know what, if anything, is missing from the Superfluous file. Regardless, the Superfluous file comprises 337 boxes of material that provide researchers with insights into original editorial policy and practice.[84]

On the negative side, the fact that the *1933 Supplement* editors failed to access the *OED1* Superfluous file meant that they missed out on finding some earlier quotations that were on slips for rejected entries in the Superfluous file. For example, there were words that the *OED1* editors deemed unfit for inclusion but that the *1933 Supplement* team chose to include. In Murray's case, this was mainly for ethnonyms such as *Kabyle*, a people of Algeria and Tunisia, and in Bradley's case, this was mainly for 'exotic' plants and animals such as *mamba*, a venomous African snake. Murray had a policy of only including ethnonyms if they had derivatives or had acquired transferred senses used generically, absolutely, or attributively. Hence, *American* was included because it was needed to explain derivatives such as *Americanism* or *Americanize*, but not enough evidence could be gathered in 1884 for derivatives of *African* (he later admitted in the preface to volume 1 that this was perhaps 'a too rigid application of first principles'), and certainly no derivatives existed for *Kabyle* in 1901, so neither was included in *OED1*.[85] The reason for Bradley's exclusion of *mamba* is less easy to explain, but had the *1933 Supplement* editors checked Bradley's slips, they would have been able to antedate their quotational evidence by fourteen years.

Each dictionary editor worked on his own part of the alphabet, usually one letter per editor, but portions of the large letter S were divided among Bradley, Craigie, and Onions. Final quotations were verified by 'library checkers', i.e. staff members whose main task was, and still is today, to check citations in the Bodleian.[86] The dictionary was published gradually in fascicles such as A–Ant in January 1884, Ant–Batten in November 1885, Batter–Boz in March 1887, until the final fascicles Wise–Worling and Worm–Wyzen were published in April 1928. The publication of fascicles was not necessarily chronological: for example, the fascicle X–Zyxt had been published by Onions in October 1921, seven years before the dictionary was finished. Depending on the size of the letter, the fascicles were gathered alphabetically and printed as volumes every few years. The final publication of letters V to Z in 1928 brought the total number of volumes to twelve.

Every slip was handled by an average of five people. Once the copy was ready for press, the slips were numbered chronologically, and sent to press in bundles of one thousand.[87] The printer date-stamped each top slip to show when it was printed, and this has proved helpful to the present study in verifying exactly when editors worked on certain entries. Using these date-stamps as indicators, the usual lag between the printer's date-stamp and final publication seems to have been about nine months, which indicates the time needed to correct various stages of proofs.

There were at least three stages in the printed form – first proof, first revise, and page form.[88] Proofs were read by the editors and selected proofreaders such as the sisters, Misses Edith and Elizabeth P. Thompson of Bath.[89] Accomplished authors themselves (Edith Thompson wrote *History of England* [1873] and Elizabeth Thompson wrote the romance novel *A Dragoon's Wife* [1907]), in addition to proofreading for Murray, the sisters read widely for the reading programme, contributing more than 15,000 quotations for the first volume alone. They continued to proofread for the dictionary until publication of the final fascicle in 1928, a few months after which Edith died. She lived long enough, however, to be present at the grand celebratory dinner with the Prime Minister at London's Goldsmiths' Hall on 6 June 1928. The guests drank Pommery Champagne and Château Margaux with their turtle soup and lamb. Because of her gender, Edith Thompson was denied a seat at the banquet and had to sit on the balcony with two other women who also gave years of devoted service, Rosfrith Murray (1884–1973) and Eleanor Bradley (1875–1950), daughters of the two deceased editors, James Murray and Henry Bradley. Given that women were to receive the vote on equal terms with men three weeks later, and women had already been awarded degrees at Oxford for eight years, it is quite surprising that they were not entitled to sit with the men at this dinner. Recalling the evening she spent on the balcony overlooking the proceedings, Rosfrith Murray wrote in a letter to the Secretary to the OUP Delegates, Robert W. Chapman (1881–1960), 'I always felt deeply that my Father would like one of his name to be "in on the finish" since this was denied to him himself.'[90]

ENDNOTES

1 Coleridge (2007).
2 Peterson (2007); Gross (1969: 169).
3 Milne (2010).
4 Trench (1857).
5 Trench (1855: 6–7).
6 Trench (1855: 7–8).
7 Trench, Furnivall, and Coleridge (1857: 944); Trench (1857: 10, 11, 22, 29–30, 44, 58, 61); Murray (1900a: 45–6).
8 Trench (1857: 11, 5).
9 Trench (1857: 4–5, 8–14).
10 Trench (1857: 4–5).
11 Coleridge (1857: 72).
12 Trench (1857: 64).
13 The scope of the ambition of the *Lexicon totius Anglicitatis* was sometimes the subject of ridicule in the midnineteenth century: an article in the *Gentleman's Magazine* in 1846 humorously referred to a word list of 'Cornish Provincial Dialect' vocabulary, 'collected and arranged by Uncle Jan Treenoodle' that will be 'a little contribution towards a "Dictionarium totius Anglicitatis"'. See 'Specimens of Cornish Provincial Dialect', *Gentleman's Magazine*, August 1846 p. 178.
14 Trench (1857: 1).
15 Trench (1857) part II, no page numbers.
16 Thanks to Bev Hunt, *OED* archivist, for verification of this.
17 See Osselton (2000) for a comparison of these three dictionaries with the *OED*.

18 Trench (1857: 59, 57, 15).
19 Ironically, Trench describes *hazle* as a verb but defines it as a noun.
20 Trench (1857: 15–16).
21 Trench et al. (1860).
22 Trench et al. (1860: 10–11).
23 Trench et al. (1860: 8, 4). Bailey (2000a: 209) records this as referring to 'Americanisms and Colonialisms', but the Bodleian version of Trench et al. (1860) does not mention 'Colonialisms'.
24 Trench (1857: 15).
25 'How the Dictionary is Made', *The Periodical* XIII, 15 February 1928, p. 15.
26 Coleridge (1860a: 39, 42, 41).
27 Appendix by Furnivall in Coleridge (1860b: 43).
28 Coleridge (1857: 77).
29 Appendix by Furnivall in Coleridge (1860b: 43).
30 MP/9/11/1862. Furnivall Circular to the Philological Society, 9 November 1862, p. 3.
31 Bickley (1911: 3).
32 Gross (1969: 171).
33 Gross (1969: 169–71); Benzie (1983: xi, 277).
34 Gross (1969: 169).
35 'The Editors and Their Staffs', *The Periodical* XIII, 15 February 1928 p. 10.
36 Bradley (1911: 7).
37 'The Editors and Their Staffs', p. 10.
38 Spurgeon (1911: 182–3).
39 OUP Archive OED Slips for *lhiamba*, *koko*, and *ju-ju*.
40 OUP Archive OED Slips for *colour-domination*, and *colour-dread*.
41 OUP Archive OED Slips for *drogherman* and *plantocracy*. Slips also showed that *Froudacity* (1889) provided quotational evidence for the entries *rationalness*, *redoubt*, *skin*, *trickster*, and *unrespectable*.
42 OUP Archive OED Slips for *tarbooshed*.
43 McKitterick (2004: 106).
44 Murray (1977: 142–5, 148–70).
45 Murray (1977: 171–4).
46 Murray (1900a: 46–7).
47 Murray (1900a: 47).
48 MP Box 30. Proofs for *abaisance*.
49 Murray (1879).
50 Murray (1880: 132).
51 Murray (1900a: 49).
52 'The Editors and Their Staffs', *The Periodical* XIII, 15 February 1928 p. 11.
53 Murray (1900a: 49).
54 Bradley (1884).
55 'Homes of the Dictionary', *The Periodical* XIII, 15 February 1928 p. 18.
56 Bradley (1884: 141–2).
57 Bradley (1904: 101, 102).
58 Bradley (1904: 104).
59 Bradley (1904: 104).
60 Bradley (1904: 104). Bradley gives no further hint as to what this new sense might be.

61 Bradley (1904: 106). Presumably, Bradley was implying in this passage that the words *squaw* and *wigwam* would receive tramlines, while the other words would not because speakers would never think of them as foreign. However, when the words *squaw* and *wigwam* were published, they were not edited by Bradley and they were not given tramlines. William Craigie published *squaw* in 1915 without tramlines, and Charles Onions published *wig-wam* in 1926 without tramlines, and, as we shall see in Chapter 5, these two men practically did away with tramlines altogether in the *1933 Supplement*.

62 OED/B/3/2/1 PP/1899/6. Letter from Murray to Cannan 1899. I was kindly alerted to this intriguing matter by Charlotte Brewer, who found this letter in the archives. We were unable to find any further reference to the matter in the OUP archives. I asked Giles Onions about his father's mysterious 'misdemeanor' in 1899 but he knew nothing about the affair, which was eight years before Onions married his mother.

63 'The Editors and Their Staffs', *The Periodical* XIII, 15 February 1928 p. 14.

64 Letter from J.R.R. Tolkien to his son Michael Tolkien, 9–10 January 1965 in Carpenter (1981: 267).

65 Personal communication with Giles Onions. Giles and his older sister, Elizabeth, were in their eighties and nineties respectively and still living in the old family home in north Oxford when I began writing this book. I visited them frequently and heard many reminiscences of their father and life growing up in literary Oxford in the early and mid twentieth century.

66 'The Editors and Their Staffs', *The Periodical* XIII, 15 February 1928 p. 13.

67 The editorial policy and practice of William Craigie is discussed further in Chapter 5.

68 OED/B/3/2/17(2) PP/1928/166. Letter from Milford to Chapman 3 May 1928.

69 'Across the Sind Desert Travellers' Tales: Lady Lawrence' *Radio Times* British Broadcasting Corporation Programmes for Wednesday, 6 June 9.15 p.m., 1 June 1928, p. 406.

70 On the omission of *radium* see Gilliver (2004).

71 Baldwin (1928: 3).

72 Work on the *OED* lay in abeyance apart from the management of dictionary files and continued reading for quotations by J. M. Wyllie, as well as cursory contributions by Kenneth Sisam (1887–1971), who was otherwise busy working as the Assistant Secretary to the Delegates until 1942, when he became Secretary to the Delegates.

73 Burchfield's editorial policy and practice are discussed thoroughly in Chapter 6.

74 Simpson and. Weiner (1989).

75 Murray (1900a: 47).

76 Murray (1977: 186).

77 Murray (1977: 186).

78 Murray (1977: 179). Many readers today simply highlight the word within the text and send the book or magazine to the *OED*, where the citations are typed by a 'data-entry assistant' into the 'Incomings Database' which editors search when they are working on an entry. Some readers still write on slips and these are still sorted in the same way they were in Murray's day – alphabetically, chronologically, and according to senses and parts of speech.

79 Murray (1977: 187).

80 Murray (1909: ii).
81 OED/MISC/91/11 n.d. 'Directions for Re-Sub-editors'.
82 Murray (1884b: 509–10). These volunteers are discussed further in Chapter 3.
83 I am indebted to Bev Hunt for giving me statistics on the number of boxes in the OUP archive.
84 See Lewis (2007: 3) for more information on the making of the Middle English Dictionary, and see Brewer (2007: 29ff.) and Mugglestone (2005) for more on the movement of slips. Craigie's work in America produced its own Superfluous file which was sent to Oxford with his other slips and stored accordingly.
85 Murray (1888: ix).
86 'How the Dictionary is Made', *The Periodical* XIII, 15 February 1928 p. 16.
87 Murray (1977: 186–7).
88 'How the Dictionary is Made', *The Periodical* XIII, 15 February 1928 p. 17.
89 'The Voluntary Workers', *The Periodical* XIII, 15 February 1928 p. 8.
90 OED/B/3/2/19. (Rosfrith) Murray to Chapman 17 June 1929.

3 James Murray and Words of the World

> It is man by man that Englishmen get the idea of a *boomerang*, a *reredos*, a *caucus*, or a *tomato*, and find a use for the name of it. Thus the English language is surrounded by a penumbra of French, Italian, Spanish, Turkish, Arabic, Hindustani, Malay, Zulu, words, some of which are "English" to some Englishmen, and undreamt of to others. At which Englishman's speech does English terminate?
>
> James Murray, Presidential Address to the Philological Society, 1880

James Murray frequently emphasized the rightful place that words of the world had in the English language, and he was committed to including them in his dictionary. 'Hardly any word from a foreign language looks odd or out of place among our home words,' he told students at Oxford University late in his career:

> We can adopt a foreign noun ... without raising awkward questions of what gender is the noun to be in English. ... We say *potatoes*, and *teas*, and *tamarinds*, and *tattoos*, and *wigwams*, and *kangaroos*, and *Rajahs*, and *quidnuncs*, without the slightest thought or doubt. So with our verbs: if we *salaam* an oriental magnate, we talk of *salaaming* him, or say we have *salaam'd* him without the slightest compunction.[1]

Murray admired the ability of English to adopt 'alien elements' and to give them English inflections and grammar. He used dictionary statistics to demonstrate the ease with which English admits foreign words:

> Some notion of the extent to which this is done is afforded by the fact that in the latest double section of the Oxford English Dictionary, which contains the words beginning with *Ta-*, and a few of those in *Te-*, it is stated that among the 1717 simple words treated, the words taken bodily from Foreign languages number 150, and that these are taken from no fewer than 55 languages, 11 European, 16 Asiatic, more than 10 Polynesian and Australian, more than 10 American North and South, and about 5 African languages.[2]

Despite pressure throughout his career to exclude words of the world from *OED1*, Murray continued to include them. It is evident from his presidential address to the Philological Society in 1880, the preface of the first volume in 1888, his lectures at Oxford in 1911, and the instances described in this chapter in which he ignored the criticism of reviewers, consultants, sub-editors, and the Delegates of the Press, that Murray's inclusive attitude in his early career remained largely unchanged in the latter part of his career.

He spoke out in favour of inclusion, and he actively put that policy into practice. Reviewers of the dictionary noted the sheer volume of foreign words (some complaining about it). The first fascicle, published in 1884, contained loanwords and neologisms from all parts of the globe: *aard-vark* and *aard-wolf*, animals from South Africa, appeared alongside new adaptations of long-existing British words, such as the South African sense of *Aaron's-beard*, 'a cultivated species of Saxifrage (S. sarmentosa) from S. Africa'. Australian English was represented by adapted senses of *acacia*, 'they form in Australia thickets called scrubs', *adansonia*, 'the Cream of Tartar Tree, or Sour Gourd of N. Australia'; *adder*, 'Death Adder of N. Australia'; and *ant-eater*, 'the aculeated, or Porcupine Ant eater (*Echidna*) of the order *Monotremata*, found in Australia'. Words from the Philippines such as *abaca*, a textile, were listed beside words from Indian English such as *aal*, a red dye; *abkari*, the sale of alcohol in India; *adjutant*, a species of stork in India; *amah*, a wet-nurse; and *amildar*, 'a native factor, manager, or agent, in India'. Murray had included a type of guinea pig from the West Indies and South America called an *agouti*; along with *alouatte*, a howling monkey from South America; and *albacore*, a fish found in the West Indies and the Pacific.

Reviewers criticized the presence of vocabulary that they considered to be 'barbarous', 'outlandish', and 'peculiar'.[3] In a review of the first volume in 1889, the *Edinburgh Review* lamented: 'they have been far too liberal in admitting to the columns of an English dictionary a multitude of words that form no part of the English language.' The interpolation of 'barbarous terms and foreign words' was seen as a sign of the corruption and decay of the English language.[4] 'In our eyes', the review stated, 'the first duty of those who devote themselves to philological studies is not only to trace the origin of language and the history of its evolution, but to defend its purity, for a corrupt and decaying language is an infallible sign of a corrupt and decaying civilisation. It is one of the gates by which barbarism may invade and overpower the traditions of a great race.'[5] A reviewer in the *Athenaeum* commented:

> A peculiar feature of the *C–Cass* section is the disproportionately large number of words derived from foreign languages outside the familiar circle of Latin, Greek, and French. e.g *caaba, cabaan, caback, caballero, cabana, cabeer, cabob, caboceer, caboose, cacafuego, cacao, cacholong, cachucha, cacique, cadenza, cadi, cadilesker, cadjan, Caffre, cafila, caftan,* &c., not to mention numerous words of Celtic origin imported in comparatively recent times from Scotland and Ireland.[6]

This list included words from English spoken in regions as diverse as India (*cabob*, a roast dish, and *cadjan*, palm leaf used for writing), West Africa (*caboceer*, a headman of a village), the West Indies (*cacique*, a chief), and North America (*caboose*, a cabin on a freight train). This anonymous reviewer was in fact Charles Fennell (1842–1916) who, at the time of writing this review, was compiling his own dictionary of foreign words, the *Stanford Dictionary of Anglicized Words and Phrases* (1892).[7] Fennell's dictionary, which is discussed fully in the next chapter, was also based on the historical method, but focused solely on foreign words.

By the end of his life, Murray was known for his inclusion of words of the world, as expressed by *The Scotsman* in 1913: 'Queer, outlandish words are quite common in Sir James Murray's dictionary, and this section [Tombal-Trahysh] has its fair share.'[8] For Murray, all these words qualified as 'English'. If a word was used in an English context, it qualified as an English word. After all, from the *OED*'s beginnings, it was considered to be a dictionary of the English *language,* not merely a dictionary written by and for the people of England. The title chosen for the dictionary was particularly important for its editors in defining its scope, and we will see that, throughout its making, this scope was often misunderstood by many, including reviewers, the media, and OUP Delegates.

In the early days of the dictionary, despite the fact that there was never any discussion of the title being anything other than 'English' (not the New *British* Dictionary nor the New *Imperial* Dictionary nor the New *National* Dictionary), the exact parameters and definition of the 'English' in the title were not always clear. Correspondence between Coleridge and Trench shows that there were changes in their understanding of the dictionary's title and remit. At first, for Coleridge, the 'English' in the title denoted England or its inhabitants, but as more Americans such as George Perkins Marsh (1801–82) – whose task was to coordinate the American readers – became involved in the project, Coleridge was forced to re-evaluate: 'The title under which we have hitherto been accustomed to announce our book – viz., that of an *English* Dictionary – is one no longer strictly applicable', he wrote in *A Letter to The Very Rev. The Dean of Westminster* in 1860, 'due to the assistance coming from Americans' who would be responsible for 'the whole of the eighteenth century literature, which probably would have a less chance of finding as many readers in England'.[9] Right from its early days then, the *New English Dictionary* would not be confined to the work of lexicographers and readers based solely in England, nor would it be limited to the language and literature of England alone. Rather, it would cover America and eventually all the English-speaking peoples of the world.

Murray's definition of English was broad, and, having grown up on the Scottish Borders, he had an appreciation of linguistic diversity, especially of dialects of English. Even before beginning work on the *OED*, Murray wrote about the corruption of language, but not in prescriptivist tones. His concerns were not the harm that external forces posed on standard British English but rather, the harm that standard English and its literary canon posed on the dialects of Britain, in particular on his own variety of Scots. Instead of calling for adherence to the canon, there is evidence that Murray challenged it, wanting to protect dialects from the 'encroaching language of literature and education'.[10] In the preface to his own dictionary of *The Dialect of the Southern Counties of Scotland* (1873), he wrote 'The local dialects are passing away. . . . Even where not utterly trampled under foot by the encroaching language of literature and education, they are corrupted and arrested by its all-pervading influence, and in the same degree rendered valueless as witnesses of the usages of the past and the natural tendencies of the present.'[11]

Right at the start of his career, before any of the dictionary had been published, Murray addressed the Philological Society about the importance of not limiting the bounds of the English language or its description in an English dictionary. Using the word *camel* and the Caribbean English word *agama*, a lizard, as illustrative examples of the imagined limits of English, Murray highlighted that:

> For one person who will turn to the dictionary to learn the meaning of *Camel*, ten will turn to learn what an *Agama* is. . . . One animal is less conspicuous and less useful than the other, therefore less widely talked about: the *Agama* has been known to Englishmen only since they settled in the West Indies, while the *camel* has been heard of ever since Christian missionaries told heathen Teutons of Oriental scenes.[12]

Murray placed his example in the grand context of the history of English, in which the language was always in a state of evolution and change: 'Both these words were once meaningless to Englishmen; both express a meaning now to those Englishmen who need to use them.'[13]

Murray had stressed that the English language was dynamic, and that no one person's English was all of English:

> The 'English language' is constantly spoken of, and written of, as if it were a definite number of words and constructions; and the question, whether a particular word or construction is 'English', is constantly settled by each man according to his own feeling and usage, as if *his* English were all of English. Then we find absurd statements in books, such as that the English language is calculated to contain 100,000 words (when 50,000 or 200,000 would be just as true), followed sometimes by a calculation as to how many of these are of native English origin, and this without definition of what is included either under 'word' or 'English word', so that mathematically put, the question assumes the highly useful form of 'What is the numerical ratio between nx2 and y3 when x and y are both indefinite quantities?'[14]

This was a common theme present in his lectures and writings throughout his life. A few years before he died, he said in a lecture at Oxford, 'How often have I heard from a man or seen a newspaper confidently assert that such a

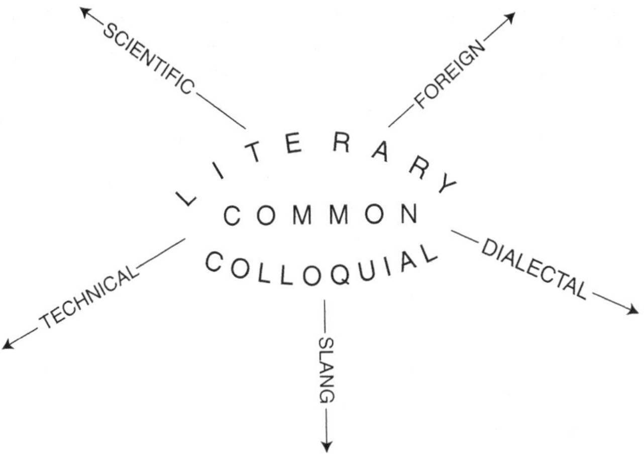

Figure 3.1 Murray's 'Circle of English' (Murray 1888: xxvi). (Credit: OUP)

word or phrase was *not English,* or perhaps that it was a vile Americanism, when the fact was merely that they were not acquainted with it, it was no part of their English, and in their ignorance they assumed that their English was all English.'[15] When asked by correspondents for advice on standard usage, Murray always replied that a speaker's individual free choice gave life and variety to language. He wrote:

Language is mobile and liable to change, and ... a very large number of words have two or more pronunciations current ... and giving life and variety to language ... it is a free country, and a man may call a *vase* a *vawse*, a *vahse*, a *vaze*, or a *vase*, as he pleases. And why should he not? We do not all think alike, walk alike, dress alike, write alike, or dine alike; why should not we use our liberty in speech also, so long as the purpose of speech, to be intelligible, and its grace, are not interfered with?[16]

In a lecture to the Philological Society in 1880, he had presented his view of English as an ink spot or 'spot of colour on a damp surface' – the centre of which is solid, discrete, and finite and the circumference of which is fuzzy, imperceptible, and infinite.[17] The bulk of an English dictionary, he said, was made up of words from the centre of the ink spot, while the rest were foreign words, slang, dialectal, technical, and scientific terms whose degree of 'Englishness' was often impossible to determine.[18] Murray refined this concept in the General Explanations that preface volume one of *OED1*, and represented it diagrammatically as a 'Circle of English' (Figure 3.1).

He acknowledged that capturing words 'on or near the frontier line' in a dictionary was a difficult and subjective process.[19] 'Our difficulty is', he told the Philological Society, 'how is this indefinitely-extended English language to be comprehended by the definite entries of a dictionary? Clearly, *never with mathematical accuracy*. In every one of these three directions the dictionary must stop *somewhere*; the exact limits will always be matters of feeling.'[20] Murray's point was not simply to highlight the subjectivity of the lexicographer's decision to include a word in the dictionary or to exclude it (though there was always an element of subjectivity), but also to note that the lexicographer's difficulty at judging these matters reflected an ambiguity inherent in the fringes of the language.

Murray was vexed by policy issues relating to when a 'fringe' word was 'English' enough to be included in an English dictionary. Although he solved the problem partially by remaining faithful to the principles of the historical method, in which each doubtful case was decided on written evidence, he still struggled lexicographically to distinguish degrees of naturalization. 'There is a wide fringe of words', he wrote, 'as to which it is difficult to say whether they ought or ought not to be treated in an English dictionary. Nearly every day this question has had to be decided. . . . Every such doubtful case has had to be settled on its own merits; with careful consideration of the evidence as to its use, and of the critical opinion of literary advisers.'[21]

Murray recognized that on a certain level the degree of a word's 'Englishness' depended on the individual speaker. As with technical and scientific words, words from indigenous languages around the world could easily be considered 'English' to one speaker and foreign gobbledegook to another:

> It is man by man that Englishmen get the idea of a *boomerang*, a *reredos*, a *caucus*, or a *tomato*, and find a use for the name of it. Thus the English language is surrounded by a penumbra of French, Italian, Spanish, Turkish, Arabic, Hindustani, Malay, Zulu, words, some of which are 'English' to some Englishmen, and undreamt of to others. At which Englishman's speech does English terminate?[22]

Murray was pioneering in his formulation of the Circle of English, as no one had previously conceptualized the relationship between different types of English vocabulary in this way. Although his model has been criticized for its inherent centre-periphery bias,[23] a version of it has endured in the recently developed field of World Englishes in which the scholar Braj Kachru has proposed a similar model for conceptualizing the relationship between different varieties of English.[24] Developed in the 1980s, Kachru's three circle model differentiated between varieties of English according to differing standards.[25] It distinguished among 'inner', 'outer', and 'expanding' circles according to whether the variety was English as a native language (ENL), English as a second language (ESL), or English as a foreign language (EFL) (Figure 3.2). It also distinguished the way in which the English language came to be important in the relevant countries. Countries in the inner circle represented the canonically privileged users that 'were the

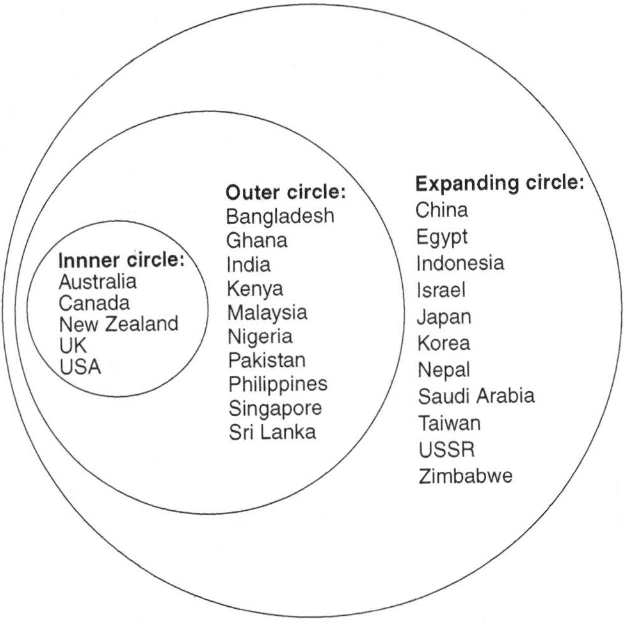

Figure 3.2 Kachru's three circles model of English (Kachru 1985: 18), reminiscent of Murray's 'Circle of English.' (Credit: CUP)

traditional cultural and linguistic bases of English', such as Britain and the United States. Countries in the outer circle were those that contextually institutionalized their Englishes' 'institutionalized non-native varieties' that 'passed through extended periods of colonization' such as Bangladesh, India, and Ghana. Countries in the expanding circle represented users who are still dependent on external norms – regions 'where the performance varieties of language are used in essentially EFL contexts' such as China, Egypt, and Korea.[26]

But Murray's Circle of English only represented the relationship between types of vocabulary; it did not solve for him the dilemma of how to deal lexicographically with words of varying degrees of naturalization. As Murray had discovered right at the start of his career, the process of borrowing becomes interesting for the lexicographer when there is a difference in the linguistic structures of the 'donor' language and 'borrowing' language, and the loanword undergoes certain adjustments, or 'nativization' of sound, orthography, meaning, or morphology. It is the lexicographer's job to *describe* these features, but his first job is to assess the loanword's use in English and to decide whether or not the word should be included at all. Once included, Murray's solution for the problem posed by foreign words of varying degrees of naturalization was to distinguish them from the rest of the vocabulary by using tramlines.

Murray anticipated that people would criticize his treatment of 'words on the fringe'; he wrote that his inclusion of these words 'will not satisfy all critics'.[27] In addition to American English terms such as *aside* meaning 'apart', *blizzard* traced back to the *Milwaukee Republican* (1881) and the *Northern Vindicator* (1860s), and *buncombe* originating in North Carolina, the volume included loanwords from languages all over the world, which gained a place in the dictionary after 'careful consideration of the evidence'.[28] He warned in the preface of volume 1: 'Opinions will differ as to the claims of some that are included and some that are excluded, and also as to the line dividing *denizens* from *naturals*, and the position assigned to some words on either side of it. If we are to distinguish these classes at all, a line must be drawn somewhere.'[29]

Opinions did differ, and throughout his career, Murray was criticized for not drawing the 'exact limits' of the fringe of English close enough to what was regarded as the centre. But the criticism did not dampen his enthusiasm for including loanwords and words from global varieties of English; he continued to include them in the dictionary and to speak out in support of their status as legitimate members of the English language. Essentially, his practice did not waver throughout his career.

Murray's view of the English language was largely and necessarily bound by the framework of the British Empire: Indian English (or 'Anglo-Indian'), South African English, Canadian English, Australian English, and New Zealand English (often grouped together as 'Austral or Australasian English') joined with British and American English to form the extent of the English language in the late nineteenth century. Murray insisted that the definition of 'Englishman' be extended to include all speakers of English around the world, regardless of variety, insisting that 'they are all forms of English'.

> The English Language is the language of Englishmen! Of *which* Englishmen? Of all Englishmen or of some Englishmen? . . . Does it include the English of Great Britain and the English of America, the English of Australia, and of South Africa, and of those most assertive Englishmen, the Englishmen of India, who live in *bungalows*, hunt in *jungles*, wear *terai* hats or *puggaries* and *pyjamas*, write *chits* instead of letters and eat *kedgeree* and *chutni*? Yes! In its most comprehensive sense, and as an object of historical study, it includes all these; they are all forms of English.[30]

Murray gained access to these words of the world by seeking them through his reading programme. This was based on the principle that the success of an historical dictionary depended on the breadth and amount of written evidence that could be gathered. He was also acutely aware that most varieties of

English around the world at that time lacked a long publishing history – especially in their own vernacular – and that such sources, if they existed, were rarely available in Britain.

In 1879, as soon as he had taken up the reins of the dictionary, Murray had issued *An Appeal to the English-speaking and the English-reading Public in Great Britain, America, and the Colonies* in which he specifically asked people around the world to read their local texts: 'American and Colonial readers we ask . . . to read for us those recent books which show the additions made to English in their respective countries, as received names for physical features, productions, &c. &c.'[31] He wanted 'a million more quotations to be contributed during the next three years, from books and authors of which a provisional List was published, to be from time to time supplemented and amended'.

There was a great response to Murray's Appeal from readers in all corners of the globe.[32] As Murray explained, 'At once some 800 volunteer readers offered themselves in Great Britain, with 400 to 500 in America, India, and the Colonies, including a few from Continental Europe, and by the labours of three meritorious workers, many thousands of books were read, and the million additional quotations furnished.'[33]

Murray's effort to seek out texts from all parts of the world indicated his loyal adherence to the original vision of Richard Chenevix Trench, a debt that Murray frequently acknowledged publicly. As he explained in a lecture at Oxford: 'At the recommendation of Dean of Westminster Archbishop Trench, the whole English-Speaking World was invited to aid in this magnificent task, and more than 2000 men and women have actually helped in systematically reading books and collecting the millions of quotations which supply the facts required.'[34]

Nine hundred quotations were submitted by Dr. Atkins in New Mexico, who read texts pertaining to general American culture and Native American tribes. His reading included Gibbs' *Tribes of West Washington* (1851), Matthews' *Hidatsa Indians* (1873), and Dall's *Tribes of the Extreme North-West* (1877). Donald Ferguson, a scholar living in Colombo, Ceylon, provided more than 500 examples of words from Sri Lanka. He read Arnold's *Light of Asia* (1879) and Robert Knox's *Historical Relation of the Island of Ceylon* (1681), which provided first quotations for *Buddha* and *puja*.

The surgeon, Dr Minor (1834–1920), contributed 3200 quotations for the dictionary. As vividly described in Simon Winchester's *The Surgeon of Crowthorne* (1998), it was twenty years before Murray realized that this faithful contributor was writing to him from Broadmoor mental asylum where he had been interned for murder.[35] Minor took up two cells in Broadmoor: one for himself and one for his collection of rare sixteenth- and seventeenth-century books. Every day he read these books for Murray and every week he sent bundles of quotations to Oxford. Murray paid tribute to Minor:

'So enormous have been Dr Minor's contributions during the past 17 or 18 years, that we could easily illustrate the last four centuries from his quotations alone.' Minor contributed hundreds of citations from travellers' tales, such as Hodges' *Travels in India* (1793), which provided first quotes for words like *durga*, a Muslim shrine, and *kunkur*, an Indian type of limestone; and Sir Thomas Herbert's *Some Yeares Travels* (1634) which first brought into English the words *Arab*, *cockatoo*, *hubble-bubble*, and *harem*.

Many loanwords and words pertaining to World Englishes were to be found in the writings of traders, explorers, and travellers, such as Richard Hakluyt (1552?–1616), or in the published works of those who edited the accounts of others, such as Samuel Purchas (bap. 1577–1626). In 1703, John Locke remarked that for 'books of travel . . . the collections made by our countrymen, Hakluyt and Purchas, are very good.'[36] And the texts of both these writers provided the *OED* with the greatest early sources of foreign words, detailing the customs, peoples, and religions of the world. Hakluyt was a geographer who published more than twenty-five travel books; his most important, *The Principal Navigations, Voiages, Traffiques and Discoveries of the English Nation, Made by sea or Over-land, to the Remote and Farthest Quarters of the Earth* (*Voyages*), was published in 1589 (the third, and most frequently quoted, edition appeared in 1600). It was a massive collection of voyage tales ranging from the fourth century to the exploits of Drake and Cavendish.

Murray requested that Hakluyt's *Voyages* be read for the dictionary by Robert Needham Cust (1821–1909), a retired civil servant living in London. Cust had spent his working life in India as the Governor-General's assistant for the north-west frontier, the magistrate of Benares, and Home Secretary to the government of India. His knowledge of Sanskrit, Persian, Arabic, and Hindi made him the perfect reader of travellers' tales for Murray, and his role as Secretary of the Royal Asiatic Society from 1878 to 1899 provided many excellent contacts, readers, and consultants for the dictionary. Cust himself published books on cultures and languages around the world,[37] none of which was read for *OED1*, but some were read for the Burchfield *Supplement*, the Additions Series, and *OED3*.

The first compilation of travellers' tales by Samuel Purchas, entitled *Purchas, his Pilgrimage*, appeared in 1613. It introduced hundreds of words that English readers had never seen before, many of which eventually became part of general parlance and took on extended meanings: *oasis* (referring originally to a fertile place in the Libyan desert), *fetish* (referring originally to sacred objects used on the Guinea coast), and *guru* (referring originally to a Hindu spiritual teacher), *pariah* (referring originally to a scheduled tribe of southern Kerala), *emu* (referring originally to a type of cassowary), and *phallus* (referring originally to an image of an erect penis). Other words in Purchas would not stand the test of time – in fact they would never appear in print elsewhere and were soon obsolete – but the editors still included them in the dictionary: *Bengalan,* Bengali; *cabal,* a wild beast of Java; *casson,* a chest; and *heathenous,* heathen. The humour of the dictionary editors is evident in the inclusion of other 'Purchasisms' that never took off, such as *fashionly,* defined by Bradley as 'subject to the sway of fashion', and *knavigation,* defined by Murray as a 'knavish invention or relation'. Since Purchas was the only evidence of the word *knavigation* ever being used, Murray marked the entry as Obsolete and etymologized it as 'Jocular, after *navigation*'.

In 1625, Purchas had published a much larger four-volume compilation of travellers' tales and accounts of the peoples and religions of the world, called *Hakluytus Post-humus, or Purchas his Pilgrims, containing a History of the World in Sea Voyages and Land travel by Englishmen and Others* (1625). Indebted to Hakluyt's papers, obtained by Purchas some time after 1616, the volumes cover accounts of English voyages to Africa, Persia, India, Asia, China, Russia, Iceland, Greenland, the Arctic, South America and North America. Murray had the four-volume text officially read by Cust and it provided first quotations for more than 250 new loanwords in *OED1*, many of which are well-known to English speakers today: *sofa*, *Koran, Bengali, couscous*, *fetwa*, *quinoa*, *yogurt,* and *kiosk.*

When Frederick Furnivall had taken over the dictionary reading programme in the 1860s, he had established a methodology that assigned readers specific letters of the alphabet so that a reader would only highlight words beginning with a particular letter.[38] When Murray inherited Furnivall's programme in 1879, he discovered that Furnivall's method had disastrous implications for the project as a whole: 'The fatal result being', Murray explained, 'that I never know whether a book reported as read was read as a whole or not, until some accident recalls the fact that of late we have not seen any quots. from the book in question.'[39] Murray revised the instructions for readers so that a text would be read for all words regardless of the initial letter.

Travellers' tales therefore formed a significant part of the reading programme, with Murray sending readers copies of Mawe's *Travels in the Interior of Brazil* (1812) and Koster's *Travels in Brazil* (1816). Fraser's *Travels in Koordistan* (1840) provided first instances of *balakhana*, an upper room in a Persian house, and *Nizam*, the Turkish regular army. Likewise, John Campbell's *Travels in South Africa* (1822) supplied quotations for *bamboos*, a wooden vessel for milk, and *pitso*, a traditional Sotho gathering. The entry *bamboos* was included by Murray with three quotations, all of which were taken from travellers' tales in South Africa (Campbell's *Travels in South Africa* [1822], Moffat's *Missionary Labours in South Africa* [1842], and Backhouse's *Narrative of a Visit to Mauritius and South Africa* [1844]). Murray would often provide each reader with books and hundreds of pre-prepared slips on which the reader could record quotations (Figure 3.3).

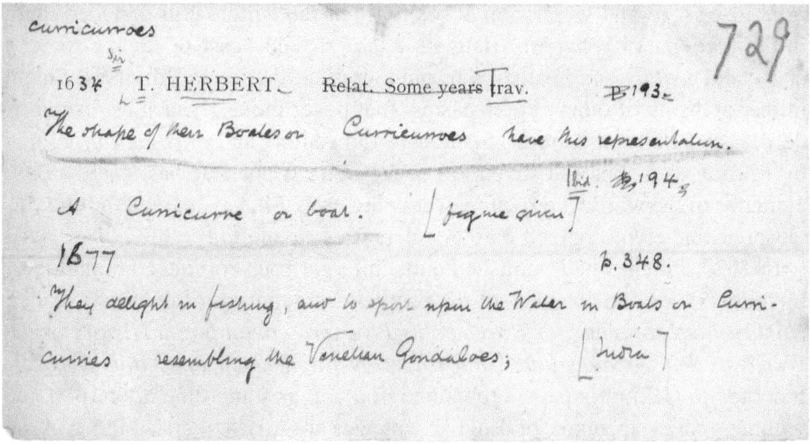

Figure 3.3 A pre-printed reader's slip filled out by Dr Minor, showing a citation for *curricurro*, a spelling variant of *corocoro*, a Malaysian boat, as used by Sir Thomas Herbert in *Some Yeares Travels* (1634). (Credit: OUP)

Hence, the coverage of words from beyond Europe depended not only on readers from around the world reading their local texts, but also on the initiative of the *OED* editors to instigate the reading of international texts, as and when they were published.[40] Readers were officially sought for such titles as R. F. Burton's *Lake Regions of Central Equatorial Africa* (1859), David and Charles Livingstone's *Narrative of an Expedition to the Zambesi and its Tributaries* (1865), A. P. Stanley's *Sinai and Palestine* (1856), Lumholtz's *Among Cannibals* (1890), and Southey's *The Curse of Kehama* (1810).[41]

From New Zealand, Rev. E. H. Cook contributed 2400 quotations of New Zealand English, and in Australia, Edward Sugden (1854–1935) and Edward Morris (1843–1902) both – over a period of forty years – sent in thousands of quotations of language in Australia. Sugden also sub-edited a portion of the letter I.[42] In the 1890s, Morris, who had moved from being Headmaster of Melbourne Grammar School to join Sugden at the University of Melbourne, realized that he had collected enough quotations to compile his own dictionary of Australian and New Zealand English. He published *Austral English* in 1898 and sent duplicates of all his quotations to the *OED*. Morris wrote in its preface:

> Dr Murray several years ago invited assistance from this end of the world for words and uses of words peculiar to Australasia, or to parts of it. In answer to his call I began to collect. . . . The work took time, and when my parcel of quotations had grown into a considerable heap, it occurred to me that the collection, if a little further trouble were expended upon it, might first enjoy an independent existence.[43]

Murray also drew on the resources of individuals with significant private collections, such as the publisher and book collector Edward Augustus Petherick (1847–1917), who had the world's largest collection of Australian books (housed now in the Australian National Library where a reading room is named after him). Petherick moved from Melbourne to London in 1870 as manager of George Robertson Booksellers and the Colonial Booksellers Agency, returning to Australia in 1908. During this time, he was in correspondence with Murray, responding to Murray's requests in *Notes & Queries* for citations, and providing him with important etymological information on Australian words. Petherick's researches enabled Murray to determine particular Australian senses of words such as *bail up*, to secure a cow while milking, and (said of bushrangers) to rob travellers, and to provide detailed entries for Australian Aboriginal words such as *boomerang,* a curve-shaped Aboriginal weapon, and *corroboree*, an Aboriginal dance ceremony.[44] Murray's etymology of *boomerang* ran to an exhaustive nineteen lines, and in order to solve a question about the original pronunciation of *corroboree*, he had gone so far as to publish a plea for help in the journal *Notes Queries*.[45]

By inviting readers from around the globe, Murray was ensuring that *OED1* was an international text. He remarked early on that the response from readers in America was much more enthusiastic than from the British public, especially within the academic community.[46] He was quoted in the *Times* in 1882 as saying that many American university professors were reading for the dictionary, and that 'we have had no such help from any college or University in Great Britain; only one or two professors of English in this country have thought the matter of sufficient importance to talk to their students about it and advise them to help us.'[47]

For those international texts that could be purchased in Britain, Murray found British readers. For instance, in the early 1880s, he sent a copy of Lady Barker's *Station Life in New Zealand* (1867) to Reverend T. Burdett in Leeds which yielded New Zealand words such as *toe-toe* (*toi-toi*), a tall reed-like grass. Similarly, John J. Thompson of London was sent a copy of John Fryer's *A New Account of East-India and Persia* (1698), the text of which provided first citations for more than sixty terms entering English in India, such as *bummalo*, an Indian fish, *cadjan*, woven coco-palm leaves, *chank*, a shell prized by Hindus, and *mussal*, a torch.

Finding the 'right readers' who would highlight the 'right words' in these texts was not always easy. Different readers highlighted different words. Nor was it clear which were the 'right words'. Murray's 'Directions to Readers for the Dictionary' provided no special guidelines for readers of texts on or from cultures outside Britain. All readers were advised to 'Make a quotation for *every* word that strikes you as rare, obsolete, old-fashioned, new, peculiar, or used in a peculiar way' and to 'Make *as many* quotations *as convenient to you* for the ordinary words, when these are used significantly, and help by the context to explain their own meaning, or show their use.'[48] But Murray did instruct some individual readers on the types of words he wanted them to watch out for in their reading. For example, he sent John J. Thompson of London a copy of John Fryer's *A New Account of East-India and Persia* (1698), and instructed him to highlight the local and peculiar rather than 'ordinary literary words': 'we should hardly quote him [Fryer] for ordinary literary words at the time, since we have so many literary writers of the same date.' Rather, Murray encouraged his reader, 'the main thing is to get the words connected with the countries visited for which Fryer is often of the earliest witness, adding to these any other antiquated, novel, or peculiar words & phrases that strike'.[49]

Some readers, as the following examples demonstrate, had a better understanding than others of Murray's sense of 'peculiar'. Murray assigned David Livingstone's *Missionary Travels and Researches in South Africa* (1857) to a Miss E. R. Blomfield of Upper Norwood in London. Murray assigned a similar book by David and Charles Livingstone, *Narrative of an Expedition to the Zambesi and its Tributaries* (1865), to be read by a Mr J. Griffith in Hereford. It is insightful to compare the nature of citations collected by Mr Griffith with those collected by Miss Blomfield. Miss Blomfield collected a good selection of 'peculiar' words, such as *banian*, a Hindu trader, *baobab*, a tree found in Africa and India, and *gnu*, a wildebeast; she also collected many 'common' words such as *fold*, *bundle*, *convert*, and *everyday*. However, no such balance was struck by Mr Griffith, whose collection was focused solely on common words or words with long histories in English such as *barter*, *bawling*, *blatter*, *boll*, *brattle*, and *brookle*.

Both texts – Livingstone's *Missionary Travels and Researches in South Africa* (1857) and the Livingstones' *Narrative of an Expedition to the Zambesi and its Tributaries* (1865) – contain roughly similar percentages of indigenous African loanwords. Typical words missed by Mr Griffith in the space of four pages in the *Zambesi* text (pages 100–4) include: *borassus,* a palm tree with large edible nuts 'of a sweet, fruity taste'; *head man*, chief of a village; *hornbill*, the bird Buceros cristatus; *Makololo*, a tribe living near Lake Nyasa; *Rundo*, a chief of a large district; *Zambesi*, a valley that bordered the Zambesi river; and *sura*, a type of palm wine which, Livingstone remarked, was 'like Champagne'.[50]

Miss Blomfield's reading of Livingstone's *Missionary Travels and Researches in South Africa* (1857) favoured the exceptional over the common, but still provided a good balance of the two, whereas Mr Griffith's reading of the Livingstones' *Narrative of an Expedition to the Zambesi and its Tributaries* (1865) favoured the common over the exceptional. Two readers can, therefore, have completely different ideas about the boundaries of

English and which words belong in an English dictionary, and their reading will have consequences for the dictionary. The lexicographer can only include words for which there is written evidence, and is therefore reliant on the readers' selections. It was vital for the *OED*'s coverage of words from around the globe that texts relating to foreign topics first of all be read, and, second, be read by readers who were sensitive to the kinds of exceptional words they contained.

James Murray's immediate context for developing this large network of readers was the British Empire. For the whole of his life, Britain had an empire, a massive 'world system' assembled by the Victorians.[51] When Murray began working on the dictionary in 1879, a 'new imperialism' was in force and the British Empire was reaching its height. The 1880s and 1890s saw a mad scramble amongst European powers for the last remaining territories in Africa and the Pacific, with Britain consolidating its hold on south, east, and central Africa. In 1882, Britain occupied Egypt, conquering the Upper Nile Valley by 1898. These decades also saw an intensification of imperial activity and imperialistic sentiments. By the beginning of the twentieth century, the British Empire covered about a quarter of the globe, stretching over twelve million square miles (out of sixty million habitable square miles across the world). It had a population of 400 million people, of which just over a tenth (41.5 million) lived in Britain.[52]

This had repercussions of course for the expansion of the English language, as linguist April McMahon notes: by the end of the eighteenth century, the scene was set 'for the building of the Empire, the development of extraterritorial Englishes in North America, Australia, and beyond . . . and a consequent quantum leap in borrowed vocabulary'.[53] Murray coordinated his network of readers across the Empire, who supplied him with new words, loanwords, and words that had originated in Britain but shifted and changed in their meaning as they had travelled with the British migrants who crossed the seas. Migration was on the increase from the 1880s, and Murray harnessed this global presence to form his reading network of over 2000 men and women by 1890.[54]

Essential to Murray's global reading network was the postal system. He sent books that he wanted read for the dictionary, and his worldwide readers sent him their slips, containing words and quotations, by mail. Murray provided so much work for the Oxford post office that they erected a special pillar box outside his house which still survives today. In general, the amount of mail being transported throughout the Empire grew rapidly with the technological innovations that enabled communications to become increasingly speedy and efficient. By 1903, letters, newspapers, and circulars weighing 12.5 million pounds were dispatched from Britain to all corners of the Empire through the post, and in turn 3.25 million pounds of mail in weight were received.[55] Steamships and railways were both vital to this postal system. Shipping lines such as P&O carried 'penny post' mail to and from all parts of the Empire. Before 1914 (which was the year before Murray died), Britain possessed 40% of the world's shipping. Railway building was a priority in almost all parts of the Empire. In India, for example, by the 1870s more than 5000 miles of track had been laid. Shipping and trains were part of an extensive communications network that also included telegraphs, cables, and wireless stations, and together they connected this vast Empire. Just as state officials, civil servants, and those engaged in trade relied on this extraordinary communication system for the increased economic success and efficient rule of the Empire, so Murray needed it for the creation of his global dictionary.

The dictionary's network of readers, like the many other influential networks of the Empire, such as those of higher education, was made possible by that vast communications system. And this network of readers was essential for the compilation of the dictionary. Gary Magee and Andrew Thompson (2010) have highlighted the importance of networks across the British Empire. Voluntary in nature, usually made up of migrants and frequently of professionals, these networks were a sort of 'cultural glue' and reinforced a sense of belonging to a worldwide British community, they argue.[56] While much of this holds true for Murray's network of readers, it is important to remember that the boundaries of his network were permeable: they stretched across the British Empire, but went beyond it. The readers' selection of words contributed to a dictionary of the English language while all the time expanding it beyond what many people thought was 'English'. Furthermore, Murray's readers were not usually in touch with each other, reinforcing the identity of Greater Britain and the Empire in one another as were, for example, the professors of the Empire's and Dominions' universities in Tamson Pietsch's recent study.[57] Murray's volunteer readers were drawn to this project, often by their attachment to Greater Britain, but also by their love of words and language.

As Murray was receiving new words, and examples of their usage, on slips from readers all over the world, so the Empire and its words were also coming to England in both high and low culture, making people of all classes conversant in a new vocabulary. Ethnographic museums, such as the Pitt Rivers Museum in Oxford, founded in 1884, displayed the artefacts of 'exotic' tribes, introducing new language to museum visitors, and the emerging disciplines of geography and anthropology (the latter established at Oxford by the dictionary's sometime consultant E. B. Tylor), explored the meaning of those newly 'discovered' cultures within the academic world. The Empire also reached a wider public in the form of newspaper reports, travel literature, visual images, music hall songs, tableaux, commercial shows and a series of exhibitions which showcased the flora and fauna, the peoples and their cultures, of even the remotest outposts of the Empire.[58] The first 'Great Exhibition' was held at the Crystal Palace in London in 1851, and it displayed a wide variety of imperial products and exhibits, such as a full-size model of a Maori *pah* or *pa*, first recorded in Cook's *Journal* and defined by Murray in *OED1* as 'a native fort or fortified camp in New Zealand'. Murray and the early editors turned to the Exhibitions and their catalogues as sources for words of the world: quotations from the Great Exhibition catalogue of 1851 provided evidence for *dinghy*, a traditional rowing boat, and *huldee*, a tumeric plant, both from Hindi; *jacaranda*, a tropical tree from Tupi-Guarani; *jambo*, an East Indies fruit tree from Sanskrit; *kauri*, a tall New Zealand tree from Maori.

Manufacturers and advertisers used imperial images (such as Imperial Leather Soap and Pears' Soap 'lightening the white man's burden' as originally described in Rudyard Kipling's poem (1899) which Murray alluded to in the preface to volume 5 H–K).[59] Adventure books by writers such as H. Rider Haggard and publications for children such as the *Boys' Own Paper* told daring tales of life in the farthest reaches of the Empire. Historians have argued about how much the culture of the Empire suffused life back home in the Metropole,[60] but the fact remains that an entirely new vocabulary was being incorporated into British life and the English language – both in Britain and the rest of the Empire, and Murray chose to embrace it.

Murray, a devoted Congregationalist Christian, had a particular interest in global missionary activities, which exposed him to new knowledge of a range of cultures.[61] His son Jowett was a missionary in China, and Murray took a keen interest in his time there, always with a view to language and the role that English played around the world. As Murray recounted,

> In a steamer in which my son travelled from Japan to China, there were two Chinese stewards one a Pekinese the other a Cantonese, who though Chinese were unable to understand each other, and had to communicate in Pidgin English. This diversity of the spoken language [in China] is a serious question in connexion with the formation of a central Chinese University about which much has been said in the last three years. At the Tientsin it has had to be solved by first teaching the students English, and then teaching them other subjects through English.[62]

Murray's son Wilfred lived in South Africa and worked at the University of Cape Town, and his daughter Elsie emigrated there in 1921.[63] Murray had visited Cape Town in 1905, and this exposed him to a particularly complex linguistic landscape. Many of Wilfred's African friends, as well as Rhodes Scholars, stayed with the Murray family in Oxford, extending James Murray's personal contact with different cultures. Although it is impossible to prove that Murray's contact with the rest of the world through his children's wide travels and his own missionary interests influenced his inclusive attitude towards the inclusion of foreign words, it seems likely that his exposure to other cultures through his own travel, curiosity, reading, researches, and family and friendship circles, widened his own domain of 'English'. As Murray articulated, 'to every man the domain of "common words" widens out in the direction of his own reading, research, business, provincial or foreign residence, and contracts in the direction with which he has no practical connexion: no one man's English is *all* English'.[64]

Murray's membership in the British and Foreign Bible Society and the Church Missionary Society gave him entrée into a community within Oxford that followed international events and welcomed missionary visitors. Several of Murray's language consultants, including James Legge (1815–97) and David Samuel Margoliouth (1858–1940), were fellow members of the Church Missionary Society.[65]

Murray made full use of his contacts and made sure he had the best advice possible for loanwords and words from World Englishes. With a reading knowledge of twenty-five languages, he defined himself as a philologist, and attributed his expertise as a lexicographer to his knowledge of philology.[66] Writing to Hucks Gibbs in 1883, he compared himself with other men of letters: 'I am not a man of letters like [Samuel] Johnson . . . but I am a Philologist, and I enter on the task of editing or writing the Dictionary with advantages due to my own especial training and my own studies, and therefore I consider myself ten times better fitted to make a Dictionary than Mr Ruskin, or Mr Carlyle or Matthew Arnold or Professor Jowett, and so a hundred times better than Dr Johnson, no Philologist, only a man of letters.'[67]

In the mid to late nineteenth century, Oxford was placed firmly in the centre of important work in philology and this naturally had an impact on Murray. He was President of the Philological Society 1878–80, 1882–84, and 1907–9, and was in frequent correspondence with the key philological figures of his day, including Walter Skeat (1835–1912), Monier Monier-Williams (1819–99), Archibald Sayce (1845–1933), David Margoliouth, Joseph Wright (1855–1930), Max Müller, and James Legge. This ensured that Murray had the best possible etymological advice for his loanword entries.

Monier Monier-Williams was Oxford's Boden Professor of Sanskrit, founder of the Indian Institute, and editor of the *Sanskrit-English Dictionary* (1872). Monier-Williams' Sanskrit dictionary was indispensable for the *OED* editors (as it still is today), and Murray also asked the author directly for advice. Although based in Oxford, Monier-Williams often wrote to Murray from his house in Bournemouth, where he did not have access to his full range of reference books but still managed to provide Murray with exemplary etymologies and advice, which Murray followed to the letter. In particular, he advised on words from Indian English such as the narcotic *bhang* which

Monier-Williams described to Murray as 'the name of the Indian Hemp plant (Cannabis Sativa) and of the intoxicating substance and beverage prepared from it. The word *bhaṅgā* in Sanskrit means "breaking, splitting" and I suppose the plant is called *bhaṅgā* because its leaves are easily split and pounded into a substance much like opium'.[68] He politely advised Murray to tone down the language of the definition: 'perhaps it might be better to describe Hashish as an "intoxicating substance" rather than as a "drug"'. Monier-Williams was quick to admit if he did not know something, and was adept at questioning Murray's definitions without appearing rude or arrogant. 'I confess I did not know it was smoked', he wrote about *bhang*, 'Your sources of information in this respect are no doubt better than mine. I have often seen the low caste natives of India stupefied with Bhang, but I was not aware that they smoked it.'[69] He went on to suggest that Murray contact Sir George Birdwood in the India Office, London, for verification on the smoking of the drug. Murray did so, and it turned out that Murray was correct: his final etymology and definition were incredibly detailed and ran to eighteen lines, complete with information that the drug leaves were not only chewed and smoked, but also 'eaten mixed up into a sweetmeat, and sometimes an infusion of them is drunk'.

Murray was also in contact with the Oxford-based Assyriologist, Archibald Henry Sayce (1845–1933), who was made Deputy Professor of Comparative Philology in 1876 and extraordinary Professor of Assyriology in 1891, a post that he held until 1914.[70] Though a specialist in the Middle East, Sayce also had an avid interest in the indigenous languages of Australia. In his book *Austral English* (1898), Edward Morris acknowledged Sayce's efforts to motivate Australian philologists to record and save Australian Aboriginal languages before they disappeared, and praised him for 'pointing out the obligation that lay upon the Australian colonies to make a scientific study of a vanishing speech'.[71] Sayce's books *The Principles of Comparative Philology* (1874) and *Introduction to the Science of Language* (1880) provided many quotations for words pertaining to cultures and languages such as *aboriginal, Uralic,* and *Sumerian,* to name just a few.

When preparing the *OED* entry for *loanword,* Henry Bradley chose two quotations to exemplify the word's use: one from A. H. Sayce's *Comparative Philology* (1874) and the other from an article by D. S. Margoliouth in *The Expositor* (1900). David Margoliouth regularly advised on Arabic terms for both *OED1* and the *1933 Supplement.* He was Laudian Professor of Arabic at Oxford from 1889 to 1937 and he corresponded with all the editors on many words relating to Arabic and Egyptian culture, such as *hygeen,* a riding camel; *medin,* an Egyptian coin; and *usnea,* a type of lichen from the Arabic word for 'moss'. His correspondence with the dictionary editors continued after Murray's death, and included glimpses of his own life and travels: advising on the word *bellum,* Margoliouth explained, 'I learned the word *balam* at Basrah, and it is noticed in Meissner's *Geschichten aus Iraq* as a local word for a sort of gondola.'[72] Margoliouth was also quick to recommend his own publications for *OED* reading: in a note on the word *sufi* he advised Onions, 'I have dealt with the origin of the name *sufi* at length in my Hibbert Lectures. It seems to me certain that it means "man of wool" i.e. ascetic.'[73] Onions followed Margoliouth's advice and the final entry refers the reader to his Hibbert Lectures entitled *The Early Development of Mohammedanism.* Margoliouth was always generous with his linguistic knowledge, informing the editors on *okea* that 'Syriac is the language by which Greek would ordinarily get into Arabic and the tendency in Syriac for a w to coalesce with a letter that follows accounts for the reduction to *ukiyyah* [from *wakiyyah*].'[74]

Before working on *OED1,* Murray had worked with the phonetician Alexander John Ellis (1814–90) on the pronunciation of British dialects, and the two men became lifelong friends. Murray was colleagues and good friends with Joseph Wright, Corpus Christi Professor of Comparative Philology and editor of *The English Dialect Dictionary* (1896–1905), and was also frequently in correspondence with Hugh Egerton (1855–1927), the first Beit Professor of Colonial History. Max Müller was one of the more vocal Delegates when it came to Dictionary policy matters. As Professor of Comparative Philology at Oxford, he was known for his theories on the laziness of speakers of 'civilized languages'.[75] As a Delegate, Müller had spoken out on many matters including the dangers of readers for the dictionary choosing exceptional over common words. As an *OED* consultant, Müller gave advice on foreign words. For example, he described *bonze,* Japanese Buddhist clergy, as a Chinese word meaning 'teacher' and 'spelt *Fǎ sze* in Chinese', that 'came to Japan with the Buddhists, and from Japan to Europe through the Dutch'.[76] He also advised Murray to 'ask Dr Legge for the correct spelling in Chinese'. This was easy for Murray because James Legge was not only the first Professor of Chinese at Oxford (a world authority on Confusianism), but he was also Murray's best friend. Legge advised Murray on all words of Chinese provenance, but his consultancy was not without its controversies. In 1889, he advised Murray that the word *chop sticks* was the equivalent of the Chinese *k'wai-tsze* meaning 'nimble boys'. 'If you saw how nimbly they are used', commented Legge, 'you would call the name a good one'.[77] Murray published the entry in 1889 with Legge's etymology, as it remains today in *OED Online* [In Chinese and in 'pigeon-English' *chop* means 'quick'; 'quick sticks' would be a kind of equivalent of the Chinese name, *k'wâi-tsze,* i.e. 'nimble boys', 'nimble ones'].

However, this etymology was later contested by the famous sinologist Herbert Giles (1845–1935), who wrote to Murray four years after the entry was published. Giles had built on Thomas Wade's romanized spelling system for Chinese to create the 'Wade-Giles' writing system which remained the official system for Chinese until 1979 when it was replaced by Pinyin. He pointed out to Murray that Legge's etymology was 'untenable' because it had confused *kuai-tzu* as a rising final tone, whereas it had no tone and was instead a nominalizing suffix.[78] Hence the etymology *kwai-tsze,* 'nimble boys', should have read *k'uai-tzu*, lit. 'haste-NOMINALIZER' = 'hasteners'. Giles later wrote again to Murray saying, 'This mistake was exposed in my *Glossary of Reference*, Shanghai, 1878. The correct explanation has been repeated in my *Chinese-English Dictionary* (p. 652), Quaritch, London, 1892.'[79] In addition, he advised that 'pigeon-English' should read 'Pidgin-English', as is the more common spelling, but none of Giles' corrections was integrated in either *OED Supplement,* and today the etymology for *chop-stick* remains as it did in 1889.

Over many years, Herbert Giles persevered in correcting the dictionary on erroneous Chinese etymologies, but not one of his suggestions was incorporated. For example, he wrote to Craigie in 1914 and pointed out that 'in the last fascicle of *The Oxford Dictionary,* under *Soy*, the Chinese *shi* should be *shu,* as you will see by reference to my *Chinese-English Dictionary*, p. 1242. No. 10.042, where the correct botanical identification is given. Also, the pronunciation of the word *Souchong* should be *soo-jong*, and not, as you have it, *soo-shong.*'[80] But again, Giles' corrections were not incorporated in either *OED Supplement* and the entry remains as it was published in 1913. It is difficult to ascertain who advised the dictionary on Chinese words after Legge's death in 1897, but it is surprising that the editors did not exploit Giles' advice, especially since he had so willingly offered his expertise on several occasions and was acclaimed worldwide for his scholarship.

The languages of Africa, Asia, and the Americas were largely covered by the expertise of James Platt, whom Murray credited in the letter K for 'many of the words from remote languages' which were 'for the first time correctly traced to their true origin'. John Thompson Platts (1830–1904) regularly advised on the etymologies of words of Persian and Hindi origin, as did Fitzedward Hall (1825–1901), a scholar of Sanskrit and Hindi whom Murray thanked for his advice on the Indian alphabet, *Devanagari*, a word which Murray described as 'on the very verge of the province of an English Dictionary'.[81] Henry Yule (1820–89), editor of the famous glossary of Anglo-Indian called *Hobson-Jobson* (1886), gave Murray copies of the proofs of *Hobson-Jobson* before it was published. Words from Slavonic languages were dealt with by William Richard Morfill (1834–1909), Professor of Russian and Slavonic Studies at Oxford; and Charles Rieu (1820–1902), Adams Professor of Arabic at Cambridge, helped with Persian and Arabic.

In addition to his philological contacts, Murray also had good lexicographic contacts. In lexicography, during the nineteenth century, new method and practice were developed in Oxford, and were expertly executed in the form of Joseph Riddle's *Dictionary of the Latin Language* (1835) and the *Greek-English Lexicon* (1843) by Henry George Liddell (1811–98) and Robert Scott (1811–87), both published by OUP. Liddell and Scott based their dictionary on Franz Passow's German dictionary *Handwörterbuch der griechischen Sprache* (1819–34). They enhanced Passow's lexicographical method, and Liddell, who was also Dean of Christ Church, shared his technique with other Oxford-based lexicographers, who, in turn, went on to train other lexicographers who eventually also worked on the *OED*. For example, as a Delegate of OUP, Liddell was instrumental in recommending Murray for the editorship and was in contact with Murray in the early days of establishing policy and preparation of specimen entries.[82] Liddell also trained Gudbrandur Vígfusson (1827–89), who had come to Oxford to turn Richard Cleasby's materials into the *Icelandic-English Dictionary* (1874). Vígfusson went on to become Reader in Icelandic at Oxford and, before his death in 1889, he trained the young lexicographer Joseph Wright.

On the whole, Murray's relations with these lexicographers was positive, but he could also be dismissive of lexicography that did not match his own high standards, territorial with his material, and highly competitive with other lexicographers such as Charles Fennell, editor of the *Stanford Dictionary of Anglicized Words and Phrases* (1892), in Cambridge. Another Cambridge lexicographer, Walter Skeat, editor of the *Etymological English Dictionary* (1879–82), was a loyal friend of Murray's who tried to appease him during the *Stanford Dictionary* controversy, which we will come to in the next chapter.

Criticism of James Murray's inclusive policy and practice by his contemporaries

In addition to the comments made in reviews of the dictionary, Murray's broad definition of English also sparked comment from his superiors at OUP, his consultants, and his sub-editors, all of whom questioned his inclusion of words of the world. The first draft section of the dictionary, A–ANT, which Murray passed on to the OUP Delegates, came back to him with instructions to 'Omit' the loanword entries '*Aardvark, Aardwolf, Ab*^{2}*, Aba, Abaca*'.[83] Murray pressed for their inclusion. As he was to articulate many years later, 'the adoption of foreign things with their foreign names is the natural process which we find adopted by people of all nations'.[84] The Delegates' view was that there was no place in an English dictionary for words unheard of in Britain, and they also urged Murray not to lengthen the dictionary unnecessarily and slow down the editing speed with 'derivatives', 'modern', and 'newspaper words'.

It was not unusual for Murray to clash with the Delegates on all manner of issues pertaining to the dictionary. Recounting one meeting with the Delegates – in which Benjamin Jowett (1817–93), who at this time was Master of Balliol, Vice Chancellor, and ex officio Delegate of the Press, was particularly insistent – Murray said, 'It soon became evident to me that they were suggestions which he [Jowett] was simply determined that I should swallow willing or unwilling. We simply had to fight every word, my wishes going for nothing; and only when I could absolutely convince him that my words were better, would he yield on anything.'[85] One issue was whether or not Murray should write his own preface, and his sub-editor, Henry Hucks Gibbs, came to his defence, pleading with Jowett to stop 'drawing the cord too tightly' with Murray.[86]

On most issues, as the text of the dictionary testifies, Murray won his battles with the Delegates. This did not mean that he did not spend a good deal of time placating his superiors, as evidenced in a letter of March 1893, which he wrote to the Secretary to the Delegates Philip Lyttelton Gell (1852–1926), reassuring him that 'I am also endeavouring by all means to abridge the work upon scientific & technical words, and to omit such occasional foreign words as have least claim to insertion.'[87] However, the Superfluous file for the letter D, which was the letter that Murray was editing in March 1893, shows no omission of foreign words, so one wonders whether Murray was saying such things merely to appease his superiors.

Time and money were the main reasons for the Delegates' concerns. They wanted Murray and his team to work faster, and ordered him to cut back on the coverage of 'fringe' vocabulary and to truncate the etymologies of borrowed words so that only the immediate host language be given, arguing that further etymologies had 'no bearing on the history of the English language'.[88] The Delegates were all too aware that longer etymologies meant more time, more space, and ultimately more money, all of which they were trying to minimize. They instructed the editors that 'the etymology of borrowed words need not be traced beyond the point at which they enter the English language'.[89] This became a long-running battle between the editors and the Delegates for most of the 1890s, with Henry Bradley coming to Murray's defence in a letter to the Delegates, in which he argued that 'there are many borrowed words of which the ultimate etymology is a matter of interest to Englishmen'.[90] The editors wanted their scholarship and the dictionary's content to reflect the advances in comparative philology and new linguistic science that had emerged in their lifetime. They also expected more from their readers than perhaps the Delegates did. Bradley explained to the Secretary to the Delegates, that 'the ordinary reader expects to learn from his dictionary what philologists have ascertained with regard to these words, or, if no certain conclusions have been reached, whether any of the current guesses are recognised by scholars as philologically admissible'.[91] In order to argue his case to the Delegates, Bradley compared *OED1* with other dictionary competitors whose etymologies were often inaccurate: 'In Webster and the *Century Dictionary*, in Ogilvie, and Cassells, he [the ordinary reader] does find an answer – often inaccurate – to his question. From our correspondence with the ablest foreign scholars we are often able to give correct information, that has not before appeared in print, with regard to the etymology of foreign words which have been adopted in English.'[92] The editors ultimately ignored the Delegates, and kept the etymologies long.

In addition to pressure from the Delegates, Murray's proofreaders were also recommending that he exclude words. The orientalist and assistant keeper of the British Museum, Russell Martineau (1831–98), who proofread for Murray, urged him in 1879:

> I should be inclined to be less liberal than you are in the insertion of words belonging to foreign languages & avowedly quoted as such in the authors you cite in support of them (e.g. apothesis is Greek, as is antisyzygy). . . . For the same reason we might have to insert Eskimo words wholesale, if we found an English book describing the parts of the huts of the Eskimos.[93]

The Greek words *apothesis,* the setting of a fractured or dislocated limb, and *antisyzygy,* union of opposites, were both published in *OED1*. In addition, one can only imagine Martineau's reaction, had he lived long enough, to witness the inclusion of numerous Inuit (Eskimo) words in *OED1*: not just well-known words such as *kayak* and *igloo,* but also less-known ones such as *tupik,* a hut or tent of skins used by Eskimo as a summer residence, and *umiak,* an Eskimo boat.

Murray received resistance from his consultants and sub-editors, many of whom, like Martineau, were specialists in cultures and languages outside Britain. A letter to Murray from the Oxford anthropologist, E. B. Tylor, who famously advocated an hierarchical view of language and culture, shows the impact of such views on the treatment of foreign words in the dictionary (Figure 3.4).[94] Tylor commiserated with Murray's task of having – as Tylor put it – 'to decide whether such outlandish words have any place in an English Dictionary'.[95] Tylor referred specifically to the word *boyuna*, a large black Brazilian snake, which came into English from Tupi (*mboiauna* < *mboia* 'cobra' + *una* 'black') in 1774 via the Portuguese, who in turn took the word to Sri Lanka where they gave an unrelated snake the same Tupi name. This caused great confusion to the editors, who could not work out at first why two unrelated species of snake in different parts of the world had the same unusual name. Tylor was questioning whether Murray should include the entry at all. Tylor's hierarchical view of language translated to a

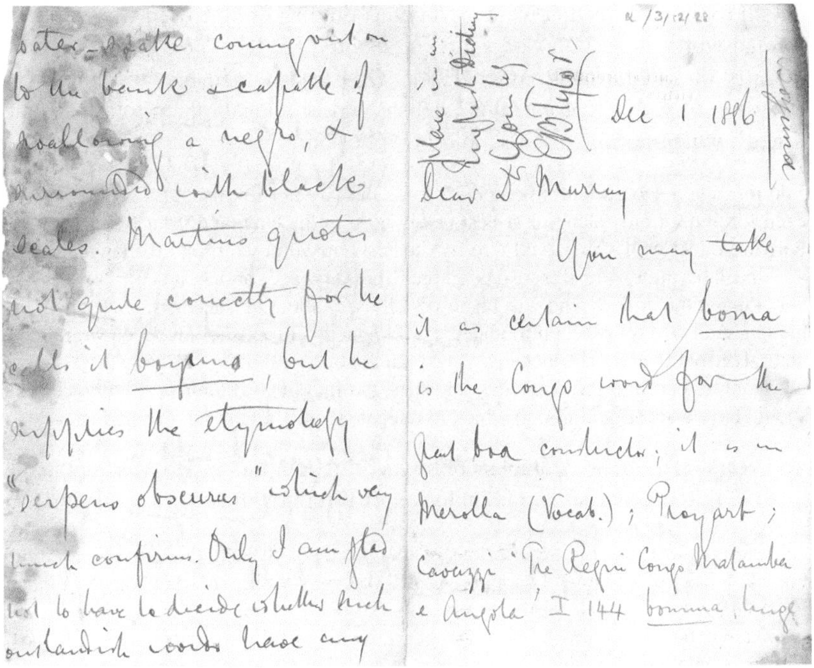
water-snake coming out on
to the bank & capable of
swallowing a negro, &
ornamented with black
scales. Martius quotes
not quite correctly for he
calls it boyuna but he
supplies the etymology
"serpens obscurus" which very
much confirms. Only I am glad
not to have to decide whether such
outlandish words have any
place in an English Dictionary.
Yours truly
EB Tylor

Dec 1 1886
Dear Dr Murray
You may take
it as certain that boma
is the Congo word for the
great boa constrictor; it is in
Merolla (Vocab.); Proyart;
Cavazzi 'The Regni Congo Matamba
e Angola' I 144 bomma, lunge

boyuna

Figure 3.4 Letter from the anthropologist, E. B. Tylor, to James Murray in which Tylor commiserates with Murray's task of having 'to decide whether such outlandish words have any place in an English Dictionary'. (Credit: OUP)

lexicographic hierarchy based on the degree of a word's 'outlandishness': less outlandish words could gain admittance to an English dictionary, but more outlandish words could not. Regardless of whether Tylor's use of the word 'outlandish' referred to an archaic sense of 'foreignness' or a more derogatory sense of 'oddness' (probably the former rather than the latter), Murray did not share Tylor's view. He ignored Tylor's advice, and published the entry *boyuna*.

Similarly, Sir William Thistelton-Dyer (1843–1928), Director of the Royal Botanic Gardens, advised Murray on exotic plant names. Writing to Murray about *pacay*, a tree and fruit of Peru, Thistelton-Dyer said, 'Markham speaks of paccay-trees otherwise the word has no place in an English Dictionary.'[96] As with Tylor's comments on *boyuna,* Murray ignored Thistleton-Dyer's recommendation and promptly published the entry *pacay*. Tylor's and Thistelton-Dyer's view was shared by Hucks Gibbs, who admitted to Frederick Furnivall in 1886 that 'I should indeed do something in cutting out all foreign words that were used not as English or borrowed words, but as foreign words in accounts of a foreign country.'[97]

Early on in Murray's career, Hucks Gibbs had urged him to rethink the inclusion of words that are 'not English' and to relegate them to a 'separate limbo', which he suggested should be 'a hot one':

> I do think you should look askance at words that are not English, and sometimes not even foreign, or only slang or at best newly born in the language from which they are borrowed. It is well – very well – to fix the first entry of a word into the language; but you must be quite sure that it has entered the language, and is not a mere vagrant knocking at the door & who will be deservedly sent about his business. . . . If you must honour such words as 'accommodated', 'accidented', 'accouche' (accouch would be a natural growth) and 'accoucheuse' by taking notice of them, in case they should ultimately creep into the language, and that you may record their first entrance, you should have a separate limbo to which to relegate them – a hot one, I should suggest.[98]

Ten years later, in 1892, Hucks Gibbs was still complaining to Murray that he was being too generous in his inclusion of foreign words:

> All foreign words used in descriptions of their own country should vanish. I open the book at a hazard 'Chaston' I suppose Acosta was only telling us what was the French for anything like a ring or mirror enclosed in a Collet. The information you give is very interesting; but if you are to curtail, that's the sort of thing to cut out. . . . Chogset. Unless people would ordinarily say 'Bring me a fried Chogset' I would have omitted it. . . . I fear mine have been what the Spaniards call Nada entre dos platos.[99]

Murray continued to ignore the views of Hucks Gibbs on the subject. The words *chaston*, a French word for the broad part of a ring in which the stone is set, and *chogset*, a Native American term for an edible fish, were included in *OED1*, the former with *Obsolete* and *Rare* labels, and the latter with a *U.S.* label. Hucks Gibbs and Murray also disagreed on the use of non-canonical sources and newspaper quotations. 'I always shared the dislike of the Delegates to the newspaper quotations unless . . . you had the name of the writer', wrote Hucks Gibbs.[100] But Murray thought the contrary, 'To the philologist and historian of language – newspaper quotations are the *most valuable* of current instances – they show how the language grows – they make visible to us the actual steps which for earlier stages we must reconstruct by inference.'[101]

There is no doubt that Murray not only believed in the inclusion of foreign words but also put his belief into practice. There are, however, three episodes that present a slightly different side to Murray and his policy on foreign words. First, Murray had ironically called himself a 'Little Englander' in a letter in 1900 that discussed the word *carnac*, an Indian elephant driver, which he had already included in the dictionary but said had 'no claim whatever to be English, either in origin, form, or use'.[102] Second, we will see in the next chapter that Murray reacted defensively in 1892 to the publication of the *Stanford Dictionary of Anglicised Words and Phrases*, dismissing it as merely consisting of 'foreign phrases, Latin quotations, and occasional words found in Travels etc.' He felt that these lay 'altogether outside our territory', even though, as we have seen, he had actually sought readers for travellers' tales, and he had gleaned hundreds of words from them.[103]

Third, another episode occurred in 1901, the period between the publication of the fascicle KAISER–KYX and the publication of volume 5 (H to K), which shows that within a few months Murray changed from boasting about the coverage of foreign words in the fascicle to apologizing defensively for it in the volume. In the preface (entitled 'Note') of the fascicle KAISER–KYX, Murray proudly asserted the presence of 'interesting words of foreign origin, often merely denizens or aliens in our language' which, he explained, 'abound all through under *Ka-, Kh-, Kl-, Ko-, Kr-, Ku-, Ky-*; we may merely instance *kangaroo, khaki, karoo, kayak, kermes, ketchup, khan, khedive, kiosk, knobkerrie, knout, kopje, Koran, kotow, koumiss, kraal, kvass*'.[104] In fact, the letter K contained double the proportion of loanwords of any other letter of the alphabet. In the preface of the fascicle, he boasted that 'many of the words from remote languages are here for the first time correctly traced to their true origin, a work in which great assistance has been rendered by Mr. James Platt, junior'.[105] This was no doubt a reference to Murray and Bradley's main argument for longer etymologies, in which they had argued to the Delegates five years earlier that the etymologies given in Websters, Ogilvie, and Cassells were often inaccurate.

However, several months later, when the contents of the fascicle were published in the full volume 5 (H to K), Murray's tone had changed and he obviously felt the need to apologize in the preface of volume 5 for the presence of so many 'exotic' words: while 'exotic words may be thought to superabound [in the volume]', he wrote, 'it would have been easy to double their number, if every such word occurring in English books, or current in English of the colonies and dependencies, had been admitted; our constant effort has been to keep down, rather than to exaggerate, this part of "the white man's burden".'[106] He warned readers that the pages of K 'contain the non-English initial combinations *Ka-, Kh-, Kl-, Ko-, Kr-, Ku-, Ky-*,'[107] and explained that the letters J and K 'contain a very large number of words adopted from Oriental, African, American, Australian, and Oceanic languages (these being phonetically usually written with J and K in preference to G and C): hence the "alien words" in J are proportionally thrice as many as in I, and one-fourth more than in H; and in K three-and-a-half times as many as in H, and seven times as many as in I'.[108] Apart from the fact that the letter K in English may have the largest number of loanwords because most languages of the world display the voiceless velar stop and choose to represent the sound orthographically with the letter K, not C, G, or Q, what is interesting in this instance is that Murray felt the need to apologize for their presence in the dictionary. His apologetic tone is surprising, especially given the proud tone he exuded in the preface of the fascicle for the same section of the alphabet. If it were true that Murray chose only to include half as many 'exotic' words as he could have, then one would expect to find slips for the rejected entries in the Superfluous file for this section of the alphabet, but an inspection reveals no such words.

One explanation is that Murray felt it necessary to justify the inclusion of so many foreign terms, by suggesting that he was in fact being prudent in his inclusion of them. He may have been attempting to pre-empt the criticism that he thought would inevitably follow the publication of a volume in which more than 13% of the words were loanwords with tramlines. If so, then his strategy worked because there were no negative reviews of the volume.

The loanword proportions were calculated by the editors on completion of each volume, and the number of tramlines was recorded in the preface of each volume (often the job assigned to Murray's daughter Hilda); there were approximately 9731 words with tramlines in *OED1*.[109] This figure equated to 4% of the total dictionary.[110] An analysis of tramlines in the dictionary letter by letter, and editor by editor, revealed two patterns:

1. Proportionally, Murray included the most loanwords (mean .05), followed by Bradley (mean .04); Onions and Craigie included the same proportion (mean .03) (Appendix 1).
2. The letter K, edited by Murray, included the most loanwords (13.4%), which was nearly double the proportion of loanwords in the second-highest letter P (6.8%), also edited by Murray (Appendix 2).[111]

Was the high proportion of loanwords in the letter K making Murray worried about, and extra sensitive to, criticism? The publication came at the same time that he wrote the letter about the word *carnac* in which he had insisted that the word had been 'excluded from the Dictionary as having no claim whatever to be English, either in origin, form, or use'. In fact he had published the entry twelve years earlier. Murray had written the letter in March 1900, at a time when he would have been busy finishing the letter K (which was published the following year, and the usual lag between final edits and publication was about nine months).

Recent criticisms of the dictionary and James Murray

If Murray's contemporaries criticized him for including too many foreign words, more recent critics have accused him of not including enough. In the

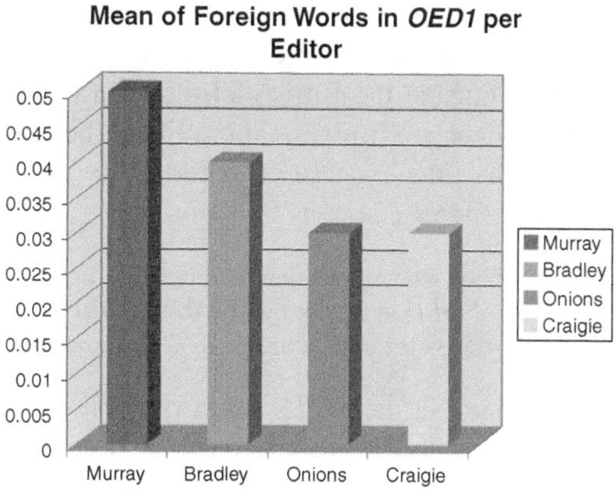

Appendix 1 The mean of inclusion of words with tramlines in *OED1* per editor (Murray 0.05, Bradley 0.04, Onions 0.03, Craigie 0.03) (See Appendix at end of book for colour version of this figure.)

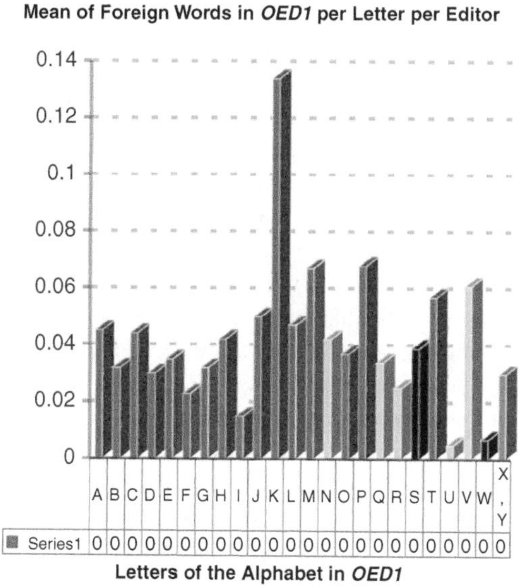

Appendix 2 The proportion of words with tramlines in *OED1* per letter per editor: Murray's letters are shown in red, Bradley's in blue, Onions' in orange, and Craigie's in yellow. The letters in black (S and V) represent ones in which more than one editor worked. (See Appendix at end of book for colour version of this figure.)

entry on Murray in the *Oxford Dictionary of National Biography*, Robert Burchfield described him as a lexicographer who 'had not given sufficient attention to the English used outside the British Isles'.[112] In many publications, as will be detailed in Chapter 6, Burchfield criticized the early editors for focusing on British English at the expense of words 'at the periphery'.[113] He stated:

> Murray preferred to fend off overseas words until they had become firmly entrenched in British use. If you open a page of *OED* at random you will find that an overwhelming majority of words and of illustrative examples are from UK sources.[114]

Burchfield's message was clear: 'in the 1870s when the policy of the Dictionary was drawn up, consensus opinion in lexicography thought of British English as the central vocabulary, and of American, Australian, etc. English as at the periphery. Information about the vocabulary of the peripheral regions made its way back to the centre by slow sailing vessel.'[115] Other scholars, such as Richard Bailey and Manfred Görlach, echoed Burchfield's message, writing in their book *English as a World Language* (1982) that 'the initial editors of the *OED* virtually excluded words not in general use in Great Britain and the United States'.[116] The international press also spread the message. Canadian newspapers reported that 'Mr Burchfield said that the dictionary's original editors resisted including foreign words'.[117]

However, such criticism is unfounded. Once the content of *OED1* is examined, it is found to contain thousands of words of the world. Murray's attitude towards these words was considered highly inclusive in his day, radical even, and his work attracted comment. In the face of such criticism, the pages of the dictionary are testament to Murray's unstinting devotion to a lexicographic policy and practice that grew out of his own system of categorization of loanwords. However, as we will see in the next chapter, when Murray's work is compared with that of a competitor in the specific area of loanwords (Charles Fennell and the *Stanford Dictionary of Anglicised Words and Phrases* [1892]), there were limits to Murray's inclusion policy. On one hand, he was not as conservative as recent criticism presents him; on the other hand, he could have gone further in his inclusion of words from beyond Britain.

More recently, Murray has also been criticized for being imperialistic, or at least for creating an imperialistic dictionary. This book does not attempt to assess whether the *OED* was an imperial project or not – that is beyond its scope – but it is worth looking briefly at these criticisms, which have been made in a variety of ways, as that is the perspective from which Murray's treatment of loanwords has often been discussed.

First, some scholars have unquestioningly taken the idea, promulgated by Burchfield and others, that Murray included low numbers of foreign words and have argued that this made Murray part of a lexicographical conspiracy to promote a Victorian mission of empire-building. Murray's plan, according to John Willinsky, author of the *Empire of Words: The Reign of the OED* (1994), was to supplant other cultures around the world by thrusting upon them a dictionary of ethnocentric words that were exemplified by purely British and canonical sources. The bias of quotations in the *OED* from the Bible and Shakespeare was part of what Willinsky called 'Britain's civilizing mission'. Suspicious of 'the Victorian enthusiasm of Murray', Willinsky has proposed that 'the dictionary is Victorian science attuned to the nation-building project.' 'It was the language of Shakespeare, after all, that was carried abroad as part of Britain's civilizing mission: "Abhorred slave, ... I pitied thee, took pains to make thee speak, taught thee each hour ... " (*The Tempest*, I.ii ... .).'[118] However, there is a more practical and straightforward explanation for the bias of quotations from the Bible, Shakespeare, Milton, Chaucer, Pope, Cowper, Walter Scott, and Tennyson: there were concordances of their work that gave the lexicographers quick and easy access to quotations. In the absence of present-day electronic databases, the nineteenth-century lexicographer used a concordance to furnish quotations for words that were missed in the dictionary's reading programme. Furthermore, Willinsky's 'civilising mission' argument relies on an idea that this book seeks to refute: namely, that the dictionary was almost entirely a work of British English. If Murray had wanted to supplant other cultures with British English, surely he would have ignored their words in preference for his own?

The work of Edward Said in *Orientalism* and a consequent school of postcolonial theorists has promoted the idea that the influence of imperialism was total and its impact entirely negative. The state – conquering, imperialistic – has been seen as total and totalizing in its power, with culture and literature simply acting as handmaidens to this project. The linguist Phil Benson, like Willinsky, believes that the *OED* was a deliberate product of this form of British imperialism. He has described the *OED* as 'more or less explicitly a project of British imperialism concerned with the consolidation of English as the dominant language of the world'. He goes on to say that 'through its documentation of the language of the British Empire ... the dictionary established itself a version of the English language as the pre-eminent language through which the world was made known'.[119] He presents a monolithic view of both Empire and the dictionary, and more specifically he ascribes a colonizing motive to the early editors' inclusion of varieties of English around the Empire. In this interpretation, Murray's inclusion of any foreign words is therefore a colonizing gesture.

These views rely on the idea that there was a fixed, specific, and overt agenda to imperialism. Both modern historians and Murray and his contemporaries present a more nuanced view of the British Empire. C. A. Bayly in his account of the creation of the modern world 'is skeptical of the exaggerated claims that many recent historians have made for the overwhelming, steam roller-like nature of the domestic and colonial state in the nineteenth century'.[120] Recent historians of the British Empire, such as John Darwin, have emphasized how the 'Empire Project' emerged more by default than by design. Darwin (2009) writes: 'Once we concede that there was nothing inevitable about the extraordinary course of Victorian imperialism, we can begin to explore the gravitational field that governed British expansion: propelling it forward in some places; holding it back in others; bending and twisting its impact; raising or lowering its costs; imposing or concealing its contemporary meaning.'[121] So we can understand the dictionary in this context: it took shape in ways that were not necessarily pre-determined, but were the result of multiple forces and a plethora of characters – each with their own ideas. Ronald Hyam (2010) says of the Empire: 'It was not a steel frame – more of a cat's cradle. … It was not an entity driven by some mythical juggernaut called "imperialism".'[122] We might well say the same thing of the dictionary. James Murray sought to incorporate the variety of new words and varieties of English that the extensive territory of the British Empire supplied, but the evidence is not there to suggest that this was part of a grand plan to make English the dominant language of the world. Rather, what the evidence shows is that Murray was often going against the wishes of his bosses and some of his colleagues, consultants, and sub-editors at Oxford University Press when he included a wide variety of words from around the world. There is no evidence that he did this with an overtly colonizing agenda.

As we consider the attitudes of James Murray and his colleagues towards the English language, and towards Britain and its Empire as a whole, it is important to remember that they were working in a time when attitudes towards the Empire were varied amongst their contemporaries. Much attention has been given to those who promoted the British Empire, but this was not universal. In his Cambridge lectures on *The Expansion of England* in 1883, given just before the British took over much of Africa (and Murray published the first fascicle of *OED1*), Seeley stated that 'we have conquered half the world in a fit of absence of mind'.[123] Bernard Porter uses Seeley's phrase as the title of his book *The Absent-minded Imperialists (2006)* to argue that apart from middle-class families with first-hand experience of the Empire, it was simply not on the radar screen of the rest of the nation until the end of the nineteenth century, culminating in the Boer War. Despite 'propaganda efforts' by Imperialists such as William Gladstone, Joseph Chamberlain, and Alfred Milner, Porter argues, it was impossible to rouse the British public from a position of ignorance about and indifference towards the Empire. While on the one hand it could be argued that this was because the fabric of the British society was too complex and disparate for a single 'imperial culture' to penetrate it, it could also be argued that the Empire itself was too large, complex, and disparate to constitute a single 'imperial culture'.

Furthermore, during the course of Murray's time as chief editor, the nature of the Empire shifted and changed. While the 1880s and 1890s saw imperial expansion at its height, the celebration of which was epitomized in the imperial theme of Queen Victoria's diamond jubilee in 1897 and the dedication of the dictionary's third volume to her as 'Empress of India', by the early twentieth century, even the most fervent of Imperialists had had their views disturbed. Britain's failure in the (Boer) war in South Africa of 1899–1902 shot down the idea of never-ending expansion and 'progress'. It was clear by the Edwardian era that Britons were no longer living in a time of colonial expansion, though immigration levels to white settler colonies such as Australia were hitting a high. The task now was to maintain and rule the territories Britain did have. This made some worried that Britain had more than it could cope with in the coming years; it made others positively queasy; yet others feigned indifference. By 1910, Australia, New Zealand, Canada, and South Africa had become self-governing, and thus Dominions rather than part of the Empire. And World War I opened up questions about Britain's role in the world: James Murray did not live to wrestle with those questions but subsequent editors of the dictionary had to face them.

Second, some scholars have criticized the dictionary for being imperialistic by looking at selected entries, in particular some definitions. Rosamund Moon, Henri Béjoint, and Lynda Mugglestone have all used the entry *canoe* to exemplify ideological biases that they believe are pervasive, in which a definition, in the words of Moon (1989), 'betrays the views of its culture, both temporal and social'.[124]

In June 1888, Murray had published the entry *canoe* with two senses, distinguishing 'a kind of boat in use among uncivilized nations' and a kind of boat 'in civilized use'. The influence of Tylor may be reflected in the language of Murray's definition of *canoe* as 'any rude craft in which uncivilized people go upon the water', referring to 'West Indian aborigines' and 'other savages' or 'pre-historic men' as opposed to 'civilized use'.

By using terminology such as 'uncivilized' and 'savages' in the entry *canoe,* the word was not impartially defined despite having a concrete referent that would lend itself to an objective definition. The notion of 'civilization' can be used in definitions, writes Mugglestone (2005), 'as a cultural marker in ways that likewise pervade the dictionary, further delineating attendant notions of inferiority and superiority, of inadequacy or its antonyms'.[125] I might add to this example of *canoe*, further instances of 'cultural binarism', in which the superior, civilized white man is contrasted with the inferior, primitive savage; for example, this is implied in the definitional language of *agriologist,* 'one who is versed in the history and customs of savages,' and *hubbub*, 'the confused shouting of a battle-cry or "hue and cry" by wild or savage races', written by Murray in 1884a[287] and 1899 respectively.[126]

Algeo (1995) has highlighted other 'national biases' relating to Britain exhibited in the *OED2* definitions of *penalty* (as a sports term that is defined using the word 'football' rather than 'soccer' – *OED3* still uses 'football') and *French fried potatoes* (defined as 'potato chips' which in America are misunderstood to be 'potato crisps').[127] Silva (2000) has referred to instances of 'parochialism' that can be found in the entries *spring* and *summer*, defined solely in terms of the northern hemisphere, and sense 8 of the entry *Act* where 'the Universities' is used to refer to Oxford and Cambridge.[128]

Mugglestone (2005) argues that the *OED*'s ideal of impartiality 'can soon fracture when faced with the historical positioning of ideologies of gender, race, and class' as further exemplified in the definitions of *gent*, the use of which was, according to Bradley's definition, a mark of 'low breeding', and of *darky* which is defined, by Murray, in terms of 'a blacky'.[129] Similarly, Brewer (2007) has criticised the definition of *white man* 2b which was defined by Onions as 'a man of honourable character such as one associates with a European (as distinguished from a negro)', but she fails to mention that this sense was labelled *U.S. slang* to differentiate its usage from the sense before it, 2a 'A man belonging to a race having naturally light-coloured skin or complexion: chiefly applied to those of European extraction'.[130] Labels such as *offensive*, *derogatory*, or *pejorative* are good ways for a lexicographer to indicate usage while still being true to a particular meaning of a word, and in addition to the *Slang* label, Onions certainly could have also added such a label to indicate that he was defining a racist usage of the word.

There are two methodological problems here. The first is to assume that the dictionary was or should be an 'impartial' project. No intellectual enterprise is ever impartial: scholars bring their context and presuppositions to their work. The dictionary is no exception. The second is in the sampling of just a few entries, or parts of entries, which is what all these scholars necessarily do. It is difficult to bring the charge of 'imperialistic' or 'racist' against the dictionary as a whole through the definitions of words in just a few entries. There are dangers in generalizing too much from isolated instances of ideological bias in definitional text. To claim that Murray is imperialistic just by looking at a few entries in the dictionary is untenable given that these are just a few entries out of hundreds of thousands of entries. If generalizations are to be drawn from definitions, then a much larger sample of entries is needed, and these entries must be examined not only for instances of bias but also instances of non-bias, especially when compared with other nineteenth-century dictionaries.[131] This has not yet been done and would make for an interesting project, though it is not the task of this book.

One of the questions lurking in all of these discussions is the extent to which the dictionary was a national project, and if so, what 'national' might have meant for the dictionary in a time of Empire. Linda Colley, in her influential work, *Britons* (2003), argued that the possession of an Empire was significant in forging a sense of 'Britishness' in the late eighteenth century. It is indeed the case that the development of the nation-state in the nineteenth century went hand in hand with the expansion of the British and other empires.[132] C. A. Bayly argues that in the later nineteenth century 'Imperialism and Nationalism were part of the same phenomenon. Nationalism and conflict in Europe made states more aware of their competitors abroad and more inclined to stake out claims and prefer their own citizens.' In other words, nationalism and imperialism were in 'a long-standing relationship with each other'.[133]

There was no common or shared understanding of the dictionary as distinctly 'national'. Many in the media and society at large, as well as academics and the Delegates, saw *OED1* as a national dictionary, but the editors had a more ambivalent understanding of the role of the dictionary in national identity, and this was rooted in their view of what constituted the English language. This should not surprise us: as literary criticism has reminded us in recent decades, the author's intention is not necessarily the same as the reader's understanding and the reception of a text.[134]

Early in the nineteenth century, dictionary makers had pitched their dictionaries as national products. Noah Webster had written *An American Dictionary of the English Language* 'for the continued increase of the wealth, the learning, the moral and religious elevation of the character, and the glory of my country'.[135] Likewise on the Continent, Littré and the Grimms wrote their dictionaries to set a national standard.

For some, the Oxford dictionary would increasingly be seen as codifying the English language in just the same way that the *Dictionary of National Biography* (*DNB*), first published a year after the first fascicle of *OED1* (in 1885), codified English history and English people. National scholarly projects such as the *OED* and the *DNB* appeared in the same century as other institutions and patterns of production and consumption in the field of the arts, which Philip Dodd interprets as 'holding the English to a single and continuous history'. The National Portrait Gallery gained a permanent home in 1896, next to the National Gallery, which had been founded in 1824; its aim was 'to aid . . . the study of national history'. Serious agitation for a National Theatre began again in the 1870s at a time when new work was produced, which could not be accommodated within the commercial theatre. It was felt that a National Theatre would 'define and (bear the drama of) the national culture and be the core from which what is of value should be disseminated to the rest of the country'. The National Trust, for the preservation of places of historic interest or natural beauty in England, Wales, and Northern Ireland, held its first meeting in 1893. Dodd places *OED1* in the same category as these national monuments, stressing that one should not 'assume that the project itself – as conceived and sustained – was ideologically neutral'. He argues: 'What the NED [*OED1*] enshrined was not the vision of a number of autonomous and equally valued histories but a national Whig history of the language, whose starting point was "1150 and its early history".'[136]

At first glance, Dodd's argument seems in tune with that of one of the dictionary's founders, Trench. In his book *English Past and Present* (1855), Trench had declared 'the care of the national language I consider as at all times a sacred trust and a most important privilege of the higher orders of society'.[137] He built on this premise in his proposal to the Philological Society in 1857, in which he said:

> A Dictionary is an historical monument, the history of a nation contemplated from one point of view; and the wrong ways into which a language has wandered, or been disposed to wander, may be nearly as instructive as the right ones in which it has travelled: as much may be learned, or nearly as much, from its failures as from its successes, from its follies as from its wisdom.[138]

On one level Trench was acknowledging the national importance of recording and describing the English language, but on another level, by acknowledging that a dictionary was the history of a nation contemplated from *one* point of view, he was preparing readers for the subjectivity and complexity of the description that would emerge; it was not the *only* point of view, but one of many points of view. By acknowledging the inherent limitations of the linear nature of a dictionary, and the subjectivity of the lexicographic process, it is as if Trench was pre-empting Dodd's criticism of *OED1*: Dodd writes, 'what such a description did was naturalise the social transmission of the language; what the NED did was to offer to establish its "evolution" and continuity, eliding the complex history of the language'.[139]

Dodd's over-arching argument was that *OED1* was just another nineteenth-century national monument, like the National Gallery, National Portrait Gallery, National Trust, and National Theatre which, he argues, enshrined national values and presented one, and only one, kind of national identity.[140] However, Dodd's view of *OED1* does not take into account the aims of the dictionary; nor does it reflect the content of the text. Just as the *DNB* included 'foreigners eminent in British life and important figures from the colonies'[141] in its pages, even more so did the *OED* cover words from outside Britain and the English language as it was developing in the colonies. These words did not need currency in British texts; as long as they occurred in English-speaking or English literary contexts, no matter how local or regional, whether those contexts were part of the British Empire or not, they gained admittance to the dictionary. In fact, by its coverage and treatment of words of the world, the *OED* succeeds in portraying more than one monolithic or Anglo-centric history of the English language.

The Delegates of the Press did, however, see the dictionary as a symbol and icon of nationhood and as guardian of the language. In assessing the dictionary early on, Max Müller wrote that 'no effort should be spared to make the work as perfect as possible' because it is 'an undertaking of such magnitude, in which one might almost say the national honour of England is engaged'.[142]

Murray never played the nation card, except on one occasion. In a plea for more British readers for the dictionary (who were outnumbered by Americans), Murray uncharacteristically positioned *OED1* as a national work, by declaring in the *Academy* in 1881 that 'We are doing for England and the English tongue a work which will be built upon, extended, and completed, but will itself never grow old; generations of Englishmen will rejoice in our light, and bless the workers who gave the light in which men shall see to do better work.'[143] This was picked up and reiterated in a nationalistic article in the *Times* the following year, in which the journalist positioned the dictionary project as a national work: 'To make a dictionary worthy of the present state of philology and of the great English nation is certainly a project of national interest.'[144]

This attempt by the Delegates, journalists, and others to harness the dictionary to the 'national honour of England' is not surprising. The fact was that the dictionary was being received into a culture that emphasized nationhood and national identity. More than the editors, then, it was the media who wanted to stress the dictionary's links to nation and national identity: 'The greatest literary undertaking of any age or any country. It is a patriotic act to order it' insisted the *Speaker*; the *Birmingham Post* wrote, 'It is impossible adequately to praise this superb work. It is one of which a great nation may well feel reasonably proud.' The *Morning Post* included 'Greater Britain' in this national pride in the dictionary: 'When this work is completed England and the English-speaking peoples of the earth will then possess a national Dictionary worthy of their language.'[145] The dictionary was being viewed and reviewed as a 'national treasure', and the marketing machinery for the dictionary was quick to exploit the praise. An advertisement placed in the *Times* on 14 June 1899, reproduced all these glowing references and also boasted of the fact that volume 3 had been dedicated, with her permission, to Queen Victoria, Empress of India.[146] This advertisement was timely, placed in the *Times* one week before fifteen thousand troops and well-wishers from around the globe had joined Queen Victoria's Diamond Jubilee procession through the streets of London. The dictionary's position as a 'national treasure' continued right to the end: reporting on its completion on 7 June 1928, the *Times* exclaimed, 'The finished Dictionary is now one of the noblest possessions that the nation has.'[147]

Murray's generous inclusion of words of the world can be regarded as either imperialistic – a way of gathering in language from the Empire, thereby responding to the notion of the nation as 'Greater Britain' and the Empire – or it can be regarded as liberal and inclusive, an attempt to be true to the premise of writing an historical dictionary that includes all, not one man's, English. One's judgement of Murray rather depends on one's perspective on, and interpretation of, Empire and one's understanding of the original remit of the project.

Murray in Oxford

Why did Murray have such an inclusive attitude towards words from the margins, and rigorously put it into practice in the way he did? One answer is that he wanted to be true to the language as it was evolving around the world, and true to a descriptive, rather than prescriptive, lexicographic remit to describe each word's origins, meaning, and usage over time. Another more speculative answer lies in Murray's own position within Oxford, especially the University, which was one of marginalization. This may have shaped his inclusive attitude, but also that attitude may in turn have helped shape the forces that made him marginalized.

If we assess Murray's place in the cultural, religious, social, and academic landscape of Oxford, we get a complex picture of someone who felt marginalized within the University of Oxford and yet was extremely active within the town of Oxford. It is difficult to know whether his exclusion from the former was the reason for his active participation in the latter, or vice versa. By the time Murray moved the dictionary project from Mill Hill to Oxford in 1885, the University was already an epicentre for linguistic and lexicographical scholarship. Murray drew on this expertise, but his contact with these scholars was largely professional, and, with the exception of James Legge, Joseph Wright, and Alexander John Ellis, Murray rarely socialized with them.

It is evident from Murray's correspondence and papers that he perceived himself to be excluded from and unappreciated by the Oxford academic community. Writing to his sons, Oswyn and Harold, about the various honours that finally flooded in towards the end of his life, Murray wrote, 'To tell the truth, my work . . . was so long so little appreciated, that I learned . . . not to care a scrap for either blame or praise.' He even expressed a reluctance to accept the accolades: 'I should prefer that my biographer should have to say, "Oxford never made him a Fellow or a D. C. L., and his country never recognized his work, but he worked on all the same, believing in his work and his duty".'[148]

In 1913, a year before Oxford honoured him with a doctorate and two years before his death, Murray gave a speech at a University event, in which he said that after thirty years in Oxford, he still considered himself to be 'only a sojourner' because his work was there.[149]

The marginal status Murray felt in the university was inversely proportional to his profile in the town of Oxford. Murray's name appeared nearly every week in the local newspaper for his attendance at various meetings and events for church, liberal party politics, and societies such as the Oxfordshire Natural History Society, the Oxford Architectural and Historical Society, and the Oxford Philatelic Society of which he was President (making use of all the exotic stamps sent by readers around the globe). He was also Chair of the Oxford Gospel Temperance Union that met weekly in the Town Hall and had annual missions in the Corn Exchange. Murray was President of the Caledonian Society of Oxford, and organized an annual banquet in the Oxford Council Chamber in honour of Robert Burns. Along with James Legge and Andrew Fairbairn (1838–1912), the Congregationalist first principal of Mansfield College, he took part in church and political events, attending the St George's Congregational Church, the Young Men's Christian Association, the Oxford Liberal Association, and the Russell Club. In one public debate on the Irish home rule crisis, Murray shared the platform in the Oxford Town Hall with James Legge, speaking in favour of home rule. His civic duties even extended to the annual prize-giving ceremonies at the Oxford High Schools for Boys and Girls.[150]

There is a tension, however, between the civic-minded Murray whose tireless activity can be traced in local newspapers, and the Murray of the University who has been presented in obituaries, biographies, and his own writings as a marginal figure. As his obituary in *The Scotsman* put it, 'He was little known in Oxford; he lived almost a life of seclusion, and apparently with little reluctance he put aside the leisure and ease of the scholar to which he was entitled.'[151] Indeed, Murray took no part in Senior Common Room life, was never made a Fellow of an Oxford college, and only received an Oxford honorary doctorate the year before his death.

In 1883, Murray had hoped to receive a doctorate ad eundem by virtue of his Edinburgh degree, but the university refused. However, his friend Benjamin Jowett, Master of Balliol College, organized an Oxford honorary MA for Murray in 1885 so that he could access the Bodleian Library, but no other privileges came with it. It has been suggested that Murray was nominated for an Honorary Fellowship at Balliol in 1885, and the Biographical Notes in the Jowett Papers list Murray as having received it in that year, but this appears to be an error since there is no record of this in the Balliol College Record nor in the Balliol Governing Body Meeting Minutes or University Calendar for 1885.[152] In 1895, Murray was hopeful that Exeter College might make him a Fellow while his fourth son Oswyn was an undergraduate, but they elected three others instead (Ingram Bywater, Regius Professor of Greek; Henry Pelham, Camden Professor of Ancient History; and Charles Parry, Director of the Royal College of Music).[153] In 1896, Balliol upgraded Murray's honorary MA to an MA by decree, which gave him college membership and the power to vote, but still did not elect him as an Honorary Fellow because that year the college instituted a rule that 'only distinguished ex-members were eligible'.[154] This included old members or previous Fellows of the college, and Murray was neither. Hence in 1896 instead of electing Murray as Honorary Fellow, the college elected Reverend Edmond Warre (1837–1920), headmaster of Eton and scholar of Balliol 1885, and Alfred Marshall (1842–1924), Cambridge economist who had been a Fellow at Balliol from 1882 to 1884.

This series of exclusions meant that Murray never belonged to the Senior Common Room culture in Oxford. As Elisabeth Murray explained about her grandfather, 'for someone not an Oxford man, and holding no college appointment, it was not easy to gain an entrée to University circles: the Colleges and their Common Rooms tended to be exclusive'.[155] Philip Howard suggests that this was because 'until Murray proved otherwise, lexicographers had been considered artisans, not scholars'.[156] But this seems to have been an attitude peculiar to Oxford, because elsewhere Murray did gain academic recognition, receiving honorary doctorates from the universities of Durham (1886), Freiburg (1896), Glasgow (1901), Wales (1902), Cape of Good Hope (1905), Dublin (1908), Cambridge (1913), and Oxford (1914). He was also a member of the British Academy, and was given membership of the Academies of Vienna, Ghent, Prussia, Leiden, and was made a foreign correspondent of the French Academy.

The odds of Murray receiving an Honorary Fellowship at Oxford should have been in his favour. After all, the Royal Commission of 1852 had dropped the requirement of Fellows to be unmarried clerics and had introduced the provision 'to elect distinguished persons to honorary Fellowships'. This meant that by the time Murray was settled in Oxford in 1885, he was theoretically eligible for Fellowship status. In practice, however, it is not surprising that he did not receive an Honorary Fellowship at this time because it was too early in Murray's career: he had only published one fascicle of the dictionary and although he had partially established his name as a philologist and lexicographer – having produced *The Dialects of the Southern Counties of Scotland* (1873), and editions of *The Minor Poems of Sir David Lyndesay* (1871), *The Complaynt of Scotland* (1874), and *The Romance and Prophecies of James of Ercildoune* (1875) – within Oxford his reputation was yet to be established.

By the time his career was established, in 1896, the rules had changed at Balliol and Murray again missed out on the honorary Fellowship because he was not an old member. There is no obvious explanation, however, why Exeter did not elect him as a Fellow in 1895. One reason could be that Murray's alliance with Benjamin Jowett thwarted his chances. Jowett was a divisive figure within the University, and as Oswyn Murray (as it happens the grandson of Oswyn and great-grandson of James) explained in *The History of the University of Oxford,* at this time in the nineteenth century 'Exeter followed the tradition of Pattison rather than Jowett.'[157] It is possible that Murray was rejected because he was seen as 'a Jowett man', but there is nothing of this sort mentioned in the College records.[158]

Would Murray have had a better chance of an Honorary Fellowship at a larger college? It appears not. At this point in the University's history, there was no correlation between size of college and number of Honorary Fellows. For example, in 1895, Magdalen College was large (with thirty Fellows) but only two Honorary Fellows; Wadham was small (with eight Fellows) but four Honorary fellows; and Exeter was of medium size but had the largest proportion of Honorary Fellows – almost as many Honorary Fellows (eleven) as Fellows (twelve).[159]

There may, of course, have been ad hominem reasons why Murray was never embraced by the University establishment. It was rare in the late nineteenth century for an Oxford don to bear Murray's characteristics: he was Scottish not English, a devout Nonconformist not an Anglican, liberal not Tory, who left school at fourteen, and was a non-smoker and a teetotaller.[160] As President of the University Total Abstinence Society, Murray was vocal in his opposition to Senior Common Room culture and what he referred to as 'otiose Oxford'.[161] Nevertheless, he did attend civic banquets and balls – he attended the Annual Mayor's Banquet at the Randolph Hotel in 1894 – so perhaps he would have attended University social events had he been invited.[162]

Murray did find solace in the company of James Legge, a like-minded don who became his closest friend. Legge had spent thirty years as a missionary in China before becoming the first Professor of Chinese at Oxford, and shared many attributes in common with Murray: both were Scottish and Nonconformist (Legge was the first Nonconformist to be appointed to an Oxford chair), and both worked long hours. In his book *The Victorian Translation of China,* Norman Girardot describes Legge as someone who 'became known at Oxford for his staunch devotion to exotic scholarship and for his quaint appearance and uncompromising routines'.[163] Legge famously rose at 3 a.m. each morning to begin his writing, and Murray spent equally long days and nights in his Scriptorium.[164] An obituary described Murray's work ethic:

> With noble self-sacrifice, he surrendered himself to his work; except his parental duties, which he scrupulously observed, he allowed nothing to come between himself

and the Dictionary. Morning, noon, and night the slips of paper on which the quotations were written were never far away from him; they were his companions at table, even at times of illness, they were near his bedside. Many a long day of twelve or fifteen hours has he spent while wrestling with the elusive meanings of a word, and the writer has found him working by lamplight in the 'Scriptorium' at nine o'clock, the slips illustrating the word on which he was engaged spread out on tables, chairs, and even round him on the floor.[165]

Letters from Murray give the impression that such diligence was rare and unappreciated in late nineteenth-century Oxford. Murray criticized Oxford dons for their laziness, and in 1885, Murray commented to Bartholomew Price that the foundations of his Scriptorium should be lower 'so that no trace of such a place of real work shall be seen by fastidious and otiose Oxford . . . where even men who work, do it in secret and pretend openly to be merely men of the world'.[166] As Murray's granddaughter described him: 'those who did not share his love of words found that his engrossment in his work made him somewhat of a bore, and on his part a natural shyness and a long habit of wasting no time, left him with little inclination to get to know casual acquaintances better. It was only those admitted to close friendship who discovered that his rugged appearance and sometimes biting tongue concealed a man described by Graham Bell as 'one of the kindest and gentlest men I ever met'.[167]

Legge was one of the few people in Oxford with whom Murray could discuss his work. There is little remaining correspondence between the two, simply because they talked in person so often. The only letters from Legge to Murray are those giving advice on Chinese words in the dictionary. The two men requested to be buried beside each other, and their neighbouring graves can be found in the Wolvercote Cemetery.

The speed with which Murray covered up any physical reminders of his unacknowledged academic prowess, however, imply that he may have secretly yearned recognition and acceptance within the Academy. After receiving his honorary Oxford MA, he wore his academic cap every day while working in relative isolation in the Scriptorium (Figure 3.5). After his knighthood in 1908, letters from Murray show that he immediately crossed out 'Dr' on his letterhead and replaced it with 'Sir'. He did this on a letter about the word *teratism* to the anthropologist Robert Ranulph Marett (1866–1943). Murray had a quotation that referred to a new sense of *teratism* coined by Marett ('That attitude of mind for which Mr. Marett has invented the term Teratism') and wanted Marett to explain the meaning. It is clear from the letter that Murray did not like Marett, perhaps because Marett was an armchair anthropologist in the same nineteenth-century vein as Tylor (in fact he was Tylor's successor as professor of Anthropology and wrote Tylor's biography [1936]). Murray ends his letter by chiding Marett: 'You ought really to have

Figure 3.5 James Murray wearing his academic cap while working on the dictionary. (Credit: G. Onions)

called our attention to it at the time! We cannot read everything or catch every word!' Marett replied, explaining the anthropological meaning of *teratism* as 'a term coined by me as an alternative to the term *Supernaturalism*, (which I prefer) which is used, in connection with my argument for a *pre-animistic* form of primitive religion, to denote the attitude of mind that attributes mystic power (*mana*) to whatever is strange and awful'.[168] For other neologisms, Marett referred Murray to the index of his book *Threshold of Religion* (1909), and recommended the word *theoplasm*, 'god-stuff or raw material out of which religious concepts are evolved', which Murray promptly included in the dictionary. Marett's reply begins 'Dear Dr Murray' with the 'Dr' scribbled out and replaced by 'Sir James', as perhaps a sly back-hander to Murray's letter which had asserted his knighted status.

It is difficult to know whether Murray's marginalization within the University influenced his involvement on its fringes and beyond, or whether his activities on the fringes influenced his marginalization. He was active in the University Extension programme and the establishment of Ruskin Hall for the education of working people.[169] Both these enterprises were associated with certain groups in the University, and certainly had Nonconformist connections: Ruskin Hall was founded by the Nonconformists Charles A. Beard and Walter Vrooman, and funded by Amne Grafflin, and key figures in the University Extension programme were Jowett, Legge, and Fairbairn. The Extension programme was an adult education movement based on the premise that it was 'an imperative duty to provide that everybody should have an education such as to draw out the faculties, whatever they might be, with which God had gifted them'.[170]

It seems that Murray attended whatever University functions and events he was eligible to attend. These events were not central to the University's activities but afforded Murray the opportunity of a degree of public visibility and prestige. For example, the local newspaper reported Murray's attendance at the 25th Annual Conference of the National Union of Teachers in 1894, in which he robed and joined the official procession of Vice Chancellor, Mayor, Senior and Junior Proctors, Heads of College, and other dignitaries as they entered the south wing of the Examination Schools and were 'greeted in a very hearty manner'.[171]

Despite exclusion from the University establishment throughout most of his career, Murray never tried to change or conform to be included. Likewise, in his work, he stayed resolute – uncompromising even – in his focus on words from the margins, and in his endeavour to include these words in the dictionary. Towards the end of his life, the University accepted him more, and in 1911 Murray gave a series of lectures to the Oxford School of English. It appears that even the media began to understand the essence of the historical method, and the brilliance of Murray's openness to foreign words and other words from the margins of English. As *The Scotsman* remarked in 1915, 'Many people have objected to his inclusion of so many slang, dialectal, or technical terms, of "mere dictionary words" or of "newspaper English", but the historical method has vindicated him and has shown how many words now classed as "good English" originated in the slang or newspaper English of past centuries, and no one can tell in this age of science, when some polysyllabic compound, like appendicitis, may not become current English.'[172]

ENDNOTES

1 Murray (1911: 16).
2 Murray (1911: 17).
3 'The Literature and Language of the Age', *Edinburgh Review,* April 1889 pp. 348 and 389; 'Review of A New English Dictionary, Vol. X Tombal-Trahysh' *The Scotsman,* 20 October 1917 p. 17; [Fennell, C. A. M.] 'Review of NED Part IV *C-Cass' Athenaeum,* 6 October 1888 p. 442.
4 'The Literature and Language of the Age', *Edinburgh Review,* April 1889 pp. 344, 348. The word 'barbarous' in relation to language in the late nineteenth century had many different meanings from the notion that words were not derived from Greek or Latin, to the idea that the language was 'unpolished, without literate

culture; pertaining to an illiterate people', as Murray published the definition in 1885. He gave an extended etymological note explaining that the sense-development of *barbarous* in ancient times was (with the Greeks) 'foreign, non-Hellenic', later 'outlandish, rude, brutal'; (with the Romans) 'not Latin nor Greek', then 'pertaining to those outside the Roman empire'; hence 'uncivilized, uncultured', and later 'non-Christian' whence 'Saracen, heathen'; and generally 'savage, rude, savagely cruel, inhuman'.

5 'The Literature and Language of the Age', *Edinburgh Review*, April 1889 p. 349.
6 [Fennell, C. A. M.] 'Review of NED Part IV *C-Cass*', *Athenaeum*, 6 October 1888 p. 442.
7 Bailey (2000b: 153).
8 'Review of A New English Dictionary, Vol. X Tombal-Trahysh', *The Scotsman*, 20 October 1917 p. 17.
9 Coleridge (1857: 72).
10 Murray (1873: preface).
11 Murray (1873: preface).
12 Murray (1880: 134).
13 Murray (1880: 134).
14 Murray (1880: 134).
15 Murray (1911: 21).
16 Quoted in Murray (1977: 189).
17 Murray (1880: 131).
18 Murray (1880: 131).
19 Murray (1888: ix).
20 Murray (1880: 133).
21 Murray (1888: ix).
22 Murray (1880: 132).
23 Benson (2001: 40–42).
24 Kachru (1985: 12–13).
25 Kachru (1985: 12–13).
26 Kachru (1985: 14, 16, 21).
27 Murray (1888: xvii).
28 'A Supplement in Preparation', *The Periodical* XIII, 15 February 1928 p. 24. Murray (1888: ix).
29 Murray (1888: xix).
30 Murray (1911: 19).
31 Murray (1879: 4).
32 Murray recorded the results of his Appeal in an appendix to his presidential address to the Philological Society in 1885.
33 MP/9/11/1910. Murray Lecture to London Institute, 9 November 1910 p. 20.
34 Murray (1903: 17). This paper was originally delivered as a public lecture in Oxford at the Clarendon Press Institute on 25 March 1890, as described in 'World of Words', *Jackson's Oxford Journal*, Saturday 30 March 1895 p. 8.
35 *The Surgeon of Crowthorne* (1998) was published in the United States under the title *The Professor and the Madman*.
36 Locke (1703), as it appears in Goldie (1997: 353).

37 Cust's linguistic publications included *Modern Languages of the East Indies* (1878), *A Sketch of the Modern Languages of Africa* (1883), and *On the Geographical Distribution of the Turki Branch of the Ural-Altaic Family of Languages* (1892). His *Modern Languages of Africa* (1883) provided quotations for many African ethnonyms like *Chagga*, *Ijo*, *Kwa*, *Koranko*, *Luba*, *Mande*, and *Tabele*, but none of these words appeared in *OED1*.
38 Knowles (2000: 32).
39 Murray quoted in Knowles (2000: 32). For this reason, I ensured in my research for this book that I verified any books read for the reading programme directly from slips, not from notebooks or lists. See McConchie (1997: 182–222) and Brewer (2000: 44) for further discussion of the unreliability of lists and notebooks of readers for the *OED*.
40 OED/MISC/13/23 as quoted in Knowles (2000: 32).
41 Titles of officially read books were determined from officially printed slips found in OUP Archive OED Slips for many entries such as *aborigen*, *cocoa*, *dhow*, *jungle*, and *nardoo*.
42 OED/B/5/4/24. Letter from Sugden to Onions March 1930.
43 Morris (1898: vi).
44 OED/BL/304/57. Letter from Petherick to Murray 11 March 1885; OED/BL/311/9. Letter from Petherick to Murray 3 November 1886; OED/BL/311/10 ii. Letter from Petherick to Murray n.d.; *OED*/BL/311/12. Letter from Petherick to Murray nd.
45 Murray sometimes sought advice and feedback on words by publishing short articles in the journal *Notes Queries*. In 1892, he enquired about the pronunciation of *corroboree*: 'I should be grateful to any one who knows the true pronunciation of this native Australian name for the festive dance of the aborigines.' He had been puzzled by the variant spelling 'caribberie' in Hunter's *Port Jackson* (1793): 'the fact that Hunter wrote *i* makes one suspect that this syllable was not distinct, and perhaps not accented' (Murray [1892: 353]). In this case, he received no feedback that explained the *i* in Hunter's 'caribberie', and the final entry for *corroboree* correctly noted 'original pronunciation uncertain'. A debate about the treatment of some Australian Aboriginal words in the *OED* can be found in Dixon (2008, 2009), Nash (2009), and Ludowyk (2009).
46 'The Philological Society's Dictionary', *Times*, 31 January 1882 p. 4.
47 'The Philological Society's Dictionary' *Times*, 31 January 1882 p. 4.
48 Numbers 5 and 7 respectively in Murray (1879), 'Directions to Readers for the Dictionary', unpaginated addendum to the *Appeal*.
49 OED/MISC/11/39. Letter from Murray to Thompson 4 October 1902.
50 Livingstone and Livingstone (1865: 100–4).
51 Darwin (2009); Bayly (2004).
52 Hyam (1999: 48).
53 McMahon (2006: 148).
54 Murray (1903: 17). This paper was originally delivered as a public lecture in Oxford at the Clarendon Press Institute on 25 March 1890, as described in 'World of Words', *Jackson's Oxford Journal*, Saturday 30 March 1895 p. 8.
55 Hyam (1999: 49).
56 Magee and Thompson (2010: 26–30).
57 See Pietsch (2010).

58 See MacKenzie (1986) for more on the role of popular culture in reflecting and disseminating imperial ideas.
59 See McClintock (1995: 32–3) on what she describes as 'commodity racism' such as the Pears' Soap campaign.
60 See Thompson (2005) for the impact of the Empire on domestic culture in Britain. Historians are divided on what kind of impact the Empire was having on British society and culture in general. Max Beloff (1969, 1989), Bernard Porter (2006), and Ronald Hyam (2010) all argue that the Empire's impact on British society and culture was almost non-existent, that the majority of British citizens showed not the slightest interest in, or knowledge of, the nation's overseas endeavours. 'The British were not an imperially minded people; they lacked both a theory of empire and the will to engender or implement one', wrote Beloff (1969: 19) in his study of British imperial decline, *Imperial Sunset 1897–1942*.
61 Murray (1977: 32).
62 Murray (1911: 31).
63 Brewer (2007: 34).
64 Murray (1888: xvii).
65 'Church Society's Anniversary', *Jackson's Oxford Journal,* 19 February 1887 p. 7; 'London Missionary Society' *Jackson's Oxford Journal* 28 May 1887 p. 8; 'London Missionary Society' *Jackson's Oxford Journal* 27 April 1895 p. 8.
66 Murray (1977: 32).
67 Jowett Papers, Balliol College Archive B8/2. Letter from Murray to Hucks Gibbs 24 October 1883.
68 OED/BL/308/4. Letter from Monier-Williams to Murray 1 April 1881.
69 OED/BL/308/4. Letter from Monier-Williams to Murray 1 April 1881.
70 Brock and Curthoys (2000: 355).
71 Morris (1898: xiii).
72 OED/MISC/317/4. Letter from Margoliouth to Driver 5 December 1928.
73 OED/MISC/115/4. Letter from Margoliouth to Onions 13 July 1915.
74 OED/AA/142. Letter from Margoliouth to Murray 22 January 1902.
75 Aitchison (2001: 153).
76 OED/B/3/1/2. Letter from Müller to Murray 15 October 1886.
77 OED/BL/324/18. Letter from Legge to Murray 2 February 1889.
78 OED/OS/18/2. Letter from Giles to Murray 16 March 1893.
79 OED/OS/18/3ii. Letter from Giles to Murray nd.
80 OED/JH/218/25. Letter from Giles to Craigie 1 January 1914.
81 OED/MISC/13/7. Letter from Murray to Fitzedward Hall 27 November 1894.
82 OED/B/3/1/1. Letter from Liddell to Bartholomew Price 10 May 1877.
83 OED/MISC/7/1. nd. 'The New English Dictionary. Suggestions for Guidance in Preparing Copy for the Press'.
84 Murray (1911: 35).
85 Jowett Papers, Balliol College Archive B8/4. Letter from Murray to Hucks Gibbs 8 November 1883.
86 Jowett Papers, Balliol College Archive B8/4. Letter from Hucks Gibbs to Jowett 10 November 1883.
87 OED/B/3/1/11. Letter from Murray to Gell 23 February 1893.
88 OED/B/3/1/2. Letter from Müller to Delegates n.d.

89 OED/B/3/1/11. Letter from Murray to Gell 23 February 1893.
90 OED/B/3/1/10. Letter from Bradley to Gell 11 April 1896.
91 OED/B/3/1/10. Letter from Bradley to Gell 11 April 1896.
92 OED/B/3/1/10. Letter from Bradley to Gell 11 April 1896.
93 MP/?/1879. Letter from Martineau to Murray, nd, but some time in late 1879.
94 Stocking (1987, 1995); Tylor (1863, 1871, and 1913).
95 OED/BL/3/12/28. Letter from Tylor to Murray 1 December 1886.
96 OED/JH/188/4/1. Letter from Thistelton-Dyer to Murray 2 May 1903.
97 OED/B/3/1/2. Letter from Hucks Gibbs to Furnivall 9 June 1886.
98 MP/20/7/1882. Letter from Hucks Gibbs to Murray 20 July 1882.
99 OED/B/3/1/6. Letter from Hucks Gibbs to Murray 2 December 1892.
100 MP/4/11/1883. Letter from Hucks Gibbs to Murray 4 November 1883.
101 MP/9/6/1882. Letter from Murray to Price 9 June 1882.
102 National Library of Scotland, MS 3219, f.158. Letter from Murray to unidentified correspondent 23 March 1900.
103 OUP/PUB/11/29. P. S. in Letter from Murray to Gell 20 October 1892.
104 Murray (1901a: i).
105 Murray (1901a: i).
106 Murray (1901b: vi). Kipling's poem, 'The White Man's Burden', was published in 1899, the same year that the Anglo-Boer War broke out in South Africa, was an appeal to the United States to assume responsibility for 'developing' (educating and governing) the Philippines (recently acquired by the United States in the Spanish-American War). It gave rise to a rhetorical expression that refers to the responsibility of the 'white' European for the 'coloured' peoples of the Empire. The expression was immediately picked up in popular culture, most saliently in an advertisement for Pears' Soap. Imperial values were playing a part in prosaic commerce, and neither Murray nor most Britons could escape their presence.
107 Murray (1901b: vi).
108 Murray (1901b: vi).
109 Murray (1977: 180). Final figures were calculated by adding the total per volume = 870 + 928 + 718 + 453 + 844 + 1343 + 1845 + 791 + 1006 + 933 = 9731 tramlines in *OED1*.
110 Total headwords in *OED1* = 243 189 and total headwords with tramlines = 9731 => 4 percent of all headwords had tramlines. This figure is based on the number of tramlines, which is a conservative estimate when one considers that not all words from outside Britain would have been given tramlines in *OED1*.
111 The proportional mean was calculated by dividing the number of headwords with tramlines per letter by the total number of headwords per letter to give the following: **A** 0.045, **B** 0.032, **C** 0.044, **D** 0.03, **E** 0.035, **F** 0.023, **G** 0.032, **H** 0.042, **I** 0.015, **J** 0.05, **K** 0.134, **L** 0.047, **M** 0.067, **N** 0.042, **O** 0.037, **P** 0.068, **Q** 0.034, **R** 0.025, **S** 0.039, **T** 0.057, **U** 0.005, **V** 0.061, **W** 0.007, **X, Y, Z** 0.03. An important factor to consider when comparing tramline counts across the English alphabet is that not all letters could ever have the same proportion of loanwords because of the simple fact that not all languages of the world have the same repertoire of sounds and orthography as English. For example, the letter K in English may have the largest number of loanwords because most languages of the

world display the voiceless velar stop and choose to represent the sound with the letter K, not C, G, or Q. Therefore, it is for these reasons, perhaps, that chances are higher that a loanword begins with the letter K, not because when Murray edited the letter K he had a stronger intention to include loanwords than at another time in his editing career. Similarly with the letter P, which is one of the smallest initial letters in an Old English dictionary, hence implying that fewer non-borrowed terms will begin with the letter P in the first place: this automatically increases the proportion of loanwords in the letter (I am grateful to Rod McConchie for this insight).

112 R. W. Burchfield (2004).

113 The nature of the criticism aimed at Murray and the early editors of the dictionary by Burchfield and others varies from focusing solely on the treatment of loanwords, or solely on the treatment of World Englishes, or on the treatment of both loanwords and World Englishes. These criticisms will all be considered together in this chapter, as many voices in one strong opposition to how words from outside Britain (loanwords and World Englishes alike) were treated by the early *OED* editors.

114 Burchfield and Aarsleff (1988: 22).

115 Burchfield Papers Deposit 2 Box 2 (OUP Archives). Lecture for Japan and Italy, 1986.

116 Bailey and Görlach (1982: 4).

117 'Wimmin and Yuppies Earn Places in Oxford Dictionary Supplement', *The Globe and Mail (Canada)*, 9 May 1986 p. 9.

118 Willinsky (1994: 90, 91, 62).

119 Benson (2001: 2, 40).

120 Bayly (2004: 249).

121 Darwin (2009: 23).

122 Hyam (2010: 21)

123 Seeley (1883: 8).

124 Moon (1989: 74). See further discussion of *canoe* in Béjoint (2000: 20–1) and Mugglestone (2000: 203).

125 Mugglestone (2005: 164).

126 I am grateful to Penny Silva for discussion on instances of cultural binarism such as *agriologist* and *hubbub*.

127 Algeo (1995: 209).

128 Silva (2000: 89).

129 Mugglestone (2005: 162–6).

130 See Brewer (2007: 207). See also Dixon (2008) for more discussions of definitions along these lines.

131 Comparing *OED1* entries with those in Webster's *American Dictionary of the English Language* (1828) illustrates the point that there are many other instances where the *OED* editor *could* have used similar phrasing, but does not. The entry for *canoe* in Webster (1828) was not dissimilar from Murray's: 1. A boat used by rude nations, formed by the body or trunk of a tree. . . . Similar boats are now used by civilised men, for fishing and other purposes. 2. A boat made of bark or skins, used by savages. Interestingly, Webster displayed similar ideological biases elsewhere in his dictionary, in entries for which Murray and his fellow

editors show no such bias. For example, taking other words that also have concrete referents and therefore lend themselves to objective definitions, Murray does not display the same biases as Webster. The word *bead,* which is defined by Webster as '2. Any small globular body, hence the glass globules used in traffic with savages', is defined by Murray as 'a small perforated body, spherical or otherwise of glass, amber, metal, wood etc., used as an ornament, either strung in a series to form a necklace, bracelet, etc., or sewn upon various fabrics.' Webster's definition of *convert* was 'to convert rude savages into civilized men', but Murray's multiple senses of *convert* showed no racially biased equivalent. Similarly, comparing Webster's definitions with those of other *OED* editors such as Charles Onions, one finds no such ideological biases: Webster defined *yell* as 'to cry out with a hideous noise; to cry or scream as with agony or horror. Savages yell most frightfully when they are rising to the first onset of battle'; whereas Onions defined it straightforwardly with no reference to other cultures or races. Webster's illustrative sentence for *wield* was 'Nothing but the influence of a civilized power could induce a savage to wield a spade', but Onions' entry contains no such bias.

132 Colley (2003).
133 Bayly (2004: 230, 228).
134 For a good summary of trends in literary criticism on how we read texts, see Eagleton (1983).
135 Webster (1828: 3).
136 Dodd (1986: 18–21).
137 Trench (1855: 4–5).
138 Trench (1857: 6).
139 Dodd (1986: 18).
140 Dodd (1986: 19–22).
141 Dodd (1986: 19).
142 OED/B/3/1/2. 1878. 'Observations by Professor Max Müller on the Lists of Readers and Books for the Proposed English Dictionary.'
143 Murray (1881: 9).
144 'The Philological Society's Dictionary', *Times*, 31 January 1882 p. 4.
145 As quoted in 'The Oxford English Dictionary', *Times*, 14 June 1899 p. 3.
146 'The Oxford English Dictionary', *Times*, 14 June 1899 p. 3.
147 'Celebrating the Dictionary' *Times* 7 June 1928 p. 17.
148 Murray (1977: 294).
149 Murray (1977: 248).
150 'Oxfordshire Natural History Society', *Jackson's Oxford Journal*, 4 February 1888 p. 8; 'Oxfordshire Natural History Society', *Jackson's Oxford Journal*, 27 January 1894 p. 8; 'Oxford High School', *Jackson's Oxford Journal*, 18 March 1893 p. 6; 'Oxford Architectural & Historical Society', *Jackson's Oxford Journal*, 15 December 1894 p. 6; 'Oxford Philatelic Society' and 'London Missionary Society', *Jackson's Oxford Journal*, 29 April 1899 p. 7. 'Gospel Temperance Mission', *Jackson's Oxford Journal*, 19 March 1887 p. 6; 'Oxfordshire Band of Hope and Temperance Union', *Jackson's Oxford Journal*, 28 September 1889 p. 8. 'Caledonian Society of Oxford', *Jackson's Oxford Journal*, 28 January 1888 p. 8; 'Burns Anniversary Dinner', *Jackson's Oxford Journal*, 2 February 1889

p. 6; 'Caledonian Society of Oxford', *Jackson's Oxford Journal*, 28 January 1893 p. 8.'Oxford High School for Boys. Distribution of Prizes', *Jackson's Oxford Journal*, Saturday 11 June 1887 p. 7.

151 'A Great Lexicographer', *The Scotsman*, Tuesday 27 July 1915 p. 17.

152 Darwall-Smith (1993: 125) incorrectly lists Murray as having received an Honorary Fellowship at Balliol in 1885. See note 133.

153 *Oxford University Calendar* 1896 London, Macmillan & Co, p. 409.

154 Jones (2005: 206fn).

155 Murray (1977: 248). She also mentions on p. 243 that Benjamin Jowett made Murray a member of Balliol College. Checking with Anna Sandler, Balliol archivist, confirms that this membership did not extend to Fellowship, and there is no evidence that Murray had college dining rights or SCR rights.

156 Howard (2002: 447).

157 Murray (2000: 339).

158 I am indebted to Juliet Chadwick, archivist of Exeter, for checking the College Minutes.

159 *Oxford University Calendar* 1896, London, Macmillan & Co.

160 The obituary for Murray in *The Scotsman*, on 27 July 1915 p. 17, described him as 'a Scot in every fibre of his being'.

161 'University Intelligence', *Jackson's Oxford Journal*, Saturday 1 December 1888 p. 5.

162 'The Mayor's Banquet', *Jackson's Oxford Journal*, Saturday 27 October 1894 p. 6.

163 Girardot (2002: 192).

164 Girardot (2002: 192).

165 'A Great Lexicographer', *The Scotsman*, 27 July 1915 p. 17.

166 MP/6/05/1885. Letter from Murray to Price 6 May 1885.

167 Murray (1977: 333).

168 OED/EP/MARE/1/2. Letter from Marett to Murray 10 December and 11 December 1910.

169 Ockwell and Pollins (2000: 675).

170 'University Extension Conference', *Jackson's Oxford Journal*, 23 April 1887 p. 8; 'Visit of University Extension Students to Oxford', *Jackson's Oxford Journal*, 11 August 1888 p. 6. Fairbairn never made Murray a member of Mansfield, but invited him to many dinners there, including a special dinner with Gladstone on 5 February 1890 ('Mr. Gladstone's Visit to Oxford', *Jackson's Oxford Journal*, 8 February 1890 p. 5).

171 'The National Union of Teachers', *Jackson's Oxford Journal*, 31 March 1894 p. 6.

172 'A Great Lexicographer', *The Scotsman*, 27 July 1915 p. 17.

4 James Murray and the *Stanford Dictionary* controversy

> The very plan of Fennell's work drove him to this method of appropriation of our work, and detraction of our results – insomuch that when met in the street his customary piece of news is 'I have found barracoon three years earlier than Murray!!!' which has become a kind of joke in Cambridge.
>
> James Murray (1889) on the making of Charles Fennell's *Stanford Dictionary of Anglicised Words And Phrases* (1892)

We have seen that James Murray formed a transnational network of *OED* collaborators, and, by actively seeking words from written sources around the world, he widened the lexicographic net to include words of the world which his contemporaries – OUP superiors, consultants, sub-editors, and reviewers – often judged too 'barbarous' or 'outlandish' for an English dictionary. This history shows that Murray believed that these words were part of the English language, and therefore deserved a place in an English dictionary. But how high a priority for Murray was their inclusion? When pushed to excise certain entries in order to save space or time, would Murray delete these entries before other subsets of the vocabulary? One way of gauging editorial priorities is to look at annotations on dictionary proofs. An editor's final changes and edits can be used as a barometer of his/her priorities, prejudices, and attitudes. With respect to foreign words, we know from Murray that he often found it difficult to decide on inclusion.[1] Add to this the pressure that he was under to work faster, to save space, and to exclude words considered too 'outlandish' for an English dictionary, and one might expect foreign words to be among the first deletions on dictionary proofs. However, an inspection of the extant dictionary proofs for letters E, F, G, and L has shown no such tendency.[2]

The proofs show that loanwords and World Englishes were no more likely to be excised than any other subset of vocabulary. This only demonstrates, however, that words from outside Britain were no less valued than other words; it does not necessarily imply that they were *more* valued than any other subset of vocabulary. While it may never be possible to gauge whether these words had priority or extra value in *OED1* editing policies and practices, it is possible to gauge how passionate Murray was about their inclusion by seeing his reaction to the suggestion that his coverage of these words be taken by another dictionary.

Early in the 1880s, such an opportunity did present itself: Murray was offered the chance to hand over his foreign materials to Cambridge's Charles Fennell and his *Stanford Dictionary of Anglicised Words and Phrases* (1892), but Murray vehemently refused to do so. The episode reveals a more complex picture of Murray's attitude towards, and treatment of, loanwords and World Englishes, as well as providing new insights into his relations with his superiors within OUP and his competitors outside OUP. This chapter confirms that Murray valued the inclusion, in fact fought for the inclusion, of words of the world in *OED1*. It compares Murray's coverage of foreign words with that of a specialist dictionary to show how much further he could have gone in his coverage, and reveals that he was territorial and competitive (and maybe even a little paranoid).

The *Stanford Dictionary* controversy

When the *Stanford Dictionary of Anglicised Words and Phrases* by Charles Fennell was published by Cambridge University Press (CUP) in September 1892, James Murray accused its editor of plagiarizing from the published sections (A–C) of *OED1*.[3] He declared that the rest of the dictionary (D–Z) showed scholarship that was 'indolent' and 'disappointingly poor'. According to Murray, Fennell's treatment of certain words was 'utterly puerile and ignorant'.[4] The *Stanford Dictionary* was a diachronic study of loanwords in English, and Murray was convinced that Fennell had stolen entries, etymologies, definitions, and quotations from *OED1*. The charge of plagiarism became a difficult issue for relations between the University Presses of Oxford and Cambridge, and they nearly ended up in court.

The incident came at a sensitive time in the *OED*'s history, just a few years after the first volume of the *Century Dictionary* (1889) was published in New York. Elisabeth Murray wrote that her grandfather 'worried that the work [*Century Dictionary*] would be a commercial rival and dangerous competitor' and 'worked himself up into a state of agitation and indignation' which provoked an accusation of plagiarism against its editor, the American, William Dwight Whitney (1827–94), and a suggestion that the Delegates take legal action.[5] In 1892, Murray and the Delegates were still smarting from the *Century Dictionary* spat and were therefore particularly sensitive to rival competitors when the *Stanford Dictionary* was published.

Born five years apart in the middle of the nineteenth century, Charles Fennell and James Murray were as different from one another as you could get. Fennell was English, Cambridge educated, and an Anglican Tory who socialized in the Senior Common Rooms of Cambridge University.[6] In contrast, Murray was Scottish, an autodidact, and non-Conformist liberal teetotaller. While Murray was never made a Fellow of an Oxford college, Fennell was a respected Classics Fellow of Jesus College, Cambridge, from the age of twenty-four, and his biographical approach to the works of the Greek poet Pindar remained unchallenged until the 1960s.[7] Murray was open to the education of women: he employed women as his sub-editors and readers on the dictionary, and his own daughter became a don at St Hilda's College, Oxford. Fennell, on the other hand, was vocally opposed to degrees for women at Cambridge: as he saw it, educating women 'would tend to impair the efficiency of our teachers and examiners'.[8] But what both these men had in common was an unrelenting work ethic and a belief that the historical method in lexicography gave all words a rightful place in a dictionary.

In 1884, just after the publication of the first fascicle A–ANT of *OED1*, Fennell told a group of philologists in Cambridge that although 'existing dictionaries recognised the necessity for giving and explaining alien words and phrases', they 'did not treat this department of lexicography systematically'.[9] By this time he had already begun systematically to compile his own dictionary of all the foreign words in English.

The idea for Fennell's dictionary originally came from the barrister and literary scholar, John Frederick Stanford (1815–80), a Fellow of the Royal Society and an old member of Christ's College, Cambridge, who, in the latter half of his life, began collecting quotations for a dictionary of anglicized words and phrases. Stanford had offered the project to the Philological Society in the 1870s but Frederick Furnivall had turned it down. Furnivall had inspected Stanford's slips, most of which were cuttings with no dates or sources, and correctly judged that the project would involve too much work to bring it to fruition.[10] These slips still exist in the Cambridge University Press archive and they are nothing more than tiny undated cuttings from unnamed newspapers, a nightmare for someone having to trace their provenance, especially in the days before searchable databases.[11]

On John Stanford's death in 1880, he bequeathed £5000 for Cambridge University to finish the job he had started.[12] Charles Fennell was chosen as the editor, and an advisory committee was assembled consisting of five distinguished Cambridge academics: the Hebrew scholar Robert Bensly (1831–93), classical scholars John Mayor (1825–1910) and John Postgate (1853–1926), the philologist and lexicographer Walter Skeat (1835–1912), and the biblical scholar William Aldis Wright (1831–1914).[13] This committee drew up a five-pronged scheme and remit for the dictionary to include all words and phrases found in English literature and borrowed from:

1. Non-European languages, e.g. *bungalow, coffee*, and *tomahawk*.
2. Latin and Greek, e.g. *aroma, genius*, and *vertigo*.
3. Modern European languages, except French, e.g. *fresco, poodle*, and *regatta*.
4. French which retain French pronunciation, e.g. *coup, gendarme*, and *vol-au-vent*.
5. French, Latin, and Greek, 'whether now altered or but imperfectly naturalised and now obsolete,'[14] e.g. *passport, pyramid*, and *syntax*.

With the intermittent help of paid assistants, Fennell produced the 800-page dictionary in ten years.[15] The project was finished on time and within budget, and sales were so strong, and CUP so impressed by Fennell's efficiency and skill, that in addition to his £3314 remuneration, the Press offered him a generous royalty share.[16]

The publication of the *Stanford Dictionary* was not celebrated by James Murray and the OUP Delegates, who had been against the project since its inception. As we shall see, Murray opposed Fennell's efforts – not because he thought there was no place for a dictionary that specialized in foreign words, but quite the contrary: he did not want a dictionary to take words that he believed had a rightful place in his own general dictionary of English. His belief that anglicized words should be treated fully in *OED1* is exemplified by his unwillingness to hand over these materials to Fennell early on in his editorship.

In 1882, before any of *OED1* was published and at the time that the Advisory Committee was drawing up the *Stanford Dictionary*'s remit, Walter Skeat wrote to Murray suggesting that the *Stanford Dictionary* could function as a kind of Supplement to Murray's dictionary by picking up the loanwords that Murray rejected.[17] Given the various constraints on Murray, which we saw in the previous chapter, Skeat's offer to Murray could have been attractive.

Skeat had presumed that Murray would welcome the opportunity to exclude words of the world – stating as examples *hacienda*, a plantation, and *tsetse*, an African insect – and was shocked by Murray's refusal. Indeed, Murray insisted that he was determined to keep his dictionary comprehensive and not to limit its scope when it came to words from outside Britain. Skeat replied apologetically: 'The mistake I made was this, that I did not know yr Dicty [*OED1*] was to be quite so comprehensive, & I honestly thought there might be words which you could afford to give away because you did not want them, & wd therefore sooner have their room than their company.'[18] Despite the fact that giving the words to Fennell's *Stanford Dictionary* would have saved Murray time and space, and therefore also money (which would have been welcomed by Murray's superiors at OUP), Murray was determined to publish them in his dictionary and refused to relinquish them to the fledgling *Stanford Dictionary* project.

As a concession to Fennell, Murray suggested that the *Stanford Dictionary* could include his 'casuals' but not his 'aliens' or 'denizens', and certainly not his 'naturals'.[19] If the *Stanford Dictionary* had only comprised casuals, i.e. 'foreign words ... not in habitual use, which for special and temporary purposes occur in books of foreign travel [and] letters of foreign correspondence',[20] it would have been very thin indeed. It is not surprising, therefore, that Fennell turned down Murray's sole offer of casuals. As Fennell explained to Murray in 1883, 'Mr *Stanford* has left copious illustrations of your "denizens" and "aliens" as well as of "casuals", so I suppose the Syndics felt they could not help including them notwithstanding your advice to the contrary. I fear we even poach on the "naturals" to some extent.'[21] After all, these were separate and independent works, and ultimately Fennell was free to include anything he wanted.

From this point on, Murray compared Fennell's work with his own whenever he could, and received secret reports on Fennell from J. H. Hessels, of St John's College, Cambridge, a disaffected Latinist whose proposal for a medieval Latin dictionary had been rejected twice by Cambridge University Press in the 1880s, the same period during which Fennell's dictionary had been generously funded.[22] Hessels provided Murray with feedback on Fennell's progress, in particular his antedatings of *OED* entries. As Murray put it, 'Fennel in fact makes our work the basis of his own, so far as his words go ... he appropriates whatever we have discovered and worked out, and then starts from that to find earlier quotations, as the justification and *raison d' etre* of his existence.' Perhaps as a means to protect himself and to prepare his superiors for a dictionary on the market that trumped *OED1* with earlier quotations, Murray reported to the Assistant Secretary to the Delegates, Charles Doble (1847–1914), in 1889, that 'the very plan of Fennell's work drove him to this method of appropriation of our work, and detraction of our results – insomuch that when met in the street his customary piece of news is "I have found *barracoon* three years earlier than Murray!!!" which has become a kind of joke in Cambridge.'[23]

Murray also got information on Fennell's progress from colleagues who attended the Cambridge Philological Society Meetings. During the compilation of the *Stanford Dictionary*, Fennell gave updates to the Cambridge Philological Society in which he sought dictionary contributions from members and often shared philological observations that emerged from his dictionary work. In 1884, he reported that English speakers 'in the sixteenth, seventeenth, and eighteenth centuries generally changed Spanish (sometimes Italian) *a*'s which they did not accent into *o*'s, such as *potato* and *tobacco*'.[24] He often used these forums as avenues to present his antedatings of *OED* evidence and to argue against some of Murray's etymological findings.[25] Skeat wrote columns in *The Academy* informing readers of Fennell's discoveries along the way, encouraging them to contact Fennell and to contribute to the dictionary's compilation.[26]

In the mid 1880s, Murray was asked to comment on a few provisional pages of *Stanford Dictionary* proofs. At this point, a small section of *OED1* had been published – the letter A and part of the letter B – and Murray observed that Fennell had taken quotations from *OED1* without acknowledgement. As Murray later recalled, Fennell had told him at the time that the quotations were 'only inserted provisionally in that proof in order to fill up gaps that would be supplied in the work itself by its own editorial staff, so as to give a provisional notion of the appearance of the book'. Murray saw no more of Fennell's text until a dictionary specimen in 1889 which he described as 'systematically appropriating our work'. Not only were quotations in the *Stanford Dictionary* taken from *OED*, but, according to Murray, the etymologies also showed 'the wholesale reproduction of my etymological work'. Murray told Doble that 'This specimen shows that he has not succeeded so much as I expected in putting dates back. In the 26 words here, he appears to have done so in 5; the others contain absolutely no information that we have not.' 'As to what can be done', wrote an exasperated Murray, 'I can unfortunately not advise. You can, I suppose do nothing legal, until he publishes.'[27]

In support of Murray, the OUP Delegates did three things to try to thwart Fennell: they tried to get the whole *Stanford Dictionary* project stopped by the Syndics of CUP; they tried to get Fennell removed from reviewing *OED1* anonymously in the *Athenaeum* journal; and they tried to stop *OED1* editors from citing or acknowledging Fennell. First of all, the OUP Delegates responded to Murray's concerns by protesting strongly to the Syndics of CUP that Fennell should not be allowed to proceed with the dictionary because of its excessive use of Murray's dictionary.[28] The Secretary to the Delegates at this time, Philip Lyttelton Gell, asked for the Syndics' assurance that they would 'guard against any excessive use of the NED [*OED1*], which the Delegates had such serious grounds for anticipating'.[29] He explained to C. J. Clay, Secretary to the Syndics, 'The enormous outlay involved in the NED renders it absolutely essential that the Delegates should protect it from any use of the original material which it contains, likely to prejudice its sale.'[30] The Syndics assured the Delegates that the *Stanford Dictionary* would not make excessive use of Oxford's dictionary.[31]

In addition to trying to stop Fennell proceeding with the *Stanford Dictionary*, the Delegates of OUP also tried to stop him reviewing *OED1* in the *Athenaeum* journal. The *Athenaeum* was a respected literary journal that anonymously reviewed *OED1* fascicles as they were published.[32] Murray and his superiors knew that Fennell was the *Athenaeum*'s anonymous reviewer. They believed that Fennell's reviews were 'unfair' and 'not impartial', and they tried to get the journal to drop Fennell as the reviewer. They argued that Fennell reviewed *OED1* 'in a way which we cannot but think unfair; contrasting it unfavourably with the Century Dictionary on points of etymology and philology'.[33] Their main complaints were that Fennell compared *OED1* with its competitors and drew attention to the *OED*'s slow rate of production. Gell warned the editor of the *Athenaeum*, 'We are shortly about to issue a new part of the "New English Dictionary", and I have been strongly urged by many Philologists of authority who take an interest in the work not to submit a copy for review in the "Athenaeum" on the ground that the previous notices [in] your columns have been made the vehicle of a personal hostility.' Gell continued:

> Independent criticism is fine, but [one] suspects that it is not impartial, which is understandable given the surmised name of the reviewer. I shall of course not comply with the suggestions made to me as to withholding the review copy, feeling quite convinced that when once your attention has been drawn to the sentiments which exist on the subject, you will be able to submit future reviews to critics whose impartiality there is no ground for disputing.[34]

OUP failed to get the journal to drop Fennell as the reviewer of the *OED*, and Fennell went on to write a total of sixty-three reviews of *OED1* in the *Athenaeum*.[35] It is true that Fennell's reviews had compared *OED1* with its competitors and had criticized its slowness of production, but it is not true that the reviews were not impartial. In fact, the reviews were actually balanced and fair and not particularly negative at all. As Bailey (2000b) put it, 'However critical he [Fennell] was of Murray the man he was consistently celebratory of Murray the lexicographer.'[36] The review which Fennell wrote immediately after Gell's letter to the Editor was particularly positive and generous in its comparison of *OED1* with the *Stanford Dictionary*. Fennell wrote:

> In many cases the articles on alien or incompletely naturalized words are better than the corresponding articles in the "*Stanford Dictionary*", as also are some of the articles on naturalized words borrowed from languages other than French, Latin, and Greek, e.g. those on 'conspectus', 'contadino', 'contre-danse', 'coracle', 'coram', 'coranto', (the dance), 'cromlech', and 'croquet', and several omissions from the "*Stanford*" are here duly supplied, e.g. 'coccagee', 'contumax', 'cordaille', 'cranreuch', 'crepon', crise', 'croche' (bud of a horn), 'crociate.'

Fennell did not, however, miss the chance to praise his own work a little also, especially his antedatings. 'On the other hand', he wrote 'the "*Stanford*" supplements the "New English Dictionary" with earlier instances of several native words, e.g. for "connexion" Elyot's "Governor", 1531, is quoted – Dr Murray's first instance being 1609, his first equivalent instance 1651, though in other respects his article is, of course, by far the better; also with earlier quotations for "consult", "consultor", "contemn", "contemplator".'[37] Indeed, once the *Stanford* was published, Fennell often compared the two dictionaries in his *OED* reviews.[38]

Did Gell's letter of complaint to the *Athenaeum* influence the tenor of Fennell's reviews? If one compares Fennell's reviews of *OED1* before and after 1893, one observes little difference. After Gell's complaint, Fennell continued to compare *OED1* with its competitors ('it is not easy to see why words given in the 'Century Dictionary', such as "constablish", "crode" = crypt (which is illustrated by a quotation), "chrome" (for It. *croma*), have not been inserted', and Fennell continued to comment on Murray's slow pace.[39] His criticism was justified, 'at this rate – namely, under 320 pages a year, Dr Murray's pace being under 250 pages a year, and Mr Bradley's slower still – we cannot expect that even with two editors the work will be completed in ten more years.'[40] Even several years afterwards, Murray was sensitive about his slow pace and in his Romanes lecture in 1900, he defensively highlighted that, 'All the great dictionaries of the modern languages have taken a long time to make; but the speed with which the New English Dictionary has now advanced nearly to its half-way point can advantageously claim comparison with the progress of any other great dictionary, even when this falls far behind in historical and inductive character.'[41]

The main difference between Fennell's reviews of *OED1* and reviews by others was the particular attention Fennell gave to the *OED*'s treatment of foreign words or words pertaining to foreign subjects.[42] His first review of *OED1* highlighted the absence of the word *African*, but was fair: 'Dr Murray has been found fault with for omitting "African", "Arimaspian", "bactrian" (sic, in a quotation from *Blackwood*); but we consider him justified in passing over the two last geographical names. It is not easy to say whether the absence of "African" can be defended in view of the insertion of "American", "Asian", "Australian".'[43] This criticism prompted Murray to address the omission of *African* in the preface to volume 1, published the following year. He wrote:

> In dealing with so vast a body of words, some inconsistencies, real or apparent, are, from the nature of the subject, inevitable. In deciding whether a word on or near the frontier line in any direction shall or shall not be included, it is not easy always to be consistent. For example, the word *African* was one of the earliest instances in which the question of admission or exclusion arose with regard to an important adjective derived from a geographical proper name. After much careful consideration, and consultation with advisers, it was decided (perhaps by a too rigid application of first principles) to omit the word, as having really no more claims to inclusion than *Algerian*, *Australian*, or *Bulgarian*.[44]

Most of Fennell's criticism in reviews showed not only deficiencies in *OED1* but also deficiencies in his own work. He often included quotations which both dictionaries had missed, as in his review of the letter P in 1907: 'Under "pirogue" Dr Murray, like the *Stanford Dictionary*, ignores Campbell's "His pirogue launched – his pilgrim begun", Gertrude of Wyoming Pt I xxviii.'[45]

Fennell's early reviews of *OED1* imply that initially he did not necessarily see *OED1* as the right place for words from outside Britain. But these reviews were written after his own dictionary was under way, so it is difficult to deduce Fennell's exact motivation.[46] Later reviews, however, show a different attitude: Fennell's comments are overwhelmingly positive regarding the inclusion of foreign words in *OED1*. He wrote: 'Foreign elements of the language are all fairly represented.'[47] He even began one review with the question '"What makes a word originally alien become English?" An answer to this question is naturally expected in a thoroughly scientific and elaborate work like the "New English Dictionary".'[48]

Nevertheless, not only did OUP try to stop Fennell proceeding with the *Stanford Dictionary* and try to remove him from reviewing *OED1*, but they also tried to stop *OED1* editors citing Fennell or the *Stanford Dictionary* in *OED* entries and prefatory material. One letter from the Assistant Secretary to the Delegates asked Henry Bradley, 'Do you think it quite necessary to acknowledge the help of Dr Fennell in your Prefatory note? Dr Fennell made use of Dr Murray's work as his basis as far as it went; and, after examining the first proofs and a portion of a clean sheet of the *Stanford Dictionary*, the Delegates thought it their plain duty to address a strong protest against his proceeding to the Syndics of the Cambridge Press.' Doble gave force to his argument by invoking the support of Gell, Murray, and Anthony Lawson Mayhew (1842–1916) who was a reader for the dictionary and chaplain of Wadham College, Oxford. Doble wrote: 'I have consulted Mr Gell on the subject, and we have no doubt that the Delegates will assert a very strong opinion as to the recognition of Dr Fennell's assistance, and their view will be shared by Dr Murray and Mr Mayhew who are cognisant of the facts.'[49] Bradley ignored Doble's request, and the preface was published with thanks to Fennell 'for several references for the article *Eureka*'.[50] Later in this chapter, I will compare the different ways in which Murray and Bradley acknowledged the *Stanford Dictionary* in *OED1*, and the ways in which it was remembered by Onions in the 1930s.

Reaction at the *OED* to the publication of the *Stanford Dictionary*

Despite the Delegates' protestations to the CUP Syndics, the *Stanford Dictionary* was published in 1892 with the inclusion of casuals, aliens, denizens, and even some naturals. Despite Murray's accusations of plagiarism and the threats of court action, the case never reached court because, when the *Stanford Dictionary* was published, Fennell acknowledged his indebtedness to *OED1* in the preface and throughout the text. He said that the complex five-pronged remit for the dictionary proved difficult for him and his contributors to follow with rigour, and therefore they depended heavily on the *OED*, especially for words belonging to the fifth section (French, Latin, and Greek words).[51]

Fennell explained in the dictionary's preface that words in the fifth section (e.g. *passport*, *pyramid*, and *syntax*) had presented the 'most serious difficulties'. He admitted that 'this portion of the work has been least satisfactory' and that he relied heavily on the expertise and etymological researches of *OED1* in preventing thirty such words appearing erroneously in the section *A–Cassz*. 'The indebtedness of the *Stanford Dictionary* to the New English Dictionary (up to *Cassz*) and to other dictionaries', Fennell wrote, 'is especially heavy with regard to these words and those treated under the fifth section of the Scheme, both as to illustrate quotations and items of vocabulary (possibly 10 percent of the latter being due to the New English Dictionary up to *Cassz*).'[52]

While sales of the *Stanford Dictionary* were strong, reviews were decidedly mixed.[53] The *New York Times* praised Fennell for getting the right balance in his selection of headwords: 'Dr Fennell has certainly . . . a fine sense of what would really be useful in such a volume and could be included without weighing it down too heavily. He has given us a dictionary of the greatest practical value and convenience for the general purposes of educated men, and one which, if it does not pretend to satisfy the erudite, is well calculated to stimulate the desire for research, and to set the investigator on the right path.'[54]

However, the boundaries of foreignness differed for different reviewers, and the *Athenaeum* and *Modern Language Notes* criticized Fennell for getting the wrong balance in headwords, especially for omitting well-known words such as *flux*, *jongo*, *myopia*, *mackintosh*, *pumpernickel*, *shaman*, *Veda*, and *zenith*.[55] 'The strange thing', wrote the anonymous reviewer in the *Athenaeum*, 'is that important and well-known foreign words . . . have been omitted while room has been found for eccentricities . . . like "dejerator", "disgusto", and "minutezzo".'[56]

The etymologies in the *Stanford Dictionary* also received mixed comments. Professor James M. Garnett at the University of Virginia praised Fennell for improving on the *OED*'s etymologies. Comparing the etymological treatment of the word *abracadabra* in both texts, Garnett wrote in the *American Journal of Philology*, 'We see here an improvement upon the NED and a reasonable etymology given for the first time in any dictionary, as far as I know.'[57] However, the *Athenaeum* and *Modern Language Notes* found Fennell's etymologies lacking in rigour. After seven pages of detailed corrections to the etymologies, the anonymous reviewer in the *Athenaeum* concluded that 'evidence has been produced sufficient to show that the '*Stanford Dictionary*' is not strong in etymology'.[58] Clarence Griffin Child (1864–1928), who later became the assistant editor of the revised *Worcester's Dictionary* but at that time was a graduate student at the University of Pennsylvania, wrote a particularly scathing review in *Modern Language Notes* that summed up the *Stanford Dictionary* as 'curiously full of error and inconsistency – useless relatively speaking for popular reference, and for scientific purposes interesting, rather than certainly instructive – but a partial record of the fact of today, and a woefully incomplete one for the fact of yesterday.'[59] In private at least, Murray also made a point of criticizing Fennell's etymologies. He wrote to Gell, complaining that in Fennell's dictionary:

> There is no real etymology; in a work of this kind dealing expressly with the foreign element, some account of the foreign word adopted was to be expected, but none is given. Thus we are not told whether the Arabic-Turkish word cited as the original of *coffee* means the beverage, the fruit, or the plant. And under *coco-nut*, there is no hint of the fact that Pg. and Sp. *coco* is a mask or bugbear and that the coco-nut is so named from the appearance of the base of the shell with its three holes and central nose-like protuberance.[60]

Outside of Britain and North America, however, speakers of other varieties of English were delighted to see many of their own words appearing in a dictionary. In India, for example, the *Stanford Dictionary* was highly praised and ranked alongside 'the great Oxford Dictionary', not – as one might have expected – alongside the *Hobson-Jobson* (1886) which had been published six years previously. Fennell's dictionary was appreciated internationally as a scholarly text. A reviewer in a prominent Indian law journal, the *Indian Jurist*, stated that the *Stanford Dictionary* was 'a very scholarly contribution to modern English lexicography, worthy, within its range, to take rank with the great Oxford Dictionary'.[61]

The publication of the *Stanford Dictionary*, and the substantial investment put into it by the prestigious Cambridge University Press, helped change both public and scholarly attitudes towards foreign words in English. Within a few years, reviewers went from criticizing the presence of 'barbarous terms and foreign words' in Murray's dictionary to highlighting the attraction that Fennell's dictionary held 'for every intelligent member of the imperial race of English-speaking men'.[62] The *Gentleman's Magazine* reported, 'it is difficult to over-estimate the value and importance of what has been accomplished [by the *Stanford Dictionary*]'.[63] As the *Athenaeum* put it, 'this book contains, as in a magic mirror, a many-coloured picture of the numberless relations of the Englishmen with the outside world, through the long course of the ages, in every quarter of the habitable world'. Fennell was likened to Noah on the Ark: 'If we could imagine a flood', wrote the

Athenaeum reviewer, 'which would sweep away every language now spoken in the world, we believe that we should find preserved for us in the ark so cunningly prepared by the Cambridge Noah many an interesting specimen of every language and important dialect.'[64]

The positive reception of Fennell's dictionary was no doubt assisted by the popularity of the recently published *Anglo-Indian Dictionary* (1885) by Whitworth and *Hobson-Jobson* (1886) by Yule and Burnell, not to mention other best sellers about the Empire such as Seeley's *The Expansion of England* (1883) and Dilke's *Problems of Greater Britain* (1890). However, it is still difficult to know whether part of the attraction of the *Stanford Dictionary* was that it allocated foreign words to their own dictionary, safely away from the possible 'contamination' that their presence in a general English dictionary, such as *OED1*, may have brought. Rather than seeing these alien words as corrupting the English language, the reviewer in the *Gentlemen's Magazine* believed that the language had 'enriched itself':

> Here are *bulbul*, redolent of Persia and Arabid; *bungalow*, from the Hindoo and Mahratta; *coffee*, coming from French from the Turkish; *gobang*, from the Japanese; *pah*, from the Maori; *proa*, from the Malay, and so forth. Almost innumberable are the languages from which we have borrowed. The list [in the *Stanford Dictionary*] includes Aramaic, Ethiopic, Dravidian, Russian, Chinese, African, and Red Indian. Many of these words are, naturally, to be found in dictionaries easy of access. Many others, however, are given in no book which the scholar can easily consult. One more merit of the book is that it is a complete guide to those French phrases which Englishmen continually misquote.[65]

All the foreign words mentioned in this review – *bulbul,* a bird known as the nightingale of the East, *bungalow*, *coffee*, *gobang*, a Japanese board game, *pah,* a fortified Maori village, *proa,* a Malaysian sailing boat – also appeared in *OED1* (e.g. *bulbul*, *bungalow*, and *coffee* were published by 1892, the others were published later: *gobang* in 1900, *pah* in 1904, *proa* in 1908). But because *OED1* was known as a general English dictionary, not a specialist dictionary of 'anglicized words and phrases', it was rarely praised for its coverage of this vocabulary. When the presence of these words was noticed in *OED1,* it was usually judged by reviewers as a decaying presence, whereas the presence of the same words in the *Stanford Dictionary* was seen by reviewers to 'enrich' the language.[66] This may well have been because notions of the decaying effect of foreign words in a general dictionary persisted into the 1890s.

Reading Murray's correspondence with Skeat, Doble, and Gell, we receive the impression that Fennell plagiarized. Going from the early *Stanford* proofs with no acknowledgement of *OED1*, to Fennell's competitive spirit driving him to boast about his antedatings in the streets of Cambridge,[67] and his own confession to Murray that he had in fact extended his inclusion policy to

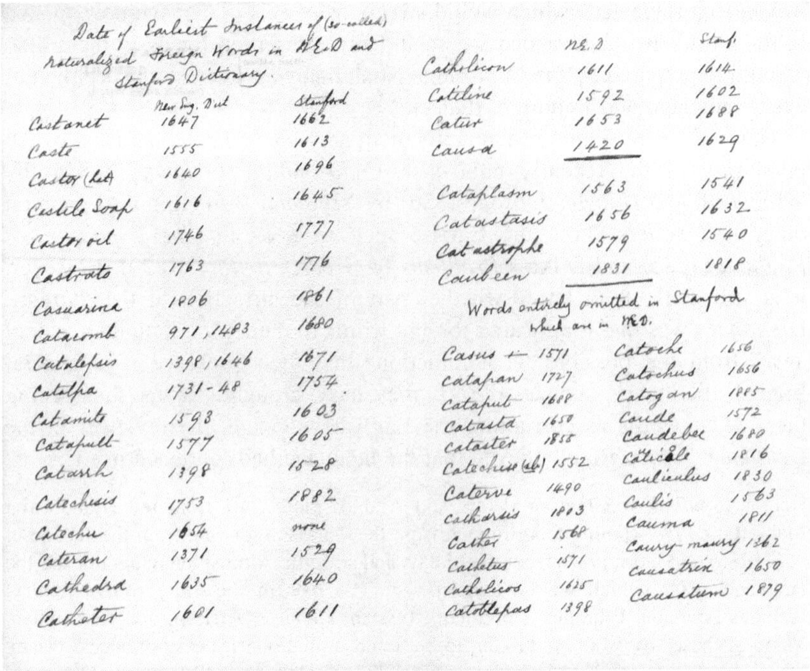

Date of Earliest Instances of (so-called) naturalized Foreign Words in N.E.D and Stanford Dictionary.

	New Eng. Dict	Stanford
Castanet	1647	1662
Caste	1555	1613
Castor (hat)	1640	1696
Castile Soap	1616	1645
Castor oil	1746	1777
Castrato	1763	1776
Casuarina	1806	1861
Catacomb	971, 1483	1680
Catalepsis	1398, 1646	1671
Catalpa	1731-48	1754
Catamite	1593	1603
Catapult	1577	1605
Catarrh	1398	1528
Catechesis	1753	1882
Catechu	1654	none
Cateran	1371	1529
Cathedra	1635	1640
Catheter	1601	1611

	N.E.D.	Stanf.
Catholicon	1611	1614
Catiline	1592	1602
Catur	1653	1688
Causa	1420	1629
Cataplasm	1563	1541
Catastasis	1656	1632
Catastrophe	1579	1540
Caubeen	1831	1818

Words entirely omitted in Stanford which are in N.E.D.

Casus ←	1571	Catoche	1656
Catapan	1727	Catochus	1656
Catapult	1688	Catogan	1885
Catasta	1650	Caude	1572
Cataster	1855	Caudebec	1680
Catechism (ab)	1552	Caticale	1816
Caterve	1490	Cauliculus	1830
Catharsis	1803	Caulis	1563
Cathar	1568	Cauma	1811
Catholus	1571	Caury-maury	1362
Catholicos	1625	Causatrix	1650
Catoblepas	1398	Causatum	1879

Figure 4.1 Murray's comparison of the first dates for fifty words following the word *Cast* in both *OED1* and the *Stanford*, along with a list of words omitted by Fennell that were in *OED1*. (Credit: OUP)

include not just Murray's aliens, denizens, and casuals but even his category of 'naturals',[68] Murray painted a convincing picture of 'Fennell as plagiarist'.

Murray presented the *Stanford* as a dictionary that starts well because the letters *A–Cast* were taken directly from the *OED*, but thereafter deteriorates into – in his words – 'puerile' and 'indolent' scholarship because Fennell had no access to any *OED1* words beyond *Cast*. In one of his letters of complaint, Murray compared the first dates for fifty words following the word *Cast* in both dictionaries, and reported to the Secretary to the Delegates that the *Stanford Dictionary* had missed half of them and those that hadn't been missed were badly treated (Figure 4.1). Murray wrote:

> Of these 50 words moreover, no less than 24 are altogether omitted in the *Stanford Dictionary*, although among the most typical words of the class with which it deals. The treatment of these words moreover shows a great falling off in fullness and accuracy; thus the historical changes in the senses of *Caste*, *Catarrh* and *Caucus* are quite missed.[69]

Murray implied to his superiors that the deterioration of Fennell's lexicographic standards, especially the etymological treatment of words, after the letter C was because Fennell did not have access to any published materials of *OED1*:

> This falling off of treatment becomes more and more marked as the work advances, and one is often astonished at the indolence with which words are dismissed, as e.g. the failure to carry *coupon* back further than 1863, when it might have been got from any financial source 40 years earlier (as we have it); and the entire omissions of the railway and hotel *coupons* of Tourists' agencies. So *couvade* begins with 1889, whereas everyone knows Dr Tylor introduced it in 1865.[70]

Murray judged Fennell's work on certain words such as *cholera* very harshly:

> In the later part of the book, it looks as if research had come to an end, and the Editor had taken such materials as came to his hand. This is seen even in earlier parts in the utterly puerile and ignorant treatment of the word *cholera*. The scholarship of the work is disappointingly poor. I expected something much better.[71]

Murray presents a scenario of plagiarism from *A–Cast*, and decline from *Cast–Z* when Fennell worked without recourse to *OED1*. A closer inspection of the texts, however, reveals quite a different picture.

Case study: a comparison of the *Stanford Dictionary* and *OED1*

In order to examine the truth of Murray's accusation that Fennell plagiarized, this case study took a sample of 23% of all first senses with quotation paragraphs in the section *A–Cast* of the *Stanford Dictionary,* and compared them with the equivalent portion of the alphabet in the *OED1*.[72] This portion of the alphabet was chosen because it was the section of *OED1* already published, and therefore the section that Fennell had access to and was accused of plagiarizing from.

The case study took a consecutive sample of all entries with quotation paragraphs in the sections *abas–arsenal* and *caaba–cantor* in the *Stanford Dictionary,* and a systematic sample of the first sense within each of these entries, and compared the quotation paragraphs with those in the equivalent portion of the alphabet in *OED1*. The total section *A–Cast* in the *Stanford Dictionary* comprises approximately 4280 entries and 3638 quotation paragraphs over 214 pages. Not every entry in the dictionary has a quotation paragraph, and because Murray's accusation of plagiarism focused on the first quotation of each quotation paragraph, the case study confined its attention to entries with quotations. Sampling was restricted to the quotation paragraph of the first sense of every entry common to both dictionaries. This quotation paragraph was compared for first dates.[73]

Therefore, all first senses (common to both dictionaries) with a quotation paragraph were extracted (831 senses) and were entered into a separate database in which each sense was analyzed according to its etymology, tramlines (in *OED1*), date of first quotation, whether the first quotation was common to both dictionaries, and if so whether the *Stanford Dictionary* acknowledged *OED1* for the shared quotation. A total of 831 entries was analyzed in this way.

The case study revealed six main findings:

1. The *Stanford Dictionary* and *OED1* shared 19% of entries in the sample.
2. The *Stanford Dictionary* antedated *OED1* in 40% of entries in the sample.
3. The *Stanford Dictionary* acknowledged *OED1* for 70% of shared first-sense quotations in the sample.
4. The *Stanford Dictionary* did not acknowledge *OED1* for 30% of shared first-sense quotations, or 6% of all entries, in the sample.
5. *OED1* antedated the *Stanford Dictionary* in 18% of entries in the sample.
6. The letters A–C in the *Stanford Dictionary* were disproportionately larger than the rest of the dictionary.

Result 1: The Stanford Dictionary *and OED1 shared 19% of entries in the sample*

The case study revealed that only 19% (19.4%) of the sample entries in *A–Cast* were common to both dictionaries. In other words, 81% of *A–Cast* in *Stanford* was unique to *Stanford* and did not appear in *OED1* (Appendix 3). It is impossible to know whether Murray was aware that the proportion of shared entries was this low, but his correspondence suggests that he had prepared a defence nonetheless. His argument was this: if the *Stanford Dictionary* had too many words in common with *OED1*, then they were obviously stolen; if there were too few words in common, then that was because they dealt with an area of the vocabulary that lay outside the remit of *OED1*. It is this second argument – that certain loanwords lay outside the domain of *OED1* – that presents a more complex picture of Murray and his policy on loanwords, and therefore demands further discussion.

While complaining to his superiors about the degree to which Fennell stole his materials, Murray also dismissed the portion of the *Stanford Dictionary* that was unique to the *Stanford* by describing it as consisting of 'foreign phrases, Latin quotations, and occasional words found in Travels etc.' He wrote to Gell: 'These lie altogether outside our territory and I have formed no judgement on the execution of this part, except that I think the last-mentioned item is far from complete . . . We come across stray instances of such words every day among our material,' he told Gell, 'which we do not use because they lie outside our domain, and which are not included in the *Stanford Dictionary*.'[74] A few years

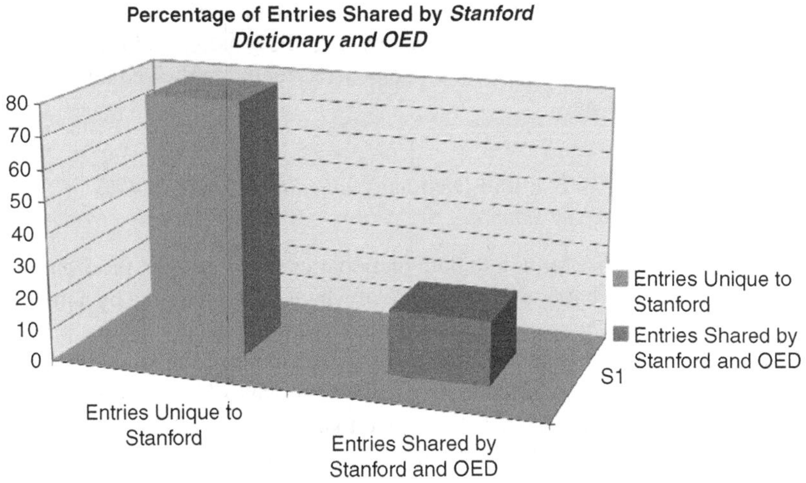

Appendix 3 Bar graph showing the proportion of shared entries (19.4%) in the sample of the section *A–Cast*. (See Appendix at end of book for colour version of this figure.)

earlier Murray had written something similar to Doble, dismissing rumours that Fennell was antedating *OED1* by admitting, 'This of course it is comparatively easy to do: he [Fennell] touches only a small part of the vocabulary, and by using our work as a *finis a quo*, and directing his energies to the restricted field of searching in a given period for particular words, he can often find earlier examples, esp. of travellers' words in the travel-literature.'[75]

Murray's dismissal of 'foreign phrases, Latin quotations, and occasional words found in Travels' as outside the domain of *OED1* warrants some attention. It is true that phrases and quotations rarely appeared as headwords for practical reasons (they were too long and had too many variations), but dismissing travellers' terms went against what is found in the actual pages of *OED1*: Murray included thousands of terms from travellers' tales, and, as discussed in the previous chapter, even sought readers for them. Therefore, it is strange that Murray should denigrate travellers' terms in Fennell's dictionary when he had gone to so much trouble to collect them for his own dictionary. Usually it was Murray justifying to his superiors the rightful place of foreign words in *OED1*, but when it came to the demolition of Fennell's work in the *Stanford Dictionary*, it seemed that even Murray was willing to change his argument.

While it makes sense that a specialist dictionary would be more comprehensive than a general dictionary, a 5:1 order of magnitude suggests that Murray did not cast his net as widely as he could have. In addition to his dismissive comments about travellers' terms, it seems that Murray applied stricter criteria than Fennell for anglicization and naturalization. One-third of the words (33.8% or 281 entries) shared by both dictionaries had tramlines in *OED1*, suggesting that while Fennell considered them 'anglicized and naturalized', Murray did not.

Result 2: The Stanford Dictionary *antedated* OED1 *in 40% of entries in the sample*

Of the 19% of words common to both dictionaries in the sample, the *Stanford Dictionary* antedated 40% of them, some of which were pre-dated by a matter of centuries, e.g. *abdest*, a Muslim rite of washing hands before prayer (antedated from 1847 to 1680), and *cannequin*, a kind of white cotton cloth from the East Indies (antedated from 1847 to 1598).[76] This did not go unnoticed by reviewers who acknowledged that while the *Stanford* took some first quotations from *OED1*, it also managed to antedate *OED1*. As Garnett highlighted in the *American Journal of Philology*: 'In some cases the earliest examples of the uses of words are taken from the NED, but in others we find earlier examples in the *Stanford*, so that this work cannot be neglected even by Dr Murray.'[77] The *Stanford Dictionary* also managed to post-date words considered obsolete in *OED1*, e.g. *amant*, a lover, was marked as *Obsolete* in *OED1*, with a final date of 1493, but this word is post-dated in the *Stanford Dictionary* by an 1828 quotation.

As we have seen, Murray was so defensive about the fact that many of his entries had been or could be antedated or post-dated by Fennell that he wrote to the Secretary to the Delegates reassuring him that, from a sample of entries taken from *Cast–Cause* (the section immediately following the published range of *OED*), *OED1* managed to antedate forty-six of the fifty words in *Stanford* (Figure 4.1). He wrote: 'I have made a list which I enclose of all the words from Cast to Cause common to the two Dictionaries in which our results differ and find that in 50 words, the N.E.D. beats him with earlier examples 46 times, and is beaten only 4 times' (Figure 4.1).[78]

Result 3: The Stanford Dictionary *acknowledged* OED1 *for 70% of shared first-sense quotations in the sample*

The verb 'to plagiarize' means 'to copy (literary work or ideas) improperly or without acknowledgement'. In other words, copying is not plagiarism if the copyist acknowledges the source even if the copying is 'improper' for being excessive and therefore copyright infringing.[79] Hence, in discerning whether Fennell plagiarized Murray, it is important to discern whether or not the *Stanford Dictionary* acknowledged *OED1* for the material they shared. The case study revealed that within the 19% of shared entries, the two dictionaries

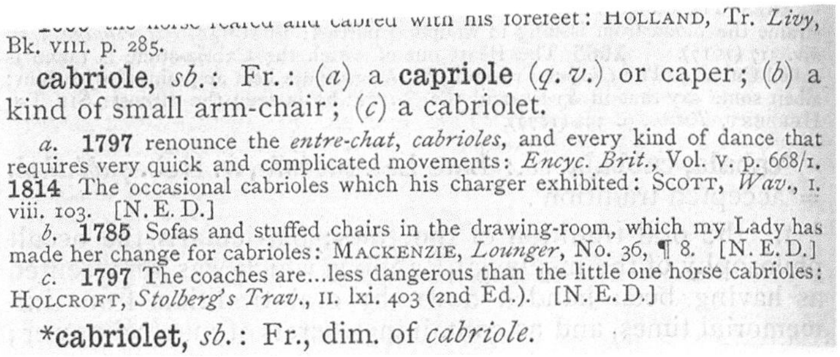

1600 the horse reared and cabred with his forefeet: HOLLAND, Tr. *Livy*, Bk. VIII. p. 285.

cabriole, *sb.*: Fr.: (*a*) a **capriole** (*q. v.*) or caper; (*b*) a kind of small arm-chair; (*c*) a cabriolet.

a. **1797** renounce the *entre-chat, cabrioles,* and every kind of dance that requires very quick and complicated movements: *Encyc. Brit.*, Vol. v. p. 668/1. **1814** The occasional cabrioles which his charger exhibited: SCOTT, *Wav.*, I. viii. 103. [N. E. D.]

b. **1785** Sofas and stuffed chairs in the drawing-room, which my Lady has made her change for cabrioles: MACKENZIE, *Lounger*, No. 36, ¶ 8. [N. E. D.]

c. **1797** The coaches are...less dangerous than the little one horse cabrioles: HOLCROFT, *Stolberg's Trav.*, II. lxi. 403 (2nd Ed.). [N. E. D.]

***cabriolet**, *sb.*: Fr., dim. of *cabriole.*

Figure 4.2 The entry for *cabriole* in the *Stanford Dictionary*, showing acknowledgement of *OED1* after three of four quotations. (Credit: CUP)

had 33% (32.7% or 272) of shared first quotations. One might presume that these were taken directly from *OED1*, and in 70% (69.9% or 190) of cases they were. We know this because Fennell tells us so; he acknowledged *OED1* by putting 'NED' in square brackets after each quotation.[80] Fennell's system of acknowledgement was thorough and rigorous: he acknowledged not only first quotations but also later quotations, some of which Fennell had antedated, e.g. *aggry*, West African glass beads; and *adeps*, soft fat, animal grease.[81]

Fennell's thorough acknowledgement of *OED1* is demonstrated well at *cabriole*, with three senses pertaining to a caper; a kind of armchair; and a horse vehicle respectively (Figure 4.2). In this entry, Fennell acknowledged *OED1* for three out of four quotations, the first one being that which Fennell antedated.

In one entry Fennell even gave Murray a personal citation in the dictionary (Figure 4.3): the quotation for the word *aphesis*, 'when an unaccented short vowel is lost at the beginning of a word', read simply as '1880 Suggested by Dr J. A. H. Murray in *Presid. Address Phil. Soc.*' This alluded to Murray's Presidential Address to the Philological Society in 1880 in which he reported, 'The Editor can think of nothing better than to call the phenomenon *Aphesis* . . . and the resulting forms *Aphetic* forms.'[82] Murray had already noted this in the entry for *aphesis* in *OED1*, published in 1885, so it is not clear whether Fennell took this note on coinage directly from the Presidential Address or the entry in *OED1*.

Most of these entries came from section five of the dictionary's remit – words from Latin, Greek, and French – for which, in addition to acknowledging *OED1* after each quotation, we saw earlier that Fennell also expressed his indebtedness in the preface for 'possibly 10 percent of vocabulary'.[83] In fact, the case study revealed that 13.3%, not 10%, of the sample was due to *OED1*, but Fennell is clearly attempting to be transparent in his indebtedness.

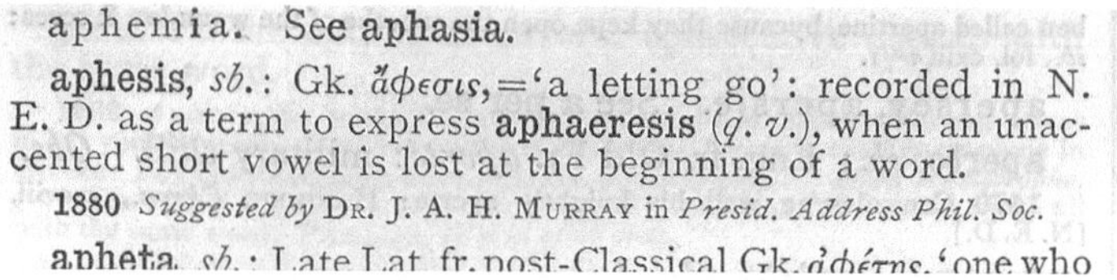

aphemia. See **aphasia.**

aphesis, *sb.*: Gk. ἄφεσις, = 'a letting go': recorded in N. E. D. as a term to express **aphaeresis** (*q. v.*), when an unaccented short vowel is lost at the beginning of a word.

1880 *Suggested by* Dr. J. A. H. Murray in *Presid. Address Phil. Soc.*

apheta, *sb.*: Late Lat. fr. post-Classical Gk. ἀφέτης, 'one who

Figure 4.3 The entry for *aphesis* in the *Stanford Dictionary*, showing Murray's coining of the term. (Credit: CUP)

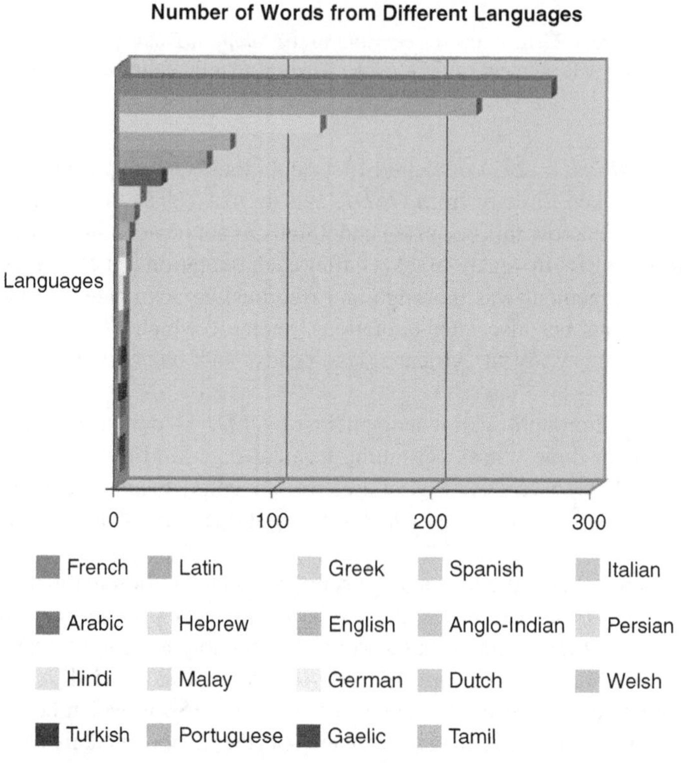

Appendix 4 Bar graph showing the provenance of words in the *Stanford Dictionary* sample. (See Appendix at end of book for colour version of this figure.)

The words belonging to section five of the *Stanford Dictionary* remit (Latin, Greek, and French) form the majority of words in the sample of *A–Cast*. The top five donor languages were French, Latin, Greek, Spanish, Italian, followed by Arabic and Hebrew (Appendix 4).[84,85]

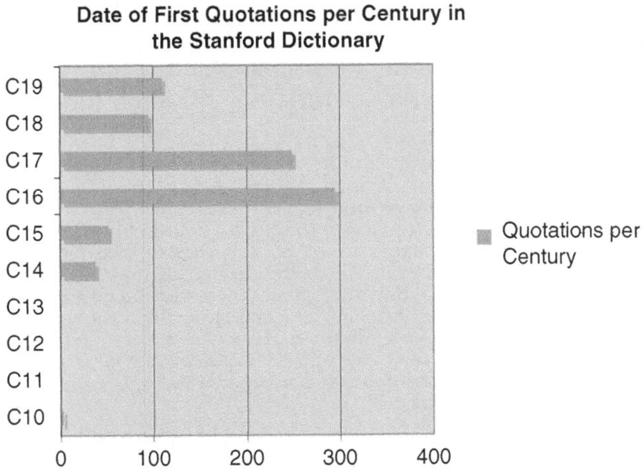

Figure 4.4 Bar graph showing the date of first quotations per century in the *Stanford Dictionary* sample.

Most of the foreign words in the *Stanford Dictionary* sample entered English in the sixteenth century, followed in frequency by the seventeenth, nineteenth, and eighteenth centuries (Figure 4.4).

Result 4: Fennell did not acknowledge OED1 *for 30% of shared first-sense quotations, or 6% of all entries, in the sample*

Given that Fennell acknowledged *OED1* in 70% of shared quotations, it is worth investigating the instances in which he did not acknowledge *OED1* in order to see why this may have been. Although these entries account for only 6% of the whole section *A–Cast*, it is still important to analyze them in order to ascertain whether Fennell did take them from Murray without acknowledgement. After all, it was this 6% of *A–Cast* in the *Stanford Dictionary* that caused Murray's fury and nearly brought OUP and CUP to court. The only way a charge of plagiarism could have been brought against Fennell is if the context implied that he meant to leave a definite impression of originality of the unacknowledged copies.

Overall, it seems that there are legitimate reasons for the lack of acknowledgement on Fennell's part. Many of the quotations – although the same source – were not copied verbatim from *OED1*. Some quotations are longer than those that appeared in *OED1*, showing that Fennell read the same source himself but did not copy the quotation wholesale from Murray, e.g. both dictionaries quote Thomas Stanley's *History of Philosophy* (1655–60) at the entry *acousmata*, 'things received on authority' (Figure 4.5). The quotation in

acousmata, *sb. pl.*: Gk.: *Philos.*: things heard, heads of Pythagorean doctrine; hence *acousmatics*, *acousmatici* (with Lat. termination), hearers, students of such dogmas, probationers.. *Rare.*

1655–60 There were many Auditors, called *Acousmaticks*, whereof he gained...two thousand by one Oration: T. STANLEY, *Hist. Philos.*, Pt. IX. p. 503/1. — of those who came to him, some were called *Mathematici*, others *Acousmatici*... The *Acousmatici* [were] they, who heard only the chief heads of learning, without more exact explication: *ib.*, p. 518/2. — The Philosophy of the *Acousmatici* consists of Doctrines without demonstrations and reasons, but that, So it must be done, and the like, which they were to observe as so many Divine Doctrines, and they did esteem those amongst them the wisest, who had most of these *Acousmata*. Now all these *Acousmata* were divided into three kinds; some tell, *what something is*; others tell, *what is most such a thing*: the third sort tell, *what is to be done*, and *what not*: *ib.*, p. 519/1. — a *Pythagorean* of the Acousmatick rank: *ib.*

[Gk. ἀκούσματα, pl. of ἄκουσμα, = 'a thing heard'.]

Figure 4.5 Entry for *acousmata* in the *Stanford Dictionary* showing an extended version of a quotation from Stanley's *History of Philosophy* that appeared in *OED1*. (Credit: CUP)

OED1 is 'They did esteem those among them the wisest, who had most of these Acousmata. Now all these Acousmata were divided into three kinds; some tell, what something is, others tell, what is most such a thing; the third sort tell, what is to be done, and what not.' The quotation in the *Stanford Dictionary* includes this portion of Stanley with the preceding three sentences, showing that although both dictionaries share the same source, Fennell did not take his quotation directly from Murray.

There are also instances where Fennell's first quotation was from the same source text as Murray's but was a different portion of that text, showing that while he may have used *OED1* as a trigger to read that particular source, he did not copy the quotation verbatim from Murray. For example, at *aphorism*, a concise statement of a scientific principle, both dictionaries quoted from Thomas Paynell's *The Regimen of Health of Salerno* (1528). Murray chose the quotation 'Galen saythe in the glose of this aphorisme, *qui crescunt*, etc..' Fennell chose the quotation 'as is sayde in the aforesayde *aphorisme*.' There are other cases where Fennell and Murray shared both the first quotation and a later quotation within the same quotation paragraph (e.g. *canaan*, land of promise) or within the same entry that has multiple senses (e.g. *accost*, to border, to approach), but Fennell only acknowledged the later quotation which implies, but of course does not prove, that he found the first quotation himself (and it just happened to coincide with Murray's). There is therefore insufficient evidence to suggest that Fennell did take the 6% of unacknowledged entries from Murray.

Legally, there is no particular threshold and no standard metric measure for plagiarism. Since Fennell acknowledged quotations from *OED1* in the majority of cases but failed to acknowledge a small proportion, it is hard to make the charge of plagiarism against him. In fact, since the text is a reference work of factual information in which snippets of literary sources are shared, one could argue that Fennell was under no obligation legally to acknowledge the research tool that allowed him to find those citations.[86]

Result 5: OED1 *antedated the* Stanford Dictionary *in 18% of entries in the sample*

If Fennell had plagiarized, surely he would not have allowed *OED1* to antedate 18% (18.3%) of entries in *A–Cast* in the *Stanford Dictionary*? Additional evidence against the claim that Fennell plagiarized Murray is the fact that *OED1* provides earlier quotations than *Stanford* for 152 words in the sample; this equates to 18.3% of the whole sample.[87] For example, the first quotation for the Arabic word *alcoran*, the Koran, in the *Stanford Dictionary* is from Chaucer (c. 1386), but is earlier in *OED1* (from Mandeville [1366]). Likewise, the first quotation for the Turkish word, *caftan*, a long tunic, in the *Stanford Dictionary* is from Hakluyt's *Voyages* (1598), but is earlier in *OED1* (from Giles Fletcher's *Of the Russe Common Wealth* (1591).

A total of 152 words, or 18.3%, of the whole sample, is a substantial proportion of first quotations that Fennell failed to take, if indeed he had plagiarized. It also goes against what Murray presented to Gell, when he wrote, 'He [Fennell] could always take our first example if he found no earlier; and did so (with or without acknowledgement) in a large proportion of his instances. Thus he was able to show always as early a quotation, and in a certain number of cases an earlier one than ours.'[88] Contrary to Murray's statement here, the case study revealed that Fennell did not always have as early a quotation as *OED1* (*OED1* antedates *Stanford* in 18% of cases), and that Fennell actually antedated *OED1* in a significant number of cases (40%).

Result 6: The letters A–C in the Stanford Dictionary *were disproportionately larger than the rest of the dictionary*

The case study revealed that the letters A–C took up 37.5% of the entire *Stanford Dictionary* and only 14.8% of the entire *OED1*, suggesting that the letters A–C in the *Stanford Dictionary* were disproportionately larger than all other letters. This could have been because Fennell took materials from *OED1* for A–C (i.e. plagiarism); it could have been a consequence of various factors such as the relative weight of letters in large source languages

(A and C in Latin, for instance);[89] or it could have been the editorial tendency to work with greater thoroughness at the beginning of the alphabet than the end, a phenomenon described as 'alphabet fatigue' by Starnes and Noyes (1946: 185) and Osselton (2007). Even if we factor out the 19% of shared words, the size of A–C drops from 37.5% to 30% of the whole, which is still a large proportion (and double that of A–C in *OED1*). The most likely explanation for this discrepancy is either the relative weight of letters in large source languages, or the phenomenon of alphabet fatigue.

The 'National Dictionary of English Language and Literature' to rival *OED1*

Two years after the *Stanford Dictionary* was published, Fennell was back in the lexicographic ring with an ambitious proposal for a 'National Dictionary of English Language and Literature'. Fennell hoped that the work would be three volumes of 1000 pages each, issued gradually in fifty monthly fascicles.[90] It is difficult to discern exactly how the dictionary's historical aims differed from those of *OED1*: '[The] National Dictionary of English Language and Literature . . . is intended to include all words and phrase-words found in English literature between 1360 A. D. and the present day.'[91] Although Fennell's prospectus said that he would not cover 'derivatives used only by modern writers or facetious coinages', it did say that it would include 'a number of words of good authority or of common speech never before registered in any dictionary', which would have encroached on the remit of *OED1*.[92]

Fennell may have judged *OED1* to be gathering too much from non-canonical sources, because he stated that his National Dictionary would gather quotations from 'full indexes of several carefully selected authors, including Chaucer, Caxton, Elyot, North, Phil. Holland, Bacon, Pope, Johnson, Burke, Thackeray, Macaulay and Ruskin'.[93] His intention to limit literary sources to the canon might account for the relatively few volumes he proposed: given that at this time *OED1* had published A–C in two volumes, Fennell's three volumes suggested a dictionary one-fifth of the size of *OED1*.

Fennell estimated the project would take six years and cost £16,000 to complete. He tried to raise funds for the project by offering subscriptions of 4 pounds, a price at the time (in 1894) that was approximately one-fifth of the price of *OED1*.[94] Despite his appeal for both readers and subscribers, even after enlisting the nominal support of distinguished Cambridge scholars such as Walter Skeat, Aldis Wright, and John Percival Postgate, he failed to attract either.[95] In 1895, Anthony Lawson Mayhew published a letter in the *Athenaeum* offering partial support for the National Dictionary as long as the dictionary confined its remit to literary sources only: 'No scientific exotic like *Ametropia* must blemish pages sacred to the Muse!' he wrote. There is no evidence to suggest that Mayhew's letter was part of an OUP plot to diminish the scope of Fennell's dictionary, but archival materials do show that, a few years earlier, Mayhew was one of the select few who were privy to Murray's accusation of plagiarism against Fennell, so it cannot be ruled out. Doble had written to Bradley, 'I have consulted Mr Gell on the subject, and we have no doubt that the Delegates will assert a very strong opinion as to the recognition of Dr Fennell's assistance, and their view will be shared by Dr Murray and Mr Mayhew who are cognisant of the facts.'[96]

Fennell's pleas for financial assistance for the National Dictionary project became desperate in 1895, and he had to face the fact that no publisher would back his proposal.[97] He made a last-ditch attempt to raise funds by issuing shares in the dictionary of £5 each, writing in the *Athenaeum*, 'I therefore appeal to persons interested in English literature to express their willingness to take shares (5*l*. each) provided that the detailed arrangements meet with their approval. [. . .] My own belief is that the capital would be returned three or four fold at least in ten years. It would especially be convenient and economical if a few persons would agree to take or place one or two hundred 5*l*. shares each.'[98] But this failed and the project had to be abandoned. Before the proposal was dropped, however, Fennell's proposal for a National Dictionary to rival *OED1* fuelled further ill feeling toward him within OUP.[99]

The impact of the *Stanford Dictionary* controversy on *OED1*

The whole 'Fennell business' – as Bradley referred to it in 1892 – left its mark on Murray and *OED1* in myriad ways.[100] Murray admitted to his superiors within the Press that he was going to make the publication of the *Stanford Dictionary* work to the *OED*'s advantage: he had the *Stanford Dictionary*'s earlier sources read for *OED1*, and reported that:

> Now that I have seen it, I do not consider that it can interfere with us in the least. If indeed the Editor had crawled on behind us, and taken advantage of each of our parts to build his structure upon, he would have considerably depreciated our work, but having had to pass us and thus show what he could do without us, his work has the opposite effect. It will also in some cases help us, by guiding us in the history of such foreign words as we may include. As at present minded, I do not intend to quote any of his examples, but I shall certainly have some of the books read whence there have been obtained earlier quotations than we have.[101]

Murray may not have originally intended to quote any of Fennell's examples, but he actually ended up quoting the *Stanford Dictionary* more than a hundred times (and more frequently than any other *OED* editor). For instance, in the first two letters edited by Murray and Bradley after 1892, both editors used quotations from the *Stanford Dictionary*, but they acknowledged it in different ways. As we have seen already, Bradley went against the advice of Doble and thanked Fennell in the preface to the letter E; in addition, he acknowledged the *Stanford Dictionary* once in the letter E (*encomienda*, an estate granted to a Spaniard in America) and twice in the letter F (*fourbe*, a cheat; *fripon*, a rogue). Murray, on the other hand, never thanked Fennell in a preface, but acknowledged the *Stanford Dictionary* for seventy-four quotations in the letter D and fifty-five quotations at the letter H. Many years later, in 1938, C. T. Onions explained how the *OED1* editors used the *Stanford Dictionary*: 'we always took what we wanted from it [*Stanford Dictionary*]. When we couldn't or didn't verify the text, we inserted "Stanf.".'[102]

Although there is no clear evidence that Murray and Fennell reconciled, there are signs in the *Athenaeum* journal in 1900 that they may have. Under an item on the etymology of *jade*, Murray wrote:

> Through the kindness of Dr. C. A. M. Fennell my attention was recently called to two passages in the English translation of 1656 of the "Letters of Voiture" in which "l'ejade" and "the ejade" are applied to a stone which the context indicated to be jade.[103]

Murray followed this by acknowledging Fennell's help in 'spotting' the new forms:

> The quotations from Voiture's letters had not been supplied by any readers for the 'New English Dictionary,' and it is due to Dr. Fennell's clever 'spotting' of them that this interesting link in the English – and still more in the French – etymology of the word has been supplied.[104]

Although this is not proof of a reconciliation, there is little chance that Murray would have written so warmly about Fennell a decade or more earlier. In fact, if anything, immediately after the 'Stanford Controversy', Murray had shown his competitive spirit by starting to list comparative tables in the prefaces of *OED1*. For example, the first table comparing *OED1*'s coverage of words and quotations with that of other dictionaries – Johnson's, Cassell's *Encyclopaedic*, *Century Dictionary*, Funk's *Standard* and Richardson's – appears in 1896 in the preface of the appropriately named fascicle DEPRAVATIVE – DISTRUSTFUL. Comparative tables appeared in every *OED* volume thereafter.

The *Stanford Dictionary* controversy revealed the territorial and competitive side of Murray. There was no way that Murray was going to share or give away his materials on loanwords and World Englishes. Not only did they deserve a place in an English dictionary, Murray insisted that they have a place in *his* dictionary and he was not happy when that place was shared by another. He did, however, temper this with ambivalence about travellers' terms and their place in the domain of *OED1* – ambivalence that was confirmed by the discrepancy in the coverage between the two dictionaries but countered by the number of travellers' terms already present in *OED1*.

By looking at Murray's relationships with his contemporaries, especially other lexicographers, we gain added insight into his commitment to words of the world. Murray's refusal to hand over all these words to another dictionary demonstrated his considered intention to include the words in his own dictionary. By comparing a portion of the *Stanford Dictionary* with the corresponding portion of *OED1*, the case study has revealed how much further Murray could have gone in his inclusion of foreign words. Fennell's work also showed that Murray's work was not perfect, i.e. it could be antedated and post-dated. Murray's accusations of plagiarism against Fennell were unfounded and could only be explained as Murray being territorial, competitive, and even a little paranoid. Weighing up all the evidence, it appears that Fennell adequately acknowledged his use of *OED1*. This did not, however, stop Murray from complaining to his superiors, and in turn, it did not stop his superiors from trying to thwart Fennell. In 1912, three years before Murray died, Edward Bensly (who had been a member of the *Stanford Dictionary* Advisory Committee) declared in *Notes & Queries* that 'the *Stanford Dictionary* does not seem to be so well known as it should be'.[105]

OUP went on to have other plagiarism cases involving their dictionaries, but no lexicographer seems to have reacted as vehemently as Murray. When the *Cassell's New English Dictionary* by Ernest Baker was published in 1919, the Secretary to the Delegates, Robert Chapman, accused Baker of plagiarizing from Henry Fowler's *Concise Oxford Dictionary* (*COD* 1911).[106] Chapman believed that Baker had taken Fowler's work wholesale, with the illustrative phrases deleted, and that the overall result was an 'unreasonably free reproduction of the framework of COD articles'.[107] Henry Fowler was not the least concerned that Baker may have copied his work. 'Most men are thieves', he wrote, 'God forbid that time should be spent on so desolating a pursuit'.[108]

ENDNOTES

1 Murray (1888: ix).
2 OUP Archive OED Proofs for Letters E, F, G, and L.
3 The publication of the *Stanford Dictionary* was announced in 'New Books and New Editions', *Times*, 17 September 1892 p. 8.
4 OUP/PUB/11/29. Letter from Murray to Gell 20 October 1892.
5 Murray (1977: 266).
6 There is no entry for Charles Fennell in the *Oxford Dictionary of National Biography*. Details of his life were gleaned from his obituary by H. B. and B. B. (1916), and details of his work were taken from Darbishire (1892), Fennell (1895a), and Fennell (1896a, b, c, d).
7 Fennell (1893b: vii, xv) outlines his approach to Pindar. The biographical approach to Pindar was challenged in the early 1960s by the bold and influential work of Elroy L. Bundy (1962). See also M. M. Willcock (1995: 19) for a summary of the

history of scholarship on Pindar. I am indebted to Nick Zair and Luuk Huitink for their advice on Fennell's scholarly work.

8 Fennell (1896b). See also Fennell (1896a, c, d).

9 'Third Meeting of the Cambridge Philological Society', *Proceedings of the Cambridge Philological Society Lent Term 1884* vol. VII, London, Trubner and Co., p. 10.

10 Ellis (1881: 7).

11 The original Stanford slips are stored in the Cambridge University Press Archive UA Pr.B.23. Other materials on the Stanford Dictionary Project can be found in the Cambridge University Press Archive UA Pr.B.4.I Correspondence Concerning Publications 1840–1901; Cambridge University Press Archive Pr.B.4.I.308–310 Letters Concerning the Stanford Dictionary 1892; Cambridge University Press Archive UA.Pr.B.13 Correspondence 1871–1947; and Cambridge University Press Archive UA Pr.V.12 Minute Book 1890–1896.

12 Ellis (1881: 7–9).

13 Fennell's appointment as editor was announced in 'Announcements', *Times,* 15 May 1883 p. 3.

14 Fennell (1892: vii).

15 'Report on the Stanford Dictionary of Anglicised Words and Phrases delivered by Alexander J. Ellis', *Transactions of the Philological Society* 19 p. 9.

16 'Cambridge, March 22', *Times,* 23 March 1893 p. 7; 'University Jottings', *The Academy,* 1 April 1893 pp. 284–5.

17 MP/15/09/1882. Letter from Skeat to Murray 1 December 1882.

18 MP/15/09/1882. Letter from Skeat to Murray 1 December 1882.

19 MP/15/09/1883. Letter from Fennell to Murray 15 September 1883.

20 Murray (1888: xix).

21 MP/15/09/1883. Letter from Fennell to Murray 15 September 1883.

22 Hessels was an authority on early printing and editor of papers in the possession of the Dutch Church in London. His proposal for the Latin Dictionary had been rejected by the Syndics of Cambridge University Press in 1882 and 1886 (see McKitterick 2004: 107). It was eventually accepted, and CUP published *An Eighth-Century Latin – Anglo-Saxon Glossary* in 1890.

23 OUP/PUB/11/29. Letter from Murray to Doble 5 June 1889.

24 'Meetings of Societies', *The Academy,* 20 December 1884 p. 416.

25 See, for example, the discussion of Fennell's criticism of Murray's entry for *-ado 2* in 'Meetings of Societies', *The Academy,* 20 December 1884 p. 416.

26 Skeat (1884: 185).

27 OUP/PUB/11/29. Letter from Murray to Doble 5 June 1889.

28 'The Delegates thought it their duty to address a strong protest against his proceeding to the Syndics of the Cambridge Press,' wrote Doble in 1891 (OUP Secretary Letterbook 1891 p. 588. Letter from Doble to Bradley 14 May 1891). A letter from Gell to Clay, 4 December 1889, refers to an original letter of complaint dated 23 November 1889, but I could not find a copy of this original letter in either the OUP or CUP archives.

29 CUPA UA Pr.B.13.G.6 Letter from Gell to Clay 4 December 1889. I am indebted to Christopher Stray and Peter Gilliver for this reference.

30 CUPA UA Pr.B.13.G.6 Letter from Gell to Clay 4 December 1889.

31 As later explained by Doble in OUP Secretary Letterbook 1891 p. 588. Letter from Doble to Bradley 14 May 1891.
32 See Bailey (2000a) for a discussion of Fennell's reviews of *OED1* in the *Athenaeum*. Also see Bailey (2000b: 253) for a description of how he inspected the office copy of the *Athenaeum* with its notations of authorship, at the City University of London.
33 OUP Secretary Letterbook 1891 p. 588. Letter from Doble to Bradley 14 May 1891.
34 OUP Secretary Letterbook 1893 p. 601. Letter from Gell to the Editor of the Athenaeum 27 May 1893.
35 These are listed in Bailey (2000b).
36 Bailey (2000b: 253).
37 [Fennell, C. A. M.] (1893a: 765–6).
38 [Fennell, C. A. M.] (1895b: 347); [Fennell, C. A. M.] (1900: 851); [Fennell, C. A. M.] (1901: 115); [Fennell, C. A. M.] (1903: 821); [Fennell, C. A. M.] '(1909: 61); [Fennell, C. A. M.] (1907: 627).
39 [Fennell, C. A. M.] '(1893a: 766).
40 [Fennell, C. A. M.] (1893a: 765–6).
41 Murray (1900a: 48–9).
42 [Fennell, C. A. M.] (1890: 207–8); [Fennell, C. A. M.] (1887: 667); [Fennell, C. A. M.] (1899: 412); [Fennell, C. A. M.] (1902: 743); [Fennell, C. A. M.] (1907a: 7).
43 [Fennell, C. A. M.] (1887: 667).
44 Murray (1888: ix).
45 [Fennell, C. A. M.] (1907a: 627).
46 [Fennell, C. A. M.] (1888b: 442).
47 [Fennell, C. A. M.] (1907: 7).
48 [Fennell, C. A. M.] (1902 743–4).
49 OUP Secretary Letterbook 1891 p. 588. Letter from Doble to Bradley 14 May 1891.
50 Bradley (1893: iv).
51 Fennell (1892: vii).
52 Fennell (1892: viii).
53 The sales were reported in 'Cambridge, March 22', *Times* 23 March 1893 p. 7; and also in 'University Jottings', *The Academy*, 1 April 1893 pp. 284–5.
54 'The Stanford Dictionary', *New York Times* 25 December 1892 p. 19.
55 Child (1893: 232); 'Review of the Stanford Dictionary of Anglicised Words and Phrases', *Athenaeum*, 18 March 1893 p. 341; also Garnett (1895: 96) criticizes the omission of *orange* 'as it is traced back to the Persian *nāranj*.'
56 'Review of the Stanford Dictionary of Anglicised Words and Phrases (First Notice)', *Athenaeum*, 18 March 1893 p. 341.
57 Garnett (1895: 95). The previous year, Garnett (1894) had also given a positive review of the *OED*.
58 'Review of Stanford Dictionary of Anglicised Words and Phrases (First Notice)', *Athenaeum*, 18 March 1893 pp. 341–2; 'Review of Stanford Dictionary of Anglicised Words and Phrases (Second Notice)', *Athenaeum*, 25 March 1893 pp. 372–3.
59 Child (1893: 115).
60 OUP/PUB/11/29. Letter from Murray to Gell 20 October 1892.
61 'Scintille Juris (Indian and English)', *The Indian Jurist Law Journal and Reporter*, 31 October 1892, vol. xvi p. 498.

62 'Review of the Stanford Dictionary of Anglicised Words and Phrases (First Notice)', *Athenaeum,* 18 March 1893 p. 341.
63 'The Stanford Bequest', *The Gentlemen's Magazine,* December 1892 p. 640.
64 'Review of the Stanford Dictionary of Anglicised Words and Phrases (First Notice)', *Athenaeum,* 18 March 1893 p. 341.
65 'The Stanford Bequest', *The Gentlemen's Magazine,* December 1892 pp. 639–40.
66 'The Literature and Language of the Age', *Edinburgh Review,* April 1889 pp. 348 and 349.
67 OUP/PUB/11/29. Letter from Murray to Doble 5 June 1889.
68 MP/15/09/1883. Letter from Fennell to Murray 15 September 1883.
69 OUP/PUB/11/29. Letter from Murray to Gell 20 October 1892.
70 OUP/PUB/11/29. Letter from Murray to Gell 20 October 1892.
71 OUP/PUB/11/29. Letter from Murray to Gell 20 October 1892.
72 The case study analyzed 831 first senses with quotation paragraphs in the *Stanford Dictionary*, which equated to 22.8 percent of the total in *A–Cast* (3638).
73 Only the first sense of multiple-sense entries in the *Stanford Dictionary* was analyzed; in other words, senses after the first sense were not analyzed. Due to the fact that the ordering of senses in the *Stanford Dictionary* is not chronological, it was necessary to ensure that this sampling technique (of choosing the first sense in an entry with a quotation paragraph, and ignoring multiple senses beyond the first) did not have a significant effect on the overall results. Therefore, every sense of a small section of the sample, *cabilliau–calidity,* was analyzed according to the same parameters. A total of 82 senses were analyzed, and the overall findings of the present study were confirmed. The sample of senses with quotation paragraphs common to both dictionaries in the case study equated to approximately 23 percent of all senses with quotation paragraphs (3638) in the section *A–Cast,* and approximately 43 percent of all senses with quotation paragraphs in the combined ranges *abas–arsenal* and *caaba–cantor* (Approx. total number of senses with quotation paragraphs in *A–Cast* = 3638. Approx. total number of senses with quotation paragraphs in the range *abas–arsenal* and *caaba–cantor* = 1921. Therefore, 831 senses with quotation paragraphs = 22.8% of *A–Cast,* and 43.2% of *abas–arsenal* and *caaba–cantor*). The alphabetical ranges *abas–arsenal* and *caaba–cantor* in the *Stanford Dictionary* include approximately 2260 entries, or 53 percent of the entries in *A–Cast* (4280).
74 OUP/PUB/11/29. P. S. in Letter from Murray to Gell 20 October 1892.
75 OUP/PUB/11/29. Letter from Murray to Doble 5 June 1889.
76 The *Stanford Dictionary* antedates 324 words out of a total of 831 in the sample = 40%.
77 Garnett (1895: 96).
78 OUP/PUB/11/29. Letter from Murray to Gell 20 October 1892.
79 I am indebted to Andrew P. Bridges of Winston & Strawn LLP for clarification on the legal definition of plagiarism.
80 The *Stanford Dictionary* and *OED* shared 272 first quotations in the sample, and the *Stanford* acknowledged *OED1* for 190 of these => 69.9%.
81 Although outside the sample, there is an instance in which Fennell over-zealously acknowledged *OED1* for a quotation that did not come from *OED1* (i.e., *calibre* sense 1a).
82 Murray (1880: 175).

83 Fennell (1892: viii).
84 The exact counts were: Flemish 1; Norse 1; Sanskrit 1; Tamil 1; Gaelic 2; Portuguese 2; Turkish 2; Welsh 2; Dutch 3; German 3; Malay 3; Hindi 5; Persian 5; Anglo-Indian 7; English 10; Hebrew 14; Arabic 27; Italian 55; Spanish 70; Greek 127; Latin 225; French 272.
85 The provenance 'English' was given in *Stanford* to words derived in English from Latin, e.g. *abductor*, *adjudicator*, and *alleviator*.
86 I am indebted to Andrew P. Bridges of Winston & Strawn LLP for advice on this point.
87 *OED1* provides earlier quotations than the *Stanford Dictionary* for 152 words in the sample (of 831); this equates to 18.3 percent of the whole sample.
88 OUP/PUB/11/29. Letter from Murray to Gell 20 October 1892.
89 I am indebted to Rod McConchie for this insight.
90 'Literary Notes', *Times,* 7 July 1894 p. 5; 'Notes and News', *The Academy,* 11 August 1894 p. 101.
91 'Notes', *The Critic,* 21 July 1894 p. 46.
92 'Literary Notes', *Times,* 7 July 1894 p. 5.
93 'Notes', *The Critic,* 21 July 1894 p. 46.
94 'The "National" Dictionary of English Language and Literature', *Times,* 26 July 1894 p. 10. *OED1* was advertised for £2 12 s. 6d per volume in 1894 (*Times,* 19 March 1894 p. 12).
95 'The National Dictionary', *Athenaeum,* 30 March 1895 p. 409.
96 OUP Secretary Letterbook 1891 p. 588. Letter from Doble to Bradley 14 May 1891.
97 'Notes', *The Critic,* 21 July 1894 p. 46.
98 Fennell (1895a: 409).
99 OUP Secretary Letterbook 1894 p. 397. Letter from Doble to Frowde 9 July 1894; OUP Secretary Letterbook 1894 p. 399 Letter from Doble to Gell 9 July 1894.
100 MP/8/03/1892. Letter from Bradley to Murray 8 March 1892.
101 OUP/PUB/11/29. Letter from Murray to Gell 20 October 1892.
102 OUP/PUB/11. Handwritten note by C. T. Onions dated 21 May 1938, on letter from Chapman to Sisam 17 May 1938. I am indebted to Chris Stray and Peter Gilliver for this reference.
103 Murray (1900b: 513).
104 Murray (1900b: 513).
105 Bensly (1912: 95).
106 McMorris (2001: 155).
107 OUPA, Oxford Pkt, 138.12, as quoted in McMorris (2001: 155).
108 As quoted in McMorris (2001: 155).

5 William Craigie, Charles Onions, and the mysterious case of the vanishing tramlines

> As in the main work [*OED1*], there has been continually present the problem of the inclusion or omission of the more esoteric scientific terms and of the many foreign words reflecting the widened interest in the conditions and customs of remote countries, and it cannot be hoped or pretended that this problem has been solved in every instance with infallible discretion.
>
> William Craigie and Charles Onions (1933),
> Editors of the 1933 Supplement

The men who succeeded Murray as editors of the *OED* were largely faithful to the lexicographic policies and practices that he had devised in the early 1880s. With respect to loanwords and World Englishes, however, the concept of naturalization – in sound, form, and meaning – changed over time, and as it turns out, in unexpected ways. In particular, the practice of putting tramlines beside headwords considered 'alien or not yet naturalized' was mysteriously dropped in the *1933 Supplement* edited by William Craigie and Charles Onions, and was reinstated for Burchfield's *Supplement* in the 1970s and 1980s.

This chapter started out to solve the mystery of the missing tramlines in the *1933 Supplement*. Just before this book went to press, this mystery was solved quite simply by a chance discovery amongst uncatalogued items in the OUP archives – two pieces of paper confirmed months of detective work. But that detective work was not wasted. The very process of trying to find an answer to the question about the tramlines revealed larger issues about attitudes towards foreign words that were behind what may have seemed an inconsequential omission of a typographical symbol.

The changes in policy and practice between the *1933 Supplement* and the versions of the *OED* that came before and after it reflected changes in policy which are instructive in understanding how attitudes to foreign words changed among the editors. By focusing on the use of tramlines in the *OED Supplements* (both the *1933 Supplement* and Burchfield's *Supplement*), we will see in this chapter how the editors were influenced by their contexts – the period in which they worked, contemporary linguistic scholarship, reception of the dictionary, their own personal interests and travels – and how it is possible to deduce their attitudes to language and culture from their lexicographic practice. It turns out that certain elements of lexicographic practice, which are intended to tell us about the words, actually tell us more about the attitudes of the lexicographers.

One of the things we saw in Chapter 3 was that Bradley and Murray differed in their view of the naturalization process. This chapter will investigate how their younger editors, Craigie and Onions, differed from them, and the best way to do this is to look at the dictionary edited by them: the *1933 Supplement.*

There is immediately one particularly striking difference between the *1933 Supplement* and *OED1*: the number of tramlines. Except for two words, tramlines were effectively abolished in the *1933 Supplement*, only to be reinstated by Burchfield in his Supplement and *OED2* (*OED3* has dropped tramlines).

Tramlines were James Murray's device to denote a word's loan status and degree of naturalization. He and the other *OED1* editors used to count up the number of tramlines in each fascicle and record them in the preface. Proportionally Murray applied the most tramlines, followed by Bradley, and Craigie and Onions who applied the same proportion each.

Why did tramlines vanish in the *1933 Supplement*? Its remit was simply to augment *OED1* with words and senses that needed correction or had not been included during its seventy-year compilation. The *1933 Supplement* editors, Charles Onions and William Craigie, had been Murray's assistants and co-editors on *OED1*; Onions since 1895 and Craigie since 1897.[1] They were both trained by Murray, and chose to apply his lexicographic methods and dictionary layout to the *1933 Supplement.* Their aim was to build on the legacy set for them by Murray, not to develop independent policies that introduced new lexicographic practices. In fact, the preface to the *1933 Supplement* quoted the original Indenture drawn up in 1879 between the Philological Society and the Delegates, which stated that the *Supplement* would be prepared 'on the same terms and in the same manner and form as the said Principal Dictionary'.[2] It is therefore striking that a central part of *OED1* policy on foreign words – the marking of loanwords – was absent from the *1933 Supplement.* This chapter seeks to solve the mystery of the vanishing tramlines in the *1933 Supplement.* It reveals that larger issues about attitudes towards foreign words in English were behind what may have seemed an inconsequential omission of a typographic symbol.

The 1933 *OED* Supplement

First it is necessary to say something about the structure of the *1933 Supplement*, about Craigie and Onions' working relationship given that they were on different sides of the Atlantic, and their editing practices. When *OED1* was finally completed in 1928, work was already under way on a supplement volume. The editors had been gathering materials for a *Supplement* for decades. In fact, since the publication of the first *OED1* fascicle in 1884, the editors of *OED1* had been slowly collecting materials for a *Supplement* – new senses and entries for, and amendments to, parts of the dictionary already published – as they progressed through the alphabet. Materials put aside for the *Supplement* were filed in what was known in-house as the 'Supplement file', which was described in the preface as 'a collection of closely-packed slips occupying some 75 linear feet of shelving'.[3] Words in the *Supplement* were restricted by the confines and purpose of the text, that is, to supplement and to amend the main text of *OED1*; therefore the structure of an entry in the *Supplement* differed slightly from *OED1*. An entry in the *1933 Supplement* was structured in one of two ways, depending on whether it was a new word (Type 1) or an addition or correction to an existing word already in *OED1* (Type 2). Type 2 entries were usually sparser in structure and shorter in length, consisting mainly of a headword and whatever the additional information was (e.g. earlier or later quotations, an added sense or variant form); they did not repeat the entry from *OED1*, therefore most of them lack pronunciations, etymologies, or definitions.

The task of editing the *1933 Supplement* was complicated by the fact that the editors lived on separate continents and communication between them was laboured.[4] Onions and his team were based in Oxford, and Craigie and his team were split between the UK and Chicago, where they were also working on the *Dictionary of American English* (1938–42).

Craigie's team consisted of (in Chicago) Mr H. J. Bayliss, Mr G. Watson, Mr M. M. Mathews; (in the UK) Mr J. M. Wyllie, Mrs Hestletine, and Miss Dorothy E. Marshall. Onions' team was double the size of Craigie's. They were experienced editors who had worked on *OED1*; half of them were women, including the daughters of Murray and Bradley: Mr J. W. Birt, Miss Eleanor Bradley (daughter of Henry), Miss E. V. V. Clark, Miss Evelyn A. Lee, Mr W. J. Lewis, Mr A. T. Maling, Miss Rosfrith Murray (daughter of James), Mr J. L. N. O'Loughlin, Mrs L. F. Powell, Mrs A. S. C. Ross (Miss E. S. Olszewska), Mr F. J. Sweatman, and Mr Walter Worrall. Onions was known to be a vigilant boss who kept his editors to a rigorous regime. Professor Eric Stanley tells an anecdote passed on to him by a member of Onions' team, Mrs Ross: whenever Onions left the office to give a lecture, the staff would all run out of the office to do their shopping or go to the dentist, pretending nothing had happened when Onions returned.[5]

On a practical level, despite the fact that Craigie's team was half the size of Onions' team, Craigie was faster at editing than Onions, handing more slips in a shorter time to the Printer. Craigie was therefore more popular with the OUP publishers.[6] An editor's production rate was calculated on the number of slips handed to the Printer each month (the goal was 4000 slips per month), and

Craigie's team typically produced copy at double the rate of Onions'.[7] There are two reasons why it was not surprising that Onions was slower than Craigie. First, Onions was editing the first part of the alphabet that needed more supplementation because it had been edited longer ago in *OED1*. The two editors managed the project by dividing the alphabet: Onions edited A–K, S, and T, and Craigie edited L–R, U–Z. The bulk of the alphabetical range assigned to Onions (A–K) had been published in *OED1* before 1901 (S and T by 1916); Craigie's range covered the second part of the alphabet most of which had recently been published in the 1920s, and therefore needed less revision.

The second reason why Onions was slower at editing than Craigie was that loanwords generally take longer to edit than other entries of the same number of senses, and Onions included over five times more loanwords than Craigie (this will be revealed in the case study in the next chapter). It is often more difficult with loanwords to find evidence in printed sources (especially overseas sources) and to trace the word's etymology, as it is more time-consuming to check its etymology and definition with a specialist of that language or culture. Loanword entries also generated fewer slips than other entries because they were more likely to be short: usually loanwords for a supplement (as opposed to a parent dictionary) will have been in English for a shorter period and therefore lack multiple senses or large quotation paragraphs. It is also rare for them to have been around long enough to form compounds, which generate a large number of slips and take up space in a dictionary.

James Murray had observed this phenomenon early on in his career. After editing the letters A and B in *OED1*, he noticed one main difference between his work and the work of previous lexicographers such as Bailey, Johnson, Webster, and Ogilvie: although the letter A had more words than B (12,183 and 10,049 respectively) and had always taken up more space than B in earlier dictionaries, in his dictionary the opposite was true: the letter A took up less space than B.[8] The reason for this is central to the nature of a diachronic dictionary: space in a diachronic dictionary is determined by the historical character of the words, not the number of headwords. 'A has a very small proportion of native English or Teutonic words, and a very large proportion of words from Latin (directly or through French), and from Greek', he wrote in the preface to the first volume of *OED1*, and 'B has a much smaller number of words from these sources, and a very large proportion of native Teutonic words.'[9]

Murray's letter A took up less space than B, but it actually had more foreign words than B (550 and 320 with tramlines respectively). For an editor, less space in a dictionary corresponds to fewer slips, but not necessarily less work or time, especially if the words are loanwords. If lexicographic progress on the *1933 Supplement* was being measured by the number of slips, and if we know that Onions included five times more loanwords than Craigie, then it is not surprising that he was judged by the Printer and his superiors as 'slower' than Craigie. If editorial progress was being measured by number of slips, then a good way to work 'quickly' would be to edit fewer loanwords. It is impossible to know if speed was a motivating factor in Craigie's decision to include fewer loanwords. What we do know is that he had an inclination towards verbosity in his dictionary writing. Early on, he had been criticized by Murray for taking up too much space. As Silva (2000) reports, 'Craigie exasperated Murray by exceeding space limits, and Murray appears to have seen his advice as being ignored.'[10] Taking up more space, of course, equated to more slips.

The larger number of loanwords included by Onions may have been a major factor in his slower pace, but this was never explained to the Printer, who was forever frustrated by the fact that Onions handed in fewer than the agreed number of one thousand slips per week.[11] Kenneth Sisam, Assistant Secretary to the Delegates, wrote a pleading note to Onions, saying, 'The position is desperate. Your programme of 1000 [slips] a week seems to have crashed, and all the Printer's arrangements and our publishing plans are in jeopardy.'[12] Onions' rate remained unchanged, and, a fortnight later, an exasperated Sisam wrote to the Printer: 'We are beating them with sticks, but one might as well beat the mist.'[13]

While the OUP publishers put pressure on Onions to increase his speed, they did at least acknowledge that he had the more difficult half of the alphabet. Robert Chapman, Secretary to the Delegates, was trying to arrange an honorary Oxford DLitt for Onions, and part of his argument to the Vice Chancellor was that 'Onions has been in charge of the most difficult part of it [the *1933 Supplement*], which is of course the earlier part, some of which was 40 years old when supplementation began. *Appendicitus* and *Aeroplane* were not in the original book.'[14]

A letter from a member of Craigie's team to Chapman gives an insight into Craigie's policy on loanwords. Explaining why Craigie had deleted *putsch* from the revised proofs, J. M. Wyllie wrote, 'It [*putsch*] is certainly in the first proof, but was deleted, if I remember rightly, on grounds that it was simply a foreign word. We had several newspaper quots [quotations] for it, all referring to one or two particular events in Germany.'[15] However, according to the editing principles set by Murray, 'foreignness' was no reason not to include a foreign word. It was one of the tasks of the lexicographer to determine the distribution and use of a foreign word: if a word were only used in reference to a particular place or context, e.g. only in Germany or relating to events in Germany, then it could still go in the dictionary. Its restricted use could be described by the lexicographer by means of regional labelling or definitional metalanguage of the kind 'In Germany'.

Another incident shows the priority given to loanwords by Onions' team. In 1932, Sisam met the American writer H. L. Mencken, who offered to publish lists of *OED* words that needed antedating in his influential journal *The American Mercury*. Following up on Mencken's offer, Sisam asked both Onions' team and Craigie's team to submit lists of words. It is insightful to compare them: Craigie's team submitted more common and basic vocabulary such as *off, office, on, open, out, peep, phony, punch,* and *put across;* Onions' team, on the other hand, submitted non-basic vocabulary and words of foreign origin such as *ichu,* Peruvian grass; *iiwi,* a Hawaiian bird; *injun,* a name for a Native American; and *Ibanag*, a language of the Philippines. The discrepancy in the content of each list did not go unnoticed by Onions' superior, who replied, 'I have had these lists typed, and am submitting them again for greater scrutiny. There are some very queer words, which will probably defeat the Americans. What, for instance, is a *iiwi*?'[16] In his letter to Mencken, Sisam accompanied the lists with a note warning him of the unusual words on Onions' list, 'I enclose you a list of words in I and O, P, Q, many of which I don't understand, with the dates of the earliest quotations we have already.'[17]

No tramlines in the *1933 Supplement*

Given that Onions and Craigie were both trained by Murray, and aimed to model the *1933 Supplement* 'on the same terms and in the same manner and form as the said Principal Dictionary',[18] it is surprising that a central part of the *OED1* policy on foreign words – the marking of loanwords – was effectively dropped from the *1933 Supplement*. Could it have been a printing error? Could the printer have mistakenly failed to insert the symbol throughout the text? If it was a printer's error, it was not consistent throughout the text because there were tramlines put on two headwords: *kadin*, a Turkish word for a woman of the Sultan's harem, and *rhexis,* a word from Latin and Greek denoting 'the breaking or bursting of the wall of a blood vessel' (Figures 5.1 and 5.2). In addition, a few entries had tramlines on the second pronunciation if it was non-naturalized (e.g. *apache,* a band of robbers in Paris; *estampage,* an impression on paper of an inscription; and *sabotage*, deliberate or organized destruction).

Why are *kadin* and *rhexis* the only headwords with tramlines in the *1933 Supplement*? A comparison with other loanwords in the volume shows no reason why they should be treated differently. The word *kadin* had a spelling that was straightforward for English orthography, and had a pronunciation (/ˈkadɪn/) that provided no difficulty for the English sound system. The word-initial stress and the length of the first vowel showed a degree of naturalization in English that differed from the original Turkish pronunciation (which

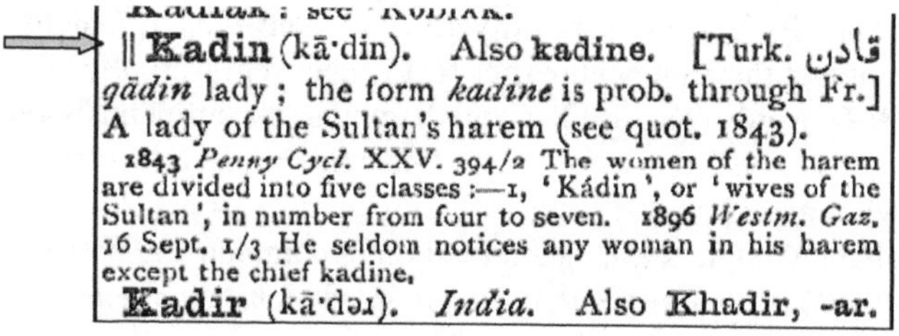
|| **Kadin** (kā·din). Also **kadine.** [Turk. قادن *qādin* lady; the form *kadine* is prob. through Fr.] A lady of the Sultan's harem (see quot. 1843).

1843 *Penny Cycl.* XXV. 394/2 The women of the harem are divided into five classes:—1, 'Kádin', or 'wives of the Sultan', in number from four to seven. 1896 *Westm. Gaz.* 16 Sept. 1/3 He seldom notices any woman in his harem except the chief kadine.

Kadir (kā·dəɹ). *India.* Also **Khadir, -ar.**

Figure 5.1 Entry *kadin* as it appears with tramlines in the *1933 Supplement*. (Credit: OUP)

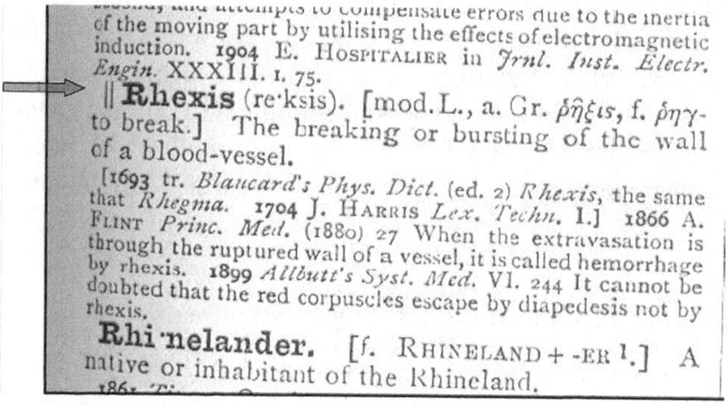
...and attempts to compensate errors due to the inertia of the moving part by utilising the effects of electromagnetic induction. 1904 E. Hospitalier in *Jrnl. Inst. Electr. Engin.* XXXIII. i. 75.

|| **Rhexis** (re·ksis). [mod.L., a. Gr. ῥῆξις, f. ῥηγ- to break.] The breaking or bursting of the wall of a blood-vessel.

[1693 tr. *Blancard's Phys. Dict.* (ed. 2) *Rhexis*, the same that *Rhegma.* 1704 J. Harris *Lex. Techn.* I.] 1866 A. Flint *Princ. Med.* (1880) 27 When the extravasation is through the ruptured wall of a vessel, it is called hemorrhage by rhexis. 1899 *Allbutt's Syst. Med.* VI. 244 It cannot be doubted that the red corpuscles escape by diapedesis not by rhexis.

Rhi·nelander. [f. Rhineland + -er 1.] A native or inhabitant of the Rhineland.

Figure 5.2 Entry *rhexis* as it appears with tramlines in the *1933 Supplement*. (Credit: OUP)

has stress on the final syllable).[19] There were examples in the *1933 Supplement* of non-naturalized pronunciations belonging to headwords without tramlines, such as *bandar,* an Indian monkey, pronounced /ˈbʌndə/ not /ˈbændə/, and *calabazilla,* a wild Mexican squash, pronounced /kælæbəˈθɪljʌ/ not /kælæbəˈzɪlʌ/. There was no obvious reason why *kadin* should have tramlines, if *bandar* and *calabazilla* did not.

It is possible to examine a variety of other features that may have led to the word *kadin* having tramlines, such as etymology, spelling variants, or citational evidence. The word *kadin* was Turkish, but so was *aoul*, 'Tartar village or encampment', and it had no tramlines. *Kadin* had a spelling variant from French (*kadine*) but so did other headwords in the volume. On the level of citational evidence, the word *kadin* only had evidence from two sources, but words on the very same page also only had two citations, such as *kabaka,* 'title of the ruler of Uganda'; *kachcheri,* 'Indian courthouse'; *Kaffrarian*, 'belonging to the country of the Kaffirs'; and *kahili*, 'Hawaiian brush-like implement', all of which lacked tramlines.

One quotation supporting *kadin* was taken from an encyclopaedia (1843 *Penny Cyclopaedia of the Society for the Diffusion of Useful Knowledge*) but encyclopaedias also provided evidence for headwords without tramlines, such as *balisaur,* 'Indian badger-like animal', and *shal,* an African fish. The other supporting quotation for *kadin* was from a newspaper (1896 *Westminster Gazette*) but, again, newspapers supported hundreds of other words in the same volume, all without tramlines.

The citations for *kadin* displayed some typographical features such as inverted commas and diacritics that in *OED1* policy often warranted tramlines. For example, the 1843 quotation displays the form 'Kádin', which is probably denoting word-initial stress rather than vowel quality, but hundreds of other loanwords in the *1933 Supplement* also shared these typographical features, and none of their headwords appeared with tramlines. For example, the headword *balakhana*, 'upper room in a Persian house', had a quotation with the form *bala hané*, and the headword *dhaman*, 'Indian rattle snake', had a quotation with the form *dhåman.*[20]

There was, therefore, nothing unique about *kadin* to warrant it having tramlines while other words did not. Similarly, if we consider the other anomalous word that appears with tramlines, *rhexis,* 'the breaking or bursting of the wall of a blood vessel', we are provided with no further clues to solving the mystery. Rather, the mystery is deepened, and it is not clear why a medical word, used in English since the seventeenth century, should be marked as 'alien or not yet naturalized', when hundreds of others in the same volume were not. A number of hypotheses could explain why: perhaps it was a printer's error; perhaps it was a conscious editorial policy decision; perhaps it was a combination of both. In order to solve this mystery, it is helpful to undertake a more detailed analysis of the text, the editors, their lexicographic policies, and their cultural context.

We saw earlier just how difficult Murray found it to draw the line between denizens and naturals, between words that qualified for tramlines and those that did not; he acknowledged in the preface to the first volume that 'opinions will differ' on the matter. Murray's successors found it just as difficult to draw that line. In the preface of the *1933 Supplement*, Onions and Craigie admitted that 'there has been continually present the problem of the inclusion or omission of the more esoteric scientific terms and of the many foreign words reflecting the widened interest in the conditions and customs of remote countries. It cannot be hoped or pretended that this problem has been solved in every instance with infallible discretion.'[21]

This caveat may have been prompted by an episode that took place just before publication in 1933, involving an adviser on words relating to India, Colonel H. G. Le Mesurier (1873–1940).[22] After reading the *1933 Supplement* proofs, Le Mesurier complained that some 'obscure' Indian words (which he had never heard of) had found their way into the dictionary, such as *chauki,* 'policeman or official; a police station', and *lunkah* 'type of cigar'. He also queried the spelling of the headword *daye* for *dai,* 'a nurse in Northern India and Persia'.[23] 'There is a really bad example in D', wrote Le Mesurier, 'The quite common memsahib's word, usually written *dai* and always pronounced dī, meaning wet-nurse, appears as *daye* pronounced dah'ī! I failed to recognize it at first.' In addition to querying *daye* for *dai,* Le Mesurier questioned the inclusion of *lunkah* and *chauki*; he reported that in all his twenty years of living in India, 'never did I hear of a lunkah'.[24]

On one level it is not surprising that Le Mesurier had not heard of a *lunkah* – after all, as Murray repeatedly said during his career, 'no one man's English is *all* English'.[25] On another level, it is perhaps surprising that Le Mesurier had never heard of *lunkah* (*lunka*) and *chauki* (*choky*), as variants of both words had already appeared in both *Hobson-Jobson* (1886) and *OED1* (*choky* was published by Murray in 1889 and *lunkah* by Bradley in 1903). The word *choky*, from Hindi *chauki,* had been substantiated in *Hobson-Jobson* by eight quotations spanning four centuries, from circa 1590 to 1810, and in *OED1* by ten quotations from 1608 to 1884 (covering three senses). The word *lunkah* had been defined in *Hobson-Jobson* as 'a kind of strong cheroot much prized in the Madras Presidency, and so called from being made of tobacco grown in the "islands" (the local term for which is *lañka*) of the Godavery Delta'. *OED1* supported *lunkah* by a solitary quotation from Conan Doyle's *Sign of Four* (1889): 'Some murder has been done by a man who was smoking an Indian lunkah.'

In India, as implied by the *Hobson-Jobson* definition, the use of the word *lunkah* was confined to southern India and the Madras Province, or 'Madras Presidency', which included Tamil Nadu, Kerala, Lakshadweep Islands, Andhra Pradesh, Orissa, Dakshina Kannada, and Karnataka. This regional localism could have been captured in the *OED1* entry by the use of definitional metalanguage of the type 'In southern India:', but Bradley did not do so. The *1933 Supplement* slips for *lunkah* no longer exist, and the word did not appear in the final *1933 Supplement* text, so it is difficult to know why the word appeared in the proofs, but perhaps Craigie (the word fell in Craigie's half of the alphabet) was going to add this metalanguage to show its regionality.

Because the word *chauki* was mainly confined to northern India and the word *lunkah* was used mainly in southern India, Le Mesurier presumed that the editors 'have been advised by someone who knows only a single Province, which is fatal'.[26] Le Mesurier suggested that Anglo-Indian words in the *OED* should be vetted by a committee of retired Indian civil servants from different regions of India, e.g. Bombay, Bengal, Madras, the Punjab, and Uttar Pradesh, but this never happened.[27] Apart from showing that he understood little about the process of creating an historical dictionary (it was usually the readers who found quotations, not the advisers), Le Mesurier was living proof of his own point: he did not know these words because he had not been exposed to their use in the regions of India from whence they came, therefore it would have been important for the *OED* editors not to rely solely on Le Mesurier's advice.

Le Mesurier complained that the word *lunkah* was so obscure that he had difficulty finding anyone in his home town of Exmouth who had heard of the word. He wrote: 'This place [Exmouth] is full of ancient Qui Hais . . . and I endeavoured to trace the word [*lunkah*]. At last I found a man of 75 who had spent forty years in India; he remembered, *as a child*, having heard the word in Madras – he called it a local word.'[28] It could be argued, of course, that this is precisely why the word *lunkah* should be in a dictionary: so that, at the very least, readers of Conan Doyle in British seaside towns, such as Exmouth, could look it up. This word's use by a high-profile writer such as Conan Doyle would have increased the word's chances of a wide readership that may well have gone to the *OED* to seek a meaning for the word.

Murray's comment on the ignorance of people who 'assumed that their English was all English' could just as easily be levelled at Britons living in the Empire who presumed that their exposure to Indian, Australian, or South African English was all Indian, Australian, or South African English.[29] The *OED* lexicographers knew that just because Colonel Le Mesurier had not heard a term, and just because other 'strays' might get into the dictionary 'because some writer in search of local colour picked them up' (as Sisam described some foreign words in the *Quarto Oxford Dictionary*[30]), the word should not automatically be excluded from an historical dictionary. Its presence in a synchronic dictionary might be questioned if its currency was in doubt, but if documentary evidence existed for its use at some point in history, then it deserved a place in an historical dictionary. This is one of the ways in which a diachronic dictionary differs from a synchronic dictionary, and in this case perhaps Le Mesurier was conflating the nature and purpose of the two; he had after all assisted Fowler on the *Concise Oxford Dictionary* and the *Pocket Oxford Dictionary*, and went on himself to edit a synchronic dictionary, the 4th edition of the *Pocket Oxford Dictionary of Current English* (1946).

Different readers could highlight different words from the same book, depending on their own understanding of the dictionary's remit and their own concepts of the borders of the English language, as the example of Miss Blomfield and Mr Griffith in Chapter 2 illustrated. A reader's subjectivity could result in loanwords and World Englishes being missed. The episode with Le Mesurier shows how different books could highlight words from different regions within the same variety of English, and those regional nuances could easily be missed by the dictionary editor who compiled the entry. The *OED* entry for *lunkah* would have benefited from the editor specifying its regional (southern) usage and from more than one solitary citation (even though it was from a high-profile author like Conan Doyle). And there is no clear reason for Onions choosing *daye* as the headword spelling for *dai* (in fact the spelling *daye* does not occur in a single one of the seven quotations, whereas the spelling *dai* occurs in the two most recent [1920 and 1927] citations). Indian English, like all varieties of English, contains variation – in register and region – and the challenge for the lexicographer is to pick up and describe these nuances.

Loanwords provided problems for the editors because of the nature of the borrowing process, a process that often involves a donor language and a borrowing language with different linguistic structures so the loanword undergoes certain adjustments, or naturalization of sound, orthography, meaning, or morphology. If tramlines were used to gauge this process of naturalization – as they clearly were used in the prefaces of each volume of *OED1* – then the question remains as to why *kadin* and *rhexis* were the only headwords with tramlines in the *1933 Supplement*. Both words had features that made them eligible for tramlines, but neither had features that made them unique and more eligible for tramlines than the other loanwords in the volume. Therefore it is highly likely that there is another reason why only these two words had tramlines.

Tramlines in the *1933 Supplement* proofs

To add further confusion to the mystery, first proofs and first-revise proofs in the *OED* archives show that at one time in its making, the *1933 Supplement* had tramlines on hundreds of words (Figure 5.4). In fact, nearly every page had a word with tramlines; words already referred to, such as *aoul* and *banda,* had tramlines (Figure 5.3).

These proofs, dated 1928 and 1929, were sent from William Craigie, based in Chicago, to his co-editor Charles Onions in Oxford.[31] Something happened between 11 September 1929 and the final publication date to explain why the tramlines disappeared in the interim.

It could be argued that since these were American proofs, they represent Craigie's tramline policy and that Onions had a 'no tramline' policy which, because he was based in Oxford, eventually won out in the end. This is not the case: in the proofs there is evidence of Onions adding tramlines to words without them. For example, he inserted tramlines by hand beside the headwords *bauera*, a plant in Tasmania, and *bauhinia*, a plant growing in the tropics of Africa and Australia (Figure 5.5).

One may argue that it is not possible to know whether these editorial marginalia were written by Onions, when in fact Onions had a team of twelve

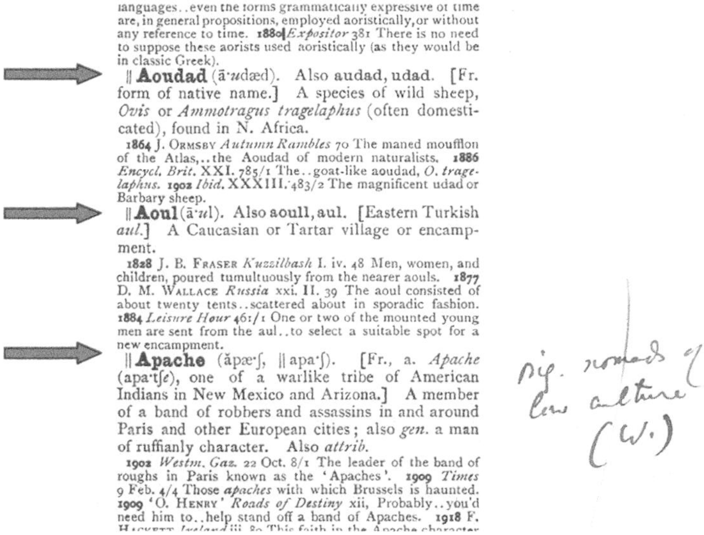
languages..even the forms grammatically expressive of time are, in general propositions, employed aoristically, or without any reference to time. 1880 *Expositor* 381 There is no need to suppose these aorists used aoristically (as they would be in classic Greek).

‖ **Aoudad** (ā·udæd). Also **audad, udad.** [Fr. form of native name.] A species of wild sheep, *Ovis* or *Ammotragus tragelaphus* (often domesticated), found in N. Africa.

1864 J. ORMSBY *Autumn Rambles* 70 The maned moufflon of the Atlas,..the Aoudad of modern naturalists. 1886 *Encycl. Brit.* XXI. 785/1 The..goat-like aoudad, *O. tragelaphus.* 1902 *Ibid.* XXXIII. 483/2 The magnificent udad or Barbary sheep.

‖ **Aoul** (ā·ul). Also **aoull, aul.** [Eastern Turkish *aul.*] A Caucasian or Tartar village or encampment.

1828 J. B. FRASER *Kuzzilbash* I. iv. 48 Men, women, and children, poured tumultuously from the nearer aouls. 1877 D. M. WALLACE *Russia* xxi. II. 39 The aoul consisted of about twenty tents..scattered about in sporadic fashion. 1884 *Leisure Hour* 461/1 One or two of the mounted young men are sent from the aul..to select a suitable spot for a new encampment.

‖ **Apache** (ăpæ·ʃ, ‖ apa·ʃ). [Fr., a. *Apache* (apa·tʃe), one of a warlike tribe of American Indians in New Mexico and Arizona.] A member of a band of robbers and assassins in and around Paris and other European cities; also *gen.* a man of ruffianly character. Also *attrib.*

1902 *Westm. Gaz.* 22 Oct. 8/1 The leader of the band of roughs in Paris known as the 'Apaches'. 1909 *Times* 9 Feb. 4/4 Those *apaches* with which Brussels is haunted. 1909 'O. HENRY' *Roads of Destiny* xii, Probably..you'd need him to..help stand off a band of Apaches. 1918 F.

Figure 5.3 First revise proofs of the *1933 Supplement*, showing tramlines on *aoudad*, *aoul*, and *apache*. (Credit: OUP)

others working with him. However, we can deduce this from a note on the previous page, in the same ink and hand, signed by Onions (Figure 5.6). The note reads: '*Bat willow* shd go in. Heard in conversn. 13/12/28 CTO.' Therefore, the mystery remains as to why all of the tramlines (except two) disappeared by the time of publication in 1933.

The reason for dropping tramlines in the *1933 Supplement*

In order to discover why the tramlines were dropped from the *1933 Supplement*, we need to fast-forward a few decades to the next Chief Editor of the *OED*, Robert Burchfield, the man whose dictionary was based on the *1933 Supplement*, and the editor who re-instated tramlines. He had noticed the missing tramlines and had asked himself this same question, as a series of three letters indicates. The first letter, dated 5 February 1963, is from Professor Eric Stanley, now Emeritus Professor of English at Oxford but then Lecturer in English at Queen Mary College, London.[32] The letter was addressed to Dan Davin, Assistant Secretary and Publisher of OUP. It was a response to a sample specimen of Burchfield's Supplement sent out to advisers in January 1963.[33] The last line of Stanley's letter says, 'It is

A NEW

ENGLISH DICTIONARY

SUPPLEMENT.

Figure 5.4 First page of revised proofs of the *1933 Supplement* showing the use of tramlines, dated 17 July 1928. (Credit: OUP)

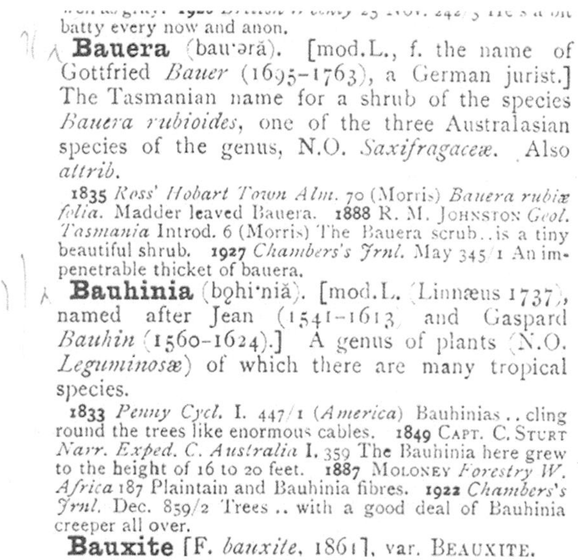

batty every now and anon.

Bauera (bau·ərǎ). [mod.L., f. the name of Gottfried *Bauer* (1695–1763), a German jurist.] The Tasmanian name for a shrub of the species *Bauera rubioides*, one of the three Australasian species of the genus, N.O. *Saxifragaceæ*. Also *attrib.*

1835 *Ross' Hobart Town Alm.* 70 (Morris) *Bauera rubiæ folia*. Madder leaved Bauera. 1888 R. M. JOHNSTON *Geol. Tasmania* Introd. 6 (Morris) The Bauera scrub..is a tiny beautiful shrub. 1927 *Chambers's Jrnl.* May 345/1 An impenetrable thicket of bauera.

Bauhinia (bǫhi·niǎ). [mod.L. (Linnæus 1737), named after Jean (1541–1613) and Gaspard *Bauhin* (1560–1624).] A genus of plants (N.O. *Leguminosæ*) of which there are many tropical species.

1833 *Penny Cycl.* I. 447/1 (*America*) Bauhinias..cling round the trees like enormous cables. 1849 CAPT. C. STURT *Narr. Exped. C. Australia* I. 359 The Bauhinia here grew to the height of 16 to 20 feet. 1887 MOLONEY *Forestry W. Africa* 187 Plaintain and Bauhinia fibres. 1922 *Chambers's Jrnl.* Dec. 859/2 Trees .. with a good deal of Bauhinia creeper all over.

Bauxite [F. *bauxite*, 1861], var. BEAUXITE.

Figure 5.5 First revise proofs of *1933 Supplement*, showing insertion of tramlines by Onions. (Credit: OUP)

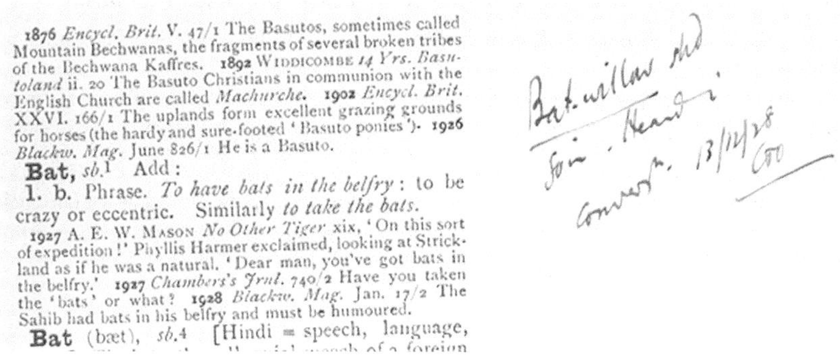

1876 *Encycl. Brit.* V. 47/1 The Basutos, sometimes called Mountain Bechwanas, the fragments of several broken tribes of the Bechwana Kaffres. 1892 WIDDICOMBE *14 Yrs. Basutoland* ii. 20 The Basuto Christians in communion with the English Church are called *Machurche*. 1902 *Encycl. Brit.* XXVI. 166/1 The uplands form excellent grazing grounds for horses (the hardy and sure-footed 'Basuto ponies'). 1926 *Blackw. Mag.* June 826/1 He is a Basuto.

Bat, *sb.*[1] Add:

1. b. Phrase. *To have bats in the belfry*: to be crazy or eccentric. Similarly *to take the bats*.

1927 A. E. W. MASON *No Other Tiger* xix. 'On this sort of expedition!' Phyllis Harmer exclaimed, looking at Strickland as if he was a natural. 'Dear man, you've got bats in the belfry.' 1927 *Chambers's Jrnl.* 740/2 Have you taken the 'bats' or what? 1928 *Blackw. Mag.* Jan. 17/2 The Sahib had bats in his belfry and must be humoured.

Bat (bæt), *sb.*[4] [Hindi = speech, language,

Figure 5.6 First revise proofs of *1933 Supplement* showing Onions' handwriting. (Credit: OUP)

probably too much to hope for the re-introduction of the symbol || for a foreign word.' Dan Davin obviously sent a copy of this letter to Burchfield, who wrote in the margin 'we will be using ||' (Figure 5.7).

Therefore, Burchfield was aware that tramlines were missing from the *1933 Supplement*, and he consciously decided to re-instate them in his *Supplement*. While Burchfield knew tramlines were missing from the *1933 Supplement*, did he in fact know why? The second letter is a copy of the first

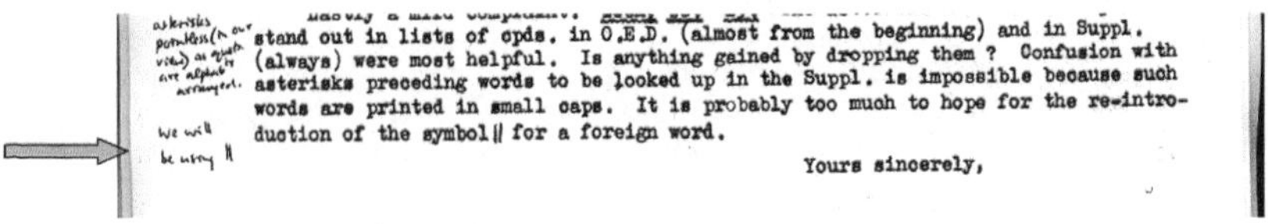
stand out in lists of cpds. in O.E.D. (almost from the beginning) and in Suppl. (always) were most helpful. Is anything gained by dropping them ? Confusion with asterisks preceding words to be looked up in the Suppl. is impossible because such words are printed in small caps. It is probably too much to hope for the re-introduction of the symbol ‖ for a foreign word.

We will be using ‖

Yours sincerely,

Figure 5.7 Extract from a letter from Eric Stanley to Dan Davin, 5 February 1963, with Burchfield's marginalia 'we will be using ‖.' (Credit: OUP)

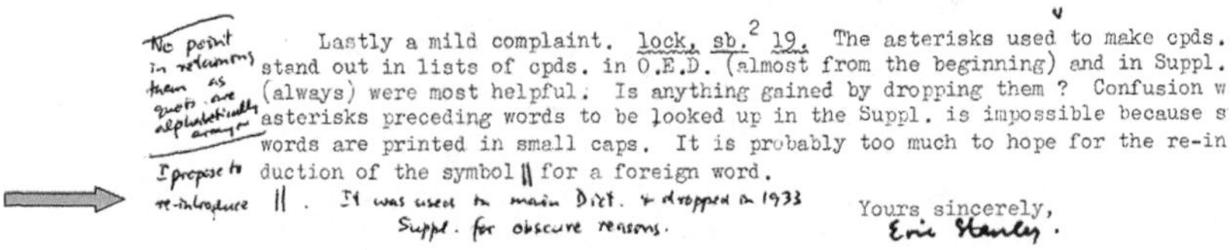
Lastly a mild complaint. lock, sb.² 19. The asterisks used to make cpds. stand out in lists of cpds. in O.E.D. (almost from the beginning) and in Suppl. (always) were most helpful. Is anything gained by dropping them ? Confusion w asterisks preceding words to be looked up in the Suppl. is impossible because s words are printed in small caps. It is probably too much to hope for the re-in duction of the symbol ‖ for a foreign word.

I propose to re-introduce ‖. It was used in main Dict. & dropped in 1933 Suppl. for obscure reasons.

Yours sincerely,
Eric Stanley.

Figure 5.8 Extract from a copy of a letter from Eric Stanley to Dan Davin, 5 February 1963, with Burchfield's marginalia, 'I propose to re-introduce ‖. It was used in main Dict. and dropped in 1933 Suppl. for obscure reasons.' (Credit: OUP)

letter with new Burchfield marginalia. He writes, 'I propose to re-introduce ‖. It was used in main Dict. and dropped in 1933 Suppl. for obscure reasons' (Figure 5.8).

A third letter explains these 'obscure reasons'. It is a copy of Dan Davin's reply to Eric Stanley, dated 7 February 1963 (Figure 5.9).[34] Davin gave Burchfield a copy, and Burchfield wrote in the margin, '‖ ought to go back. Was dropped in 1933 when SPE was flourishing – they preached a doctrine of 'pure English' which I could not accept – writing 'tamber' for *timbre*, etc. R.W.B.' Davin replies 'I agree about ‖'.

The *OED* and the Society for Pure English (SPE)

Burchfield's three letters show that he consciously decided to re-instate tramlines in his four-volume *Supplement*, and that he believed they were dropped from the *1933 Supplement* because of the influence of the Society for Pure English (SPE). This Society had strong connections with the *OED* and in order to learn more about it, we need to go back to 1913, when four leading intellectuals gathered in the home of Poet Laureate, Robert Bridges (1844–1930), at Boar's Hill on the outskirts of Oxford, to discuss the future of the English language. Bridges and three friends – the *OED* editor, Henry Bradley, the Oxford professor of English Sir Walter

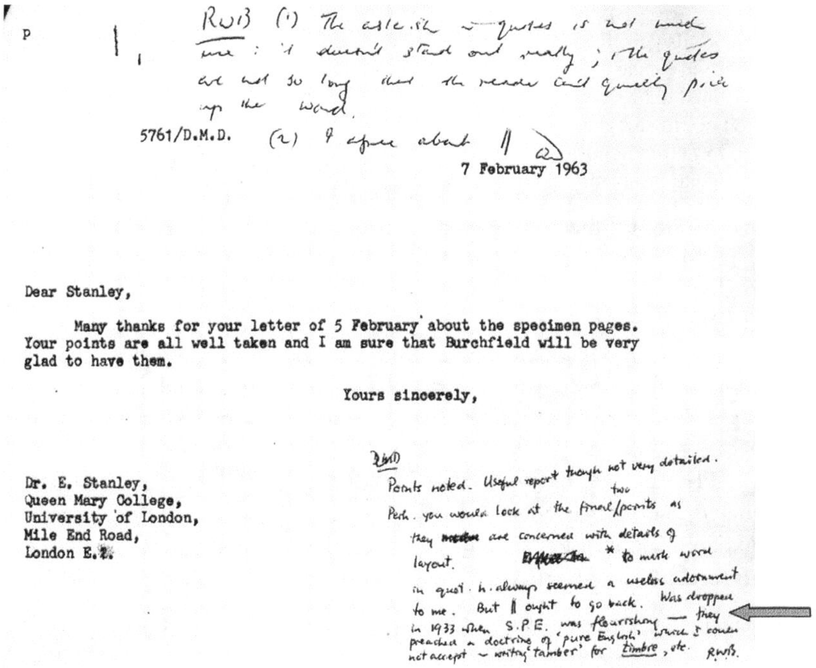

P

RWB (1) The asterisk ~ quotes is not much use: it doesn't stand out really; & the quotes are not so long that the reader can't quickly pick up the word.

5761/D.M.D. (2) I agree about ||

7 February 1963

Dear Stanley,

Many thanks for your letter of 5 February about the specimen pages. Your points are all well taken and I am sure that Burchfield will be very glad to have them.

Yours sincerely,

Dr. E. Stanley,
Queen Mary College,
University of London,
Mile End Road,
London E.1.

RWB
Points noted. Useful report though not very detailed.
Perh. you would look at the final/two points as they are concerned with details of layout. * to mark word in quot. h. always seemed a useless adornment to me. But || ought to go back. Was dropped in 1933 when S.P.E. was flourishing — they preached a doctrine of 'pure English' which I could not accept ~ writing 'tamber' for timbre, etc. RWB.

Figure 5.9 Copy of a letter from Dan Davin to Eric Stanley, 7 February 1963, with Burchfield marginalia, '|| ought to go back. Was dropped in 1933 when SPE was flourishing – they preached a doctrine of "pure English" which I could not accept – writing "tamber" for *timbre*, etc. R.W.B.' (Credit: OUP)

Raleigh (1861–1922), and the literary critic Logan Pearsall Smith (1865–1946) – were concerned that foreign words entering English were not being properly assimilated. With the aim that words should not retain their foreign spelling and pronunciation in English, they founded a society called 'The Society for Pure English' (SPE) whose initial membership consisted of Britain's literary elite and eventually grew internationally. Their concern was that 'our borrowed terms are now spelt and pronounced, not as English, but as foreign words, instead of being assimilated, as they were in the past, and brought into conformity with the main structure of our speech'.[35] Hence, the reference to 'pure English' in the title did not mean that English speakers should not borrow foreign words, but rather, once they did borrow them, they should assimilate them and pronounce and spell them as they would other English words, that is, without a foreign accent, diacritics, or italics.

Logan Pearsall Smith described the Society's foundation in this way:

A few of us were talking one afternoon in that home of leisurely conversation, the library of Chilswell [Robert Bridges' home in Boar's Hill] – the date must have been somewhere in January 1913 – about the state of the English language and the dangers which seemed to be threatening it under modern conditions. How would it be possible, we asked . . . to safeguard our inherited form of speech from some at least of these dangers, to help defend its integrity and beauty, and make it, perhaps, into an even more adequate means of expression for modern ideas?[36]

The first list of SPE members included prominent figures such as Walter de la Mare, E. M. Forster, and Thomas Hardy. OUP and the *OED* were well-represented: not only was *OED* editor Henry Bradley a founder, but Murray and Craigie were also members, along with the Fowler brothers, and Horace Hart, Controller of OUP and author of the style guide *Hart's Rules*. The SPE existed until 1953, and during its forty years of existence it published a series of sixty-six tracts containing articles and comments on all aspects of the English language.

The SPE was not only concerned that foreign words were not being assimilated, but that 'even words that were once naturalized are being now one by one made un-English, and driven out of the language back into their foreign forms.' Moreover,

The mere printing of such words in italics is an active force towards degeneration. The Society hopes to discredit this tendency, and it will endeavour to restore to English its old reactive energy; when a choice is possible we should wish to give an English pronunciation and spelling to useful foreign words, and we would attempt to restore to a good many words the old English forms which they once had, but which are now supplanted by the original foreign forms.[37]

These concerns were in reaction to a fashion in the late-nineteenth century to pronounce and spell foreign words as they would be spelled and pronounced in their donor language. Bridges and his colleagues displayed a sense of paternalistic responsibility to their language. If English was spreading at such a fast rate as a global language, then its speakers had a responsibility to maintain its quality, they argued. 'The English language is spreading all over the world', wrote Bridges, 'this is a condition over which we have no control. It . . . entails a vast responsibility and imposes on our humanity the duty to do what we can to make our current speech as good a means as possible for intercommunication of ideas.'[38] It is not surprising, then, that the SPE gradually attracted the attention of English speakers around the world. The final list of SPE members, recorded in 1946, shows that the Society had taken on a truly international membership, with 40% of its membership outside Britain: for example, individual members in Iraq, Egypt, New Zealand, Brazil, and Argentina; and university library memberships in North America, Australia, Sri Lanka (Ceylon), and India.[39]

Concerned that words such as *confrere, congee, cortege, dishabille, distrait, ensemble, fete, flair, mellay* (now *melee*), *nonchalance, provenance, renconter* were 'being driven out of the language', Logan Pearsall Smith urged other members of the SPE to anglicize foreign words and to naturalize their pronunciation. 'Members of our Society', he wrote, 'will, we hope, do what is in their power to stop this process of impoverishment, by writing and pronouncing as English such words as have already been naturalized, and when a new borrowing appears in two forms they will give their preference to the one which is most English. . . . If we are to use foreign words (and, if we have no equivalents, we must use them) it is certainly much better that they should be incorporated in our language, and made available for common use.'[40]

The SPE led a successful campaign in the 1920s to assimilate loanwords in English by consciously reforming their spelling and pronunciation. In 1920, they recommended that *role, debris, detour, depot* should drop their diacritics and that *rendezvous, dilettante,* and *vogue* should not be italicized. 'The printing in italics and the restoration of foreign accents', wrote Pearsall Smith, 'is accompanied by awkward attempts to revert to the foreign pronunciation of these words, which of course much lessens their usefulness in conversation.'[41] He warned that foreign words risked disappearing from use if they were not naturalized in sound and spelling. 'Sometimes this, as in *nuance*, or *timbre*, practically deprives us of a word which most of us are unable to pronounce correctly; sometimes it is merely absurd, as in "envelope", where most people try to give a foreign sound to a word which no one regards as an alien, and which has been anglicized in spelling for nearly two hundred years.'[42]

In November 1923, the SPE circulated a table of Rules to national newspapers, leading journalists, and prominent writers. The table listed alternative spellings for 'foreign forms and French words in italics', such as *debris* for *débris, bandits* for *banditti, medieval* for *mediæval*, and *formulas* for *formulæ*. The Rules were adopted by the editors of the *Times* and the *London Mercury*.[43]

It is important to consider how the SPE and their campaign might have influenced William Craigie and Charles Onions, particularly in their role as editors of the *1933 Supplement*. After Bradley's death in 1923, Craigie increased his involvement with the Society. He joined the committee in 1925, the same year he moved from Oxford to Chicago, and he remained actively involved until its end. Craigie contributed articles to ten tracts between 1927 and 1946 and kept the SPE going (in his role as Secretary) during the war years.[44] Onions never joined the SPE, but he contributed to five tracts between 1924 and 1931.[45] Onions' son, Giles Onions, believes the reason his father never joined was financial: with ten children to support,

Charles Onions never paid subscriptions of any sort.[46] The two editors wrote on topics as diverse as British English, Scottish English, and American English (Craigie),[47] and French words in English (Onions).[48] Their colleagues at OUP wrote on the finer points of particular lexis (Bradley), English syllabification (Sisam), Oxford English (Chapman), and English usage in newspapers (Henry Fowler).

Given Onions' and Craigie's close involvement with the SPE, it seems likely that Burchfield was right when he said in his third letter that tramlines in the *1933 Supplement* were 'dropped in 1933 when SPE was flourishing – they preached a doctrine of "pure English" which I could not accept – writing "tamber" for *timbre*, etc. R.W.B.'

The Word *timbre* and the SPE's influence on the *OED*

In referring to the word *tamber,* Burchfield was not simply making a random reference, but was, rather, recalling a particular controversy of the 1920s, for which the SPE was still remembered at the time of his writing in the 1960s, and which indicated, in sharp form, SPE policy and its effects on a generation of literary figures, including the editors of the *OED*. Robert Bridges had sparked debate in 1920, when he had challenged England's literary set, and 'professors and doctors of music', to pronounce the word *timbre* as an English word, not as a French word. 'Now how is this word to be Englished?' he asked in an SPE tract, 'is the spelling or pronunciation to stand?'[49] The word had already been described in the pages of *OED1* as 'the character or quality of a musical or vocal sound'. James Murray had published the entry for *timbre* n^3 in 1912 with tramlines and a French pronunciation '(tẽñbr').' According to the dictionary, *timbre* was first used in print by Charlotte Brontë in *Shirley* (1849): 'Your voice ... has another "timbre" than that hard, deep organ of Miss Mann's.' Unusually for *OED* practice, Murray highlighted the word's French pronunciation by adding a comment at the end of the etymology that read 'the word has passed into English use retaining its French pronunciation'. Of all the French words that entered English in 1879, retaining their pronunciations (for example, *boulevardier* or *soufflé),* it is curious that Murray should only make a point of stressing the French pronunciation of *timbre.*

Bridges and the SPE were recommending that English speakers start pronouncing *timbre* as /'tæmbəɹ/ and spelling it as 'tamber'. He wrote:

> We generally use *timbre* in italics and pronounce it as French ... the English pronunciation of the letters of *timbre* is forbidden by its homophone ... whereas our English form of the French sound of the French word would be approximately *tamber*; and this would be not only a good English-sounding word like *amber* and *clamber*, but would be like our *tambour* which is *tympanum* which again is *timbre*. So that if our professors

and doctors of music were brave, they would speak and write *tamber*, which would be not only English but perfectly correct etymologically.[50]

The following year, Brander Matthews (1852–1929), Professor of Dramatic Literature at Columbia University, wrote an article on 'The Englishing of French Words' in which he supported Bridges' suggestion: 'I can only register here my complete concurrence with the opinion expressed in Tract III of the Society for Pure English – that the English form of the French sound of the word [timbre] should be tamber.'[51]

In 1922, an anonymous SPE correspondent wrote saying that she or he was 'impatiently awaiting' the 'practical adoption' of tamber.[52] Other SPE supporters also took to the task of writing and pronouncing *timbre* as *tamber*. For example, Roger Fry (1866–1934), a member of the SPE and the man responsible for bringing post-Impressionist art to England, used 'tamber' in the *Nation and Athenaeum* when he wrote about French art: 'The local colours here maintain a separate and distinct quality almost as definite throughout their various changes as the tambers of flute, oboe, and violin in a symphony.'[53] However, the SPE's conscious reform did not escape criticism. The following week a letter of complaint appeared in the same journal under the title 'Tamber':

> Mr Roger Fry has every reason to disport himself as he pleases. In spelling 'timbre' as he does, he has behind him ... the authority of Mr Logan Pearsall Smith (SPE Tract III), supported by a correspondent in Tract X, the analogies being amber, camber, and chamber. Thus it is not by chance but by principle that Mr Fry is trying to impose upon us a pronunciation – not a spelling only – which all those from whom I have inquired dislike ... Most people, I am almost sure, if they say timbre rather than tone or quality, pronounce it in French, even if it be in what Mr Eliot would call demotic French. I suspect that Mr Fry does also. Why try to standardize an unusual pronunciation?[54]

The letter was from Bonamy Dobrée (1891–1974), an English scholar and drama critic who ten years later was to become Professor of English Literature at Leeds University. He ended the letter with a humorous quip: 'So is it not, Sir, a vain, as well as an ungainly thing, to timpre with our spelling?'[55] In disagreeing with the use of *tamber* for *timbre*, Dobrée was clearly against one of the SPE's core objectives – as he put it – to 'try to standardise an unusual pronuniciation', and yet he was listed as a member of the Society in 1933 and 1942.[56] Although a good friend of many other members, Dobrée was not listed as a member in 1919, and no list of members exists between 1920 and 1933, so it is impossible to find out whether he was a member at the time of writing his letter to the *Nation and Athenaeum* in 1926. It is difficult to find out whether Dobrée changed his views on systematic linguistic naturalization between the time of writing his letter in 1926 and being listed as a member of SPE in 1933. But it is worth noting that he wrote the letter just after finishing a year of teaching at East London College (London University) and editing Congreve's *Comedies* (1925), and just before leaving London for four years in Cairo as Professor of English at the Egyptian University. Though hypothetical, it is not improbable that Dobrée's stint in Egypt changed his view on foreign words in English.

In 1929, Richard Capell of the *Daily Mail* published an article about music entitled 'Let's Have Plain English!', in which he suggested replacing *timbre* with 'tamber', *quartet* with 'foursome', and spelling *cello* as 'chello' and *oboe* as the Old English 'hoboy'' The *Musical Times* responded by recommending that 'the red badge of courage should be bestowed on the journalist who deliberately writes "tamber", and an even higher reward should be devised for the one who is more logical, and (like Mr Capell with chello) anglicises the spoken word and bravely called it "timber".'[57]

Writing 'tamber' for *timbre* never really caught on in general use, but continued in certain domains, such as linguistics. Perhaps influenced by the SPE campaign, the phonetician Daniel Jones changed his spelling of *timbre* to 'tamber' in between the second and third editions of his *Outline of English Phonetics* published in 1922 and 1932 respectively. For example, in describing a resonance chamber he wrote in 1932, 'The tamber of this sound depends on the length of the part of the cylinder projecting beyond the piston.'[58] The same passage appeared ten years earlier in the earlier edition, before the *timbre* controversy reached its height, with the spelling *timbre*, 'The quality (timbre) of this sound depends on the length of the part of the cylinder projecting beyond the piston.'[59]

The different editions of Jones' famous *English Pronouncing Dictionary* also show the possible influence of the SPE. The 1917 (first) edition only has an entry for *timbre* not 'tamber', but the 1937 (fourth) edition has entries for both *timbre* and *tamber*.[60] In the first edition, he lists three different pronunciations for timbre: first, /tɛmbr/; second, the pronunciation /tæmbə/ which appears in square brackets denoting that it is 'the less frequent form'; and a third variant /tɛ:br/ in parentheses reserved for 'borrowed foreign words which are pronounced in the foreign way or nearly so by many of the persons referred to in §7 of the Introduction' (i.e. 'Southern English persons whose men-folk have been educated at the great public boarding-schools').[61] The later (1937) edition lists one pronunciation for *tamber* /ˈtæmbə/, and makes no changes to the three variant pronunciations for *timbre* listed in the first edition.

It is not easy to gauge to what extent Jones was influenced by the SPE in his rendering of the pronunciation of *timbre*. After all, Jones' inclusion of *tamber* in the 1930s may solely be a reflection of the word's widespread use in the media and academia. On the other hand, the word's use may not have been so widespread had it not been for the SPE's conscious efforts to reform its spelling and pronunciation. It is always difficult to disentangle use and policy when they coincide historically. Other linguists followed Daniel Jones, such as John Rupert (J. R.) Firth, who was his colleague in the Department of Phonetics at University College London.[62] He and Jones appear never to have joined the SPE, but Jones did contribute to four SPE tracts between 1919 and 1946.[63]

Given that both Craigie and Onions were involved with the SPE in the 1920s, it is likely that they shared its policy on the assimilation of loanwords and therefore possible that this manifested itself in new *OED* policy for the *1933 Supplement*. For example, one way, lexicographically, of showing a word's assimilation in English would be not to differentiate it from other words, that is, not to give it a different status by marking it with tramlines denoting that it was 'alien and not yet naturalized'.

Can we be sure that Burchfield's explanation was right? Charles Onions' son, Giles, says that for the last eight years of his father's life (between 1957 and 1965) Robert Burchfield cycled to the Onions family home most afternoons to visit his father. It is worth noting that two days passed between the second and third letters (5 and 7 February 1963; Figures 5.7 and 5.8 respectively) discussed earlier, in which Burchfield went from writing that tramlines were 'dropped in *1933 Supplement* for obscure reasons' to writing that tramlines were 'dropped in 1933 when SPE was flourishing – they preached a doctrine of "pure English" which I could not accept – writing "tamber" for *timbre*, etc. R.W.B.' Though this is merely conjectural, it is possible that during these two days, Burchfield visited Onions and heard about tramline policy and the influence of the Society for Pure English from Onions himself.

Murray had published *timbre* in *OED1* in 1912, a year before the SPE was founded, with tramlines and a non-naturalized French pronunciation '(tē̃nbr')'. The entry had no mention of the alternate spelling *tamber* nor pronunciation /ˈtæmbəɹ/, until it was added by Burchfield in 1986. Indeed, Burchfield had found enough evidence (especially in texts pertaining to linguistics, such as Daniel Jones' *Phoneme* [1950] and John Wells' *Jamaican Pronunciation in London* [1973]) to warrant a new entry for *tamber* and an amendment for the entry *timbre* which read 'Delete ‖ and add: Now also with pronun. (tæmbəɹ).' The SPE had long ceased to exist, but Burchfield's treatment of *timbre* in 1986 finally coincided with SPE's recommendations of 1920: tramlines on *timbre* were dropped, an anglicized pronunciation was added, and a new anglicized spelling, *tamber*, was given its own entry in the *OED*.

Implementation of the decision to drop tramlines in the 1933 *Supplement*

The Society for Pure English and its push for the assimilation of loanwords in English seem to have influenced the lexicographic policy of the editors of the *1933 Supplement*. If dictionary proofs included tramlines in 1929, the question remains as to when exactly Craigie and Onions implemented their new policy of assimilation and decided to drop tramlines.

The last proofs with tramlines are dated 11 September 1929. The first proofs without tramlines are dated 2 July 1930. Therefore, the decision to drop tramlines was made between these dates. In this crucial nine-month period, Craigie and Onions exchanged thirteen letters, but none mentioned tramlines.[64] However, three of them do refer to a visit to Oxford that Craigie and his wife Jessie made in August 1929, in particular a meeting with Onions on 3 August. This was a month before the final proofs containing tramlines were printed. It is possible that Craigie and Onions discussed tramline policy on this date; if this was the case, it was too late to change the next proofs, but a 'no tramline' policy was put into practice thereafter.

The *OED* and the BBC advisory committee on spoken English

In the period between these two sets of proofs, Onions joined the BBC Advisory Committee on Spoken English, and his reaction to its workings gives an insight into his view of language at the time. Founded in 1926 and chaired by Robert Bridges, this committee was formed with the aim of 'evolving some sort of standard English which might be adopted by all BBC stations'.[65] The BBC Advisory Committee was closely allied to the SPE: Robert Bridges was joined by Logan Pearsall Smith on the committee of both, and they arranged for the SPE to publish the pronunciation recommendations of the BBC Advisory Committee as *SPE Tracts*. Moreover, both bodies shared the same policy on the assimilation of loanwords, as articulated in the first meeting of the BBC Advisory Committee: 'foreign words in common use should be Englished and where their sounds approximated English sounds the original sounds should be respected, e.g. Chauffer, and in proper names, Shoobert, but Mose-art, Reams (Rheims).'[66]

Onions joined the BBC Advisory Committee on Spoken English in early 1930, but his membership became controversial and was short-lived. A few months after Onions joined, Robert Bridges died and the Nobel Laureate George Bernard Shaw (1856–1950) took over the chair. While Onions agreed with the committee's initial policy on the assimilation of loanwords, under Shaw's leadership the committee took a strongly prescriptive and proscriptive direction, which Onions refused to follow. He and Shaw clashed in their general approaches to language. With Onions on the committee, Shaw felt that 'the Committee wobbles and will not take on an authoritative position; so that it ends too often in our giving our hallmark to ugly and slovenly English simply because it is common and paying no attention at all to beauty of sound and rhythmical value'.[67] In Onions' own words, 'it was with misgiving that I accepted the invitation to join the BBC Advisory

Committee on Pronunciation, because it seemed to me there was a danger of its being regarded as a kind of academy for the regulation of the English language. And this, inspite of all disclaimers, it is virtually taken to be, though it pretends in fact only to give directions to announcers ... The misgivings which I felt when I joined the Committee have only been intensified by experience.' Referring obliquely to Shaw as a 'distinguished amateur', Onions complained that 'it is odd that in no other department than that of language – one's own language – would the distinguished amateur be tolerated'.[68]

Within two years of joining the BBC Advisory Committee, Onions resigned. His resignation was a sensitive issue for the BBC. The director-general, Sir John Reith, was concerned that the authority of the BBC Advisory Committee would be permanently damaged if Onions went public with his criticism. Onions agreed to keep his reasons private, and the BBC merely reported that 'his work prevents him from continuing with us.'[69] According to Shaw, the real reason for Onions' resignation was neither his exasperation with Shaw nor his workload, but rather Onions' unreasonable expectation to be paid for his contribution to the Committee, a scenario that is believable knowing how much Onions struggled to provide for his large family on a lexicographer's salary. Writing to Reith a couple of years after the episode, about reimbursements for Committee members, Shaw said: 'I think that in the case of members domiciled at universities outside of London, we ought to pay railway fares. A first class return ticket and afternoon tea, in addition to our most distinguished consideration, might prevent them from following the example of Onions and asking why the BBC, wallowing in millions (as they all believe) should not pay them a thousand a year apiece for teaching us how to speak with an Oxford accent.'[70]

This episode provides a glimpse into Onions' attitude towards language in the same period that tramlines disappeared from the *1933 Supplement* proofs. Unlike some of his contemporaries, Onions refused to be part of 'an academy for the regulation of the English language', in the same way perhaps that he refused to judge certain foreign words in the *1933 Supplement* as 'alien or not yet naturalized' by marking them with tramlines.

The Society for Pure English and the BBC Advisory Committee on Spoken English were both started by Robert Bridges, and both promulgated his doctrine for the assimilation of loanwords. The significant involvement of Craigie and Onions in these bodies suggests that they shared Bridges' view on loanwords, but can we say that this was the reason for the absence of tramlines in proofs after September 1929? It seems a likely explanation, but two other pieces of evidence should be taken into account before coming to any final conclusion, precisely because this other evidence may work against that explanation. The first appears in a letter from one of Craigie's staff, J. M. Wyllie, who wrote in April 1933, on the cusp of the publication of the *1933 Supplement*, 'The use of the symbol ‖ to denote alien words has been dropped in the *Supplement*, for reasons which I do not know and which, I believe, Sir William Craigie does not know either.'[71]

Wyllie's task was to prepare Craigie's work for the printers, so at first glance one might think his statement carries considerable weight. But, as we saw with his comments on *putsch*, the value of his evidence is questioned when one considers that Wyllie was not based in Chicago with Craigie; rather he was based in Aberdeen, Scotland, working by himself, and he had only begun working on the project in May 1929, merely a few months before the last proofs appeared with tramlines.[72] His new status, his youth (he was just 22 years old at the time), and the fact that he lived in Scotland would have put him out of the loop on senior editorial policy decisions at that time.

So it is no surprise that Wyllie wrote that he did not know why tramlines had been dropped. Furthermore, it is not clear how effectively Wyllie communicated with the other editors. He stayed in contact with the OUP publishers, who at the start were very supportive of him, but his isolation from the other editors and, more importantly, from their lexicographic policies and practices was an issue that worried them. Kenneth Sisam, Assistant Secretary to the Delegates, expressed concern in a letter to Craigie in 1930: 'Wyllie is working hard, but gets practically no support from the others and badly needs a month or so of extra guidance.'[73] Wyllie remained in Aberdeen for the first two years of his work on the *1933 Supplement*, before moving to Oxford in April 1931. Once in Oxford, he did not join Onions' team, but remained a member of Craigie's team. In the end, then, Wyllie's statement comes down to his own opinion, and his phrase 'I believe' with regard to Craigie's position on the matter may well indicate his lack of real knowledge about editorial policy. The marginalization that Wyllie experienced while working on the *1933 Supplement* seemed to dog him throughout his life: he kept the dictionary reading programme going, virtually solo, until Burchfield took over in 1957. By this time, he had suffered several nervous breakdowns, helped in no part by the death of two of his children and disappointment at having to wait ten years before being appointed sole editor of the *Oxford Latin Dictionary* (after Alexander Souter's death in 1939, Wyllie was appointed co-editor with Cyril Bailey until 1949). During the war, he had worked as a cryptographer at Bletchley Park and wrote the *Bletchley Park Cryptographic Dictionary* (1944).[74] In 1965, he (self-)published a book of slanders against OUP entitled *The Oxford Dictionary Slanders: The Greatest Scandal in the Whole History of Scholarship*.[75]

Appendices

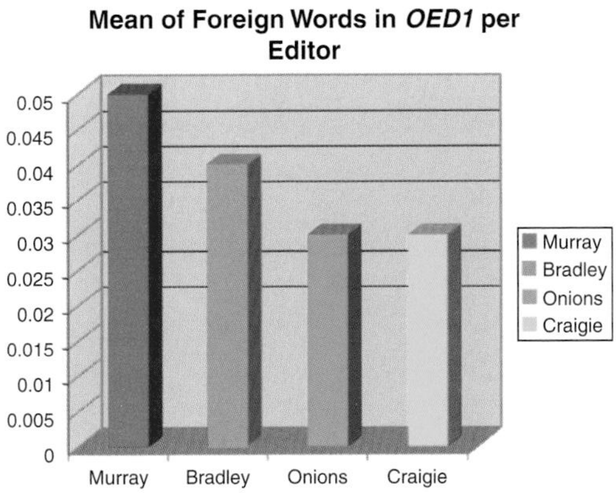

Appendix 1 The mean of inclusion of words with tramlines in *OED1* per editor (Murray 0.05, Bradley 0.04, Onions 0.03, Craigie 0.03)

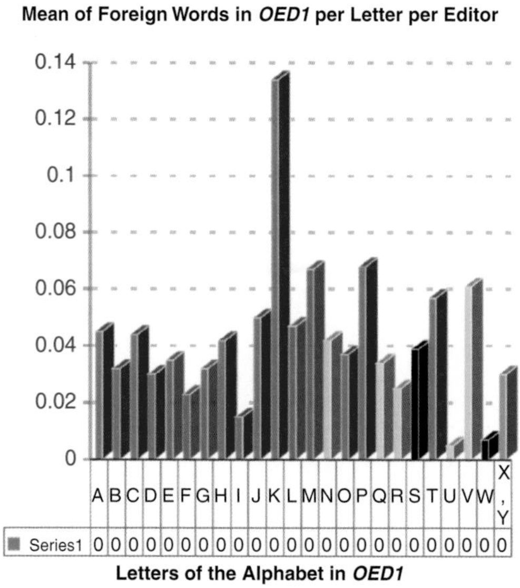

Appendix 2 The proportion of words with tramlines in *OED1* per letter per editor: Murray's letters are shown in red, Bradley's in blue, Onions' in orange, and Craigie's in yellow. The letters in black (S and V) represent ones in which more than one editor worked.

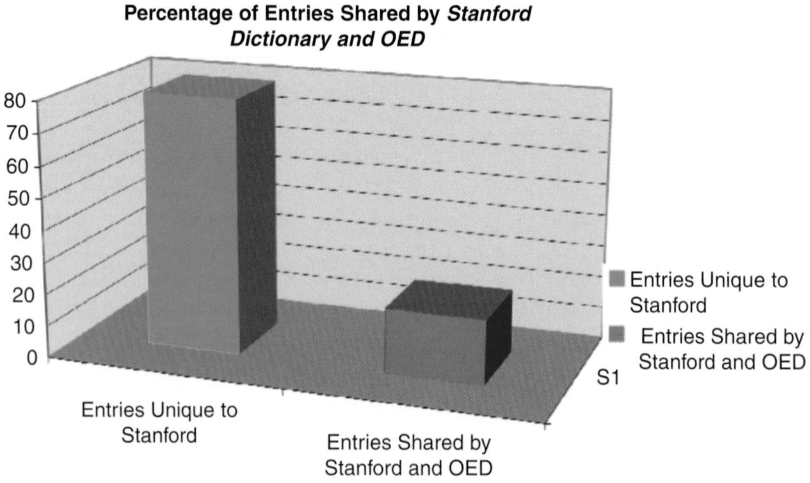

Appendix 3 Bar graph showing the proportion of shared entries (19.4%) in the sample of the section *A–Cast*.

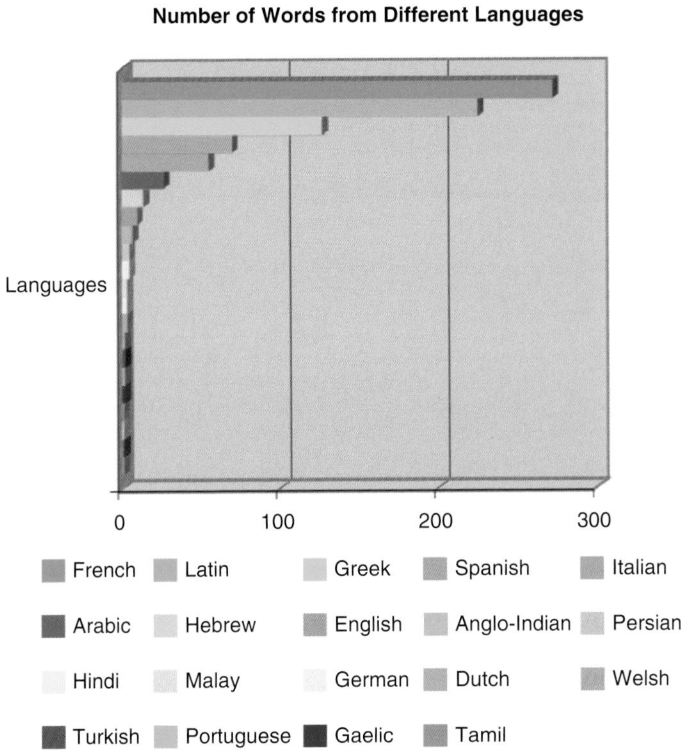

Appendix 4 Bar graph showing the provenance of words in the *Stanford Dictionary* sample.

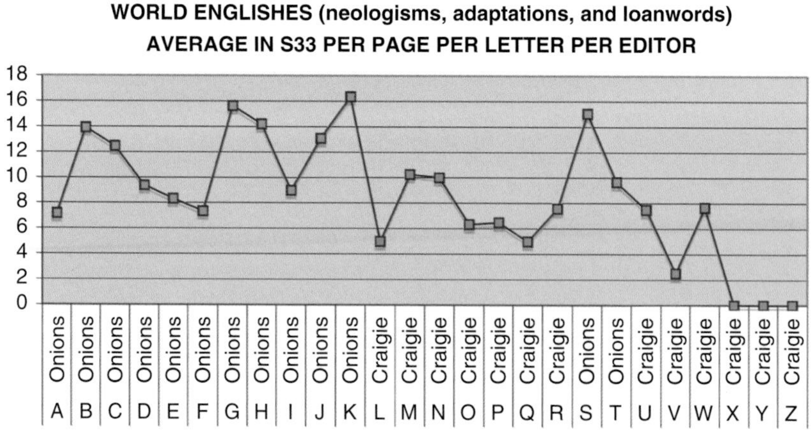

Appendix 5 Line graph showing the average number of loanwords and World Englishes in the *1933 Supplement* per page per letter per editor. Letters edited by Onions are marked by orange dots, and letters edited by Craigie are marked by blue dots. N.B. the peak in the second half of the alphabet (letters S and T edited by Onions).

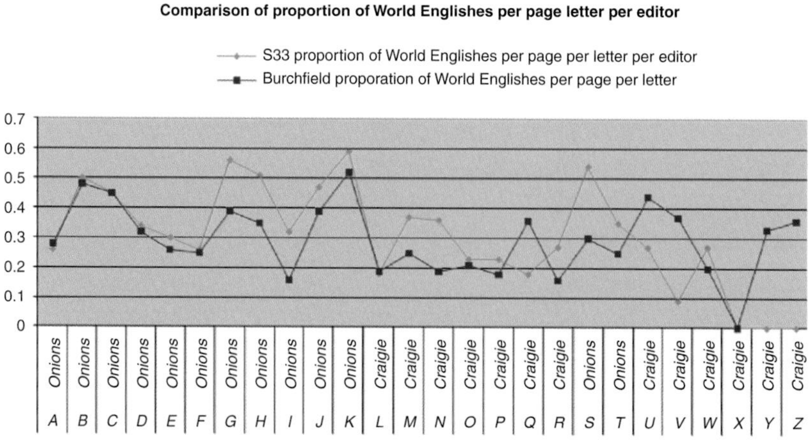

Appendix 6 Line graph showing the proportion of World Englishes (neologisms, adaptations, and loanwords) in the *1933 Supplement* (orange line) compared with that in Burchfield's *Supplement* (blue line).

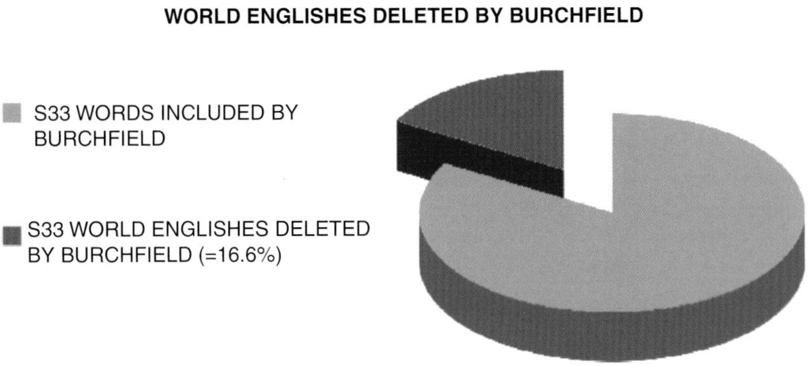

Appendix 7 List of entries deleted from the *1933 Supplement* sample by Burchfield in his *Supplement*. The case study revealed that Burchfield deleted 17% (16.6%) of the sample.

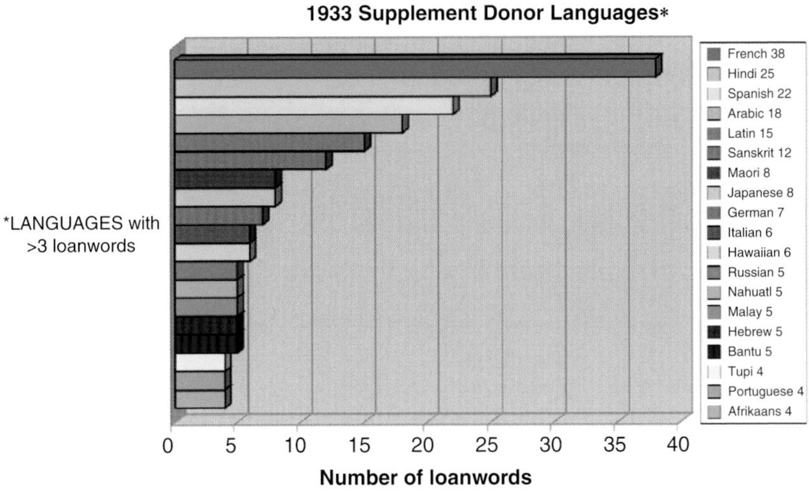

Appendix 8 Bar graph showing *donor languages that contributed more than three loanwords in the *1933 Supplement*.

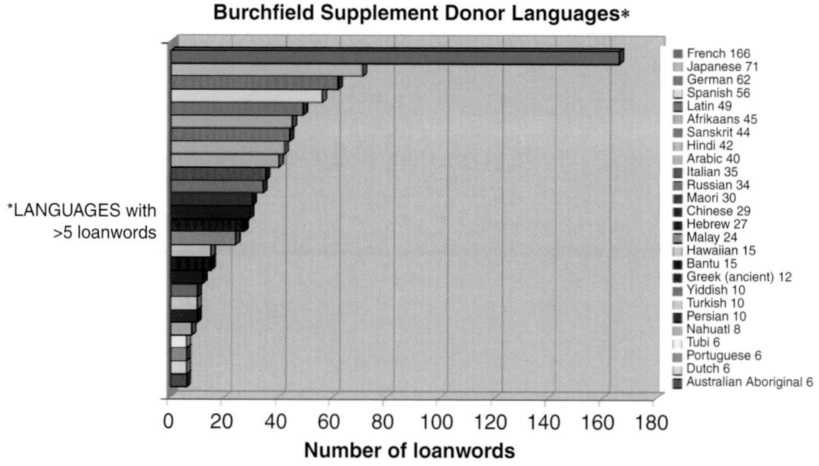

Appendix 9 Bar graph showing *donor languages that contributed more than five loanwords in Burchfield's *Supplement*.

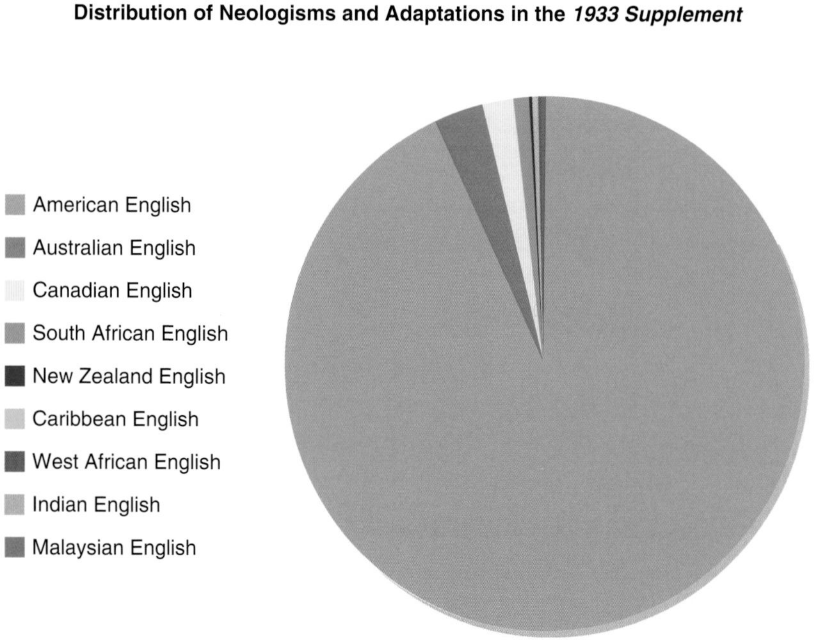

Appendix 10 Pie chart showing the proportional representation of neologisms and adaptations in the *1933 Supplement*.

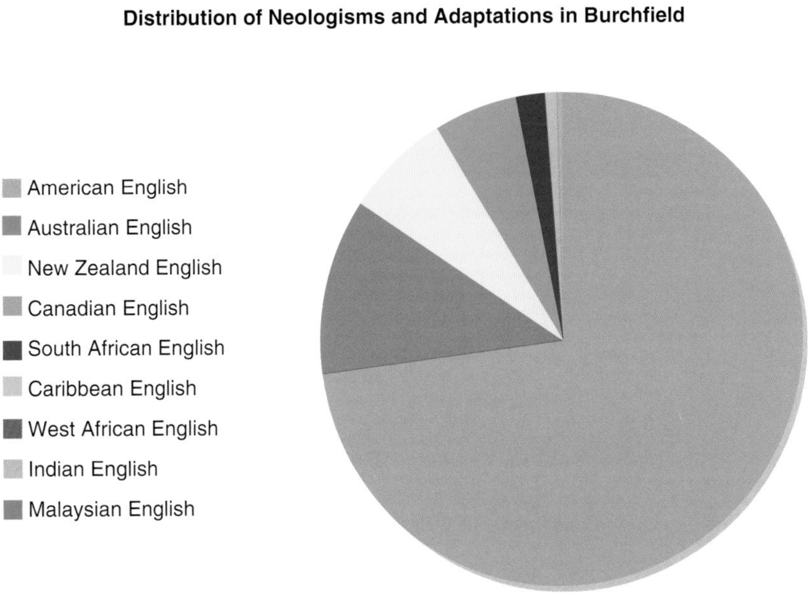

Appendix 11 Pie chart showing the proportional representation of neologisms and adaptations in Burchfield's *Supplement*.

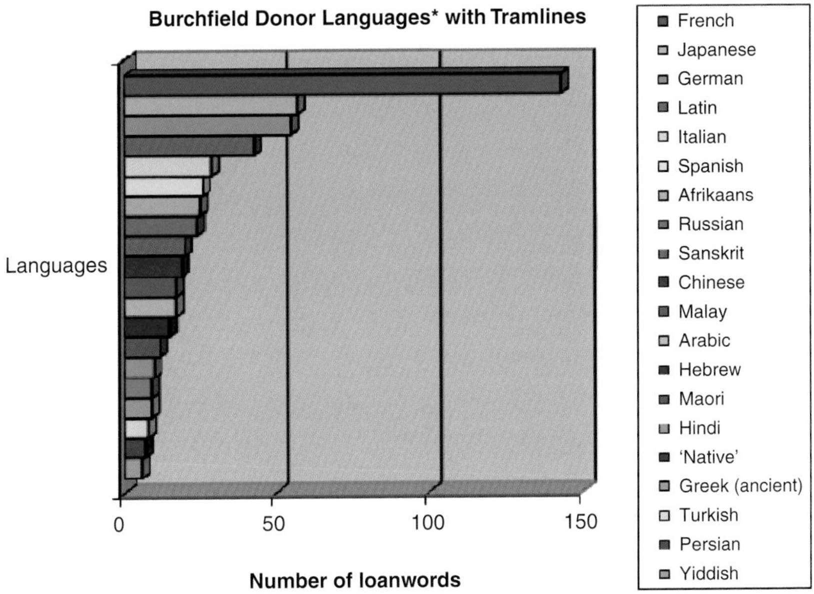

Appendix 12 Bar graph showing the top ten donor languages (that contributed more than five loanwords) given tramlines in Burchfield's *Supplement*.

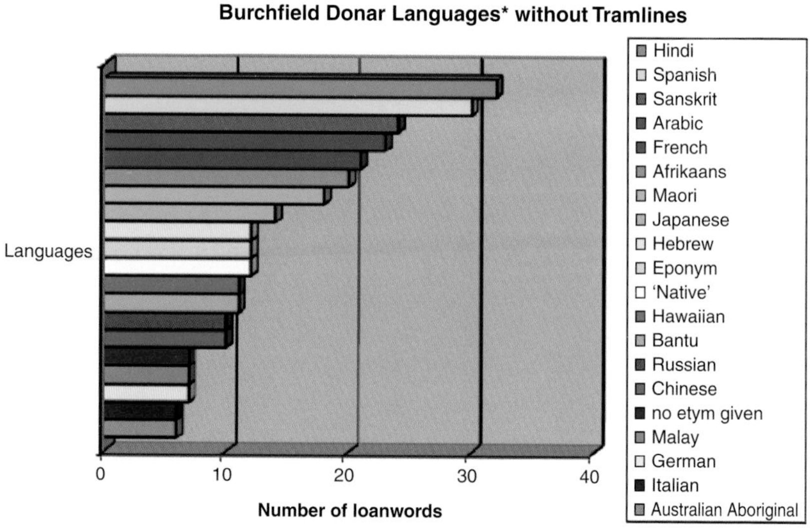

Appendix 13 Bar graph showing the top ten donor languages (that contributed more than five loanwords) not given tramlines in Burchfield's *Supplement*.

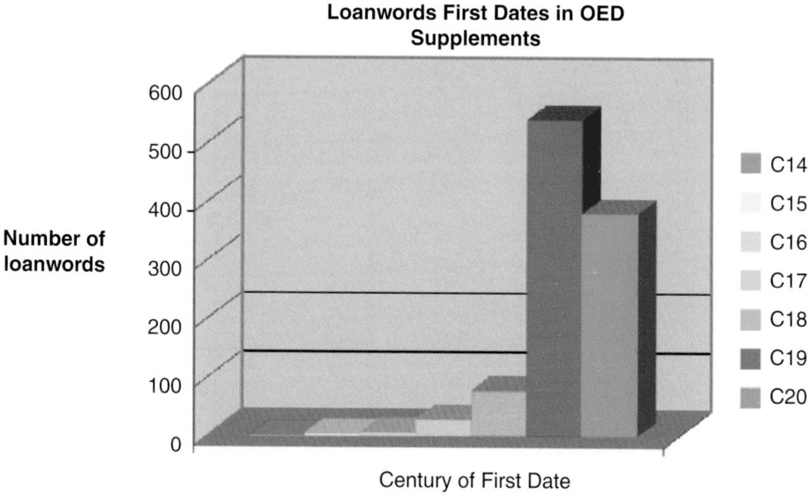

Appendix 14 Bar graph showing the first dates of loanwords in the sample.

Charles Onions and the use of tramlines in the *Shorter Oxford English Dictionary*

The second piece of evidence we should consider is found within the pages of the *Shorter Oxford English Dictionary*. The *Shorter Oxford* was published in the same year as the *1933 Supplement*; it was also edited by Charles Onions, and it appears *with* tramlines on loanwords that 'retain their foreign appearance and to some extent their foreign sound'.[76]

At first glance, it would seem that Onions had put tramlines on loanwords in the *Shorter Oxford*, but not on loanwords in the *1933 Supplement*. However, this would be ignoring the fact that ten years earlier, in 1923, the *Shorter Oxford* was nearly complete (letters A–T, and V) and one-third of its pages had already been sent to the Printers, thereby setting the style for the rest of the dictionary. The *Shorter Oxford* was strictly an abridgement of *OED1*; its remit was 'to present in miniature all the features of the principal work', including tramlines.[77]

The editor of the *Shorter Oxford* in 1923 was not Charles Onions, but rather William Little, who died later that year just five letters short of completion. With one-third of the text already sent to press with tramlines, the future editors simply followed suit. Little's successors were Henry Fowler (letters U, X, Y, Z) and Jessie Coulson (letter W). Therefore, whatever Craigie and Onions decided about *OED* loanword policy in 1929, it would have no bearing on the pages of the *Shorter Oxford* that were prepared by Fowler and Coulson.

Furthermore, although Onions was later listed as the editor of the *Shorter Oxford*, in reality he had had a peripheral supervisory role in its making. His editorial input was minimal. The OUP Publishers added his name to the title page at the last minute for reasons they described as 'commercial'. As Kenneth Sisam expressed it in a memo to Onions a couple of months before publication: 'From a purely commercial point of view, Little's name carries no weight, Fowler's carries great weight, Mrs Coulson's must go in if Fowler's does, and we trust a great deal to your name on the title page. However do your worst!'[78] Onions complained to Sisam that by listing him on the title page beside Fowler and Coulson, his name took 'only a tertiary place among "the Editors".' Hence, just before publication, Onions was promoted on the title page to sole editor.[79] The presence of tramlines in the *Shorter Oxford*, therefore, tells us little about their absence in the *1933 Supplement* because a large portion of the *Shorter Oxford* text was already printed before 1929, and although Onions' name appears as editor, his editorial contribution was minimal.

And so, to return to the *1933 Supplement*: after 1929, the use of tramlines to signal a word's alien status was abandoned by both Onions and Craigie. The symbol '‖' continued to be used by Craigie, but it carried a different meaning:

Craigie used the symbol in the *Dictionary of American English* (1938–44) to denote 'that the term or sense is known only from the passage cited and may be an individualism'.[80] Onions did not use tramlines, or any other symbol to denote a word's loan status, in his *Oxford Dictionary of English Etymology* (1966).

But the question remains as to why *kadin* and *rhexis* were the only two words with tramlines in the *1933 Supplement*. If they were an oversight, with their tramlines slipping through unnoticed, it was an oversight on the part of both editors, since they divided the alphabet: *kadin* fell in Onions' part of the alphabet (A–K, S, and T) and *rhexis* fell in Craigie's (L–R, U–Z). Similarly, the few words with tramlines on the second pronunciation also span both portions of the alphabet (*apache* and *estampage* fell in Onions' part of the alphabet, and *sabotage* in Craigie's). The presence of tramlines on these two words (as opposed to none) also goes against the argument that perhaps it was a printer's typographical policy (or error); after all there are also no paragraph marks ¶ in the *1933 Supplement* which denoted 'erroneous or catachrestic' usage (but unlike tramlines, this paragraph mark was not a feature of the 1929 proofs).

Solving the mystery of the vanishing tramlines

As this book was going to press, my colleague at the *OED*, Peter Gilliver, emailed me to say that he had found uncatalogued documents in the OUP archives that may solve this tramline mystery, at least partially. He had found two letters between Burchfield and Onions that were written a few years before Burchfield's communication with Eric Stanley. The letters confirmed that the tramlines had been omitted for a reason, and not by accident. On 9 December, 1959, Burchfield had written to Onions with his own query about the missing tramlines:

> We have noticed that the sign ‖ is not used in *OED Supplement* for words that are not naturalized (*Borné*, *Brisé*, *Gedackt*, etc.) – at least not before the headwords. It is used (?occasionally, ?often) within entries – as under *Bouquetier*, *Comme il faut*, where in each case one of the possible pronunciations is so marked – and ‖ is included in the List of Abbreviations, Signs, &c. on p. viii. Was there a reason for this significant change from the policy followed in *OED* itself?[81]

Burchfield had asked Onions the exact question I would have liked to ask him. I was, therefore, keen to read Onions' reply:

> I made no use in the *OED Supp.* of the symbol ‖ because I found, or thought I found, that not a few entries in [the] main work could not with full certainty be so marked & that in the Suppt very many words [footnote (by Onions himself): i.e. an excessive number] could not improperly be so. The symbol was, I think, retained by Wyllie, but I don't see any examples. Another device that I discarded was "faint" type for less important entries, which had been extensively used in the main work. My view was

that such words had no place in a substantial supplement, but you will find many examples in Wyllie's work, e.g. *potentialness, potholing*.[82]

Onions' explanation tells us that tramlines were not used because it was simply too difficult to assess, in so many cases, whether a word should have tramlines or not. This was the problem James Murray had faced, of course, when determining the fuzzy boundaries of his 'circle of English'. This confirms that tramlines were excluded as a matter of conscious policy rather than any other reason – such as a printer's error – and reminds us once again that the dividing line between 'alien' and 'non-alien' words is never clear cut.

We can deduce that those principles were acted on between the stage of first-revise proofs (September 1929) and final publication in 1933. Once a no-tramline policy was decided, we can presume – without further evidence – that it was merely an oversight that tramlines were not deleted from two words.

If I had found these letters amongst the stacks of uncatalogued boxes of material in the OUP archives earlier, I might have chosen not to write this chapter, but I would have missed an important discovery in the process. As it is, the lack of evidence compelled me to look at the question from a number of different angles, one of the most revealing being that of the SPE. This investigation opened up strong ties between Onions and Craigie, when they were editors of the *OED*, and the SPE. It indicates the ways in which they were trying to grapple with the issue of alien and non-alien words within the intellectual milieu of their time. The conclusion I deduced from this research – that the policies of the SPE influenced the editors' decision to drop tramlines – still stands as highly likely. This was the reason given by Burchfield, and Burchfield was in frequent communication with Onions and therefore in a position to know; but in the absence of any written statement by Onions or Craigie, we can never be certain.

This whole mystery shows that certain elements of lexicographic practice that are intended to tell us about the words, sometimes tell us more about the attitudes of the lexicographers. Changes in the lexicographic practice of Charles Onions and William Craigie reflected changes in their attitudes towards words from outside Britain. In the next chapter, we turn our attention to Burchfield and seek to discover exactly how his policy and practice on words of the world compared with that of his predecessors.

ENDNOTES

1 An overview of the different editors of the *OED* is given in Chapter 2.
2 Craigie and Onions (1933: v).
3 Craigie and Onions (1933: v).
4 A more general account of the differences between the working practices of Craigie and Onions is given in Brewer (2007: 24–33).

5 Professor Eric Stanley, personal communication, Oxford, 15 May 2007.

6 OED/B/3/10/3. Progress Reports for the 1933 Supplement; Letters between the OUP Printer and Sisam and Chapman.

7 OED/B/3/10/3. Progress Reports for the 1933 Supplement.

8 Murray (1888: vii).

9 Murray (1888: vii).

10 Silva (2000: 82).

11 OED/B/3/10/3 Progress Reports for the 1933 *Supplement*.

12 OED/B/3/10/3 Letter from Sisam to Onions 15 September 1931.

13 OED/B/3/10/3 Letter from Sisam to Johnson 25 September 1931.

14 OED/B/3/2/21 Letter from Chapman to the Vice Chancellor 30 November 1932.

15 OED/B/3/2/22. Letter from Wyllie to Sisam 12 December 1933.

16 OED/B/3/10/4 MISC 393/89/ii. Letter from Sisam to Charles Onions 6 May 1932.

17 OED/B/3/10/4 MISC 393/89/ii. Letter from Sisam to Mencken 6 May 1932.

18 Craigie and Onions (1933: v).

19 I am indebted to Dr Celia Kerslake for advice on the pronunciation of *kadin* in Turkish.

20 1882 O'Donovan *Merv Oasis* I. xxii. 369 Above the arch was a square-topped room known as the *bala hané*, which served as quarters for the better class of travellers, as well as a kind of watch tower and look-out station; 1927 *Chambers's Jrnl.* 493/2 The dhåman, though not poisonous, turns a somersault and hits you with its tail.

21 Onions and Craigie (1933: v).

22 See the section on 'The Enthusiastic Amateur: Colonel H. G. Le Mesurier' in Brewer (2007: 69–75). After reading Brewer (2007) I have revised my original interpretation of the correspondence between Le Mesurier, Fowler, Sisam, and Onions as previously articulated in Ogilvie (2008a: 31, 2008b: 7), both of which went to press before Brewer's book was published.

23 OED/B/3/10/4 (2) MISC/393/196ii. Letter from Le Mesurier to Fowler 10 January 1933; OED/B/3/10/4 (2) MISC/393/194. Letter from Fowler to Sisam 11 January 1933; OED/B/3/10/4 (2) MISC/393/195. Letter from Sisam to Onions 13 January 1933; OED/B/3/10/4 (2) MISC/393/197 Letter from Sisam to Fowler 13 January 1933; OED/B/3/10/4 (2) MISC/393/198. Letter from Le Mesurier to Sisam 16 January 1933.

24 OED B/3/10/4 (2) MISC/393/196. Letter from Le Mesurier to Fowler 10 January 1933.

25 Murray (1888: xvii).

26 OED B/3/10/4 (2) MISC/393/196. Letter from Le Mesurier to Fowler 10 January 1933.

27 Brewer (2007: 70).

28 OED B/3/10/4 (2) MISC/393/196. Letter from Le Mesurier to Fowler 10 January 1933.

29 Murray (1911: 21).

30 OED/B/3/10/4 (2) MISC/393/197. Letter from Sisam to Fowler 13 January 1933.

31 Proofs consist of 'first proof' and 'first revise' dated 7 July 1928, 17 July 1928, 15 October 1928, 12 September 1928, 27 September 1928, 20 December 1928, 3 Jan 1929, 6 March 1929, 22 March 1929, 13 April 1929, and 11 September 1929.

32 Burchfield Papers Deposit Supplement BB2/5. Letter from Stanley to Davin 5 February 1963.
33 The sample specimen consisted of words from LO – LOCK, described by Burchfield and Aarsleff (1988: 49) as 'the range of entries that filled a complete page in the 1933 Supplement. ... It faithfully reflected the progress that we – three assistants and myself – had made at the time'.
34 Burchfield Papers Deposit Supplement BB2/5. Letter from Davin to Stanley 7 February 1963.
35 Bridges (1919: 7).
36 Pearsall Smith (1931: 481).
37 Bridges (1919: 7).
38 Bridges (1925a: 4).
39 Forty-two of the SPE's 104 members were outside Britain.
40 Pearsall Smith (1920: 4).
41 Pearsall Smith (1920: 4).
42 Pearsall Smith (1920: 4–5).
43 Bridges (1925b: 65).
44 Craigie wrote articles for *SPE Tracts* published in 1927, 1937, 1940–42, 1944–46 (*SPE Tracts* 27, 48, 50, 56, 57, 58, 59, 63, 64, 65).
45 Onions contributed to *SPE Tracts* 18, 19, 24, 36, and 61.
46 Giles Onions, personal communication, Oxford, 17 August 2007.
47 *SPE Tracts* 27, 50, 56, and 57.
48 *SPE Tract* 61.
49 Bridges (1920: 11).
50 Bridges (1920: 11).
51 Matthews (1921: 8).
52 'Notes and Correspondence' *SPE Tract* X 1922 p. 26.
53 Fry (1926: 776).
54 Dobrée (1926: 804).
55 Dobrée (1926: 804).
56 A list of SPE members in 1933 includes Bonamy Dobrée of Menham Priory, Harleston, Norfolk. A list of SPE members in 1942 includes Bonamy Dobrée of Leeds University.
57 'Feste' (1929: 886).
58 Jones (1932: 30).
59 Jones (1922: 16).
60 The second and third editions do not have headword entries for 'tamber'.
61 Jones (1917: viii).
62 Jones (1932: 20), Hubbell (1951: 46), Firth and Rogers (1937: 1065).
63 Jones contributed to four *SPE Tracts* (published in 1919 [*SPE Tract* 1], 1933 [*SPE Tract* 40], 1943 [*SPE Tract* 60], and 1946 [*SPE Tract* 66] respectively). Firth and Jones do not appear on any SPE member lists. For contributions to SPE by Daniel Jones, see 'Notes and Correspondence' *SPE Tract* 24 1924 pp. 127–8.
64 OED/B/3/4/2. The archives at the University of Birmingham and the National Library of Scotland, Edinburgh, do not contain any relevant material in this period.
65 BBC R6/196/1a. File 1 1926–1927.
66 BBC R6/196/1b. Minutes of First Meeting 5 July 1926.

67 BBC R6/146/4c. Letter from Shaw to Lloyd James 30 September 1932.
68 BBC R6/146/4b. Letters from Onions to Lloyd James 3 January, 28 February, and 12 June 1932.
69 BBC R6/196/6. Correspondence of Reith and Lloyd James 1932–1934.
70 Letter from Shaw to Reith 22 June 1934 (Laurence [1988: 376]).
71 SOED/1933/16/5ii. Letter from Wyllie to Sisam 21 April 1933.
72 Onions and Craigie (1933: vi). Wyllie's appointment to work on the 1933 *Supplement* is described in Wyllie (1965: 111) and in Brewer (2007).
73 OED/B/3/2/19. Letter from Sisam to Craigie 7 May 1930.
74 See Wyllie's cryptographic dictionary at www.codeandciphers.org.uk/documents/cryptdict.
75 See Brewer (2007) for more on Wyllie and his work after 1933.
76 Onions (1933: vii).
77 Onions (1933: v).
78 OUP/MISC Remainder SOED. Letter from Sisam to Onions 21 October 1932.
79 OUP/MISC Remainder SOED. Letter from Onions to Sisam 21 November 1932. Onions wrote to Sisam: 'It is a little odd that my name takes only a *tertiary* place among "the Editors". (Did I pass that?).'
80 Craigie and Hulbert (1938: xiv). James Murray referred to such hapax legomena as 'nonce words', and labelled them in the *OED1* as '*nonce-wd*'.
81 OED/16/OED Supplement Policy 1958–72. Letter from Burchfield to Onions 9 December 1959.
82 OED/16/OED Supplement Policy 1958–72. Letter from Onions to Burchfield 4 January 1960.

6 Robert Burchfield and words of the world in the *OED Supplements*

> It is exceedingly difficult to draw the line or leave out words. To ignore a country or a subject when compiling a dictionary would be like leaving some gold unmined.
>
> Robert Burchfield (1986), Editor of the dictionary from 1957 to 1986

James Murray and the early editors were committed to including words of the world in *OED1*. They sought readers of international texts, consulted experts in the languages of the world, and applied the historical method so that this subsection of the vocabulary was treated with the same rigour and thoroughness as the rest of the English lexicon. Murray's personal commitment to foreign words was confirmed by the *Stanford Dictionary* controversy and challenged by the comprehensive coverage of Fennell's dictionary. Murray's successors, William Craigie and Charles Onions, continued the legacy started by Murray but, over time, changed their attitudes towards the anglicization of foreign words by dropping the use of tramlines in the *1933 Supplement*. Although they admitted in the preface of the *1933 Supplement* that it was difficult to decide on which foreign words to omit or include, this chapter seeks to discover how many they did include and how their work compared with that of their successor, Robert Burchfield. After all, it was Burchfield who was most vocal in the 1970s against the coverage of loanwords and World Englishes by his predecessors. And it is Burchfield who is renowned today for being the first *OED* editor to open the pages of the dictionary to words supposedly neglected by his predecessors.[1] But was Burchfield as inclusive in practice as he claimed in theory?

First, it is necessary to highlight the differences between a supplement dictionary and its parent dictionary. A parent dictionary has a relatively balanced representation of different types of vocabulary – common, literary, slang, foreign or scientific terms – but a supplement dictionary is limited to vocabulary that was either not included in the main dictionary or needs amendment. It is not possible to compare with any statistical rigour the coverage of types of vocabulary in a supplement dictionary with its parent dictionary because the remit of each text is too dissimilar. For example, we cannot compare with any statistical rigour the coverage of foreign words and

World Englishes in Burchfield's *Supplement* with the coverage in *OED1* because the remit of each text was too dissimilar. If we want to compare Burchfield's work with that of his predecessors, we must compare it with the work of the editors of the *1933 Supplement*. As supplements to *OED1*, both texts shared the same aims and remit, and therefore potentially the same balance of vocabulary.

This chapter therefore compares Burchfield's treatment of words of the world with that of his predecessors, Craigie and Onions. It examines in detail over nine thousand dictionary entries (10% of each dictionary) across nineteen parameters. The results reveal unexpected trends in the individual editorial practices of the editors of the *OED Supplements*, often in marked contrast to their stated policies, and, moreover, contrary to received scholarship on the topic.

Burchfield and his image as champion of words of the world

If you were to ask anyone working on the *OED* today which editor from the past included the most loanwords and World Englishes, they will probably say 'Robert Burchfield', the New Zealander who edited the four-volume *Supplement to the Oxford English Dictionary* (1972–86). This was certainly my own view when I went to work on the *OED*. Both scholarship and the popular press have presented him as the champion of words of the world. This is because it was the opinion of Burchfield himself and he let it be known in his writings, his public lectures, and his media interviews. But my own work on the dictionary and further analysis of the text showed this not to be true.

When it came to World Englishes and loanwords, Burchfield was quick to distance himself from the lexicographic policies and practices of his predecessors. He openly criticized Murray, Bradley, Onions, and Craigie for their neglect of words from beyond Britain. 'Readers will discover by constant use of the *Supplement*', Burchfield wrote in the preface to the first volume of his *Supplement* (1972), 'that the written English of regions like Australia, South Africa, and India have been accorded the kind of treatment that lexicographers of a former generation might have reserved for the English of Britain alone.'[2] Promoting his completed *Supplement* in 1986, Burchfield toured the globe and told the media in numerous countries that his treatment of vocabulary from outside Britain was unprecedented. Not only did he claim to bring a fresh focus on lexical items from around the world that were neologisms and adaptations of existing English forms, but he also claimed to bring a new emphasis on loanwords. He presented to the media a new democratic attitude towards language, in which words from Chinese and Russian were as welcome in English as words from Romance and Germanic languages. Speaking on *News Hour* on the radio in New York on 27 May 1986, Burchfield said, 'The final volumes, S to Z – or S to Zed, as they would say – begins with the word *se*, a Chinese stringed instrument, and ends with *Zyrian*, a Russian tribe.'[3] A review in the journal *English World-wide* declared that Burchfield 'kept his promise . . . the number of words from Hawaiian and Maori alone is impressive.'[4] Speaking at a symposium at the Library of Congress in Washington in 1986, Burchfield told the audience that 'Murray preferred to fend off overseas words until they had become firmly entrenched in British use.'[5] Tom McArthur (1993) repeated Burchfield's message and congratulated him for 'noting that an *OED* editor no longer has the freedom or right to fend off items of English that are not entrenched in (and canonized by) British acceptance'.[6]

Burchfield's criticisms of his predecessors for ignoring loanwords were repeated by the Press. The *Globe and Mail* in Canada reported that 'Mr. Burchfield said the dictionary's original editors resisted including foreign words "until they had become firmly entrenched in British use," and that some words were treated "almost like illegal immigrants".'[7] Philip Howard in the *Times* declared that '[Murray's] successor, born and educated at Wanganui, New Zealand, has a more liberal and realistic attitude to overseas Englishes and loanwords from foreign languages.'[8] The *New Leader,* a liberal political magazine based in New York, hailed Burchfield's 'new aproach':

> The new approach is to be saluted, as is the even greater deinsularization Burchfield doesn't bother to mention: Innumerable words from foreign languages that have surfaced in English texts make a massive showing. Thus we get in rapid succession *Seilbahn* from Germany, *Sejm* from Poland, *selamlik* from Turkey. A German word such as *Sehnsucht,* defined as "yearning, wishful longing," is obviously totally at home in an English dictionary, as the many quotations from distinguished sources attest, but what is truly commendable is the hospitality extended to less traveled words.[9]

From the beginning of the project, Burchfield had referred to himself and this editorial team as 'the new explorers' whose lexicographic efforts were pioneering not only in the history of English dictionary-making but also in the European tradition: 'We have ventured into areas unexplored by Dr Johnson and Dr Murray, and excluded on principle by compilers of French dictionaries. For example, our second volume will contain many of the words used by American blacks. As each new wave of vocabulary advances we advance towards it.'[10] Claiming that his team had corrected the failures of his predecessors, Burchfield wrote in the preface: 'We have made bold forays into the written English of regions outside the British Isles, particularly into that of North America, Australia, New Zealand, South Africa, India, and Pakistan.'[11]

Burchfield's message also spread quickly throughout the scholarly community, prompting praise such as that in *American Speech,* 'When the supplement is complete it will deserve the label *International* more fully than *Webster's Third.*'[12] Donald B. Sands in *College English* went so far as to assert that '"Bold forays" are confirmed by the number of exotic attestations that appear page after page – attestations, for example, drawn from *The Boston Traveler, The Cape Times, The Springfield* (Mass.) *Weekly Republican, The Daily Columnist* (Victoria, B.C.), *The Village Voice, The New Yorker.*'[13] Richard Bailey and Manfred Görlach, in *English as a World Language* (1982), stated that 'while the initial editors of the *OED* virtually excluded words not in general use in Great Britain and the United States, their successors have recognized the international dimension of English by what the editor [Burchfield] calls "bold forays into the written English of regions outside the British Isles, particularly that of North America, Australia, New Zealand, South Africa, India, and Pakistan".'[14] Scholarly reviews of the *OED* highlighted that Burchfield was 'determined to include as much non-English English as possible'.[15]

Contrasting it with his own *Supplement*, Burchfield presented the *1933 Supplement* as inadequate on every level:

> Subject by subject, word class by word class, the first *OED Supplement* was a riffraff assemblage of casual items, in no way worthy of the magnificent monument to which it formed an extension.[16]

In order to emphasize the pioneering aspect of his own democratic approach to language and culture, Burchfield presented an image of his predecessors as typically Victorian in their view of language and culture. In his biography of Murray in the *Oxford Dictionary of National Biography*, he wrote,

> Later editions of the dictionary have departed from Murray's basic principles in only two important ways. He had not given sufficient attention to the English used outside the British Isles, whereas since the 1972–86 supplement the OED has attempted to cover the language as it is written and spoken throughout the world. And, as was to be expected of a Victorian lexicographer, Murray drew a veil over all coarse words: none of the ancient 'four-letter' words was included in his dictionary.[17]

According to Burchfield, Murray and his editors had Anglocentric views of the world that influenced their policies and encouraged a lexicographic practice that excluded 'the vocabulary of the peripheral regions'.[18] Burchfield told audiences in Japan and Italy that 'in the 1870s when the policy of the Dictionary was drawn up, consensus opinion in lexicography thought of British English as the central vocabulary, and of American, Australian, etc. English as at the periphery. Information about the vocabulary of the peripheral regions made its way back to the centre by slow sailing vessels'.[19] Burchfield stressed that 'the *OED* was shown at once to be a product of the Victorian and Edwardian period, and not up-to-date at all'.[20]

In turn, newspapers reiterated the message that Burchfield was opening the doors of an outdated 'Victorian *OED*' to previously ignored sections of English vocabulary. Peter Ackroyd (1987) reported in the *Times*: 'As is appropriate in a post-imperial addition to a Victorian *OED*, Dr Burchfield has included West Indian English, Indian English, South African English, and all those other productive but no longer exotic variants.'[21] Burchfield said that he offered a thorough supplementation that included new quotations from non-British sources: 'we are treating the English of all English-speaking regions. Nabokov and Salinger are quoted as freely as Graham Greene and Anthony Powell, and it is the same with Canadian, Australian, Indian, West Indian, and South African writers.'[22] The *Dallas Morning News* applauded the fact that 'Burchfield sought to expand entries from other English-speaking countries.'[23]

One perspective is to say that Burchfield deserves praise for the way in which he publicly promoted the status of World Englishes. This came at a time – in the 1970s and 1980s – when there was a shift in public perceptions of the validity of words previously considered marginal, and Burchfield's role as a public intellectual was instrumental in this shift. During the period in which Burchfield compiled and edited his *Supplement*, linguists began to study the similarities and differences between varieties of English. The study of 'World Englishes' became a discrete field of linguistics with the advent of specialized journals such as *English World-Wide* (1980–) and *World Englishes* (1981–),[24] and the publication of books on the topic such as those by Trudgill and Hannah (1982), Bailey and Görlach (1982), Platt et al. (1984), and Kachru (1986). Burchfield's democratic message on New York public radio in 1986 that 'English everywhere had to be given the same treatment' seemed to be in step with developments in the wider field of English studies.[25] For example, the journal *World Language English* changed its name to *World Englishes* in 1985 and designed a new logo 'WE', which served to indicate that, in the words of Tom McArthur (1993), 'there is a club of equals here, where the journal in its earlier incarnation tended to centre upon the standard language and the standards of language of south-eastern England'.[26]

Burchfield's principal criticism of Murray was that his policy on words of the world was too insular. According to Burchfield, the main difference between his policy and that of Murray was 'my decision to try to locate and list vocabulary of all English-speaking countries, and not merely that of the United Kingdom. . . . At a time when the English language seems to be breaking up into innumerable clearly distinguishable varieties, it seemed to me important to abandon Murray's insular policy and go out and find what was happening to the language elsewhere.'[27]

Given Burchfield's context this was a believable, if inaccurate, message; he was editing nearly a century after Murray. The English that Burchfield faced in the 1970s was very different from that which had confronted earlier editors. Not only were there more World Englishes being spoken, but they were becoming more accessible than ever before.[28] From the 1960s onwards, Anglophone countries began instituting policies in education, legislation, voting rights, and co-official languages that can be said to reflect a changed sentiment on English. During Burchfield's chief editorship of the *OED*, Fred Cassidy and Robert Le Page had published a *Dictionary of Jamaican English* (1967); Walter Avis in Canada had published the *Dictionary of Canadianisms* (1967); Jean Branford in South Africa was writing *A Dictionary of South African English* (1978); and Bill Ramson in Australia and Harry Orsman in New Zealand were gathering materials for the *Australian National Dictionary* (1988) and the *New Zealand Dictionary of English* (1997) respectively. In the 1960s, '70s, and '80s, each of these editors corresponded with Burchfield and sent him slips and information about words from their regions, in the same way that Edward Morris had sent slips and information to Murray in the 1890s from Australia while compiling his dictionary *Austral English* (1898). Burchfield also enlisted the help of a contributor from South Africa, Mr N. van Blerk, while the latter was on long-service leave in Oxford, and paid for him to work on South African entries in the dictionary for four months in 1960.[29]

A number of factors, therefore, conspire to support the image of Robert Burchfield as the champion of World Englishes in the *OED*. He had unprecedented access to World Englishes via a network of international lexicographers; he was himself a speaker of a variety (New Zealand English); and, as we have seen, he made it known in his writings, lectures, and interviews that within the pages of his *Supplement* 'the written English of regions like Australia, South Africa, and India have been accorded the kind of treatment that lexicographers of a former generation might have reserved for the English of Britain alone.'[30]

It was my own experience of working on the *OED* that made me question Burchfield's story. Two key aims of this study are to investigate the relationship between a lexicographer's policy and practice, and to assess the coverage of loanwords and World Englishes in the *OED*. Hence we turn now to a case study that examines Burchfield's treatment of loanwords and World Englishes in the dictionary, in order to see if his practice matched his policy.

Case study: loanwords and World Englishes in the *OED supplements*

This case study examines the treatment of loanwords and World English in the *OED Supplements*. After outlining the case study's purpose, sample, and method, I show how general trends and patterns of lexical borrowing in English are reflected in the sample in the form of donor-language statistics and loanword phases. I demonstrate how the process of nativization can be traced in a dictionary entry by analyzing a loanword's pronunciation, etymology, inflectional morphology, grammatical gender, pluralization, class, and semantic field. We saw in the first chapter that written citations, showing how a word is used in context, form the basis of all decisions in historical lexicography. It was therefore vital for the case study to examine the quotation paragraphs of every loanword and word from World English in the sample, in order to determine exactly what aspects of the quotational evidence influenced lexicographic practice. Each word was assessed according to the type of source, variant forms (spelling variants), first date, number of quotations in a quotation paragraph, use of square brackets on first quotation, and typographical features such as italics, inverted commas, brackets (with gloss), and diacritics. Hence the case study was able to examine how factors such as typography and time-depth combine with a word's own features to influence a lexicographer's practice of applying tramlines, labels, definitional metalanguage, and non-naturalized renderings of pronunciation. The results will offer an alternative perspective to that usually assumed in scholarship on the *OED Supplements*.

Case study purpose

The primary objective of this case study was to examine and compare how each of the *OED Supplement* editors (Burchfield, Craigie, and Onions) treated World Englishes and loanwords. This entailed assessing a 10% sample of Craigie and Onions' single-volume *1933 Supplement* and comparing it with a sample of Burchfield's four-volume *Supplement* (1972–1986). I assessed each word's status as 'loanword' or 'World English', including its eligibility for tramlines, and compared it with the treatment it actually received by an editor. The second objective was to test the widespread assumption, articulated by Bailey and Görlach (1982), that 'while the initial editors of the *OED* virtually excluded words not in general use in Great Britain and the United States, their successors have recognized the international dimension of English by what the editor [Burchfield] calls "bold forays into the written English of regions outside the British Isles, particularly that of North America, Australia, New Zealand, South Africa, India, and Pakistan".'[31]

Case study sample

The *1933 Supplement* was the base text for Burchfield's *Supplement*, so it provides the perfect text for comparison. I took a sample of 9364 entries, or 10% of each dictionary (2427 entries from the *1933 Supplement* and 6937 entries from Burchfield *Supplement*).[32] These entries were not all taken from the same letter or section of the dictionary, but were chosen randomly from 10% of each letter of the alphabet. The same sections of the alphabet were compared for each dictionary. This method of sampling across the entire alphabet minimized biases towards, or against, the sound systems and orthographies of particular donor languages. For example, it minimized the chance of a 'variety glut': a skew *towards* words from a given variety of English such as only choosing a portion of the letter D that might contain a surfeit of Indian English and Hindi words beginning with *dh-* (e.g. *dhak,* an Indian tree; *dhaman,* rat snake; *dhamnoo,* an Indian tree; *dhan,* rice in its husk; *dhandh,* lake or swamp; *dhania,* coriander seed; *dharna,* mode of extorting payment; *dhobi*, washer man; *dhol,* Indian drum; plus thirteen more words); or only choosing a portion of the letter V with a surfeit of South African English and Afrikaans words beginning with *vaa-* (e.g. *vaalhai,* South African tope; *vaaljapie*, young wine; *vaalpens,* member of the Kalahari tribe). Conversely, it minimized the chance of a 'variety void': a skew *against* words from a given variety of English that may lack certain sounds or representations of sounds such as choosing L when there is no /l/ in Japanese, or choosing W when there is no /w/ in Russian.

The sample also ensured a balanced representation of lexicographic work by all editors over all time periods, thereby accounting for the fact that in the *1933 Supplement,* Onions edited A–K, S, T, and Craigie edited L–R, U–Z, and Burchfield published his *Supplement* gradually over fourteen years: A–G in 1972, H–N in 1976, O–Scz in 1982, and Se–Z in 1986. The random selection within each letter meant that certain sections yielded no results, e.g. no lexical items were extracted from X – XANTHINE, but this balanced out over the entire sample. It also protected against results being skewed by possible 'alphabet fatigue', the phenomenon described in Chapter 4 whereby lexicographers work with greater thoroughness at the beginning of the alphabet than at the end.[33] In the case of the *1933 Supplement,* which had two editors who split the editing task according to certain letters, the sampling technique allowed for alphabet fatigue within each editor's range. De Schryver (2005) describes the reverse phenomenon in other dictionaries in which some lexicographers treat individual entries with more thoroughness towards the end of the alphabet, and this sampling technique would also safeguard against such biases.

Apart from starting at the beginning of each letter, random samples were taken from within each letter of Burchfield's *Supplement* and then matched in the *1933 Supplement*. The beginning of each letter was included in the sample in order to compare differences in the treatment of loanwords and World Englishes within each letter of the alphabet, starting at the beginning. In retrospect this condition did not reveal any patterns in lexicographic practice, so it ended up being a redundant measure, but that could not be predicted at the beginning of the case study and in itself tells us that all editors were constant in their treatment within each letter. A random number generator was used to calculate each step of the sample, alternating between 'number of pages' and 'page number'.[34]

All results and calculations were also calibrated in order to account for differences in size and content of the respective texts. It would have been wrong to presume that there was a direct proportional relationship between the relative sizes of Burchfield's *Supplement* (four volumes) and the *1933 Supplement* (single volume); that is, to presume that Burchfield's dictionary was four times the size of the latter. In fact, Burchfield's *Supplement* was a little less than three, not four, times larger than the *1933 Supplement*. The relative sizes of each letter of the alphabet were also factored into calculations in order to give proportional figures that account for alphabet fatigue and the fact that some letters, such as C and S, account for a disproportionate number of English words.

Definitions of 'World Englishes' and 'loanwords' in the case study

Before moving on to the case study methodology, it is important to remind ourselves of the specific meanings of 'World Englishes' and 'loanword'. This is particularly relevant for the case study, because the semantic scope of these terms had an impact on which words were selected from the sample and therefore which words comprised the database. Jespersen's ground-breaking analysis of French loanwords in *OED1*, *Growth and Structure of the English Language* (1905), provided a precedent for the dangers of skewed sample selection. Using sections of *OED1* that had been published by that date, he took the first hundred French words in the letters A–G and the first fifty in the letters I and J. However, he inadvertently skewed the results by the decision to exclude words listed with fewer than five quotations. This applied to many nineteenth-century loans because *OED* editors rarely gave more than four quotations per century, and thus Jespersen's results provided a misleading overview both of the coverage of French loans in the *OED* and of the continued influence of French upon English.

This case study aimed to be as inclusive as possible in the selection of loanwords and words from World Englishes. Lexical items referred to as 'World Englishes' fall into four broad categories: neologisms, adaptations, fossilizations, and loanwords (or 'retentions'). Neologisms consist of newly formed English lexemes which include compounds, phrasal verbs, and hybrids. The term 'adaptation' is used to refer to English terms that have undergone semantic shifts. Fossilizations are words that have died out of use in British English but are preserved in the variety of World English.

Loanwords are broadly interpreted in this study as words that are borrowed into English and which, according to Murray's criteria, would be classified by *OED* editors as denizens, aliens, or casuals. These loanwords fall into two main types: borrowings that are restricted to one particular region or variety of

English (e.g. *pak pai*, in Hong Kong: a car used illegally as a taxi; *ogi*, in Nigeria: a kind of maize meal; or *dadah*, in Malaysia: illegal drugs) and borrowings that have entered English globally and are not restricted to one particular region or variety (e.g. *typhoon, okra, bamboo*). The former are often referred to as 'retentions' because they are seen by speakers of the English variety to be retained, rather than borrowed, from the indigenous language.[35]

There is often no clear boundary between loanwords and other lexical items in World Englishes. This ambiguity was evident in the newspaper articles quoted at the beginning of this chapter, in which it was often difficult to discern if the journalist was praising Burchfield for his coverage of loanwords, his inclusion of lexical adaptations or neologisms, or a combination of all three. In order to accommodate the widespread and varied assumptions of Burchfield's role as champion of World Englishes, this case study needed to be as broad and comprehensive as possible, thereby considering not only neologisms and adaptations from World Englishes, but loanwords as well.

Given the strong media response to Burchfield in America, and taking into account the emphasis Burchfield gave to Americanisms in his interviews and writings, it was also important for the case study to investigate the treatment of American English and to include it in its definition of a variety of English, although American English and British English share a common core that most scholars would describe as 'International English'.[36] The *OED* editors marked all Americanisms with a regional label *U.S.* or *N. Amer.*, in the same way that they marked other lexical items from World Englishes by region (*S. Afr.*, *Austral.*, or *N.Z.*).

Case study method

From the sample of 9364 words, all World Englishes and loanwords were extracted (1918 words) and were entered into a separate database in which each word was compared according to its features, its quotational evidence, and its lexicographic treatment (Table 1). A word's 'features' included its pronunciation, orthography, etymology, region, semantic field, plurality, and age. A word's 'quotational evidence' was the type and amount of written evidence, and the typographic features of the evidence (i.e. whether or not the word appeared in citations with italics, inverted commas, or brackets). A word's 'lexicographic treatment' was the presence or absence of tramlines, labelling, metalanguage, and square-bracketed quotations. A total of 1918 lexical items was analyzed in this way.

The method used to select words considered 'alien or not yet naturalized' was based on the same method of categorization of loanwords devised by James Murray. Words were selected according to their 'tramline eligibility' and their likely qualification as casuals, aliens, or denizens. I then examined

Table 1. Summary of parameters of the case study.

Features of the Word	
Pronunciation	*Is the pronunciation naturalized?*
Orthography	*Is the word's spelling naturalized? Does it include diacritics?*
Variant forms	*Is there more than one spelling variant?*
Etymology	*What is the word's provenance?*
Region	*From which region of the world does the word come?*
Semantic field	*To which semantic field does the word belong?*
Word class	*Is the word a noun, verb, or adjective?*
Plurality	*Was the word borrowed with the plural marking of its donor language?*
Grammatical gender	*Does the word demonstrate variants with the grammatical gender of its donor language?*
Age	*When did the word enter English?*
Quotational Evidence	
Number of quotations	*How many citations are in the quotation paragraph?*
Type of source	*Are all the citation sources of the same type (i.e. all travellers' tales, newspapers, encyclopaedias)?*
Italics	*Does the word appear in italics in the citations?*
Inverted commas	*Does the word appear in inverted commas in the citations?*
Gloss in brackets	*Is the word followed by a gloss in brackets in the citations?*
Lexicographic Treatment	
Tramlines	*Is the word marked with tramlines?*
Labelling	*Is there a regional or subject label?*
Metalanguage	*Is the word defined with the use of metalanguage?*
Square-bracketed quotations	*Are any quotations square-bracketed?*

their lexicographic treatment, most especially the use of tramlines. I say '*likely* to qualify' because this process proved as difficult as it must have been for the editors themselves.

A word was usually given tramlines if it appeared in citations with typographical features such as italics (e.g. *sedekah*, Malaysian alms; *kiack*, a Burmese Buddhist temple), inverted commas (e.g. *maya*, illusion; *sampan*, an African insect), diacritics (e.g. *matelassé*, French silk), or brackets with a gloss (e.g. *pagri*, an Indian turban). Most words with a non-naturalized pronunciation were given tramlines (e.g. *timbre* n.[3], the quality of a sound, appeared in *OED1* with French pronunciation [tēṅbr’]), as were many words with non-naturalized variant spellings (e.g. *tee*, a Burmese umbrella, with spelling variant *htee*), with foreign plural marking (e.g. Hebrew plural *mezuzoth* for *mezuzah*, a sacred Jewish text; Akan plural *abosom* for *obosom*, an Akan god), or with marking of grammatical gender (e.g. *yaksha*, a Sanskrit term in Indian mythology for a class of deities, appears with two feminine variants *yakshī* and *yakshiṇī*).

Tramlines were never put on a loanword if it was an acronym, ethnonym (name of a language or people), toponym (named after a place), eponym (named after a person), or trademark. Hence there were no tramlines on words such as *Chipewyan,* a North American Indian language and people*;* *Iatmul*, a people of Papua New Guinea; or *Kabyle,* a Berber language and people. Nor were there tramlines on *Kurrichane,* a kind of South African bird named after a town in western Transvaal; or *Ushak*, a kind of rug named after a town in Turkey, or *Nabeshima,* a kind of Japanese porcelain named after a family in feudal Japan. But there were tramlines on some words that demanded 'special' attention because they were extended uses of toponyms such as *Pont l'Évêque,* a French cheese named after a town in Normandy, which appeared with tramlines and a French pronunciation.

Burchfield based the structure of his *Supplement* volumes on that of the *1933 Supplement*: entries are structured in one of two ways depending on whether it is a new word (Type 1) or an addition to an existing word already in *OED1* (Type 2). Typically being sparser in structure and shorter in length, Type 2 entries consisted mainly of a headword and whatever the addition is (e.g. earlier or later quotations, an added sense or variant form); they did not repeat the entry from *OED1*, therefore most of them lacked pronunciations, etymologies, and definitions. Burchfield never put tramlines on Type 2 (presumably because they already had them in *OED1*), so I excluded Type 2 from the sample, except for fifteen 'special cases' in which the lexicographer's comments related to tramlines, such as instructions to delete tramlines from *OED1* headword (e.g. *abattoir, svelte*); instructions to add tramlines to additional senses (e.g. *damassé*); or instructions to add tramlines to additional variants (e.g. *qadi, qaimaqam*).[37]

Because Burchfield made the decision to reinstate tramlines on words without them in the *1933 Supplement*, Murray's original categories were important for him to understand and master. Documents in the *OED* archives reveal that, in private at least, Burchfield struggled to understand Murray's system of casuals, aliens, denizens, and naturals.[38] One box of papers contains his attempts to reproduce and learn Murray's categories, complete with diagrams, arrows, and circles showing the connections between the categories. Burchfield's musings on paper suggest that he struggled to negotiate the boundaries between Murray's categories. Whether or not a word was 'alien or not yet naturalized' was often difficult to determine. This is more a reflection of the complex pattern of borrowing in English rather than the functionality of Murray's system. Murray's system is even more commendable when we consider the fact that he devised it in the early 1880s, when comparative philology and work on borrowing was a relatively new science.

Case study results

The case study revealed that the *1933 Supplement* included proportionally more (5.4%) loanwords and World Englishes than Burchfield's *Supplement.* Of the 10% sample of each dictionary, 25.8% of Burchfield's *Supplement* was loanwords and World Englishes, as compared with 31.2% of the *1933 Supplement.*[39]

The case study revealed six main findings relating to the treatment of loanwords and World Englishes in both *OED Supplements*:

(1) Burchfield was not the *OED* editor who included the most World Englishes and loanwords; proportionally, Charles Onions included more World Englishes and loanwords than both Burchfield and Craigie.
(2) The *1933 Supplement* had a higher proportion of loanwords and World Englishes, including American English, than Burchfield's *Supplement.*
(3) Burchfield deleted 17% of World Englishes and loanwords in the *1933 Supplement.*
(4) Burchfield reinstated tramlines on words without them in the *1933 Supplement*, thereby assigning them a new 'alien' status.
(5) Analysis of loanwords revealed that the *1933 Supplement* sample had loanwords from forty-four donor languages (most came from French, Hindi, Spanish, and Arabic). Burchfield's *Supplement* sample had loanwords from eighty languages (most came from French, Japanese, German, and Spanish).
(6) Analysis of neologisms and adaptations showed that a total of nine varieties of English were represented in both *Supplement* samples. The only difference in the representation of World Englishes in both *Supplements* was that Burchfield had proportionally more New Zealand English than Canadian English and South African English.

These six main findings will be discussed in the next sections, followed by a discussion of other findings relating specifically to Burchfield's lexicographic policies and practices on loanwords, as well as observations pertaining to trends in borrowing and the lexicographic practice used to accommodate and describe such trends.

Burchfield was not the OED editor who included the most World Englishes and loanwords; proportionally, Charles Onions included more World Englishes and loanwords than both Burchfield and Craigie.

If we calculate the average number of loanwords and World English words that were included by each editor of the *Supplements* (Onions, Craigie, and Burchfield) in relation to the total number of words per page per letter of the alphabet, we get a surprising result: 0.42, 0.19, and 0.29 respectively. In other words, proportionally, Charles Onions put in 45% more loanwords and World Englishes than Burchfield and 121% (over double) more than Craigie, and Burchfield included 53% more than Craigie (Figure 6.1).

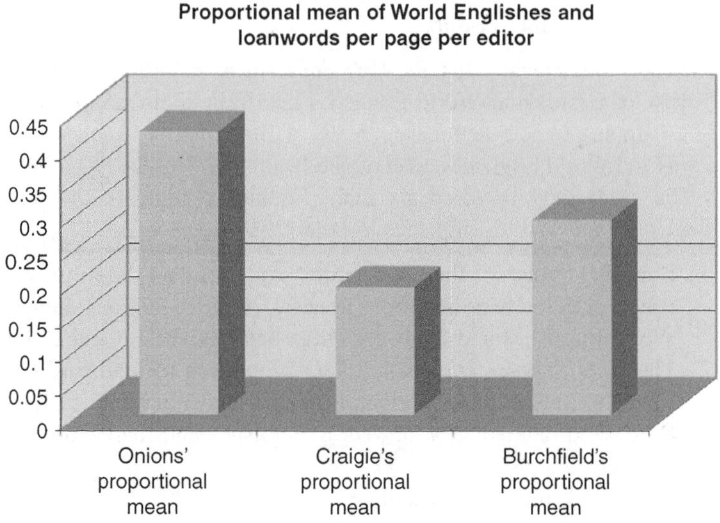

Figure 6.1 Bar graph showing the proportion of World Englishes and loanwords per page per editor (Onions 0.42, Craigie 0.19, Burchfield 0.29)

If we compare the sections of the alphabet of the *1933 Supplement* edited by Onions (A–K, S, and T) with the sections edited by Craigie (L–R, U–Z), we see that the peak in the second half of the alphabet (Craigie's portion) corresponds to the letters S and T, which were edited by Onions (Appendix 5).

When the proportion of World Englishes and loanwords in the *1933 Supplement* is compared with the proportion in Burchfield's *Supplement*, we see that Onions outstrips Burchfield on every letter except A (0.26:0.28) and C (equal proportions). Craigie and Burchfield are equal in the proportion of their coverage of World Englishes and loanwords in X, but Craigie outstrips Burchfield on every other letter except U, V, Y, and Z (Appendix 6).

Isolating loanwords in the sample, Onions outstrips both Craigie and Burchfield on his proportion of loanwords: he included 12% more than Burchfield and 533% (over five times) more than Craigie. Burchfield included 466% (over four times) more loanwords than Craigie.

If we separate the proportion of World English neologisms and adaptations included by Onions, Craigie, and Burchfield per page per letter of the alphabet (0.23, 0.16, 0.12 respectively) from the proportion of loanwords (0.19, 0.03, and 0.17 respectively), we get the following results: Onions included 92% more World English neologisms and adaptations than Burchfield and 44% more than Craigie, and Craigie included 33% more than Burchfield.

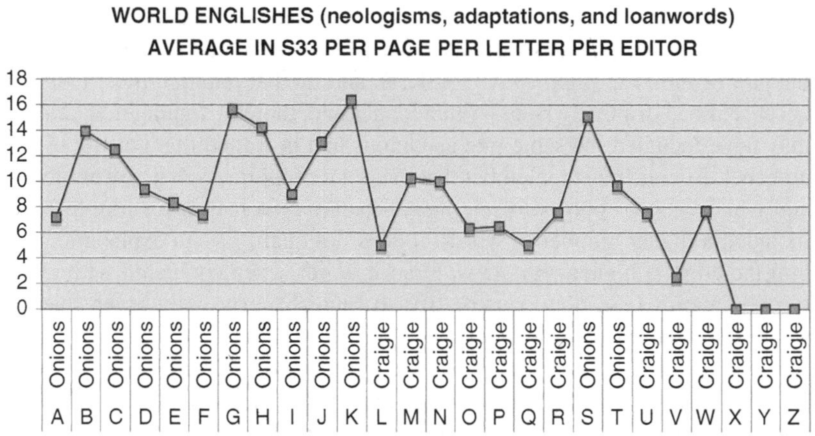

Appendix 5 Line graph showing the average number of loanwords and World Englishes in the *1933 Supplement* per page per letter per editor. Letters edited by Onions are marked by orange dots, and letters edited by Craigie are marked by blue dots. N.B. the peak in the second half of the alphabet (letters S and T edited by Onions). (See Appendix at end of book for colour version of this figure.)

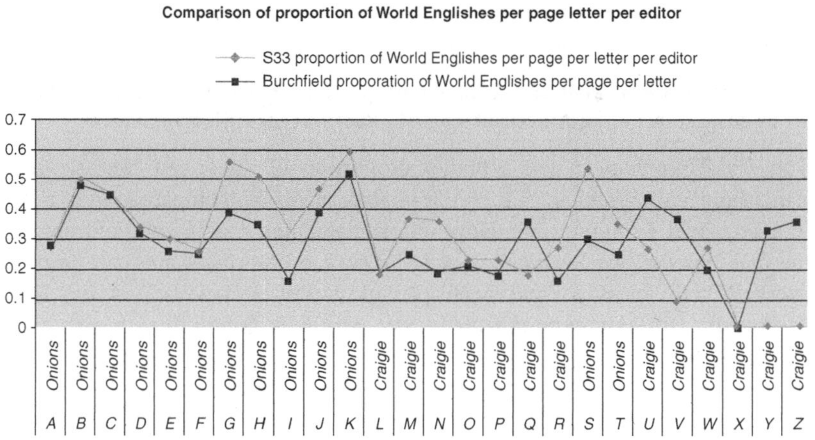

Appendix 6 Line graph showing the proportion of World Englishes (neologisms, adaptations, and loanwords) in the *1933 Supplement* (orange line) compared with that in Burchfield's *Supplement* (blue line). (See Appendix at end of book for colour version of this figure.)

When comparing Onions with Craigie, one might be tempted to infer that Onions' larger proportions were due to the fact that he had responsibility for the part of the *1933 Supplement* (A–K, S, and T) that required most revision because it had originally been written longer ago, thereby arguing that Craigie may have included the same rate as Onions had he edited that portion of the alphabet. But one must remember that these are proportions, not raw numbers, and while Onions' portion of the alphabet may be a reason for him to have included a higher number of words, it does not qualify as an explanation for him including a higher *proportion* of such words when compared with other types of words (e.g. non-loans or British English), especially given that no such bias occurred in *OED1*.

It must be highlighted that this is the only part of the vocabulary (World English neologisms and adaptations) in which Craigie includes a higher proportion than Burchfield. Craigie's inclusion of neologisms and adaptations coincides with the liberal policy of inclusion he displayed in his work on Americanisms (i.e. American neologisms and adaptations), in particular the dictionary he wrote with James Hulbert, *Dictionary of American English on Historical Principles* (1939–44). As articulated in the dictionary preface, Craigie and Hulbert had a liberal policy of inclusiveness: '[*The Dictionary of American English*] includes, however, not only words and phrases which are clearly or apparently of American origin, or have greater currency here than elsewhere, but also every word denoting something which has a real connection with the development of the country and the history of its people.'[40]

The *1933 Supplement* had a higher proportion of loanwords and World Englishes, including American English, than Burchfield's Supplement.

The *1933 Supplement* had a higher proportion of American English than Burchfield's *Supplement,* i.e. no less than 95% as compared with 81% in Burchfield's *Supplement.* How unfortunate then that Burchfield spread the message that his *Supplement* was the first to describe American English properly. His message had been picked up by reviewers and by Tom McArthur (1993), who commented: 'as a result, in noting this change from the first editor's policy, American reviewers of the fourth *Supplement* commented that at last their variety of the language was being properly catalogued in the great book'.[41]

One might assume on the face of it that the substantial coverage of American English in the *1933 Supplement* was due solely to Craigie, who had access to American English materials through his joint role as editor of the *Dictionary of American English,* having moved to Chicago in 1925. This would surely have had something to do with it, and, indeed, early on in the planning for the *1933 Supplement* it was proposed that Craigie would provide the 'Americana' for the dictionary. Was Craigie therefore responsible for all

Onions' American entries? An inspection of the slips for these American entries shows that while some slips were written by Craigie or his assistants, the vast majority were not. Onions also wrote several letters to Craigie requesting information on American words he wanted to include. Unless Craigie sent Onions a list of words and quotations from America which Onions then wrote onto his own slips – an unprecendented practice and one for which there is no such evidence in the archives – then it appears that Onions was responsible for the majority of his American entries, not Craigie.

Burchfield deleted 17% of all World Englishes and loanwords in the *1933 Supplement*

The case study revealed that Burchfield deleted World Englishes and loanwords that were included in the *1933 Supplement*. The deletion of entries went against all *OED* policy before and since: usually, once a word is added to the *OED*, it remains forever. If a word becomes obsolete, it is marked with a small dagger beside the headword, but *OED* policy is that it is never removed from the dictionary.

Nevertheless, Burchfield deleted 17% of all neologisms, adaptations, and loanwords in the *1933 Supplement* sample (Appendix 7). Loanwords accounted for 20% of Burchfield's deletions, and neologisms and adaptations accounted for 80%. This is surprising given Burchfield's reassurance in the preface that 'nearly all the material in the *1933 Supplement* has been retained here, though in revised form'.[42] And even more surprising given his comment in *Newsweek* that 'It seemed obvious to me that the vocabulary of all English-speaking countries abroad should receive proper attention,' and his insistence to the *Dallas Morning News* that 'it is exceedingly difficult to draw the line or leave out words. To ignore a country or a subject when compiling a dictionary would be like leaving some gold unmined.'[43]

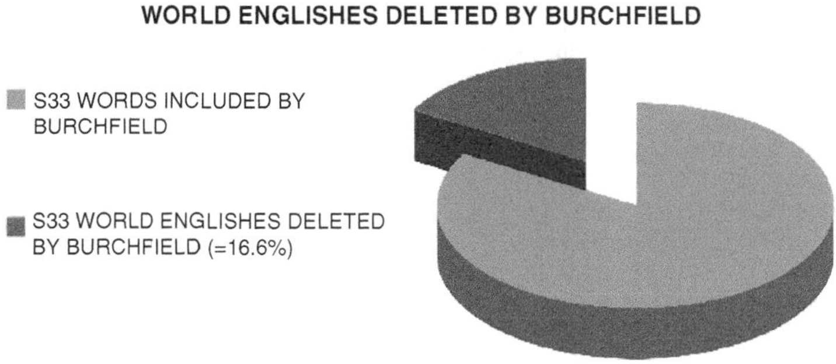

Appendix 7 List of entries deleted from the *1933 Supplement* sample by Burchfield in his *Supplement*. The case study revealed that Burchfield deleted 17% (16.6%) of the sample. (See Appendix at end of book for colour version of this figure.)

Table 2. Sample of words deleted by Burchfield from the 1933 supplement. *These words, Burchfield was going against* OED *policy.*

aberglaube	calaboose	danchi	juba
about and about	calculate *v.*	dicky, *n*	labour, *n.*
apex, *v.*	calico flower	die, *n2*, to make	machine-oven
apex-right, *n.*	calico-back	a die of it	milk sociable
aposaturnium	calico-bass	Doosuti	milk-and-molasses
appeaseless, *adj.*	calico-tree	eagle, *n.*	milk-sick
bake-kettle	call-box	ear-corn	milk-sickness
bake-oven	calling card	easternmost,	Mohawk *v.*
baldness	call-meeting	*adj.*	myal
bale-rope	calloused *ppl adj*	fandangle, *v.*	nap, *n3*
balisaur	cart-wheel	fanning, *vbl n.*	negro-car
bancal	casa	frog-farm, *n.*	pail, *n.*
batten *v2*	chancer, *v.*	frog-pond	pin-hook
batter *v2*	chancery, *v.*	front door	pinkling, *n.*
beagle-hound	chaparral	front, *n.*, to get	sancho, *n2*
Boviander	chermany	in front of	sand-draw
bowery	cherry birch	oneself	seater
bowie *n2*	chesser, *n.*	frontier colt	section, *n.*
bowman's root	chessy, *adj2*	gad	sedge boat
bow-wood	chestnutting,	ghetchoo	seed-cake
box (out), *v1*	*vbl n.*	ghost-racket	seerhand
box elder	chic, *adj.*	gift book-store	shake, *v.*, to shake
box, *v1*	chicaric	gift enterprise	on to
boxing, *vbl n.*	chicken, *n1*	gift store	shal
box-stew	chicken-eater	gift-deed	shammatha
box-stoop	chicken-thief	gift-tree	shape, *n2*
boyam	chief hare	gouger, *n.*	shave, *n2*
brace *v2*	chill, *n.*	gouging, *vbl n.*	shebbel
brace, *n4*, to	chimney- sweeper	gourd fiddle	sheller, *n2*
take a brace	chin stuff	government	shelter-house
brag *n1*	chinche	goy-blamed,	sours, *n.*
cabbage land	chinked *ppl adj.*	*pa pple*	swaly, *adj2*
cabinet finish	chinking, *vbl n1*	haciendero	swamp fuchsia
cabinet furniture	chinkle	Highlander, Arctic	swampy, *adj.*
cabinet shop	chinook, *v.*	Highlander	swear off, *n.*
cabinet ware	chip hat	hill-side *attrib.*	taa
cabinet work	chipper	huff *v.*	tab, *n1*
cain, *n2*, what	dairy, *n.*	iboga	tacuacine
in Cain	dajaksch	igloowik	user, *n2*
cake, *v.*	dalle, *n2*	iztli	wading-place
calabazilla	dance-cellar	jack-hunting	wake-up

World English neologisms and adaptations comprised 80% of Burchfield's deletions. These fell into four types of entries: full entries (e.g. American English *wake-up*, a golden-winged wood-pecker); added examples which antedated existing entries and could change a word's provenance from British to American (e.g. *chestnutting*, the gathering of chestnuts, remains a British activity in the *OED* despite the *1933 Supplement* finding earlier American examples of usage); added examples which post-dated existing entries and could show that a British word was no longer obsolete or rare because it was fossilized in American English (e.g. the *1933 Supplement* entry for American English *beagle-hound*, meaning a beagle, showed that the British use, last recorded in 1552 in the *OED*, was recorded in American usage in the twentieth century); and combinations of both antedatings and post-datings (e.g. the *1933 Supplement* entry for American English *chancer*, a verb meaning 'to tax', provided a 114-year antedating and four later quotations showing that it was still used in the twentieth century).

All World English neologism and adaptation deletions from the *1933 Supplement* sample were Americanisms, except one term from Australian English, *swamp fuchsia*, a plant species defined by Craigie as '*Eremophilia maculata* of Queensland'. Most of the deletions displayed only one quotation, but 12% of the sample displayed more than one quotation and long histories, e.g. the Americanism *government*, referring to the governing body of a college, had five quotations in a variety of sources dating from 1787 to 1908; *frog-pond* had seven quotations dating from 1635 to 1891; and *wading-place*, used to refer to a ford, had five quotations dating back to 1598. The list shows that the deletions belonged to all parts of speech.

Loanwords accounted for 20% of all Burchfield's deletions in the sample. If a loanword appeared in the *1933 Supplement* with only one or two quotations, and if these quotations came from encyclopaedias or dictionaries, then in most cases (but not all) Burchfield deleted the word. For example, *balisaur*, an Indian badger-like animal, only had one quotation taken from the *Cassell's Encyclopedic Dictionary* and was deleted by Burchfield.

But it is not always clear why Burchfield deleted certain words from the *1933 Supplement*. For example, *shape*, n^2 a Tibetan councillor, appears in the *1933 Supplement* with three quotations from a variety of sources; and *boviander*, the name in British Guyana for a person of mixed race living on the river banks, appears in the *1933 Supplement* with four quotations taken from a selection of sources (books, newspapers, and travellers' tales), showing the word used in full English contexts, such as the 1899 quotation 'A boviander with whom he could chat about hunting and fishing on the rivers' taken from James A. Rodway's *In Guiana Wilds: A Study of Two Women* (Figure 6.2).

Similarly, there is no obvious reason why Burchfield deleted *danchi*, a Bengali shrub, which appears in the *1933 Supplement* with three quotations

9 Oct. 2/1 The garden, with odorous bouvardias all awake.

Boviander (bōu·viændəɹ). [Etym. doubtful.] A name given in British Guiana to the people of mixed race who live on the river-banks.

1875 VENESS *Ten Yrs. Mission Life Brit. Guiana* 10 Some families of mixed race, called 'Bovianders', whose progenitors—of negro extraction—had intermarried with the Indians. 1882 *Timehri* June 145. 1895 *Sat. Rev.* 21 Dec. 828 The 'boviander' is almost amphibious...He may be a pure negro, a mulatto, or an indistinguishable compound of black, red, and white races, but, whatever his ancestry, he is always at home on or in the water. 1899 RODWAY *Guiana Wilds* 21 A boviander with whom he could chat about hunting and fishing on the rivers.

Figure 6.2 The entry *boviander* in the *1933 Supplement*, deleted by Burchfield in his *Supplement*. (Credit: OUP)

handed from the foeman's land—without..scalps to dance.

Danchi (dɒ·ntʃi). Also **dhanicha, dhunchee, dhun-chî, dunchee.** [Bengali.] A tropical shrub, *Sesbania aculeata*; also, the bast fibre obtained therefrom.

a 1815 ROXBURGH *Flora Indica* 571 Cultivation of the Dhunchi plant. 1866 *Treas. Bot.* s.v. *Sesbania*, *S. aculeata*, the Danchi of India, is an erect slightly branched annual. 1887 MOLONEY *Forestry W. Afr.* 312 'Dhunchee' or 'Danchi'...Cultivated about Calcutta during the rains.

Figure 6.3 The entry *danchi* in the *1933 Supplement*, deleted by Burchfield in his *Supplement*. (Credit: OUP)

taken from a selection of plant and forestry books showing the word used in full English contexts, and arguably comparable to the Bengali and Hindi word *dhan*, rice in the husk, which Burchfield did not delete from the *1933 Supplement* (where it also appeared with three quotations comparable to those at *danchi*) (Figure 6.3).

Burchfield's deletions were not confined solely to World Englishes and loanwords, and further study is needed to identify what proportion of all deletions belonged to other vocabulary. Until further detailed study, we can only estimate the proportion by comparing the 17% figure of this case study with a smaller case study done by Hans Heinrich Meier in 1979. In a review of Burchfield's 1972 *Supplement* (S72), Meier took a sample of 100 entries in the letter D and compared it with the same portion in the *1933 Supplement* (S33). He reported that 'S72 is here found to completely omit some items from S33, viz: dimplingly, +Dinarian, dine in, +Dingar, dingled, +Diocletian'.[44] Meier (1979: 649) calculated that this equated to a deletion rate of 22% of his sample. Three of Burchfield's six deletions in Meier's sample were foreign words or derivatives of foreign words: *Dinarian*, denoting a division of Triassic rocks named after a mountain in Dalmatia; *Dingar*, a wild bee of East India; and *Diocletian*, denoting the persecution of Christians named after a Roman Emperor. Although Meier's sample of 100 words was too small to be statistically comparable with my own case study findings, taking the two together does suggest that loanwords and World Englishes do account for the majority of deletions. However, further research is needed to be able to assert this with any authority and statistical reliability.

Because Burchfield's *Supplement* did not entirely replace the *1933 Supplement*, the latter should not be dispensed with. But Burchfield thought otherwise. He predicted in his preface to the first volume that the *1933 Supplement* 'will in future descend, along with other rarely consulted works, into the vaults of the larger libraries'.[45] Burchfield's message was characteristically echoed by reviewers: Donald B. Sands remarked in *College English* that 'Uutimately [sic.] libraries may retire the *Supplement* of 1933 from their active reference shelves', and A. J. Aitken stated in the *TLS* that 'the entire contents of [the *1933 Supplement*] which it [Burchfield's *Supplement*] will incorporate and so supersede'.[46] Again, we see reviewers and journalists relying on Burchfield's account of his dictionary, and echoing his message.

In spite of the fact that Burchfield deleted 17% of all World Englishes and loanwords in the *1933 Supplement*, the language of his definitions is generally more culturally sensitive than that found in the *1933 Supplement*. For example, Burchfield rephrases uses of the word 'natives' in the *1933 Supplement*: *chiragh* was defined in the *1933 Supplement* as 'A primitive lamp used by natives in India', but Burchfield changed the definition to 'A primitive lamp used in India and adjacent countries'. Similarly, *kahuna*, which is defined in *1933 Supplement* as 'A Hawaiian witchdoctor' was defined by Burchfield as 'A Hawaiian priest or minister; an expert or wise man'.

Despite Burchfield's efforts to use more culturally sensitive language in definitions, his etymologies rarely differed from those in the *1933 Supplement*, and both dictionaries used the general term 'native name' when an exact donor language was not known (e.g. *kau kau*, a New Guinea sweet potato; *luluai*, a village headman in New Guinea; *palang*, a penis piercing in

Borneo and the Philippines). In a few cases, Burchfield managed to specify the donor language otherwise given as 'native name' in the *1933 Supplement* (e.g. Burchfield specifies the etymology of *ukulele*, a Hawaiian guitar < Hawaiian; and *ponga*, a New Zealand fern < Maori). The *1933 Supplement* sometimes only gave a country name for an etymology, 'Angola' for *ife*, a liliaceous plant; or 'Brazil' for *jacitara*, a South American palm; but Burchfield changes these to 'Native name' and 'Tupi' respectively. It was rare in the sample to find the two dictionaries with different etymologies for a word, but it did happen (e.g. the *1933 Supplement* has *kakur*, a barking deer < Javanese, but Burchfield's *Supplement* has *kakur* < Hindi).[47]

Burchfield reinstated tramlines on words without them in the *1933 Supplement*, thereby assigning them a new 'alien' status.

The case study reaffirmed what has already been revealed in the previous chapter: the editors of the *1933 Supplement* dropped tramlines to distinguish a word as 'alien or not yet naturalized', but Burchfield reinstated them.[48] It seems likely that Onions and Craigie were influenced by the doctrine of assimilation of foreign words promulgated by the Society for Pure English. Their practice of not marking words with tramlines coincides with that of the current editors of *OED3* who believe that if a word is used in an English context, then it is an English word and should not be treated differently. Ironically, Burchfield removed the tramlines from *rhexis,* one of the two words with tramlines in the *1933 Supplement*; he antedated and marked the medical sense as obsolete, and added a new biological sense 'the fragmentation of a cell'.

Burchfield added tramlines to many words, such as the Malaysian English word *sambal*, a spicy condiment; the South African English word *aasvogel*, a South African vulture; the Indian English word *gadi*, a cushioned throne; the Japanese word *kuruma*, a rickshaw; and the New Zealand English word *taiaha*, a Maori club (weapon). By reinstating tramlines, Burchfield was opening himself to criticism similar to that which he had placed on the earlier editors: it could be seen as pushing these words back to the outer circle of naturalization and treating them 'almost like illegal immigrants'. This suggests that he was working to a set of differing standards within the lexicon, much like those editors whom he had blamed for thinking 'of British English as the central vocabulary, and of American, Australian, etc. English as at the periphery'. This is all the more surprising given that Burchfield wrote in the preface of his dictionary:

> Words more or less restricted to North America, Australia, New Zealand, South Africa, the West Indies, and so on, were treated almost like illegal immigrants [by earlier editors]. All that has been changed and, as far as possible, equality of attention has been given to the sprawling vocabulary of all English-speaking countries.[49]

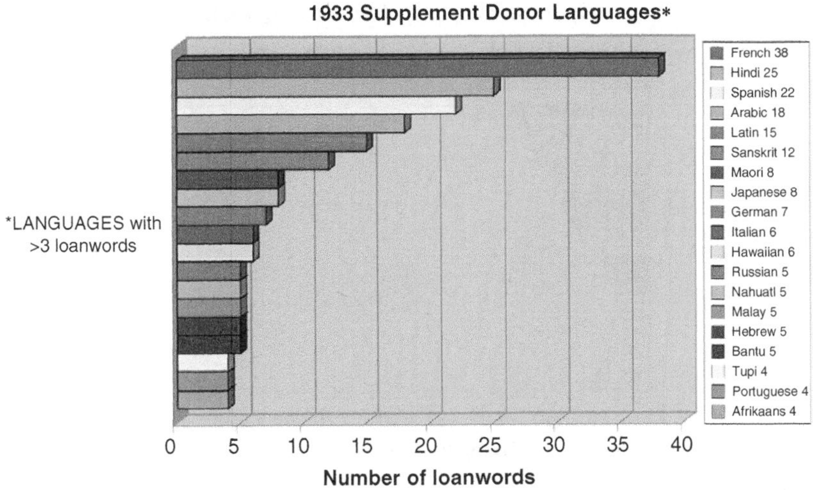

Appendix 8 Bar graph showing *donor languages that contributed more than three loanwords in the *1933 Supplement.* (See Appendix at end of book for colour version of this figure.)

The *1933 Supplement* sample had loanwords from forty-four donor languages (most came from French, Hindi, Spanish, and Arabic). Burchfield's *Supplement* sample had loanwords from eighty languages (most came from French, Japanese, German, and Spanish).

It is estimated that 6800 languages are spoken in the world today, and the case study revealed that 81 (less than 2%) of these are donor languages of loanwords in the samples.[50] Most loanwords in the *1933 Supplement* came from French, Hindi, Spanish, and Arabic (Appendix 8). Most loanwords in Burchfield's *Supplement* came from French, Japanese, German, and Spanish (Appendix 9). The samples showed the presence of more donor languages in Burchfield's *Supplement* (80 languages) than the *1933 Supplement* (44 languages), but this is to be expected given that the Burchfield sample was nearly three times larger than the sample taken from the *1933 Supplement* (6937 words and 2427 words respectively).

Overall, the *1933 Supplement* included 66% more World English neologisms and adaptations than Burchfield's *Supplement* in the sample. Analysis of neologisms and adaptations showed that a total of nine varieties of English were represented in both *Supplements*. The only difference in the representation of World Englishes in both *Supplements* was that Burchfield had proportionally more New Zealand English than Canadian English and South African English.

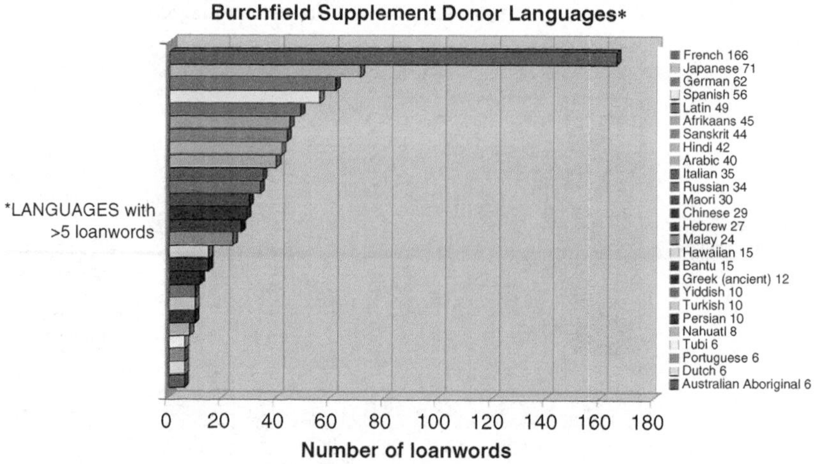

Appendix 9 Bar graph showing *donor languages that contributed more than five loanwords in Burchfield's *Supplement*. (See Appendix at end of book for colour version of this figure.)

If we exclude loanwords, and only consider the treatment of World English neologisms and adaptations in each *Supplement*, we see that, taking the mean per page per letter of the alphabet, the *1933 Supplement* includes 66% more neologisms and adaptations than Burchfield's *Supplement*.[51] This goes against the general view that Burchfield's *Supplement* was the first to make 'bold forays into written English of regions outside the British Isles', or as Brewer (1993) put it: Robert Burchfield had been 'determined to include as much non-English English as possible'.[52] It certainly puts into question the assertion by Weiner (1987) that Burchfield's coverage of World Englishes virtually amounted to the equivalent of a collection of World English dictionaries:

> The description of the [Burchfield's] *Supplement*'s coverage of the language of these areas, or at least of the major five (the United States, Canada, Australia, New Zealand, and South Africa) as a series of 'forays' is rather too modest. In fact, the *Supplement*'s coverage is so full that it is not far from equivalent to a collection of dictionaries of their contemporary vocabulary.[53]

Altogether, nine varieties of English were represented in both *Supplements*: American English, Australian English, Canadian English, Caribbean English, Indian English, Malaysian English, New Zealand English, South African English, and West African English. As already noted, the *1933 Supplement* had a higher proportion of American English than Burchfield's *Supplement* (95% and 81% respectively).

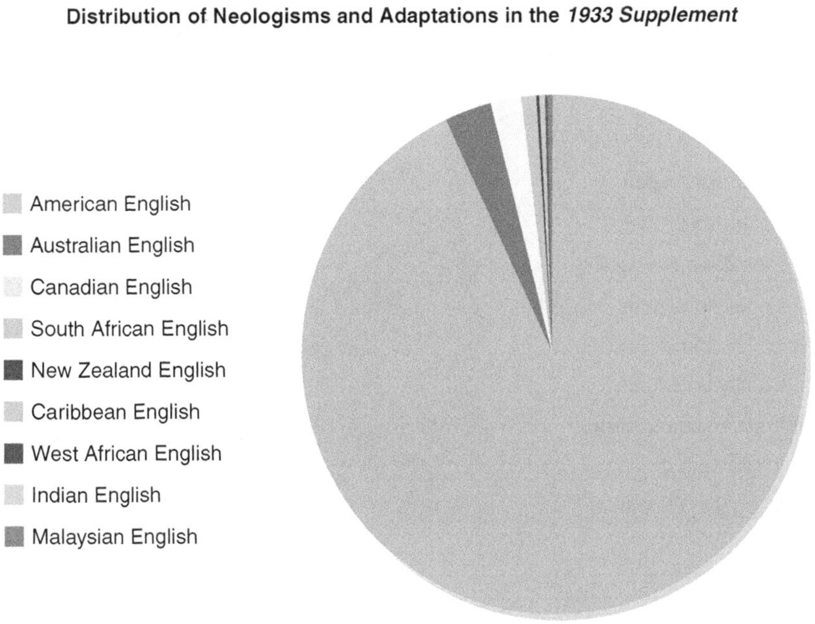

Appendix 10 Pie chart showing the proportional representation of neologisms and adaptations in the *1933 Supplement*. (See Appendix at end of book for colour version of this figure.)

The only difference in the representation of World Englishes in both *Supplements* was that Burchfield had proportionally more New Zealand English than Canadian English and South African English (Appendix 10 and Appendix 11). This slight bias towards New Zealand English may be explained by the fact that Burchfield was a New Zealander by birth and lived in New Zealand until the age of twenty-six, when he went to Oxford as a Rhodes Scholar in 1949.

There is a clear bias in both *Supplements* in coverage of words from American, Australian, New Zealand, and Canadian English. These are words from countries that Phillipson (1992) describes in his book *Linguistic Imperialism* as rich and dominant 'core English-speaking countries' as opposed to poorer 'periphery English-speaking countries'. It could be argued, therefore, that the *OED*'s coverage of this vocabulary prioritized them in a way that added to Phillipson's concept of 'linguistic imperialism' in which 'the dominance of English is asserted and maintained by the establishment and continuous reconstitution of structural and cultural inequalities between English and other languages'.[54] Phillipson defines these 'structural inequalities' as material properties such as institutions and financial allocations, and 'cultural

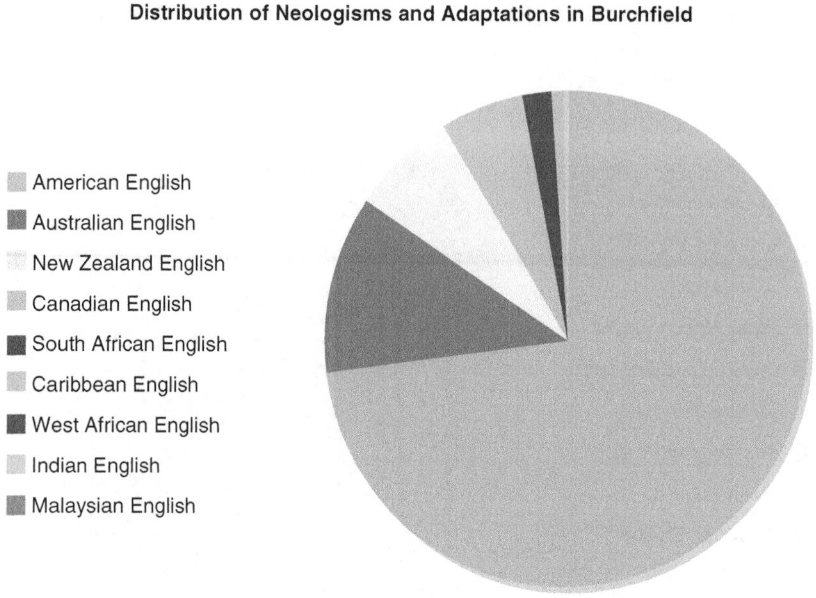

Appendix 11 Pie chart showing the proportional representation of neologisms and adaptations in Burchfield's *Supplement*. (See Appendix at end of book for colour version of this figure.)

inequalities' as immaterial or ideological properties such as attitudes and pedagogic principles.[55]

Adherents of the linguistic imperialism theoretical approach might want to argue from the results of this case study that the *OED* supported and contributed to such structural and cultural inequalities between different varieties of English. They might suggest that the bias of words from 'core English-speaking countries' in the *OED*, such as Australian English and New Zealand English, had contributed to allocation of more material resources to benefit those who are proficient in speaking 'core' Englishes, as was demonstrated in the amount of resources invested in publishing national and historical dictionaries such as the *National Australian Dictionary* (1988) by Bill Ramson and the *Dictionary of New Zealand English* (1997) by Harry Orsman. However, this argument is not supported by the fact that resources were also invested in publishing the *Dictionary of South African English* (1996) by Penny Silva and the *Dictionary of Caribbean English Usage* (1996) by Richard Allsopp, both dictionaries of Phillipson's 'peripheral' English.

The discrepancies in coverage of different Englishes, and the relatively low proportion of words from Caribbean English and African varieties of English (including West African English but excluding South African English) in particular, was highlighted by one reviewer of the first volume of Burchfield's *Supplement*. 'There appears to be little trace of the literary English of Black Africa, of the Caribbean, and nearer home, of Scotland' wrote A. J. Aitken in the *TLS*.[56] But such criticism was rare, and generally no one noticed the discrepancies in coverage between varieties of English. A. J. Aitken also pointed out that while the *OED* marked lexical items particular to regional varieties of English with abbreviated labels such as *Austral., Canad., N.Z.,* and *S. Afr.*, it did not mark items specific to Britain with a label such as 'U.K.' He called this 'latent elitism or parochialism (albeit inherited from *OED*)' and a 'blind spot in the *Supplement*'s appreciation of the regional distribution of word-usages':

> Whereas we are told that *apartment* is chiefly *N. Amer.* and corresponds to *flat* in British use, no converse note is provided under *flat*. Whereas *chip* (=(potato) *crisp*) is *chiefly U.S.*, neither *chip* (= *French fried*) nor (potato) *crisp* is labelled. *baby-carriage, cuff* (for 'turn-up'), *gasoline* and the rest are all labelled *U.S.*, but *bonnet* (of a car), *caravan, (the) gents,* and many other Briticisms are unlabelled either here or in the *OED*.[57]

In 1995, John Algeo criticized the *OED* for failing to label Briticisms, an oversight which Algeo insisted made the *OED* 'the worst offender of all dictionaries in biased labelling'. He observed that the *OED* 'makes no effort to identify uses that are restricted to the tight little island, or to its former dependencies in the Commonwealth'. The single omission of 'Brit' or 'U.K.' labels in the *OED* led Algeo to the extreme conclusion that 'this is the most egregious example of national bias in any English dictionary claiming to be international in scope'.[58] Algeo's criticism is harsh because it fails to account for the *OED*'s liberal inclusion of World Englishes in the first place, and its consistent use of labels and metalanguage in definitions for these entries.

That said, it is true that if the *OED* were to follow Aitken and Algeo's recommendation of labelling Briticisms, then it would be oriented as a truly international dictionary. The third edition of *OED* has not taken up such a proposal, but if regional Oxford dictionaries are anything to go by, then there might be a change of policy in the future. The *Australian Concise Oxford Dictionary* (3rd ed.) introduced 'Aust.' labels for Australianisms in 1997. This practice could be interpreted in two different ways: as a positive development because, as the preface stated, 'users of dictionaries are entitled to know if a particular word or meaning is geographically limited'; or as a negative development because by not marking a word as explicitly Australian, Australian lexicographers were taking their words as default, in the same way that the *OED* was taking Briticisms as default. The editor, Bruce Moore, explained it thus:

> Given the struggle during most of the twentieth century for Australian English to gain acceptance as a dialect in its own right, it is understandable that lexicographers in the 1980s and early 1990s felt that by not explicitly marking Australianisms as such they were giving appropriate status to those Australianisms (on the grounds that dictionaries produced in Britain did not use a *Brit.* label for specifically British words and meanings, and the dictionaries produced in the United States did not use a *US* label for specifically American words and meanings).[59]

The benefits to linguistic research are obvious, as Moore remarks: 'our decision to mark Australian words and meanings has been instructive in revealing the extent of the Australian lexicon.'[60] Indeed, 'Brit.' labels would allow linguists to comment on the extent of the British lexicon. However, the lexicographic task of introducing 'Brit.' labels into the *OED* would be immense, because the lexicographer would have to ensure that the word was strictly limited in use to Britain. This is easy to gauge for British dialects, but incredibly difficult – if not impossible – for terms that might appear to be confined to British use but in fact may also be used elsewhere in the world, especially in the postcolonial world. Tracing this kind of global usage in today's world is near impossible and any error in being too restrictive in labelling would open the *OED* editors to further criticism of national bias.

In addition to the six main findings of the case study, there were other observations relating to the treatment of loanwords that are worthy of discussion because they contribute to our general understanding of loanwords in English, and the *OED* editors' attitudes towards them. In particular, by analyzing Burchfield's eligibility criteria for tramlines and his actual use of tramlines, we gain insight into the borrowing process in English, and his understanding of it. While other studies such as Dekeyser (1986), Jucker (1994), Coleman (1995), Fischer (1997), Nevalainen (1999), Bauer (2001), Mair (2001), Markus (2001), and Hoffman (2004) use historical dictionaries as discrete corpora from which to comment on lexical change in English over time, no study has used the *OED Supplements*. This is no doubt because neither *Supplement* can be searched electronically, and therefore requires time-consuming manual examination. Another reason may be that the remit of the supplement, as opposed to the parent dictionary, is too restrictive to provide a balanced and useful corpus for general observations on lexical change. However, targeted corpora – in this case of vocabulary that was not included in *OED1* – are still useful. And this study opens the way for future study that could test the usefulness of such a corpus by comparing these results with a similar case study based on the complete corpus of *OED2* or *OED3*.

The case study revealed that a loanword's etymology had no direct bearing on Burchfield's inclusion policy or tramline policy. In other words, when it came to the task of judging a word as 'alien or not yet naturalized', Burchfield

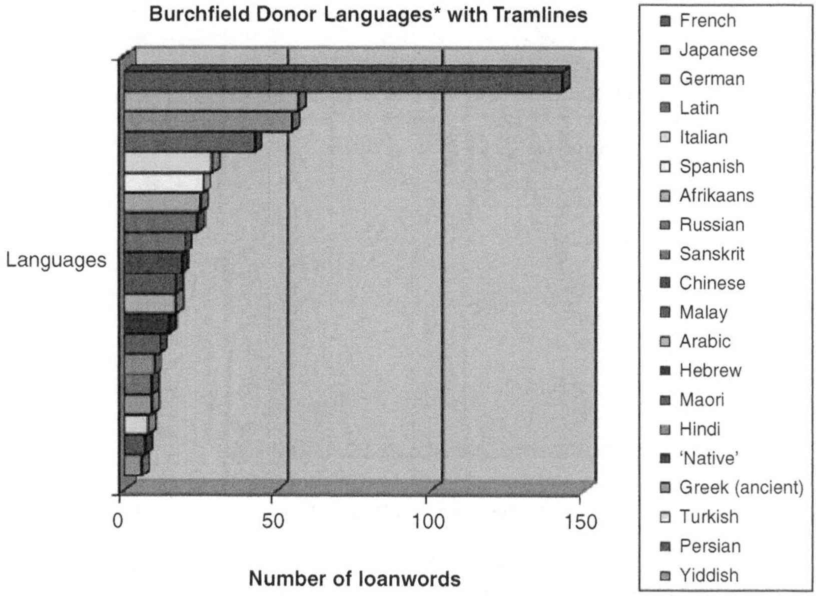

Appendix 12 Bar graph showing the top ten donor languages (that contributed more than five loanwords) given tramlines in Burchfield's *Supplement*. (See Appendix at end of book for colour version of this figure.)

had no bias against or for words from certain languages. Other features such as the word's pronunciation, and its typographic form in quotations, were more influential on his policy.

There were no instances in the case study sample where every word from a particular language (that contributed over five words) was given a tramline in Burchfield's *Supplement*, which suggests no blatant biases existed against a certain language.[61] The top ten donor languages in Burchfield's *Supplement* are not the top ten recipients of tramlines. For example, the top ten donor languages (regardless of tramlines) were French, Japanese, German, Spanish, Latin, Afrikaans, Sanskrit, Hindi, Arabic, Italian. The order changes for donor languages with tramlines: French, Japanese, German, Latin, Italian, Spanish, Afrikaans, Russian, Sanskrit, and Chinese (Appendix 12). Hindi and Arabic drop out of the top ten; Russian and Chinese move in, and Italian moves up from tenth place to fifth. The top ten donor languages without tramlines in Burchfield's *Supplement* are: Hindi, Spanish, Sanskrit, Arabic, French, Afrikaans, Maori, Japanese, Hebrew, and Hawaiian (Appendix 13).

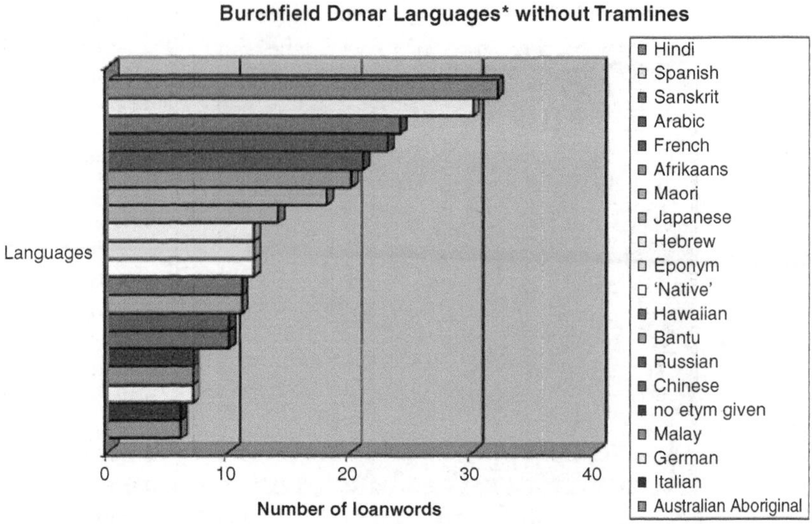

Appendix 13 Bar graph showing the top ten donor languages (that contributed more than five loanwords) not given tramlines in Burchfield's *Supplement*. (See Appendix at end of book for colour version of this figure.)

The case study revealed that the nativization, or naturalization, process played a large part in Burchfield's editorial policy and practice relating to loanwords. The degree of a word's nativization was determined from various factors that included pronunciation and typographic features such as italics, inverted commas, diacritics, and a gloss in brackets. With respect to pronunciation, a key factor in the success of a lexical borrowing is whether or not the word is pronounceable. Non-naturalized pronunciation was the second most important factor influencing Burchfield's decision to add tramlines to a headword. The appearance of the headword in italics in quotations was Burchfield's number one reason for tramlines.

English speakers use strategies to naturalize pronunciations such as accommodating donor sounds to the most similar sounds in English, or manipulating the spelling of a loanword to conform with the English sound system or orthography. Most loanwords go through a period of nativization, and the lexicographer must often describe a dynamic situation in which a loanword is partially nativized. This is often the case if a loanword has two or more pronunciations, one that is more authentic to the donor language and one that is more authentic to English. In the first volume of *OED1*, Murray made an interesting observation on how speakers naturalize loanwords: they naturalize words from unfamiliar languages more quickly than words from languages they know. For example, as he wrote in the preface of the first volume of the dictionary, 'words from French and the learned languages, especially Latin, which are assumed to be known to all the polite, are often kept in the position of denizens for centuries: we still treat *phenomenon* as Greek, *genus* as Latin, *aide-de-camp* as French.'[62]

The pronunciation of each word in the case study sample was examined in order to discern whether non-naturalized pronunciation was a feature that Burchfield recorded, and if so whether it influenced lexicographic practice such as tramlines. In more than half the sample (57%), a non-naturalized pronunciation was given and 69% of these occurred with tramlines on the headword. In most cases only the non-naturalized pronunciation was given, but if a naturalized pronunciation was also given, then it appeared before the non-naturalized pronunciation.

Both the *1933 Supplement* and Burchfield's *Supplement* used the same pronunciation system devised by Murray in *OED1*. Unlike IPA, this system marked stress with a raised dot '·' *after* the syllable, and provided for non-naturalized sounds by using special symbols never used for naturalized words. For example, the key to pronunciation in both *Supplements* has a separate column for eight 'foreign and non-southern' consonants such as **χ** for German a*ch* /aχ/, **γ** for north German sa*g*en /za·γên/, and **k**ʸ for Afrikaans baardmanne*tj*ie /ba·rtmanəkʸi/, and it has tramlines beside eleven vowel symbols reserved for 'foreign (or earlier English) words' such as ǁ*e* for French attach*é* and ǁö for German Köln.

For the case study, I took naturalized pronunciations as default (unmarked) and only recorded non-naturalized pronunciations. A pronunciation qualified as 'non-naturalized' if it satisfied one of three criteria:

(1) it appeared with tramlines within the pronunciation brackets, or
(2) it comprised symbols listed in the key to pronunciation as reserved solely for 'foreign and non-Southern' consonants and 'foreign (and earlier English)' vowels, or
(3) it showed stress patterns typical of the donor language and atypical of English (e.g. word-final stress in Hebrew words such as *taharah*).

Seventeen entries in the case study sample appeared without tramlines on the headword but with tramlines solely on the pronunciation, and all these were included in the database, for example, *baardman* (Afrikaans pronunciation), *hartal* (Hindi pronunciation), *kabuki* (Japanese pronunciation), *kainga* (Maori pronunciation), *sacaton* (Mexican Spanish pronunciation), *sabotage* (French pronunciation), *sambal* (Malay pronunciation). In these cases the tramlined pronunciation appeared after the naturalized pronunciation.

In addition to typographic reasons (especially italics in the quotation) and non-naturalized pronunciation, other factors influencing Burchfield's use of tramlines included pluralization, grammatical gender, and variant spellings. The pluralization of each noun in the samples was examined in order to assess whether the word was borrowed with the plural marking of its donor language. The results showed that sixty-four words, 6% of the total sample, had this marking. These came from a spread of languages, for example, Japanese -Ø (*shaku,* a Japanese measure of length); Ashanti *a-* (*obosom*, an Akan god); Hebrew *-im* (*moshav*, a village in Israel); Russian *-i* (*ispravnik*, a Tsarist Russian chief of police); Latin *-i* (*miles gloriosus*, a character in Renaissance comedies) and *-a* (*judicatum*, a philosophical proposition); French *-aux* (*cheval de bataille*, an obsession); Italian *-e* (*frottola*, a type of fifteenth-century Italian popular song) and *-i* (*bozzetto*, a sketch for a larger painting); Afrikaans *-e* (*saaidam*, a basin of land used for irrigation); German *-en* (*übermensch*, a super human), *-e* (*nachtlokal*, a German nightclub), *-er* (*wunderkind*, a child prodigy), and *-n* (*rohrflöte*, an organ stop). A word marked with a foreign plural did not, however, guarantee the corresponding presence of tramlines. Tramlines appeared on the headwords of 79% of words with foreign pluralization, and in none of these cases was pluralization the sole reason for tramlines.

Pluralization was not the only marked feature of donor languages in the case study sample. Two loanwords, *yaksha* and *voyant*, also demonstrated variants with the grammatical gender features of their donor languages. *Yaksha,* a Sanskrit term in Indian mythology for a class of deities, appears with two feminine variants, *yakshī* and *yakshi-ṇī*. The adjective *voyant,* a French word meaning 'showy, gaudy, flashy', also demonstrated a variant form denoting the feminine *voyante*. Both words had tramlines, but grammatical gender in the donor language may not have been the sole reason for this because both words also displayed many other features that made them eligible for tramlines, such as non-naturalized pronunciation and typographical features.

Forty percent of the loanwords in the case study sample had one or more variant spelling. Tramlines appeared on the headword of 45% of these. Not all loanwords that occurred in the *1933 Supplement* appear in Burchfield's *Supplement* with the same spelling. In most cases this is because more quotational evidence was found for the Burchfield entry, and the headword chosen by Burchfield was the most frequent. For example, the Hawaiian plant, *ieie,* appeared as *ie* in the *1933 Supplement* but as *ieie* in Burchfield *Supplement* because most quotations showed the latter spelling. Similarly, the Hindi word for a flood plain appears as *kadir* in the *1933 Supplement*, but as *khadar* in Burchfield's *Supplement.*

In most instances, the editor did not recognize diacritics as a significant factor of variance. For example, the entry for the Hindi greeting, *namaskar,* lists the variants *namashkar* and *namaskara* but ignores the variant *namaskāra* in the first quotation. There was also no differentiation between variants with hyphens and those without; for example, the entry for *kala azar,* a tropical disease of Assam, ignores the variant *kala-azar* that occurs in four out of six quotations. Initial capital letters were a significant factor of variance; for example, the entry for the Japanese minister, *Rōjū,* lists *rōjū* as a variant. The highest number of variants listed is eleven for the Romani self-designation, *didicoi.* Some variants in Burchfield had tramlines beside them (e.g. ‖ *incomunicado*), but the headword, *incommunicado,* had no tramlines.

Despite ignoring diacritics as a basis for spelling variance, Burchfield does not ignore them for choice of headword spelling. In fact, in many cases he favoured a spelling with diacritics regardless of quotational frequency (e.g. *rézbányite,* a mineral deposit, *shahāda,* the Muslim profession of faith), or he lists two headwords with the diacritic spelling first (e.g. *rézel, rezel*; *piñata, pinata*). Burchfield's preference for headwords that preserve the orthography of the donor language is most obvious if we compare the spelling of the headwords in the *1933 Supplement* with the spelling of the same words in his *Supplement.* For example, the Angolan plant called *ife* in the *1933 Supplement* becomes *ifé* in Burchfield's *Supplement,* while only one of the three quotations bears the diacritic.

Burchfield takes this preference to its extreme with the headword *κατ' ϵζοχηv,* the Greek phrase meaning 'pre-eminently' (*kat' exochen*) (Figure 6.4). Admittedly, the word is spelled as *κατ' ϵζοχηv* in all five quotations, and, describing it as 'the more usual form of katexochen', Burchfield has included it to supplement the entry *katexoken* in *OED1*, but it is extraordinary that Burchfield chose the Greek-script form for the headword spelling. It is certainly the only entry in the *OED* to have a non-Roman script headword. In light of the fact that all non-Roman scripts that appeared in the etymologies of the *1933 Supplement* were deleted in Burchfield's *Supplement,* Burchfield's decision to include a headword with non-Roman script is particularly puzzling.

In fact, Burchfield's dropping of all non-Roman scripts was the main difference between etymologies in the *1933 Supplement* and Burchfield's *Supplement.* The *1933 Supplement* had followed the convention of *OED1* to gloss etymons using the writing system of the donor language, but Burchfield dropped this practice. For example, the etymology for *balakhana,* a room in a Persian house, in the *1933 Supplement* had both the Persian (Arabic) script and the roman equivalent, but Burchfield drops the Persian script and only gives the roman form. In cases such as *balalaika,* a Russian guitar, in which the *1933 Supplement* gives only the Russian (Cyrillic) script with no roman equivalent, Burchfield drops the Russian script and provides no roman form (i.e. the etymology is simply '[Russ.]').

(a)

|| **κατ' ἐξοχήν** (kăte·ksokīn, -kēin). More usual form of KATEXOKEN. [Gr. phr.] Pre-eminently, par excellence.

1588 A. FRAUNCE *Lawiers Logike* sig. ¶¶1v The Romayne Lawe, which Iustinian calleth the Cyuill law *κατ'εξοχην*, (as Homer is called the Poet). **1698** J. SERGEANT *Non Ultra* (in *Monist* XXXIX, 1929) 605. § 21

(b)

Which Propositions being..most fully and Properly such we do therefore, *κατ'ἐξοχην*, call Identical. **1841** MILL *Let.* 1 Mar. in *Works* (1963) XIII. 466 Poetry *κατ'ἐξοχήν* or poet's poetry as opposed to everybody's poetry. **1865** —— *Exam. Hamilton's Philos.* xx. 402 If any general theory of the sufficiency of Evidence and the legitimacy of Generalization be possible, this must be Logic *κατ'ἐξοχήν*. **1879** W. JAMES *Coll. Ess. & Rev.* (1920) 88 Schopenhauer ..says that Intuition..'is knowledge *κατ'ἐξοχήν*'.

Figure 6.4 Entry for the word *kat' exochen* appears in Burchfield's *Supplement* with the headword in the Greek alphabet *κατ' εζοχην*. (Credit: OUP)

In order to observe if editors of either dictionary had any bias towards certain types of cultural borrowings, I allocated a semantic field to each word (e.g. music, food, law, or plants), observed the number of words in each category in both dictionaries, and also compared the number of tramlines on words in Burchfield's categories. Some categories were already marked in the form of entry labels such as 'Ballet' (e.g. *changement de pieds,* a ballet jump, *soutenu*, a ballet movement); 'Chess' (e.g. *Zugzwang*, a forced move in chess; *zwischenzug*, an interim move in chess); 'Geology' (e.g. *gaize,* a type of sandstone; *pahoehoe*, a type of volcanic lava), 'Dressmaking' (e.g. *balayeuse*, a frill beneath a hem), 'Botany' (e.g. *bouvardia*, a Mexican plant), and 'Music' (e.g. *cabaletta,* a short aria; *zoppa*, a syncopated rhythm).

In Burchfield's *Supplement*, most semantic fields had a balanced number of tramlines (i.e. tramlines on about half the words in each semantic field), except 'Geology' and 'Judaism' (with tramlines on -hird) and Latin expressions and Latin and German philosophical terms (with tramlines on virtually all of them). There were virtually no tramlines on plant names, except those from Afrikaans, Japanese, and Maori (but not Hindi, Bantu, or Tupi). All nine Russian political terms had tramlines.

When the loanwords of both dictionaries were sorted according to their respective semantic fields, and compared according to the first dates of their quotational evidence, there emerged certain patterns of borrowing, or

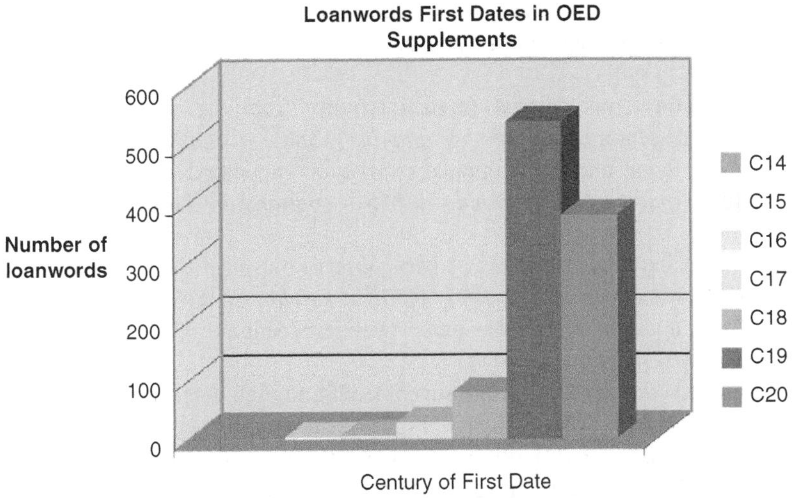

Appendix 14 Bar graph showing the first dates of loanwords in the sample. (See Appendix at end of book for colour version of this figure.)

'loanword phases'. History shows that groups of loanwords entered English in phases, depending on language contact and the importance of particular semantic fields at different times.[63] The case study revealed that the sample contained evidence of lexical borrowings in certain semantic fields. But before discussing the loanwords' phases that emerged when the data were sorted by semantic field, donor language, and first date, it is important to note that a first date in the *OED* is, as Murray recognized, rarely the exact first instance of a word's usage. 'The word was spoken before it was written', stated Murray in his presidential address to the Philological Society in 1884, 'the written instance is, in most cases, evidence, not that the word was then coming into use, but that it was already established and known to readers generally.'[64] Unless a word is known to be coined by a particular author in a particular text, it can usually be antedated. Nevertheless, the first date does provide a general barometer of usage and popularity, and it can therefore be used as a rough gauge of when a loanword entered English. The following patterns emerged in the samples of both *Supplements* (Appendix 14):

- Most words in the case study sample had first-date quotations from the nineteenth century.
- Most words in the case study sample came from French in the eighteenth and nineteenth centuries, in the fields of food and cooking (*soupe* [1767], *rognon* [1828], *chiffonade* [1877], *noix* [1845]), and the late nineteenth

century from clothing and fashion (*fanchon* [1872], *cache-peigne* [1873], *casaquin* [1879]), and culture and society (*milieu* [1854], *piou-piou* [1854], *roi soleil* [1890]).

- Most Latin terms entered English steadily from the fourteenth to the eighteenth century (*ignotum per ignotius* [1386], *ut supra* [1450], *ab extra* [1642]). Legal and philosophical expressions appeared in the nineteenth century (*pacta sunt servanda* [1855], *cogitandum* [1866], *cogitatum* [1878]).
- German contributed loanwords pertaining to music in the eighteenth and nineteenth centuries (*rohrflöte* [1773], *Tafelmusik* [1876], *nachschlag* [1879]), and politics in the early twentieth century (*Götterdämmerung* [1909], *Macht-politik* [1916]).
- Japanese words entered in the seventeenth and eighteenth centuries in the area of food (*tai* [1620], *katsuo* [1727][65]); in the nineteenth century in the area of art (*ukiyo-e* ([1879], *yamato* [1879]), and martial arts (*judo* [1889], *ju-jitsu* [1875]); and in the late nineteenth and early twentieth centuries in the areas of culture (especially theatre *nogaku* [1916], *katsuramono* [1916], and society *kabane* [1890], *Eta* [1897], *maiko* [1891]).
- Hindi words for plants and animals entered English predominantly in the nineteenth century (*babul* [1824], *dhoona* [1846], *bandar* [1885]).
- Sanskrit words pertaining to religion in general, and Hinduism and Buddhism specifically, entered English mainly in the eighteenth century (*maharisha* [1785], *vajra* [1788], *Saman* [1798]).

These loanword phases can be summarized in ten points:

1. Most plant and animal terms came from Afrikaans and Hindi in the nineteenth century.
2. Most architecture terms came from French and German in the nineteenth and twentieth centuries.
3. Art terms were borrowed into English in the nineteenth and twentieth centuries from French, Japanese, or Italian.
4. Bird names were borrowed into English mainly from Hawaiian and Afrikaans in the eighteenth and nineteenth centuries.
5. Types of boats were borrowed into English from Arabic and Malay in the nineteenth and early twentieth centuries.
6. Buddhism terms were borrowed in the nineteenth and twentieth centuries from either Sanskrit, Tibetan, or Japanese.
7. Food and drink terms predominantly came from French in the eighteenth and nineteenth centuries, and from Italian and Japanese in the nineteenth and twentieth centuries.
8. Clothing terms came from French in the eighteenth and nineteenth centuries.

9. Dance terms (especially ballet terms) came from French in the eighteenth and nineteenth centuries, and from Spanish in the nineteenth century.
10. Fish and food terms came from Afrikaans in the eighteenth and nineteenth centuries.

Borrowing varies across word classes. It is generally believed that nouns are more readily borrowed than any other word class, followed by adjectives and verbs. The closed sets of pronouns and conjunctions are rarely borrowed. The data in the case study support these generalizations: 99% of the loanwords were nouns, 0.8% adjectives (e.g. *bahuvrihi,* of or relating to a Sanskrit grammatical term; *sacré,* holy; *voyant*, showy) and 0.2% verbs (e.g. *Mohawk*, to masquerade as a Mohawk, although this was probably coined in English from the noun, rather than borrowed). None of the loanwords belonged to basic or core vocabulary, a category that is generally known to resist change and borrowing.[66]

Loanwords enter a language for historical, political, and cultural reasons. For example, an increase in trade and business links in the postwar era would have contributed to greater linguistic exchange. The rise in German and Japanese loanwords in Burchfield's *Supplement* (they ranked eighth and ninth in the *1933 Supplement* but ranked third and second, respectively, in Burchfield's *Supplement*) is possibly a consequence of the world war of the intervening years. The words may have existed in English long before the war (e.g. half the German words have first quotations pre-dating 1914, and the majority of the Japanese words pre-date the twentieth century[67]), but, as is often the case with loanwords, international events highlight loanwords and bring them into wider usage, and hence to the lexicographer's attention.

Some World English terms were exchanged between varieties of English and used in new war contexts. For example, the British forces fighting in the Sudan in 1885 coined the term *fuzzy-wuzzy* to refer to the Sudanese warrior; the term was made famous by Rudyard Kipling's poem of this title published in 1890, but was similarly applied by speakers of Australian English to Papua New Guineans in World War II.[68]

There are instances of borrowing between varieties in the other direction too, i.e. many loans entered World Englishes before finding their way into more general British English usage. Australian English borrowed terms from the languages of the regions it had contact with through war: Walter Hubert Downing remarked in the preface to *Digger Dialects* (1919), his famous dictionary of words used by Australians in World War I: 'Australian slang is not a new thing; but in those iron years it was modified beyond recognition by the assimilation of foreign words, and the formulae of novel or exotic ideas.'[69] One example from the sample is *iggri*, an exclamation meaning 'hurry up!', borrowed from Arabic *ijri*, hurry (imperative form of the verb jarā, to run) by the troops serving in Egypt and the Middle East during World War I.

Words also come to a lexicographer's attention through personal experiences. Interesting patterns emerge if we compare inclusion of loanwords from certain donor languages with events in the life of the lexicographer. For example, is there an increase in loanwords from Chinese after Burchfield's journey to China in 1979? In order to determine this, we must compare the number of Chinese words in the sample from volume III *O–Scz* (1982) and volume IV *Se–Z* (1986) with the number of Chinese words in the earlier volumes (1972, 1976). The results show more than three times as many Chinese words in Burchfield's *Supplement* after his journey to China.[70] However, it is worth noting that a natural bias in the Chinese sound system may account for many words in the sample beginning with a letter in the second half of the English alphabet: the longest letters in the Chinese dictionary are S, X, Y, and Z.[71] Therefore, it is difficult to know for sure how profoundly his visit to China influenced the treatment of Chinese words in the Burchfield *Supplement*.

The true champion of loanwords and World Englishes in the *OED Supplements*: Charles Onions

We have seen in this chapter that the practice of implementing the lexicographic policy on foreign words that was devised by Murray in the 1880s was complicated and far from clear cut. Murray struggled with these words, and so did his successors, Craigie, Onions, and even Burchfield himself. Recent criticism of the early *OED* editors had its origins with Burchfield. He contrasted himself with his predecessors, and portrayed himself as an advocate for words of the world in the *OED*, a message that was repeated by media and scholars alike.

In 1997, the widespread perception of Burchfield as supporter of World Englishes led to his appointment as general editor of the volume devoted to World Englishes in the six-volume *Cambridge History of the English Language* (1997), but his editorial treatment of the subject disappointed some of his contemporaries. Despite Burchfield's sustained public rhetoric extolling equal status for all varieties of English, the structure of the volume was indicative of the Burchfield we have seen in this chapter. Part one was devoted to 'regional varieties of English in Great Britain and Ireland' and part two was allocated to a category he labelled 'Overseas English' in which he grouped together the English of Australia, the Caribbean, New Zealand, South Africa, and South Asia. By separating British English from 'Overseas English', Burchfield exhibited a bias quite contrary to his rhetoric: a view of British English as the centre, and varieties of Englishes spoken elsewhere as the peripheral 'other'. When Burchfield toured Italy and Japan in 1986, he had criticized his predecessors for positioning 'British English as the central vocabulary' and other Englishes 'at the periphery'. A decade later, however, Burchfield instituted the same dichotomy with its implied hierarchy in the *Cambridge History of the English Language*.

The volume was criticized for the neglect of varieties of English spoken in West Africa (Nigeria), East Africa (Kenya, Tanzania), and South East Asia (Singapore, Malaysia, Hong Kong).[72] Reviewing the volume for the *Journal of Linguistics*, James Milroy (1997) wrote, 'failure to cover more world varieties must be counted as a defect'.[73] Kingsley Bolton (1999) in *World Englishes* reiterated the concerns of others in the field that the structure of Burchfield's volume and his choice of chapters 'led to a somewhat skewed and uneven representation of Englishes worldwide, with an obvious over-emphasis on the British Isles and its former "settler" colonies'.[74] But Burchfield justified his selection by saying that 'at an early stage of the planning of the volume, round about 1984, it was decided, after much discussion, that the forms of English spoken and written in numerous other overseas regions had received too little attention from linguistic scholars to form a satisfactory part of this volume.'[75] A reviewer in *Linguistics* was not convinced by Burchfield's excuse: 'This is certainly not a very convincing argument, given the fact that books such as Bailey and Görlach (1982), Pride (1982), and Platt et al. (1984) had already shown the way when this decision was made (in 1984!).'[76] As another reviewer put it, 'the whole field of world Englishes in the last 15 years has greatly outpaced the original conception of the volume'.[77]

Burchfield's volume on World Englishes drew attention to what Kingsley Bolton referred to as 'a central myopia in the Burchfield view of English'. Suggesting that World Englishes, and the substantial body of literature on them, had grown beyond Burchfield's vision and imagination, Bolton gave his review the suggestive title 'World Englishes – the way we were', referring to his belief that Burchfield's volume 'hearkens back to a much earlier era': Burchfield's view of English was more 'the way we were' than 'the way we are'.[78]

The scholarship on World Englishes that emerged in the 1980s focused on the complexity of the historical, ideological, and functional diversity of varieties of English. Tom McArthur (1998) described it as a revolution that never quite extended beyond the academic community: 'A revolution took place in the world of English Studies . . . but beyond this significant but limited academic world the shift in perspective has hardly been noticed, and even within that world it is not yet banner headlines.'[79] He surmised that scholars had 'moved on from a cautious pluralism in the early 1980s to an increasingly confident assertion of multiplicity and distinctiveness by the close of the decade'. Ironically, this case study has shown that Burchfield spoke confidently of the multiplicity and distinctiveness of World Englishes, but did not put it into practice; his predecessors, on the other hand, spoke humbly of their struggle with the representation of such words, but their practice showed a recognition of the multiplicity and distinctiveness of the English language.

This is not to ascribe mendacity to Burchfield: he seems to have believed what he said. In a radio interview on *News Hour* in New York on 27 May 1986, when asked how he went about updating 'English English', Burchfield described his policy as 'slightly rebellious':

> Well, [The *OED*] is a very British English work with occasional American words let in, as it were, by special grace and favor. I am a colonial – a New Zealander – and that didn't seem to me to be the right way to go about it. And I thought it really not right to follow too conservative a policy. English was burgeoning everywhere, especially in the United States, but also in Australia and Canada and elsewhere. And I pursued a policy – a slightly rebellious policy. I had no idea it would lead me to take 29 years to carry out this policy, but I decided that English everywhere had to be given the same treatment.[80]

Burchfield may have regarded his *policy* on World Englishes as 'slightly rebellious', but this case study has shown that his lexicographic *practice* was not. He was, however, proclaimed as the first editor to open the pages of the *OED* to words of the world, and this myth continues to the present day. On his death in 2004, an obituary in a New Zealand newspaper declared, 'The furore he raised by his liberal inclusion of foreign and slang words in supplements to the Oxford dictionaries . . . never deterred him from a course he believed was correct.' Burchfield, it concluded, 'continued to maintain that English as a living and international language must be flexible enough to change and to encompass words, expressions and conventions from all parts of the globe'.[81]

In *Lost for Words* (2005), Lynda Mugglestone did not question the old story that 'Burchfield's *Supplements* began a policy of lexicographic redress which is still in operation.'[82] Nor in the *Treasure-House of the Language* (2007) did Brewer survey the dictionary text when she perpetuated the image of Burchfield's triumph of World Englishes by a section devoted to the topic. She described how Burchfield's policy on World Englishes went from being conservative in the early 1960s to being liberal in the early 1970s. He had initially stated in 1962 that 'no systematic treatment of Commonwealth sources is being attempted but Australian, New Zealand, and South African words already in *OED* will be joined by a relatively small number of additional words and senses which now seem to deserve a place in *OED* pending the preparation of regional dictionaries of various kinds of English'. But by the time the first volume was published in 1972, Brewer claims that Burchfield's policy on World English 'had changed radically' so that his *Supplement* was, in his words, 'the natural repository for all of it'.[83] Relying on Burchfield's word, and quoting his 'bold forays into the written English of regions outside the British Isles', Brewer argues that his mind was changed by David Crystal's proposal for a 'Dictionary of the English-Speaking Peoples'. Crystal presented his proposal to the Linguistics Association of Great Britain and the Colloquium of British Academic Phoneticians, but the project never came to fruition. The proposal certainly had vision, and Brewer claimed that it had influence on Burchfield's treatment of World Englishes. She documents Burchfield's reaction to Crystal's speech in a memo of 15 November 1967, and argues that he had been so 'disturbed by the boldness of Crystal's proposal' that a seed had been planted in Burchfield's mind 'that grew and prospered' into generous coverage of World English in the *OED*.[84] Although the idea may have grown and prospered in Burchfield's mind, thereby informing his policy and rhetoric, this chapter has shown that it did not influence his actual lexicographic practice, which remained more faithful to his original vision in 1962 than to Crystal's vision in 1967 of a dictionary for all English-speaking peoples.

In 2008, the *Oxford Dictionary of National Biography* published a new entry for Robert Burchfield which was written by the current Chief Editor of the *OED,* John Simpson. It gave a familiar take on Burchfield and his coverage of World Englishes: 'Burchfield's New Zealand background made him particularly conscious that the *Supplement* should enhance the *OED*'s coverage of international varieties of English, and the achievement of this remains one of his legacies to the dictionary.'[85] In addition, the new website for *OED Online*, officially launched in November 2010, reiterates that one of Burchfield's 'valuable contributions to the Dictionary's expansion' was 'broadening its scope to include words from many countries including North America, Australia, New Zealand, South Africa, India, Pakistan, and the Caribbean'.[86]

This scholarly and journalistic take on Burchfield's coverage of words of the world stems from Burchfield's own perception, his self-promotion, and his many interviews. But when we look at the actual dictionary, we get a different picture. By deleting 17% of World Englishes and loanwords from the *1933 Supplement*, Burchfield banished words from around the world that had previously earned a rightful place in the lexicographic canon. And by reinstating tramlines on words without them in the *1933 Supplement*, Burchfield afforded words a new alien status in the *OED*.

Although Burchfield was vital in helping to shift public perceptions of the validity and importance of World Englishes, his claims for what he had done in the *Supplement to the OED* simply were not true. The step of making – as Burchfield (1972: xiv) put it – 'bold forays into the written English of regions outside the British Isles' should actually be attributed to Charles Onions, not Robert Burchfield.

ENDNOTES

1 Simpson (2008); Brewer (2009b).
2 Burchfield (1972: xv).
3 'Interview with Burchfield on the Macneil/Lehrer' *News Hour*, New York, Tuesday 27 May 1986.
4 Görlach (1990: 312).
5 Burchfield and Aarsleff (1988: 22).
6 McArthur (1993: 332).
7 'Wimmin and Yuppies Earn Places in Oxford Dictionary Supplement', *The Globe and Mail (Canada)*, 9 May 1986 p. 9.
8 'Yetis, Yuppies, and Wimmin', *Times*, 8 May 1986 p. 12.
9 'A Supplement to the Oxford English Dictionary', *The New Leader*, 68 1 December 1986 p. 5.
10 Burchfield (1977: 61).
11 Burchfield (1972: xiv).
12 Sledd (1973: 46).
13 Sands (1976: 718).
14 Bailey and Görlach (1982: 4).
15 Brewer (1993: 326).
16 Burchfield (1989: 117).
17 Burchfield (2004). It is true that Murray and the early editors had not included 'coarse words' such as *fuck* or *cunt* which were later added by Burchfield. See Burchfield (1972), 'Four-letter Words and the OED', *TLS*, 13 October p. 1233, and discussion of Burchfield's *TLS* article in Sands (1976: 715–17).
18 Burchfield Papers Deposit 2 Box 2. Lecture for Japan and Italy, 1986.
19 Burchfield Papers Deposit 2 Box 2. Lecture for Japan and Italy, 1986.
20 Burchfield (1989: 190).
21 Ackroyd (1987: 22).
22 Burchfield (1977: 61).
23 'The Last Word on Words: Supplement to Oxford English Dictionary Finished', *Dallas Morning News*, 8 June 1986 p. 13.
24 The journal *World Englishes* began in 1981, but it was called *World Language English* until July 1985.
25 'Interview with Burchfield on the Macneil/Lehrer' *News Hour*, New York, Tuesday 27 May 1986.
26 McArthur (1993: 334).
27 Burchfield (1986: xi).
28 Graddol (1999: 68).
29 OED/PB/ED/012865 OP 1712. OUP paid Mr N. van Blerk £100 for four months' work while on long-service leave in Oxford.
30 Burchfield (1972: xv).
31 Bailey and Görlach (1982:4).
32 The *1933 Supplement* calculation is based on the estimated total number of headwords in the 1933 Supplement = 28 entries per page x 867 pages = 24 276 headwords. The Burchfield *Supplement* calculation is based on the total number of

headwords (69, 372) in the Burchfield *Supplement* as recorded in Simpson and Weiner (1989: xii).

33 See Coleman and Ogilvie (2009) for further discussion of sampling techniques. Alphabet fatigue is discussed by Starnes and Noyes (1946: 185) and Osselton (2007).

34 Starting with the total number of pages of 10% of each letter, a random number of pages was generated to be examined from the first page of each letter. This result was then deducted from the total number of pages of 10% of that letter, and used as the maximum (minimum being constant 1) for the next random number of pages to be examined, until the number generated was greater than or equal to the number of pages remaining to be sampled. Between each of these calculations, the page range for that letter of the alphabet in Burchfield's *Supplement* was entered into the random number generator to give the next page number to be examined. All these figures were entered into a database, and then sorted alphabetically. The random number generator used to generate the random sample was the 'True Random Number Generator' at www.random.org.

35 Mesthrie and Bhatt (2008: 110).

36 See Romaine (1998: 26) for more discussion on 'International English'.

37 There is one exception to this rule: the entry *kaïd* in Burchfield's *Supplement* is marked with tramlines despite also having them in *OED1*; this was classified as a 'special case' in my criteria so I included it in the database.

38 Burchfield Papers Deposit 2 Box 2. nd. Murray's System of Casuals, Aliens, Denizens, and Naturals.

39 In other words, of the 6937 entries examined in the Burchfield sample, 1787 of them classified as loanwords and words from World Englishes, as compared with 757 entries in the *1933 Supplement* sample of 2427 entries.

40 Craigie and Hulbert (1938: preface).

41 McArthur (1993: 332).

42 Burchfield (1972: v).

43 Lehman and Foote (1986: 74); 'The Last Word on Words: Supplement to Old English Dictionary finished' *Dallas Morning News* 8 June 1986 p. 13.

44 Meier (1979: 649).

45 Burchfield (1972: v).

46 Aitken (1973: 90).

47 The early citations for *kakur* refer to an Indian context, so, although the word exists in both Hindi and Javanese, Burchfield's etymology is probably more accurate as the source language of the borrowing into English.

48 As already discussed in the previous chapter, only two words appeared with tramlines in the *1933 Supplement: kadin*, a Turkish word for a woman of the Sultan's harem, and *rhexis*, a Greek and Latin word for the rupture of a blood vessel.

49 Burchfield (1986: ix).

50 Comrie (2001: 19) estimates over 6000 languages. Donor languages in *1933 Supplement* = 44 languages. Donor languages in Burchfield's *Supplement* = 80 languages. My calculations => 81 donor languages comprise 1.35% of 6000 languages.

51 This calculation is based on the proportional means of 0.23 Onions, 0.16 Craigie, 0.12 Burchfield, which equates to 0.2 for *1933 Supplement*, 0.12 for Burchfield's *Supplement*.
52 Brewer (1993: 326).
53 Weiner (1987: 32). This view is repeated by Price (2003b).
54 Phillipson (1992: 47).
55 Phillipson (1992: 47).
56 Aitken (1973: 90).
57 Aitken (1973: 90).
58 Algeo (1995: 208).
59 Moore (1997: v).
60 Moore (1997: v–vi).
61 For example, none of the six loanwords from Australian Aboriginal languages (*callop, nannygai, pindan, quokka, yakka, yandy*) gets tramlines and conversely, all three loanwords from Thai (*baht, farang, samlor*) get tramlines, but I consider these samples too small to be significant.
62 Murray (1888: xxvi).
63 McMahon (1994: 201).
64 Murray (1884: 517).
65 In 1727, John Gaspar Scheuchzer (1702–29) translated Engelbert Kaempfer's *History of Japan* from Dutch into English, thereby introducing many Japanese words such as *adzuki, kirin, Mikado, samurai,* and *Zen*.
66 Hock (1991: 385).
67 Breakdown of first-date quotations for 62 German words: C18 1 + C19 26 + C20 35 = 61; breakdown of first-date quotations for 71 Japanese words: C17 2 + C18 6 + C19 31 + C20 32 = 71.
68 'Fuzzy Wuzzy' first appeared in *Departmental Ditties, Barrack Room Ballads and Other Verses*, United States Book Company, New York, 1890. Laugesen (2005: ix) states that *fuzzy wuzzy* was likely to have been generated independently by Australians, but fails to demonstrate how.
69 Downing (1919: 7).
70 Chinese words in Burchfield sample: vols. I and II (A–N) = 7; vols. III and IV (O–Z) = 23.
71 I am indebted to Mike Clark of the Chinese-English Oxford Dictionary Project for verification that the longest letters in the Chinese dictionary are S, X, Y, and Z.
72 Aitchison (1997: 74), Stephan (1995: 1196).
73 Milroy (1997: 175).
74 Bolton (1999: 406).
75 Burchfield (1997: 3–4).
76 Stephan (1995: 1196).
77 Bolton (1999: 411).
78 Bolton (1999: 411).
79 McArthur (1998: 67).
80 'Interview with Burchfield on the Macneil/Lehrer' *News Hour*, New York, Tuesday 27 May 1986.
81 'Robert Burchfield', *The Christchurch Press,* 24 July 2004 p. 18.
82 Mugglestone (2005: 217).

83 Brewer (2007: 197–200).
84 Brewer (2007: 198).
85 Simpson (2008) 'Burchfield, Robert William (1923–2004)', *Oxford Dictionary of National Biography* online edn Oxford University Press, January 2008 [http://www.oxforddnb.com/view/article/93833, accessed 19 Jan 2008].
86 See http://oed.com/public/editors/dictionary-editors#burchfield.

7 Conclusion

Samuel Johnson defined *lexicographer* as 'a writer of dictionaries; a harmless drudge that busies himself in tracing the original, and detailing the signification of words', and there is truth in that. Day after day, the lexicographer works on words beginning with the same letter – *padishah*, *padkos*, *padmasana*, *pahareen*, *pahit*, *paho*, *pahoehoe*, *pajero*, *pakalolo*, *pakeha* . . . But that process is never exactly 'harmless', to use Johnson's language – which is to say it is never neutral. Every decision a lexicographer makes has consequences, and those consequences are almost always political, reflecting the values of the individual editor and his or her context: to include a word or not; to give all pronunciations – naturalized or foreign; to list every way that word has ever been spelt; to trace its etymology back to its furthest source or to stop at the donor language to English; to define using metalanguage or a regional label; to include quotations from regional and local sources or only British publications; to include quotations from spoken sources. These are all steps in the dictionary-making process and each has political and cultural implications which readers, journalists, and scholars will happily criticize and pull apart.

When I went to work at the *OED* in 2001, I arrived with the common belief that the *OED* was, and had been until the 1970s, a distinctly British product in its making and its content. But my editing of words from outside Europe, which was my remit as an editor at the *OED*, gave a different impression, and as I explored papers in the OUP archives and analyzed the actual text, I began to see the dictionary in a whole new light. This has consequences for an oft-told tale.

Burchfield told a story of 'progress': that the early *OED* editors, living and working at the height of the British Empire, were conservative in their policy and practice relating to words of the world, and he was the post-colonial hero who opened the pages of the dictionary to these words for the first time. Because Burchfield told this story not only as Chief Editor of the *OED*, but also as a New Zealander, no one questioned it.

This book has shown that the editors of *OED1* – Murray, Bradley, Craigie, and Onions – actively sought words of the world, and included them in the dictionary despite pressures from inside and outside OUP to exclude them. We have seen that the editors of the *1933 Supplement* included loanwords and World Englishes in higher proportions than their successor, Burchfield, who reinstated tramlines and deleted 17% of loanwords and World Englishes in the *1933 Supplement*. Burchfield's claims about himself have therefore been refuted by statistical evidence. This is not, as I stated earlier in the book, to attribute mendacity to Burchfield; he believed he was doing what he said he was doing. But it reminds us, crucially, that a lexicographer's practice may not match his or her policy or rhetoric, and it demonstrates the value of combining quantitative analysis with qualitative.

The purpose of this book has not been to judge whether the *OED* was ethnocentric and imperialistic (a question that has been addressed by other scholars); nevertheless, it has recognized that the British Empire and the postcolonial era provided the respective contexts in which *OED1* and Burchfield's *Supplement* were written. Thus, the early editors have been revealed as less conservative in their policy and practice with regard to seeking and including in the dictionary words of the world than usually assumed, and Burchfield less the champion of these words than has been claimed. Three consequences of this are: to question whether Murray was the wholly imperialistic editor that some have suggested he was, while recognizing that the inclusion of more 'foreign' words can be used *both* to argue that the dictionary was an imperialistic product *and* the exact opposite case; to question whether Burchfield was the champion of colonial and postcolonial English that he said he was; and to find an unlikely hero in Charles Onions.

These findings therefore question a smooth story from imperialism to postcolonialism, in which coverage of words of the world has improved in the *OED*. My hope is that the conclusions presented here may suggest new directions for further research in the areas of ethnocentrism and the *OED*, even though it has been outside the remit of this study to pursue those questions. The foundations of past research and arguments, which based their critique on this story of progress and used it as a barometer of the editors' attitudes towards race, language, and culture, may have to be re-evaluated.

The founders of the *OED* succeeded in creating an entirely new dictionary, 'no patch upon old garments, but a new garment throughout'. They strove to satisfy Furnivall's instruction to 'fling our doors wide! All, all, not one, but all, must enter.' In 1900, Murray gave a lecture in Oxford in which he wondered whether the art of dictionary-making could evolve beyond the system he had established so effectively at the *OED*. 'It is never possible to forecast the needs and notions of those who shall come after us; but with our present knowledge it is not easy to conceive what new feature can now be added to English Lexicography . . . in the Oxford Dictionary, permeated as it is through and through with the scientific method of the century,

Lexicography has for the present reached its supreme development.'[1] Modern-day lexicographers wonder if technology and the vast collections of text available to us at the touch of a button might revolutionize lexicography forever. It has succeeded in revolutionizing our ability to search for words quickly and to track frequency of usage and 'culturomics' over time, but the disambiguation of senses and the vital trigger of which word we should be searching for still remains the indispensable duty of assistants and volunteer readers around the globe. No computer can replace a contributor like Mr Chris Collier in Australia, Mr Donald Ferguson in Colombo, Rev E. H. Cook in New Zealand, or Dr Atkins in New Mexico. The *OED* will always be indebted to its international contributors who supported, and continue to support, the Oxford lexicographers in producing a truly global product.

ENDNOTE

1 Murray (1900a: 49).

Bibliography

UNPUBLISHED SOURCES

British Broadcasting Corporation (BBC) Written Archives Centre, Reading, UK

BBC R6/196/1a. File 1 1926–1927.
BBC R6/196/1b. Minutes of the First Meeting 5 July 1926.
BBC R6/196/4a. Letters from Onions to Lloyd James 3 January 1932 and 28 February 1932.
BBC R6/146/4b. Letter from Onions to Lloyd James 12 June 1932.
BBC R6/146/4c. Letter from Shaw to Lloyd James 30 September 1932.
BBC R6/196/6. Correspondence of Reith and Lloyd James 1932–1934.

Cambridge University Press Archive, University of Cambridge, UK

CUPA UA Pr.B.23. Stanford Slips.
CUPA UA Pr.B.4.I. Correspondence Concerning Publications 1840–1901.
CUPA UA Pr.B.4.I.308–310. Letters Concerning the Stanford Dictionary 1892.
CUPA UA Pr.B.13. Correspondence 1871–1947.
CUPA UA Pr.B.13.G.6. Letter from Gell to Clay 4 December 1889.
CUPA UA Pr.V.12. Minute Book 1890–1896.

Jowett Papers, Balliol College Archive, Oxford, UK

B8/2. Letter from Murray to Hucks Gibbs 24 October 1883.
B8/4. Letter from Murray to Hucks Gibbs 8 November 1883.
B8/5. Letter from Hucks Gibbs to Jowett 10 November 1883.

Murray Papers, Bodleian Library, Oxford, UK

MP/9/11/1862. Furnivall Circular to the Philological Society 9 November 1862.
MP/?/1879. Letter from Martineau to Murray, n.d., but sometime in late 1879.
MP/9/6/1882. Letter from Murray to Price 9 June 1882.
MP/20/7/1882. Letter from Hucks Gibbs to Murray 20 July 1882.
MP/15/09/1882. Letter from Skeat to Murray 1 December 1882.
MP/15/09/1883. Letter from Fennell to Murray 15 September 1883.
MP/4/11/1883. Letter from Hucks Gibbs to Murray 4 November 1883.

MP/6/05/1885. Letter from Murray to Price 6 May 1885.
MP/9/06/1886. Letter from Hucks Gibbs to Furnivall 9 June 1886.
MP/8/03/1892. Letter from Bradley to Murray 8 March 1892.
MP/9/11/1910. Murray Lecture to London Institute 9 November 1910.
MP/10/1883. Letter from Skeat to Murray October 1883.
MP/1903. Murray Lecture to the London Institute 'The World of Words and Its Explorers' 1903.
MP Box 30. Proofs for *abaisance*.

National Library of Scotland, Edinburgh, UK

National Library of Scotland, MS 3219, f.158. Letter from Murray to unidentified correspondent 23 March 1900.

Oxford University Press Archives, Oxford, UK

Burchfield Papers Deposit 2 Box 2. 1986. Lecture for Japan and Italy.
Burchfield Papers Deposit 2 Box 2. n.d. Murray's System of Casuals, Aliens, Denizens, and Naturals.
Burchfield Papers Deposit Supplement BB2/5. Letter from Stanley to Davin 5 February 1963.
Burchfield Papers Deposit Supplement BB2/5. Letter from Davin to Stanley 7 February 1963.
OED/16/OED Supplement Policy 1958–72. Letter from Burchfield to Onions 9 December 1959.
OED/16/OED Supplement Policy 1958–72. Letter from Onions to Burchfield 4 January 1960.
OED/AA/142. Letter from Margoliouth to Murray 22 January 1902.
OED/B/3/1/1. Letter from Liddell to Price 10 May 1877.
OED/B/3/1/2. Letter from Hucks Gibbs to Furnivall 9 June 1886.
OED/B/3/1/2. Letter from Max Müller to Murray 15 October 1886.
OED/B/3/1/2. Letter from Max Müller to Delegates nd.
OED/B/3/1/2. 1878. 'Observations by Professor Max Müller on the Lists of Readers and Books for the Proposed English Dictionary.'
OED/B/3/1/6. Letter from Hucks Gibbs to Murray 2 December 1892.
OED/B/3/1/10. Letter from Bradley to Gell 11 April 1896.
OED/B/3/1/11. Letter from Murray to Gell 23 February 1893.
OED/B/3/2/17(2) PP/1928/166. Letter from Milford to Chapman 3 May 1928.
OED/B/3/2/19. (Rosfrith) Murray to Chapman 17 June 1929.
OED/B/3/2/19. Letter from Sisam to Craigie 7 May 1930.
OED/B/3/2/21. Letter from Chapman to the Vice Chancellor 30 November 1932.
OED/B/3/2/22. Letter from Wyllie to Sisam 12 December 1933.
OED/B/3/4/2. Letters between Onions and Craigie between 11 September 1929 and 2 July 1930.
OED/B/3/10/3. Progress Reports for the 1933 Supplement.
OED/B/3/10/3. Letter from Sisam to Charles Onions 15 September 1931.
OED/B/3/10/3. Letter from Sisam to Johnson 25 September 1931.

OED/B/3/10/4 MISC 393/89/ii. Letter from Sisam to Onions 6 May 1932.
OED/B/3/10/4 MISC 393/89/ii. Letter from Sisam to Mencken 6 May 1932.
OED/B/3/10/4 (2) MISC/393/194. Letter from Fowler to Sisam 11 January 1933.
OED/B/3/10/4 (2) MISC/393/195. Letter from Sisam to Onions 13 January 1933.
OED/B/3/10/4 (2) MISC/393/196. Letter from Le Mesurier to Fowler 10 January 1933.
OED/B/3/10/4 (2) MISC/393/197. Letter from Sisam to Fowler 13 January 1933.
OED/B/3/10/4 (2) MISC/393/198. Letter from Le Mesurier to Sisam 16 January 1933.
OED/B/5/4/24. Letter from Sugden to Onions March 1930.
OED/B/7/4/8. Miscellaneous newspaper clippings about the progress and publication of *OED1*.
OED/BL/3/12/28. Letter from Tylor to Murray 1 December 1886.
OED/BL/304/57. Letter from Petherick to Murray 11 March 1885.
OED/BL/308/4. Letter from Monier-Williams to Murray 1 April 1881.
OED/BL/311/9. Letter from Petherick to Murray 3 November 1886.
OED/BL/311/10 ii. Letter from Petherick to Murray n.d.
OED/BL/311/12. Letter from Petherick to Murray n.d.
OED/BL/324/18. Letter from Legge to Murray 2 February 1889.
OED/EP/MARE/1/1. Letter from Murray to Marett 10 December 1910.
OED/EP/MARE/1/2. Letter from Marett to Murray 11 December 1910.
OED/JH/188/4/1. Letter from Thistelton-Dyer to Murray 2 May 1903.
OED/JH/218/25. Letter from Giles to Craigie 1 January 1914.
OED/MISC/7/1.n.d. 'The New English Dictionary. Suggestions for Guidance in Preparing Copy for the Press.'
OED/MISC/11/39. Letter from Murray to Thompson 4 October 1902.
OED/MISC/13/7. Letter from Murray to Hall 27 November 1894.
OED/MISC/91/11 n.d. 'Directions for Re-Sub-editors.'
OED/MISC/115/4. Letter from Margoliouth to Onions 13 July 1915.
OED/MISC/317/4. Letter from Margoliouth to Driver 5 December 1928.
OED/OS/18/2. Letter from Giles to Murray 16 March 1893.
OED/OS/18/3ii. Letter from Giles to Murray n.d.
OED/PB/ED/012865 OP 1712. Payment of £100 for Mr N. van Blerk.
OUP Archive OED Proofs for Letters E, F, G, and L.
OUP Archive OED Slips (stored alphabetically).
OUP/MISC Remainder SOED. Letter from Sisam to Onions 21 October 1932.
OUP/MISC Remainder SOED. Letter from Onions to Sisam 21 November 1932.
OUP/PUB/11/29. Letter from Murray to Doble 5 June 1889.
OUP/PUB/11/29. Letter from Murray to Gell 20 October 1892.
OUP/PUB/11. Handwritten note by C. T. Onions dated 21 May 1938, on letter from Chapman to Sisam 17 May 1938.
OUP Secretary Letterbook 1891: 588. Letter from Doble to Bradley 14 May 1891.
OUP Secretary Letterbook 1893: 601. Letter from Gell to the Editor of the *Athenaeum* 27 May 1893.
OUP Secretary Letterbook 1894: 397. Letter from Doble to Frowde 9 July 1894.
OUP Secretary Letterbook 1894: 399. Letter from Doble to Gell 9 July 1894.
SOED/1933/16/5ii. Letter from Wyllie to Sisam 21 April 1933.

Published works

Ackroyd, P. 1987. 'Map of the Sea of Words.' *Times* 16 July: 22.

'Across the Sind Desert Travellers' Tales: Lady Lawrence' *Radio Times* British Broadcasting Corporation Programmes for Wednesday 6 June 9.15 p.m. June 1 1928: 406.

Adams, M. 1995. 'Sanford Brown Meech at the Middle English Dictionary.' *Dictionaries* **16**: 151–85.

1998. 'Credit Where It's Due: Authority and Recognition at the Dictionary of American English.' *Dictionaries* **19**: 1–20.

'A Great Lexicographer.' *The Scotsman* 27 July 1915: 17.

Ainsworth, R. 1736. *Thesaurus Linguae Latinae Compendiarius, or a compendious Dictionary of the Latin Tongue, designed for the use of the British nations: in three parts.* London, Knapton.

Aitchison, J. 1997. 'Review of the Cambridge History of the English Language.' vol. V, English in Britain and Overseas: Origins and Development. Edited by Robert Burchfield.' *Review of English Studies* **48**: 74–5.

Aitchison, J. 2001. *Language Change: Progress or Decay?* 3d ed. Cambridge University Press.

Aitken, A. J. 1973. 'Modern English from A to G.' *TLS* 26 January: 90.

Algeo, J. 1995. 'British and American Biases in English Dictionaries' in B. B. Kachru and H. Kahane *Cultures, Ideologies, and the Dictionary*. Lexicographica Series **64** Tübingen, Max Niemeyer Verlag: 205–12.

Alsopp, R. 1996. *Dictionary of Caribbean English Usage*. Oxford University Press.

'Announcements.' *Times* 15 May 1883: 3.

Aristotle. [1928]. *On Topics (Topica and De sophisticis elenchis)*, transl. W. A. Pickard Cambridge, Oxford, Clarendon Press.

Ashcroft, B., G. Griffiths, and H. Tiffin (eds.) 2005. *The Post-Colonial Reader* 2nd ed. London, Routledge.

'A Supplement in Preparation.' *The Periodical XIII* 15 February 1928: 23–4.

'A Supplement to the Oxford English Dictionary.' *The New Leader* **68** (1) December 1986: 5.

Bailey, N. 1721. *An Universal Etymological English Dictionary*. London, E. Bell.

Bailey, R. W. 1991. *Images of English*. Ann Arbor, University of Michigan Press.

2000a. '"This Unique and Peerless Specimen": The Rreputation of the OED,' in L. Mugglestone (ed.) *Lexicography and the OED*. Oxford University Press: 207–27.

2000b. 'Appendix III: The OED and the Public' in L. Mugglestone (ed.) *Lexicography and the OED*. Oxford University Press: 253–84.

2009. 'National and Regional Dictionaries of English' in A. P. Cowie (ed.) *The Oxford History of English Lexicography* vol. **I**. Oxford, Clarendon Press: 279–301.

Bailey, R. W. and M. Görlach (eds.) 1982. *English as a World Language*. Ann Arbor, University of Michigan Press.

Bailey, R. W. and J. L. Robinson (eds.) 1973. *Varieties of Present-Day English*. New York, Macmillan.

Baker, P. 1988. 'Notes. A Supplement to OED: Se-Z and the Concise Oxford Dictionary of English Etymology.' *Notes & Queries* June: 148–54.

Baker, S. 1868. *Tributaries of Abyssinia*. London, Macmillan and Co.

Baker, S. J. 1945. *The Australian Language*. Sydney and London, Angus and Robertson Ltd.

Baldwin, S. 1928. 'The Prime Minister The Rt. Hon. Stanley Baldwin, P.C., M.P., proposing the health of the Editor and Staff of the Oxford English Dictionary.' *Oxford English Dictionary 1884–1928 Speeches Delivered in the Goldsmiths' Hall 6 June 1928* Oxford, Clarendon Press: 3–11.

Bamgbose, A. 1998. 'Torn Between the Norms and Innovations in World Englishes.' *World Englishes* **17** (1): 1–14.

Barber, C. 1997. *Early Modern English*. Edinburgh University Press.

Bauer, L. 2001. *Morphological Productivity*. Cambridge University Press.

Baugh, A. C. 1935. 'The Chronology of French Loan-Words in English.' *Modern Language Notes* **50** (2): 90–3.

Baycroft, T. and M. Hewitson (eds.) 2006. *What is a Nation? Europe 1789–1914*. Oxford University Press.

Bayly, C. A. 2004. *The Birth of the Modern World, 1780–1914: Global Connections and Comparisons*. Oxford University Press.

Béjoint, H. 2000. *Modern Lexicography*. Oxford University Press.

Beloff, M. 1969, 1989. *Imperial Sunset: Britain's Liberal Empire, 1897–1921* **2** vols. London, Methuen.

Bensly, E. 1912. 'Letters' *Notes & Queries* **II S. VI.** 3 August: 95.

Benson, P. 2001. *Ethnocentrism and the English Dictionary*. London, Routledge.

Benzie, W. 1983. *Dr. F. J. Furnivall: Victorian Scholar Adventurer*. Norman, Pilgrim Books.

Bickley, F. 1911. 'Memories of F. J. Furnivall' in *Frederick James Furnivall: A Volume of Personal Record*. London, Henry Frowde: 1–4.

Bisong, J. 1995. 'Language Choice and Cultural Imperialism: a Nigerian Perspective.' *ELT Journal* **49** (2): 122–32.

Bloomfield, L. 1935. *Language*. London, George Allen and Unwin.

Bolton, K. 1999. 'World Englishes –The Way We Were. Review of *The Cambridge History of the English Language*. vol. V, *English in Britain and Overseas: Origins and Development*. Edited by Robert Burchfield.' *World Englishes* **18** (3): 393–413.

2005. 'Symposium on World Englishes Today (Part II) Where WE Stands: Approaches, Issues, and Debate in World Englishes.' *World Englishes* **24** (1): 69–83.

2006. 'World Englishes Today' in B. B. Kachru, Y. Kachru, and C. L. Nelson (eds.) *Handbook of World Englishes*. Oxford, Blackwell: 240–69.

Boyer, A. 1702. *Dictionnaire royal* **2** vols. La Haye, chez Adrian Moetjens.

Bradley, H. 1884. 'Review of A New English Dictionary on Historical Principles.' *The Academy* (Second Notice) 1 March: 141–2.

1893. *A New English Dictionary on Historical Principles Letter E*. Oxford University Press

1904. *The Making of English*. London, Macmillan.

1911. 'Memories of F. J. Furnivall' in *Frederick James Furnivall: A Volume of Personal Record*. London, Henry Frowde: 4–9.

Branford, J. 1978. *A Dictionary of South African English*. Oxford University Press.

Brantlinger, P. 1988. *Rule of Darkness: British Literature and Imperialism*. Ithaca, Cornell University Press.

Brewer, C. 1993. 'The Second Edition of the Oxford English Dictionary.' *Review of English Studies* **44**: 313–42.

2000. 'OED Sources' in L. Mugglestone (ed.) *Lexicography and the OED*. Oxford University Press: 40–58.

2006. 'Eighteenth-Century Quotation Searches in the Oxford English Dictionary' in R. W. McConchie, O. Timofeeva, H. Tissari, and T. Saily (eds.) *Selected Proceedings of the 2005 Symposium on New Approaches in English Historical Lexis (HEL-LEX)*. Somerville, MA, Cascadilla Proceedings Project: 41–50.

2007. *Treasure-House of the Language: The Living OED*. New Haven and London, Yale University Press.

2009a. 'The OED Supplements' in A. P. Cowie (ed.) *The Oxford History of English Lexicography* vol. **I**. Oxford, Clarendon Press: 260–78.

2009b. 'R. W. Burchfield' in H. Stammerjohann (ed.) *Lexicon Grammaticorum*. Berlin, Walter de Gruyter (pre-publication copy so no page numbers).

Bridges, R. 1919. 'Original Prospectus' in *SPE Tract No. 1* (October 1919) part **6** (i). Oxford, Clarendon Press.

1920. *'Notes to the Above' SPE Tract No. III*. Oxford, Clarendon Press: 10–12.

1925a. *'The Society's Work' SPE Tract No. XXI*. Oxford, Clarendon Press: 1–17.

1925b. *'New Spellings' SPE Tract No. XXII*. Oxford, Clarendon Press: 65–6.

Brock, M. G. and M. C. Curthoys (eds.) 2000. *The History of the University of Oxford: Nineteenth-Century Oxford* vol. **VII** Part 2. Oxford University Press.

Brown, J. M. and W. R. Louis (eds.) *The Oxford History of the British Empire. The Twentieth Century* vol. **IV**. Oxford University Press.

Brutt-Griffler, J. 2002. *World English: A Study of its Development*. Clevedon, Multilingual Matters.

2005. 'Globalization and Applied Linguistics: Post-imperial Questions of Identity and the Construction of Applied Linguistics Discourse.' *International Journal of Applied Linguistics* **15** (1): 113–15.

Bundy, E. 1962. 'Studia Pindarica.' *University of California Studies in Classical Philology* **18** (1 and 2).

1986. *Studia Pindarica (reprint of 1962 fascicles)*. Berkeley and Los Angeles, University of California Press.

Burchfield, R. W. 1972, 1976, 1982, 1986. *A Supplement to the Oxford English Dictionary* vols. **I–IV**. Oxford, Clarendon Press.

1972. 'Four-letter Words and the OED' *TLS*. **13** October 1972: 1233.

1977. 'The New Explorers' in D. Abse, et al. *More Words*. London, B.B.C.: 59–72.

1989. *Unlocking the Language*. London, Faber & Faber.

(ed.) 1997. *The Cambridge History of the English Language. English in Britain and Overseas: Origins and Development* vol. **V**. Cambridge University Press.

2004. 'Murray, Sir James Augustus Henry 1837–1915' *Oxford Dictionary of National Biography*. Oxford University Press, September 2004; online edn, May 2007 [http://www.oxforddnb.com/view/article/35163, accessed 27 April 2008].

Burchfield, R. W. and H. Aarsleff 1988. *The Oxford English Dictionary and the State of the Language*. Washington, DC, Library of Congress.

'Burns Anniversary Dinner.' *Jackson's Oxford Journal* 2 February 1889: 6.

Butterfield, J. 2008. *A Damp Squid: The English Language Laid Bare*. Oxford University Press.

Bynon, T. 1977. *Historical Linguistics*. Cambridge University Press.
'Caledonian Society of Oxford.' *Jackson's Oxford Journal* 28 January 1888: 8.
'Caledonian Society of Oxford.' *Jackson's Oxford Journal* 28 January 1893: 8.
'Cambridge, March 22.' *Times* 23 March 1893: 7.
Cardim, F. c.1584. *Do Clima e Terra do Brasil* fl. 16v.
Carpenter, H. 1981. *Letters of J. R. R. Tolkien*. London, George Allen and Unwin.
Cawdrey, R. 1604. *A Table Alphabeticall Conteyning and Teaching the true Writing and Understanding of Hard Usuall English wordes facsimile reproduction Gainesville, Scholars' Facsimile and Reprints* [1963].
'Celebrating the Dictionary.' *Times* 7 June 1928: 17.
Cheshire, J. (ed.) 1991. *English Around the World: Sociolinguistic Perspectives*. Cambridge University Press.
Child, C. G. 1893. ' Review of the Stanford Dictionary of Anglicised Words and Phrases.' *Modern Language Notes* 8: 114–21.
'Church Society's Anniversary.' *Jackson's Oxford Journal* 19 February 1887: 7.
Clarke, C. 1897. 'A Propos.' *Notes & Queries* VIII S. XII 17 July: 48.
Cogo, A. 2008. 'English as a Lingua Franca: Form Follows Function.' *English Today* **24** (3): 58–61.
Coleman, J. 1995. 'The Chronology of French and Latin Loan-Words in English.' *Transactions of the Philological Society* **93**: 95–124.
2004a. *A History of Cant and Slang Dictionaries Volume 1: 1567–1784*. Oxford University Press.
2004b. *A History of Cant and Slang Dictionaries Volume II: 1785–1858*. Oxford University Press.
2009. *A History of Cant and Slang Dictionaries Volume III: 1859–1936*. Oxford University Press.
Coleman, J. and S. Ogilvie. 2009. 'Forensic Dictionary Analysis: Principles and Practice.' *International Journal of Lexicography* **22**: 1–22.
Coleridge, E. 2007. 'Coleridge, Herbert (1830–1861)', rev. John D. Haigh, *Oxford Dictionary of National Biography*, Oxford University Press, 2004; online edn, May 2007 [http://www.oxforddnb.com/view/article/5883, accessed 28 June 2011]
Coleridge, H. 1857. 'A Letter to The Very Rev. The Dean of Westminster from Herbert Coleridge, Esq.' *Transactions of the Philological Society* **4** (2): 71–8.
1860a. 'Observations on the Plan of the Society's Proposed New English Dictionary.' *Transactions of the Philological Society* **7**: 152–68.
1860b. 'On the Exclusion of Certain Words from a Dictionary' (with an Appendix by F. J. Furnivall). *Transactions of the Philological Society* **7**: 37–44.
Colley, L. 2003. *Britons: Forging the Mation 1707–1837*. London, Pimlico.
Collins, B. and I. M. Mees 2003. *Daniel Jones Selected Works: Unpublished Writings and Correspondence* vol. **8**. London, Routledge.
Comrie, B. 1998. 'Languages' in *Encarta Encyclopedia* CD-ROM, Microsoft.
2001. 'Languages of the World' in M. Arnoff and J. Rees-Miller (eds.) *Handbook of Linguistics*. Oxford, Blackwell: 19–42.
Considine, J. 2009. 'Literary Classic in OED Quotation Evidence.' *Review of English Studies*, advanced access published online 5 April, 2009: 1–19.
Coote, E. 1596 *The English Schoole-Maister*. Menston, The Scholar Press Limited Facsimile [1968].

Craigie, W. A. and C. T. Onions 1933. *A New English Dictionary on Historical Principles. Founded on the Materials Collected by the Philological Society.* Edited by James A. H. Murray, Henry Bradley, William A. Craigie, and C. T. Onions. *Introduction, Supplement, and Bibliography.* Oxford, Clarendon Press.

Craigie, W. A. and J. R. Hulbert 1938–44. *Dictionary of American English on Historical Principles* **4** vols. London, Oxford University Press.

Creighton, M. 1896. *The Romanes Lecture: The English National Character.* Oxford, Clarendon Press.

Crewe, W. (ed.) 1977. *The English Language in Singapore.* Singapore, Eastern Universities Press.

Crystal, D. 1967. 'Report of the Pilot Scheme for the Proposed "Dictionary of the English-Speaking Peoples"' unpublished document at <http://www.davidcrystal.com/David_Crystal/lexi.htm>

1985. 'How Many Millions? The Statistics of English Today.' *English Today* **1** (1): 7–9.

1997. *English as a Global Language.* Cambridge University Press.

2003. *Cambridge Encyclopedia of the English Language* 2d ed. Cambridge University Press.

2004. *The Stories of English.* London, Allen Lane.

2008. 'Two Thousand Million?' *English Today* **24** (1): 3–6.

Curr, E. M. 1886. *The Australian Race: Its Origin, Languages, Customs* 4 vols. London, Trubner and Co.

Curzan, A. 2000. 'The Compass of the Vocabulary' in L. Mugglestone (ed.) *Lexicography and the OED.* Oxford University Press: 96–109.

Darbishire, H. D. 1892. 'Review of Fennell's Indo-European Vowel-System.' *The Classical Review* **6**: 56–8.

Darwall-Smith, R. 1993. *Balliol College Library: The Jowett Papers.* Abingdon, Thomas Leech Ltd.

Darwin, J. 2009. *The Empire Project: The Rise and Fall of the British World-System, 1830–1970.* Cambridge University Press.

Davies, A. 1996. 'Review of Linguistic Imperialism: Ironising the Myth of Linguicism.' *Journal of Multilingual and Multicultural Development* **17** (6): 485–96.

Dekeyser, X. 1986. 'Romance Loans in Middle English: A Reassessment' in D. Kastovsky and A. Szwedek (eds.) *Linguistics Across Historical and Geographical Boundaries* vol. I. Berlin, Mouton de Gruyter: 253–65.

de Schryver, G.-M. 2005. 'Concurrent Over- and Under-treatment in Dictionaries – The Woordeboek van Afrikaanse Taal as a Case in Point.' *International Journal of Lexicography* **18**: 47–75.

Dilke, C. W. 1868. *Greater Britain: A Record of Travel in English-speaking Countries during 1866 and 1867,* vols. **I and II.** London, Macmillan and Co.

1890. *Problems of Greater Britain.* London, Macmillan and Co.

Dixon, R. M. W. 2008. 'Australian Aboriginal Words in Dictionaries: A History.' *International Journal of Lexicography* **21** (2): 129–52.

2009. 'Australian Aboriginal Words in Dictionaries: Response to Nash.' *International Journal of Lexicography* **22** (2): 189–90.

Dobrée, B. 1926. 'Tamber' in *The Nation and the Athenaeum* vol. **38** (24): 13 March: 804.

Dodd, P. 1986. 'Englishness and the National Culture' in R. Colls and P. Dodd (eds.) *Englishness: Politics and Culture 1880–1920*. London, Croom Helm: 1–28.

Dowling, L. 1982. 'Victorian Oxford and the Science of Language.' *PMLA* **97** (2): 160–78.

Downing, W. H. 1919. *Digger Dialects*. Oxford University Press.

Dryden, J. 1679. 'Defence of the Epilogue, or An essay on the Dramatick Poetry of the Last Age. Troilus and Cressida: or Truth Found out too Late, a Tragedy' in *The Critical miscellaneous prose works of John Dryden*, 1800, vol. **2 of 4**.

Eagleton, T. 1983. *Literary Theory: An Introduction*. Minneapolis: University of Minnesota Press.

Elliot, I. 1934. *Balliol College Register 1833–1933* 2d edn. Oxford University Press.

Ellis, A. J. 1881. 'Report on the Stanford Dictionary of Anglicised Words and Phrases delivered by Alexander J. Ellis.' *Transactions of the Philological Society 1880–1* **18**: 7–9.

Fallon, H. 2004. 'Comparing World Englishes.' *World Englishes* **23** (2): 309–16.

Feldman, D. 1989. 'The Importance of Being English: Jewish Immigration and the Decay of Liberal England' in D. Feldman and G. Stedman Jones (eds.) *Metropolis-London: Histories and Representations since 1800*. London, Routledge: 56–84.

Fennell, C. A. M. 1887.'Review of NED parts II and III.' *Athenaeum* 21 May: 667.

1888a. 'Review of A New English Dictionary, Part IV Bra–Byz.' *Athenaeum* 6 October: 441–2.

1888b. 'Review of NED Part IV C–Cass.' *Athenaeum* 6 October: 442.

1890. 'Review of NED part V Cast–Clivy.' *Athenaeum* 15 February: 207–8.

1892a. *The Stanford Dictionary of Anglicised Words and Phrases*. Cambridge University Press.

1893. 'Review of NED Part IV Clo–Consigner and Part VII *Consignificant-Crouching*.' *Athenaeum* 2 December: 765–6.

1893b. *Pindar, the Oympian and Pythian Odes*. Cambridge University Press.

1895a. 'The National Dictionary.' *Athenaeum* No. 3518 30 March: 409.

1895b. 'Review of NED.' *Athenaeum* 14 September: 347.

1896a. 'Degrees for Women.' *Athenaeum* 26 January: 149.

1896b. 'Cambridge Degrees for Women.' *Athenaeum* 21 March: 381.

1896c. 'Cambridge Degrees for Women.' *Athenaeum* 4 April: 448.

1896d. 'Cambridge Degrees for Women.' *Athenaeum* 27 June: 845.

1899. 'Review of NED vol V.' *Athenaeum* 23 September: 412.

1900. 'Review of NED vol. V.' *Athenaeum* 29 December: 851.

1901. 'Review of NED Jew-Kairine.' *Athenaeum* 27 July: 115.

1902. 'Review of NED Leisureness–Lief.' *Athenaeum* 14 June: 743–4.

1903. 'Review of NED R–Reactive.' *Athenaeum* 19 December: 821.

1907a.'Review of NED N–Niche.' *Athenaeum* 5 January: 7.

1907b. 'Review of NED Piper – Polygenistic.' *Athenaeum* 25 May: 627.

1909. 'Review of NED vol. VIII.' *Athenaeum* 17 July: 61.

'Feste' 1929. 'Ad Libitum.' *The Musical Times* **70** 1 October: 884–6.

Firth, J. R. and B. B. Rogers 1937. 'Structure of the Chinese Monosyllable in a Hunanese Dialect (Changsha).' *Bulletin of the School of Oriental Studies* **8**: 1055–74.

Fischer, A. 1997. 'The Oxford English Dictionary on CD-ROM as a Historical corpus: To wed and to marry Revisited' in U. Fries, V. Müller, and P. Schneider (eds.) *From Ælfric to The New York Times: Studies in English Corpus Linguistics*. Amsterdam, Rodopi: 161–72.

Fishman, J. A. 1977. 'The Spread of English as a New Perspective for the Study of Language Maintenance and Language Shift' in J. A. Fishman, A. Cooper, and A. Conrad (eds.) *The Spread of English: the Sociology of English as an Additional World Language*. Rowley, Newbury House: 329–36.

1995. 'Dictionaries as Culturally Constructed and as Culture-Constructing Artifacts: the Reciprocity View as Seen from Yiddish' in B. B. Kachru and H. Kahane (eds.) *Cultures, Ideologies, and the Dictionary* Lexicographica Series **64**. Tübingen, Max Miemeyer Verlag: 29–34.

Fishman, J. A., A. Conrad, and A. Rubal-Lopez (eds.) 1996. *Post-imperial English*. Berlin, Mouton de Gruyter.

Fishman, J. A., R. Cooper, and A. Conrad (eds.) 1977. *The Spread of English: The Sociology of English as an Additional Language*. Rowley, Newbury House.

Fox, S. 1886. 'The Invasion of Foreign Paupers.' *Contemporary Review* June 1886: 859.

Fry, R. 1926. 'Art: The French Gallery.' *The Nation and the Athenaeum* **38** (23): 6 March: 775–7.

Gainer, B. 1972. *The Alien Invasion: The Origins of the Alien Act of 1905*. London, Heinemann.

Garnett, J. M. 1894. 'Review of the New English Dictionary.' *American Journal of Philology* **15**: 82–5.

1895. 'Review of the Stanford Dictionary of Anglicised Words and Phrases.' *American Journal of Philology* **16** (1): 93–7.

Gilliver, P. 2004. 'That Brownest of Brown Studies: The Work of the Editors and In-house Staff of the Oxford English Dictionary in 1903.' *Dictionaries* **25**: 44–64.

Girardot, N. J. 2002. *The Victorian Translation of China*. Berkeley and Los Angeles, University of California Press.

Gladstone, W. 1878. *England's Mission*. London, John Hodges.

Goldie, M. (ed.) 1997. *Locke: Political Essays*. Cambridge University Press.

Goodland, G. 2008. *'Continual Plodders: Contextualising Shakespeare's First Uses in the OED.'* Unpublished paper presented at Hel-Lex2. Finland, 25–27 April, 2008.

Gordon, R. G. 2005. *Ethnologue: Languages of the World*. 15th edn., Dallas, SIL International.

Görlach, M. 1988. 'English as a World Language: The State of the Art.' *English World-Wide: A Journal of Varieties of English* **10** (1): 279–313.

1990. 'Review of The Oxford English Dictionary. 2d ed. eds. John Simpson and Edmund Weiner.' *English World-Wide: A Journal of Varieties of English* **11** (2): 310–14.

1991. *Englishes*. Amsterdam, John Benjamins.

1997. 'Review of Penny Silva, managing editor, A Dictionary of South African English on Historical Principle.' *International Journal of Lexicography* **10**: 336–8.

'Gospel Temperance Mission.' *Jackson's Oxford Journal* 19 March 1887: 6.

Gott, R. 1989. 'Little Englanders' in R. Samuel (ed.) *Patriotism: The Making and Unmaking of British National Identity* vol. **1.** London, Routledge: 90–103.

Graddol, D. 1997. *The Future of English?* London, The British Council.
1999. 'The Decline of the Native Speaker' in D. Graddol and U. H. Meinhof (eds.) *English in a Changing World: AILA Review* **13**: 57–68.
Grant, A. P. 2009. 'Loanwords in British English' in M. Haspelmath and U. Tadmor (eds.) *Lexical Borrowing in Cross-linguistic Perspective*. Berlin, Mouton de Gruyter (pre-publication copy so no page numbers).
Grant White, R. 1880, *Every-day English*. London, Kessinger.
Greenbaum, S. (ed.) 1996. *Comparing English Worldwide*. Oxford, Clarendon Press.
Gross, J. 1969. *The Rise and Fall of the Man of Letters: Aspects of English Literary Life since 1800*. London, Lowe & Brydone.
Hall, C. and S. Rose (eds.) 2006. *At Home with the Empire*. Cambridge University Press.
Hanks, P. 2006. 'English Lexicography' in K. Brown (ed.) *Encyclopedia of Language and Linguistics* 2d ed. Oxford, Elsevier: 184–94.
Harris, R. 1982. 'Review of R. W. Burchfield A Supplement to the OED Volume 3: O–Scz.' *TLS* 3 September: 935–6.
Hart, H. 1896. *Rules for Compositors and Readers Employed at the Clarendon Press . . . revised by Dr. J. A. H. Murray and Mr Henry Bradley*. Oxford, Clarendon Press.
H.B. and B.B. 1916. *J. C. C. S. (Jesus College Cambridge Society) Annual Report*. Cambridge University Press.
Hickey, R. (ed.) 2004. *Legacies of Colonial English*. Cambridge University Press.
Hobson, J. A. 1901. *The Psychology of Jingoism*. London, Grant Richards.
1902. *Imperialism: A Study*. London, James Nisbet.
Hock, H. H. 1991. *Principles of Historical Linguistics*. New York, Mouton de Gruyter.
Hoffman, S. 2004. 'Using the OED Quotations Database as a Corpus – a Linguistic Appraisal.' *ICAME Journal* **28**: 17–30.
'Homes of the Dictionary.' *The Periodical* **13** 15 February 1928: 18.
'How the Dictionary is Made.' *The Periodical* **13** 15 February 1928: 15–17.
Howard, P. 1986. 'Yetis, Yuppies, and Wimmin.' *Times* 8 May: 12.
2002. 'Murray, Sir James' in J. Wintle (ed.) *Makers of Nineteenth Century Culture* vol. **II**. London, Routledge: 447.
Hubbell, A. F. 1951. 'Daniel Jones on the Phoneme.' *American Speech* **26**: 44–6.
Hughes, G. 2000. *A History of English Words*. Oxford, Blackwell Publishing.
Hyam, R. 1999. 'The British Empire in the Edwardian Era' in J. M. Brown and W. R. Louis (eds.) *The Oxford History of the British Empire. The Twentieth Century* vol. **IV**. Oxford University Press: 47–63.
2010. *Understanding the British Empire*. Cambridge University Press.
'Interview with Burchfield on the Macneil/Lehrer' News Hour. New York, 27 May 1986.
Jenkins, J. 2007. *English as a Lingua France: Attitude and Identity*. Oxford University Press.
Jespersen, O. 1905. *Growth and Structure of the English Language*. Leipzig, Teubner.
Johnson, H. T. 1899. 'The Black Man's Burden.' *Voice of Missions* **7** April 1899: 63–4.
Johnson, S. 1747. *The Plan of a Dictionary of the English Language; addressed to the Right Honourable Philip Dormer, Earl of Chesterfield*. London, J. and P. Knapton.

1755. *Dictionary of the English Language*. London, J. and P. Knapton.
1755. *A Dictionary of the English Language* **2** vols. republ. facsimile, 1st edn. London, Folio Society [2006].

Jones, D. 1917. *An English Pronouncing Dictionary*. London, Dent and Sons.
1922. *An Outline of English Phonetics* 2d ed. Cambridge, Heffer and Sons.
1932. *An Outline of English Phonetics* 3d ed. New York, Dutton and Co.
1937. *An English Pronouncing Dictionary* 4th ed. London, Dent and Sons.
1946. 'Some Observations on English Speech: Lecture to the English Association, Jan. 25th, 1946' in B. Collins and I. M. Mees (2003) *Daniel Jones Selected Works: Unpublished Writings and Correspondence* vol. 8 section 11. (no page numbers)

Jones, J. 2005. *Balliol College: A History* 2d edn. Oxford University Press.

Jucker, A. H. 1994. 'New Dimensions in Vocabulary Studies: Review Article of the Oxford English Dictionary (2d edn) on CD-ROM.' *Literary and Linguistic Computing* **9/2**: 149–54.

Kachru, B. 1985. 'Standards, Codification, and Sociolinguistic Realism' in R. Quirk and H. G. Widdowson (eds.) *English in the World*. Cambridge University Press: 11–30.
1986. *The Alchemy of English: The Spread, Functions, and Models of Non-native Englishes*. Oxford, Pergamon.
2001. 'World Englishes and Cultural Wars' in T. C. Kiong, A. Pakir, B. K. Choon, and R. B. Goh (eds.) *Ariels: Departures and Returns*. Singapore, Oxford University Press: 392–414.

Kachru, B. B., Y. Kachru, and C. L. Nelson (eds.) 2006. *The Handbook of World Englishes*. Oxford, Blackwell Publishing.

Kinloch Cooke, C. (ed.) 1903. 'Official Report of the Allied Colonial Universities Conference.' *The Empire Review* 5 August.

Kirkpatrick, A. 2007. 'Linguistic Imperialism? English as a Global Language' in A. Pauwels and M. Hellinger (eds.) *Handbook of Applied Linguistics* vol. **9**. Berlin, Mouton de Gruyter: 333–64.

Kitson Clark, G. S. R. 1965. *The Making of Victorian Britain*. London, Routledge.

Knowles, E. 2000. 'Making the OED: Readers and Editors. A Critical Survey' in L. Mugglestone (ed.) *Lexicography and the OED*. Oxford University Press: 22–39.

Kortmann, B. and E. Schneider 2004. *A Handbook of Varieties of English* 2 vols. Berlin, Mouton de Gruyter.

Kubicek, R. 1999. 'British Expansion, Empire, and Technological Change' in A. Porter (ed.) *The Oxford History of the British Empire: The Nineteenth Century* vol. III. Oxford University Press: 247–69.

Labouchere, H. 1899. 'The Brown Man's Burden.' *Literary Digest* 25 February: 219.

Langford, P. 2000. *Englishness Identified*. Oxford University Press.

Laugesen, A. 2005. *Diggerspeak: The Language of Australians at War*. Melbourne, Oxford University Press.

Laurence, D. H. (ed.) 1988. *Collected Letters Bernard Shaw: 1926–1950* vol. **4**. New York, Viking.

Lehman, D. and D. Foote. 1986. 'The Last Word in Dictionaries.' *Newsweek* 2 June: 74.

Leonard, J. W. 1908. *'Child, Clarence Griffin' Who's Who in Pennsylvania: A Biographical Dictionary* 2d ed. New York, L. R. Hamersly and Co.: 141–2.

Lewis, R. E. 2007. *Middle English Dictionary Plan and Bibliography* 2d ed. Ann Arbor, University of Michigan Press.

'Liberal Meeting in the Corn Exchange.' *Jackson's Oxford Journal* 17 December: 6.

'Literary Notes.' *Times* 7 July 1894: 5.

Livingstone, D. 1857. *Missionary Travels and Researches in South Africa*. London, John Murray.

Livingstone, D. and C. Livingstone 1865. *Narrative of an Expedition to the Zambesi and its Tributaries; and the Discovery of the Lakes Shirwa and Nyasa*. London, John Murray.

'London Missionary Society.' *Jackson's Oxford Journal* 28 May 1887: 8.

'London Missionary Society.' *Jackson's Oxford Journal* 27 April 1895: 8.

'Lord Jersey at the Young Men's Christian Association.' *Jackson's Oxford Journal* 2 June 1894: **8**.

Ludowyk, F. 2009. 'Boomerang, Boomerang, Thou Spirit of Australia!' *Ozwords* **18** (2): 1–3.

Luna, P. 2005. 'The Typographic Design of Johnson's Dictionary' in J. Lynch and A. McDermott, *Anniversary Essays on Johnson's Dictionary*. Cambridge University Press: 175–97.

MacKenzie, J. M. (ed.) 1986. *Imperialism and Popular Culture*. Manchester University Press.

Magee, G. B. and A. S. Thompson 2010. *Empire and Globalisation: Networks of People, Goods, and Capital in the British World c. 1850–1914*. Cambridge University Press.

Mair, C. 2001. 'Early or Late Origin for Begin + V-ing? Using the OED on CD-ROM to Settle a Dispute between Visser and Jespersen.' *Anglia* **119**: 606–10.

Malone, J. L. 1878. 'Specimen of the Language of the Extinct Sydney Tribe.' *Journal of the Anthropological Institute* **7**: 262–83.

Mandler, P. 2006. *The English National Character*. New Haven and London, Yale University Press.

'Map of the Sea of Words.' *Times* 16 July 1987: 22.

Markus, M. 2001. 'Linguistic Commercialism in and around the Paston and Cely Letters. An OED and Corpus-Based Approach.' *Journal of English Linguistics* **29** (2): 162–78.

Marshall, P. J. 1996. 'Imperial Britain' in P. J. Marshall (ed.) *The Cambridge Illustrated History of the British Empire*. Cambridge University Press: 318–37.

Martin, B. 1749. *Lingua Britannica Reformata; or, A New English Dictionary*. London, J. Hodges.

Matthews, B. 1921. *' The Englishing of French Words.' SPE Tract No. V* Oxford, Clarendon Press.

McArthur, T. 1987. 'The English Languages?' *English Today* **11**: 9–11.

1993. 'The English Language or the English Languages?' in W. F. Bolton and D. Crystal (eds.) *The English Language*. London, Penguin: 323–41.

2002. *The Oxford Guide to World English*. Oxford University Press.

McClintock, A. 1995. *Imperial Leather: Race, Gender, and Sexuality in the Colonial Contest*. London, Routledge.

McConchie, R. W. 1997. *Lexicography and the Physicke*. Oxford, Clarendon Press.

McKitterick, D. 2004. *A History of Cambridge University Press: New Worlds for Learning 1873–1972* vol. **3**. Cambridge University Press.

McMahon, A. 1994. *Understanding Language Change*. Cambridge University Press.

2006. 'Restructuring Renaissance English' in L. Mugglestone (ed.) *Oxford History of English*. Oxford University Press: 147–77.

McMorris, J. 2001. *The Warden of English: The Life of H. W. Fowler*. Oxford University Press.

'Meetings of Societies.' *The Academy* 20 December 1884: 416.

Meier, H. H. 1979. 'Review of A Supplement to the Oxford English Dictionary.' *English Studies* **60**: 648–60.

Mesthrie, R. and R. M. Bhatt 2008. *World Englishes: The Study of New Linguistic Varieties*. Cambridge University Press.

Meyer, C. 2002. *English Corpus Linguistics: An Introduction*. Cambridge University Press.

Milne, K. 2010. 'Trench, Richard Chenevix (1807–1886)', *Oxford Dictionary of National Biography*, Oxford University Press, 2004; online edn, May 2010 [http://www.oxforddnb.com/view/article/27702, accessed 28 June 2011]

Milroy, J. 1997. 'Review of the Cambridge History of the English Language. Vol. V, English in Britain and Overseas: Origins and Development. Edited by Robert Burchfield.' *Journal of Linguistics* **33** (1): 171–5.

Mitchell, A. G. 1946. *The Pronunciation of English in Australia*. Sydney, Angus and Robertson Ltd.

Moag, R. F. 1982. 'The Life Cycle of Non-Native Englishes: A Case Study' in B. B. Kachru (ed.) *The Other Tongue: English across Cultures*. Urbana, University of Illinois Press: 270–90.

Moon, R. 1989. 'Objective or Objectionable? Ideological Aspects of Dictionaries' in M. Knowles and K. Malmkjær (eds.) *Language and Ideology ELR Journal* (New Series) vol. **3** English Language Research. University of Birmingham: 59–94.

Moore, B. 1997. *Australian Concise Oxford Dictionary* 3d ed. Melbourne, Oxford University Press.

2008. *Speaking Our Language*. Melbourne, Oxford University Press.

Morris, E. 1898. *Austral English*. London, Macmillan and Co.

Mossé, F. 1943. 'On the Chronology of French Loan-Words in English.' *English Studies* **25**: 33–40.

'Mr. Gladstone's Visit to Oxford.' *Jackson's Oxford Journal* 8 February 1890: 5.

Mufwene, S. S. 2001. *The Ecology of Language Evolution*. Cambridge University Press.

Mugglestone, L. 2000. '"An Historian not a Critic": The Standard of Usage in the OED' in L. Mugglestone (ed.) *Lexicography and the OED*. Oxford University Press: 189–206.

2003. 'Proof and Process: The Making of the Oxford English Dictionary' in M. Dossena and C. Jones (eds.) *Insights into Late Modern English*. London, Peter Lang: 107–27.

2004. 'Departures and Returns: Writing the English Dictionary in the Eighteenth and Nineteenth Centuries' in F. O'Gorman and K. Turner (eds.) *The Victorians and the Eighteenth Century*. London, Ashgate: 144–62.

2005. *Lost for Words: The Hidden History of the Oxford English Dictionary*. New Haven and London, Yale University Press.

2009. 'The Oxford English Dictionary' in A. P. Cowie (ed.) *The Oxford History of English Lexicography* vol. **I**. Oxford, Clarendon Press: 230–59.

Murray, J. A. H. 1873. *The Dialect of the Southern Counties of Scotland*. London, Asher and Co.

1879. *An Appeal to the English-Speaking and English-Reading Public in Great Britain, America and the Colonies*. Oxford, Clarendon Press.

1880. 'Ninth Annual Address of the President to the Philological Society, delivered at the Anniversary Meeting Friday 21st of May, 1880.' *Transactions of the Philological Society 1880–1* **18**: 117–75.

1881. 'Shaksperian Illustrations and the Philological Society's Dictionary.' *The Academy* 1 January 1881: 9.

1884a. *A New English Dictionary on Historical Principles*. Part I. A–ANT. Oxford, Clarendon Press.

1884b. 'Thirteenth Annual Address of President to the Philological Society.' *Transactions of the Philological Society 1882–4* **19**: 501–31.

1888. *A New English Dictionary on Historical Principles* Vol. **I** A and B. Oxford, Clarendon Press.

1892. 'Corroboree.' *Notes & Queries* **VIII S. I** 30 April: 353.

1900a. *The Romanes Lecture: The Evolution of English Lexicography*. Oxford, Clarendon Press.

1900b. 'The Etymology of Jade (the Mineral).' *Athenaeum* 20 October: 513.

1901a. *'Note' A New English Dictionary on Historical Principles KAISER – KYX*. Oxford, Clarendon Press.

1901b. *'Preface' A New English Dictionary on Historical Principles* vol. **V**, H to K. Oxford, Clarendon Press.

1903. *'The World of Words and Its Explorers.'* Unpublished lecture delivered to the London Institute (MP Box 26).

1909. *'Preface' A New English Dictionary on Historical Principles* vol. **VII**, O and P. Oxford, Clarendon Press.

1911. *'Lectures I, II, and V to Oxford School of English.'* Unpublished lectures delivered to the University of Oxford School of English (MP Box 27).

Murray, K. M. E. 1977. *Caught in the Web of Words*. New Haven and London, Yale University Press.

Murray, O. 2000. 'Ancient History, 1872–1914' in M. G. Brock and M. C. Curthoys (eds.) *The History of the University of Oxford: Nineteenth-Century Oxford* Vol. **VII** part 2. Oxford University Press: 339–60.

Nash, D. 2008. *'An "unsaleable bent stick", boomerangs, and yardsticks' Posted on Transient Languages and Cultures Blog*, University of Sydney, on 6 October, 2008 12:00 PM; update 14/10/08 and 19/10/08. <http://blogs.usyd.edu.au/elac/2008/10/an_unsaleable_bent_stick_boome_1.html#c544435>

2009. 'Australian Aboriginal Words in Dictionaries: A Reaction.' *International Journal of Lexicography* **22** (2): 179–88.

Nevalainen, T. 1999. 'Early Modern English Lexis and Semantics' in R. Lass (ed.) *The Cambridge History of the English Language: Early Modern English* 1476–1776 vol. **III**. Cambridge University Press: 332–458.

Nevalainen, T. and I. Tieken-Boon Van Ostade 2006. 'Standardisation' in R. Hogg & D. Denison (eds.) *A History of the English Language*. Cambridge University Press: 271–311.

'New Books and New Editions.' *Times* 17 September 1892: 8.

'North Ward Liberal Association.' *Jackson's Oxford Journal* 30 March 1889: 6.

'Notes.' *The Critic* 21 July 1894: **46**.

'Notes and Correspondence.' *SPE Tract No.* **10** 1922: 26.

'Notes and Correspondence' *SPE Tract No.* **24** 1924: 127–8.

'Notes and News.' *The Academy* 11 August 1894: 101.

Ockwell, A. and H. Pollins 2000. '"Extension" in All its Forms' in M. G. Brock and M. C. Curthoys (eds.) *The History of the University of Oxford: Nineteenth-Century Oxford* vol. VII part **2.** Oxford University Press: 661–88.

Ogilvie, S. 2004. 'From 'Outlandish Words' to 'World English': The Legitimization of Global Varieties of English in the Oxford English Dictionary' in G. Williams and S. Vessier (eds.) *Proceedings of the Eleventh Euralex International Congress*. Euralex 2004. Lorient, France. vol. II. Universite de Bretagne-Sud: 651–8.

2008a. 'Rethinking Burchfield and World Englishes.' *International Journal of Lexicography* **21**: 23–59.

2008b. 'The Mysterious Case of the Vanishing Tramlines: James Murray's Legacy and the 1933 *OED Supplement.' Dictionaries* **29**: 1–22.

2010. 'The OED and the Stanford Dictionary Controversy: Plagiarism or Paranoia?' in Michael Adams (ed.) *Cunning Passages, Contrived Corridors: Unexpected Essays in the History of Lexicography*. Milan, Polimetrica: 85–109.

Onions, C. T. 1933. *The Shorter Oxford English Dictionary*. Oxford, Clarendon Press.

Onions, C. T. and W. A. Craigie 1933. *The Oxford English Dictionary Supplement*. Oxford, Clarendon Press.

Orsman, H. 1997. *Dictionary of New Zealand English*. Oxford University Press.

Osselton, N. 2000. 'Murray and his European Counterparts' in L. Mugglestone (ed.) *Lexicography and the OED*. Oxford University Press: 59–76.

2007. 'Alphabet Fatigue and Compiling Consistency in Early English Dictionaries' in J. Considine and G. Iamartino (eds.) *Words and Dictionaries from the British Isles in Historical Perspective*. Cambridge Scholars Publishing: 81–90.

'Oxford Architectural and Historical Society.' *Jackson's Oxford Journal* 15 December 1894: 6.

'Oxford High School for Boys. Distribution of Prizes.' *Jackson's Oxford Journal* 11 June 1887: 7.

'Oxford High School.' *Jackson's Oxford Journal* 18 March 1893: 6.

'Oxford Philatelic Society' and 'London Missionary Society.' *Jackson's Oxford Journal* 29 April 1899: 7.

'Oxfordshire Band of Hope and Temperance Union.' *Jackson's Oxford Journal* 28 September 1889: 8.

'Oxfordshire Natural History Society.' *Jackson's Oxford Journal* 27 January 1894: 8.

'Oxfordshire Natural History Society.' *Jackson's Oxford Journal* 4 February 1888: 8.

Oxford University Calendar 1896. London, Macmillan and Co.

Parkes, M. B. 1992. *Pause and Effect: An Introduction to the History of Punctuation in the West*. Aldershot, Scolar Press.

Payne, T. 1795. *A catalogue of books in various languages and in every branch of science and learning; comprising several valuable collections lately purchased which are to be sold . . . by Thomas Payne*. London.

Pearsall Smith, L. 1920. 'A Few Practical Suggestions.' *SPE Tract No.* **3**: 1–9.

1931. 'Recollections' *SPE Tract No.* **35**: 481–502.

Pennycook, A. 1994. *The Cultural Politics of English as an International Language*. London, Longman.

2007. *Global Englishes and Transcultural Flows*. London, Routledge.

Peterson, W. S. 2007. 'Furnivall, Frederick James (1825–1910)', *Oxford Dictionary of National Biography*. Oxford University Press, 2004; online edn, May 2007 [http://www.oxforddnb.com/view/article/33298, accessed 28 June 2011]

Phillipson, R. 1992. *Linguistic Imperialism*. Oxford University Press.

2009. *Linguistic Imperialism Continued*. New York and London, Routledge.

Pietsch, T. 2010. 'Wandering Scholars? Academic Mobility and the British World, 1850–1940.' *Journal of Historical Geography* **36**: 377–87.

Platt, J., H. Weber, and M. L. Ho 1984. *The New Englishes*. London, Routledge.

Porter, A. 1999. 'Introduction: Britain and the Empire in the Nineteenth Century' in A. Porter (ed.) *The Oxford History of the British Empire: The Nineteenth Century* vol. **III.** Oxford University Press: 1–30.

Porter, B. 2004. *The Absent-minded Imperialists*. Oxford University Press.

Price, J. 2003a. 'Of Course it's English, it's in the Dictionary!' in TRANS. Internet-Zeitschrift für Kulturwissenschaften. No. 15/2003 <http://www.inst.at/trans/15Nr/06_1/price15.html>

2003b. 'The Recording of Vocabulary from the Major Varieties of English in the Oxford English Dictionary' in C. Mair (ed.) *The Politics of English as a World Language*. Amsterdam, Rodopi: 119–38.

(ed.) 1982. *New Englishes*. Rowley, Newbury House Publishers.

Proceedings of the Philological Society (Monthly Abstract of Proceedings) 16 January 1880.

Quirk, R. 1962. *The Use of English 2nd. impr*. London, Longmans.

Quirk, R. and H. G. Widdowson (eds.) 1985. *English in the World*. Cambridge University Press.

Q. V. 1897. 'A Propos' *Notes & Queries* **VIII S.** XII. 9 October: 290.

Ramson, W. S. 1966. *Australian English*. Canberra, Australian National University Press.

1988. *Australian National Dictionary*. Melbourne, Oxford University Press.

'Review of A New English Dictionary, vol. X Tombal-Trahysh.' *The Scotsman* 20 October 1913: 17.

'Review of Stanford Dictionary of Anglicised Words and Phrases (First Notice).' *Athenaeum* 18 March 1893: 341–2.

'Review of Stanford Dictionary of Anglicised Words and Phrases (Second Notice).' *Athenaeum* 25 March 1893: 372–3.

Richardson, C. 1836–7. *A New Dictionary of the English Language* **2** vols. London, William Pickering.

'Robert Burchfield.' *The Christchurch Press* 24 July 2004: 18.

Romaine, S. 1998. *Cambridge History of the English Language* vol. **IV** *1776–1997*. Cambridge University Press.

Rooney, K. and A. Soukhanov 1999. *Encarta World English Dictionary*. New York, St. Martin's Press.

Said, E. 1994. *Culture and Imperialism* London, Vintage.

Sands, D. B. 1976. 'Review of A Supplement to the Oxford English Dictionary vol. I A–G.' *College English* **37** (7): 710–18.

Saraceni, M. 2008. 'English as a Lingua Franca: Between Form and Function.' *English Today* **24** (2): 20–6.

Schäfer, J. 1980. *Documentation in the OED*. Oxford, Clarendon Press.

Schneider, E. W. (ed.) 1997. *Englishes Around the World* **2** vols. Amsterdam, John Benjamins.

2003. 'The Dynamics of New Englishes: From Identity Construction to Dialect Birth.' *Language* **79** (2): 233–81.

2007. *Postcolonial English: Varieties around the World*. Cambridge University Press.

'Scintille Juris (Indian and English).' *The Indian Jurist Law Journal and Reporter XVI* 31 October 1892: 498.

Seeley, J. R. 1883. *The Expansion of England: Two Courses of Lectures*. London, Macmillan and Co.

Shea, A. 2008. *Reading the OED*. New York, Penguin.

Shephard, B. 1986. 'Showbiz Imperialism: The Case of Peter Lobengula' in J. M. Mackenzie (ed.) *Imperialism and Popular Culture*. Manchester University Press: 94–112.

Silva, P. 2000. 'Time and Meaning: Sense and Definition in the OED' in L. Mugglestone (ed.) *Lexicography and the OED*. Oxford University Press: 77–94.

Simpson, J. and E. Weiner (prepared by) 1989. *The Oxford English Dictionary* 2d ed. vol. 1. Oxford, Clarendon Press.

Simpson, J. 2000-. OED *Online*. 3d ed. Available to subscribers at www.oed.com.

2008. 'Burchfield, Robert William (1923–2004)', *Oxford Dictionary of National Biography* online edn, Oxford University Press, January 2008 [http://www.oxforddnb.com/view/article/93833, accessed 19 Jan 2008].

Skeat, W. 1884. 'Jury-Mast.' *The Academy* 619 March: 185.

Sledd, J. H. 1973. *'Un-American English Reconsidered'* *American Speech* 48 (1): 46–53.'Specimens of Cornish Provincial Dialect.' *Gentleman's Magazine* August 1846: 178.

Spencer, J. (ed.) 1971. *The English Language in West Africa*. London, Longman.

Spurgeon, C. 1911. *'Memories of F. J. Furnivall' in Frederick James Furnivall: A Volume of Personal Record*. London, Henry Frowde: 182–7.

Starnes, D. W. T. and G. E. Noyes 1946. *The English Dictionary from Cawdrey to Johnson 1604–1755*. Chapel Hill, University of North Carolina Press.

Stephan, C. 1995. 'Review of The Cambridge History of the English Language. vol. V, English in Britain and Overseas: Origins and Development. Edited by Robert Burchfield.' *Linguistics* **33** (6): 1196–1201.

Stocking, G. 1987. *Victorian Anthropology*. New York, Free Press.

1995. *After Tylor: British Social Anthropology, 1888–1951*. Madison, University of Wisconsin Press.

Stockwell, R. and D. Minkova 2001. *English Words: History and Structure*. Cambridge University Press.

Summerfield, P. 1986. 'Patriotism and Empire: Music-hall Entertainment, 1870–1914' in J. M. Mackenzie (ed.) *Imperialism and Popular Culture*. Manchester University Press: 94–112.

Swift, J. 1712. 'A Proposal for Correcting, Improving, and Ascertaining the English Tongue, in a Letter to the Most Honourable Robert Earl of Oxford and Mortimer, Lord High Treasurer of Great Britain,' first printed in May 1712, in *The Works of Jonathan Swift* vol. **2** (1841). London, Henry Washbourne.

Taylor, D. 1993. *Hardy's Literary Language and Victorian Philology*. Oxford, Clarendon Press.

'The Editors and Their Staffs.' *The Periodical XIII* 15 February 1928: 10–15.

'The Home Rules Question.' *Jackson's Oxford Journal* 12 May 1888: 7.

'The Last Word on Words: Supplement to Old English Dictionary finished.' *Dallas Morning News* 8 June 1986: 13.

'The Literature and Language of the Age.' *Edinburgh Review* April 1889: 342–50.

'The "National" Dictionary of English Language and Literature.' *Times* 26 July 1894: 10.

'The Marquis of Ripon in Oxford.' *Jackson's Oxford Journal* 4 March 1893: 8.

'The Mayor's Banquet.' *Jackson's Oxford Journal* 27 October 1894: 6.

'The National Dictionary.' *Athenaeum* 30 March 1895: 409.

'The National Union of Teachers.' *Jackson's Oxford Journal* 31 March 1894: 6.

'The Philological Society's Dictionary.' *Times* 31 January 1882: 4.

'The Stanford Dictionary.' *New York Times* 25 December 1892: 19.

'The Stanford Bequest.' *The Gentlemen's Magazine* December 1892: 639–40.

'The Voluntary Workers.' *The Periodical XIII* 15 February 1928: 6–9.

'The Whole Irish Question.' *Jackson's Oxford Journal* 4 June 1887: 5.

'Third Meeting of the Cambridge Philological Society' Proceedings of the Cambridge Philological Society Lent Term 1884 vol. VII. London, Trubner and Co.: 10.

Thomason, S. G. and T. Kaufman 1988. *Language Contact, Creolization, and Genetic Linguistics*. Berkeley and Los Angeles, University of California Press.

Thompson, A. S. 2005. *Empire Strikes Back: The Impact of Imperialism on Britain from the mid-Nineteenth Century*. New York, Pearson Longman

Tongue, R. K. 1974. *The English of Singapore and Malaysia*. Singapore, Eastern Universities Press.

Trench, R. C. 1851. *On the Study of Words: Lectures Addressed (originally) to the Pupils at the Diocesan Training School, Winchester*. London, J. W. Parker and Son.

1855. *English Past and Present*. New York, Redfield.

1857. 'On Some Deficiencies in our English Dictionaries.' *Transactions of the Philological Society* 1857 **4** (2): 1–70.

Trench, R. C., F. Furnivall, and H. Coleridge 1857. 'Collections for a New Dictionary of the English Language.' *Athenaeum* 25 July: 944–5.

Trench, R. C., T. Goldstücker, T. H. Key, T. Watts, H. Wedgwood, F. J. Furnivall, F. Pulszky, and H. Coleridge 1860. *Canones Lexicographici, or Rules to be Observed in Editing the New English Dictionary of the Philological Society*. Philological Society Miscellaneous Papers, London, the Philological Society.

Troy, J. 1994. *The Sydney Language [Flynn, A.C.T., the author] Produced with the assistance of the Australian Dictionaries Project and the Australian Institute of Aboriginal and Torres Strait Islander Studies.*

Trudgill, P. and J. Hannah 1982. *International English: A Guide to Varieties of Standard English*. London, Edward Arnold.

Turner, G. W. 1966. *The English Language in Australia and New Zealand*. London, Longman Press.

Tylor E. B. 1863. 'Wild Men and Beast Children.' *Anthropological Review* **1** (1): 21–32.

1871. *Primitive Culture: Researches into the Development of Mythology, Philosophy, Religion, Art, and Customs* vol. **I**. London, John Murray.

1913. *Primitive Culture: Researches into the Development of Mythology, Philosophy, Religion, Art, and Customs* vol. **I**. 5th ed. London, John Murray.

'University Extension Conference.' *Jackson's Oxford Journal* 23 April 1887: 8.

'University Intelligence.' *Jackson's Oxford Journal* 1 December 1888: 5.

'University Jottings.' *The Academy* 1 April 1893: 284–5.

Viereck, W., E. Schneider, and M. Görlach 1984. *A Bibliography of Writings on the Varieties of English 1965–1983*. Amsterdam, John Benjamins.

'Visit of University Extension Students to Oxford.' *Jackson's Oxford Journal* 11 August 1888: 6.

Watts, T. 1850. 'On the Probable Future Position of the English Language.' *Transactions of the Philological Society 1848–49 and 1849–50* vol. **IV** London, Richard and John E. Taylor: 207–14.

Webster, N. 1828. *An American Dictionary of the English Language* facsimile ed. 2002 San Francisco, California, Foundation for American Christian Education.

Weiner, E. 1987. 'The New OED and World English.' *English Today* **11**: 31–4.

1990. 'The Federation of English' in C. Ricks and L. Michaels (eds.) *The State of the Language*. Berkeley and Los Angeles, University of California Press: 492–502.

Whitwhorth, G. C. 1885. *An Anglo-Indian Dictionary: A Glossary of Indian Terms used in English, and of Such English or other Non-Indian terms as Have Obtained Special Meanings in India*. London, Kegan Paul, Trench & Co.

Willcock, M. M. 1995. *Pindar Victory Odes: Olympians 2, 7, 11; Nemean 4; Isthmians 3, 4, 7*. Cambridge University Press.

Williams, C. 2006. 'The United Kingdom: British Nationalism during the Long Nineteenth Century' in T. Baycroft and M. Hewitson (eds.) *What Is a Nation? Europe 1789–1914*. Oxford University Press: 272–92.

Willinsky, J. 1994. *Empire of Words: The Reign of the OED*. Princeton University Press.

'Wimmin and Yuppies Earn Places in Oxford Dictionary Supplement.' *The Globe and Mail (Canada)* 9 May 1986: 9.

Winchester, S. 1998. *Surgeon of Crowthorne*. London, Viking.

Wong, J. 2008. 'Review of Edgar Schneider Postcolonial English.' *Language in Society* **37** (5): 756–60.

Wyllie, J. M. 1965. *The Oxford Dictionary Slanders: The Greatest Scandal in the Whole History of Scholarship Guernsey*. Barras, St Andrews.

'Yetis, Yuppies, and Wimmin.' *Times* 8 May 1986: 12.

Zgusta, L. (ed.) 1992. *History, Language, and Lexicographers*. Tübingen, Max Niemeyer.

Index